DYNASTIC CHA

Dynastic Change: Legitimacy and Gender in Medieval and Early Modern Monarchy examines the strategies for change and legitimacy in monarchies in the medieval and early modern eras.

Taking a broadly comparative approach, *Dynastic Change* explores the mechanisms employed as well as theoretical and practical approaches to monarchical legitimisation. The book answers the question of how monarchical families reacted, adjusted, or strategised when faced with dynastic crises of various kinds, such as a lack of a male heir or unfitness of a reigning monarch for rule, through the consideration of such themes as the role of royal women, the uses of the arts for representational and propaganda purposes, and the impact of religion or popular will. Broad in both chronological and geographical scope, chapters discuss examples from the 9th to the 18th centuries across such places as Morocco, Byzantium, Portugal, Russia, and Western Europe, showing readers how cultural, religious, and political differences across countries and time periods affected dynastic relations.

Bringing together gender, monarchy, and dynasticism, the book highlights parallels across time and place, encouraging a new approach to monarchy studies. It is the perfect collection for students and researchers of medieval and early modern monarchy and gender.

Ana Maria S. A. Rodrigues is a specialist in medieval queenship. She has recently edited, with M. Santos Silva and A. Leal de Faria, four volumes on the marriages of the Portuguese royal house (*Casamentos da Família Real Portuguesa*, Lisbon, Círculo de Leitores, 2017–18). She is an associate professor at the University of Lisbon.

Manuela Santos Silva is an adjunct-professor at the University of Lisbon and specialist in Western medieval monarchy and gender. She has recently edited, with Ana Maria S. A. Rodrigues and A. Leal de Faria, four volumes on the marriages of the Portuguese royal house, and before that, with Ana Maria S. A. Rodrigues and Isabel dos Guimarães Sá, 18 volumes on the queens of Portugal.

Jonathan Spangler is a specialist in the history of monarchy, particularly of France. His previous monographs include *The Society of Princes* (2009), and he is currently completing a survey of the lives of second sons in the French monarchy. He is Senior Lecturer in Early Modern History at Manchester Metropolitan University, and Senior Editor of *The Court Historian*.

Themes in Medieval and Early Modern History

This is a brand-new series which straddles both medieval and early modern worlds, encouraging readers to examine historical change over time as well as promoting understanding of the historical continuity between events in the past, and to challenge perceptions of periodisation. It aims to meet the demand for conceptual or thematic topics which cross a relatively wide chronological span (any period between c. 500–1750), including a broad geographical scope.

Series Editor: Natasha Hodgson, Nottingham Trent University.

Available titles:

War in the Iberian Peninsula, 700–1600
Edited by Francisco García Fitz and João Gouveia Monteiro

Writing War in Britain and France, 1370–1854: A History of Emotions
Edited by Stephanie Downes, Andrew Lynch and Katrina O'Loughlin

Drama in Medieval and Early Modern Europe: Playmakers and Their Strategies
Nadia Thérèse van Pelt

Florence in the Early Modern World
Nicholas Baker and Brian Maxson

Dynastic Change: Legitimacy and Gender in Medieval and Early Modern Monarchy
Edited by Ana Maria S. A. Rodrigues, Manuela Santos Silva and Jonathan Spangler

www.routledge.com/Themes-in-Medieval-and-Early-Modern-History/book-series/TMEMH.

DYNASTIC CHANGE

Legitimacy and Gender in Medieval and Early Modern Monarchy

Edited by Ana Maria S. A. Rodrigues, Manuela Santos Silva and Jonathan Spangler

Routledge
Taylor & Francis Group
LONDON AND NEW YORK

First published 2020
by Routledge
2 Park Square, Milton Park, Abingdon, Oxon OX14 4RN

and by Routledge
52 Vanderbilt Avenue, New York, NY 10017

Routledge is an imprint of the Taylor & Francis Group, an informa business

British Library Cataloguing-in-Publication Data
A catalogue record for this book is available from the British Library

Library of Congress Cataloging-in-Publication Data
A catalog record has been requested for this book

ISBN: 978-1-138-49055-0 (hbk)
ISBN: 978-1-138-49057-4 (pbk)
ISBN: 978-1-351-03514-9 (ebk)

Typeset in Bembo
by Swales & Willis Ltd, Exeter, Devon, UK

MIX
Paper from responsible sources
FSC www.fsc.org FSC™ C013985

Printed in the United Kingdom
by Henry Ling Limited

CONTENTS

ILLUSTRATIONS

Figures

Tables

CONTRIBUTORS

Charlotte Backerra is an assistant professor in Early Modern European History at the University of Göttingen, having previously taught Early Modern and Modern History at the universities of Mainz, Stuttgart, and Darmstadt. Her projects cover the role of dynasties in politics and culture, premodern international relations, and intelligence and espionage of European powers. Her PhD thesis on Imperial–British relations has been published as *Wien und London, 1727–1735. Internationale Beziehungen im frühen 18. Jahrhundert* (2018), and she has co-edited a volume of *Transnational Histories of the "Royal Nation"* (2017).

Isabel de Pina Baleiras is a history researcher interested in political and social power of the Middle Ages. Currently she holds a PhD fellowship at the University of Lisbon – Faculty of Arts (FLUL), and is a collaborator with the Medieval Studies Institute of the New University of Lisbon. The theme for her dissertation is the study of the political power of King Fernando of Portugal and Queen Leonor Teles and the role of the higher nobility in royal policy, 1367–85. In 2012, she published the biography *Uma rainha inesperada, Leonor Teles* [*An Unexpected Queen, Leonor Teles*], which was awarded the Lusitania Prize of the Portuguese Academy of History in 2012.

Caitlin Brady Carter is an assistant professor in the Department of Modern Languages at Fort Hays State University in Kansas. Her recently completed doctoral research (University of Colorado, Boulder) examined the fundamental role drama played in the formation of royal identity in the Spanish Baroque era by examining gender, sexuality, politics, and royal disability during the regency of Mariana of Austria for her son, Carlos II.

Jolanta Choińska-Mika is a professor at the University of Warsaw. Her specialism is the parliamentary history of the Polish-Lithuanian Commonwealth, its political culture, and the relationships between localities and central power.

Anna M. Duch is the lead for World History at Columbia State Community College, Tennessee, where she recently completed the creation of a new online Early World History course. Dr. Duch graduated from the University of York, UK, in 2016 with a PhD entitled "The Royal Funerary and Burial Ceremonies of Medieval English Kings, 1216–1509". She has recently published an essay, "Bodies in Constant Motion: The Burials and Reburials of the Plantagenet Dynasty, c. 1272–1399", in *Fourteenth Century England X* (2018).

Alexandra Karagianni is a postdoctoral graduate of Byzantine art and archaeology from Aristotle University of Thessaloniki (Greece). She has obtained two master's degrees, one in Byzantine art and archaeology from Aristotle University of Thessaloniki and one in Roman and Gothic art from the Université de Paris I Panthéon-Sorbonne. Her PhD, "The Cross in Byzantine Monumental Painting: Its Function and Dogmatic Content", has been published by the Byzantine Research Centre of Thessaloniki (2010).

Katarzyna Kuras is an assistant professor at the Jagiellonian University in Cracow. Her research focuses on the history of the Polish-Lithuanian Commonwealth in the early modern period and in particular the court of Queen Marie Leszczyńska of France in the eighteenth century.

Paula Almeida Mendes obtained her PhD in Portuguese Literature and Culture from the Faculty of Arts, University of Porto. She is a researcher at CITCEM (Centro de Investigação Transdisciplinar Cultura, Espaço e Memória/Center for Transdisciplinary Research Culture, Space and Memory) at the University of Porto, as a member of the group Religious Sociabilities and Practices. She is currently a Postdoctoral Fellow of the Foundation for Science and Technology. Her research focuses on the history and literature of spirituality, and the history of books and reading. Recent works include: *Paradigmas de Papel: a edição de "Vidas" de santos e de "Vidas" devotas em Portugal (séculos XVI-XVIII)* (2017); and "'Aa mais excellẽte & suprema Princesa & senhora do mũdo.' Sobre algumas dedicatórias a D. Catarina de Áustria (1507–1578)", in *Mulheres em rede/Mujeres en red. Convergências lusófonas*, Dimitri Almeida et al., eds (2018).

Penelope Nash is an honorary associate at the Medieval and Early Modern Centre, University of Sydney, Australia. Her book *Empress Adelheid and Countess Matilda: Medieval Female Rulership and the Foundations of European Society* (2017) compares two successful medieval women for their relative ability to retain wealth and power in the midst of the profound social changes of the eleventh century. Her most recent publications include a chapter on the households of elite medieval women, "Maintaining Elite Households in Germany and Italy, 900–1115", in *Royal and Elite Households* (2018); "Jane Austen and Medieval Women: What on Earth Did They Have in Common?", *Sensibilities* 56 (2018); "Insular Influences on Carolingian and Ottonian Literature and Art", in *Prophecy, Memory and Fate in the Early and Medieval Celtic World* (2019); and the forthcoming "Italy and her [German] Invaders", in *Murder and Mayhem* (2020) (about Otto III's and Frederick Barbarossa's early tours of Italy).

Cinzia Recca is a lecturer in Early Modern History at the University of Catania. Her area of research is the European Enlightenment. She has published several studies on the figure of Queen Maria Carolina of Naples through the analysis of unpublished sources, notably *The Diary of Maria Carolina of Naples, 1781–1785: New Evidence of Queenship at Court* (2017); and "The Eagle Eye of the Habsburg Family on the Kingdom of Naples: Lights and Shadows of Queen Maria Carolina at Court", in *Forgotten Queens in Medieval and Early Modern Europe: Political Agency, Myth-Making and Patronage* (2018).

Fatima Rhorchi is an associate professor at Moulay Ismail University, Meknes, Morocco, and a member of the Groupe de Recherche Interdisciplinaire des Etudes Féminines et du Genre. She received her PhD from Sidi Mohamed Ben Abdellah University in Fez in 2005. Fatima teaches courses on general linguistics, cultural/gender studies and translation. Her research focuses on higher education, gender studies, and history. Her relevant publications include a chapter on one of the forgotten queens of Morocco, "Consorts of Moroccan Sultans: Lalla Khenata Bint Bakkar, A Woman With Three Kings, 1727–1754", in *Queenship in the Mediterranean* (2013).

Lledó Ruiz Domingo is a graduate student in History at the University of Valencia, completing a PhD project on queenship in the Late Middle Ages in the Crown of Aragon which looks specifically at the processes of construction of the institutional figure of the queen consort.

Cathleen Sarti is a postdoctoral researcher at the University of Oxford. Her research focuses on political culture in early modern Northern Europe. Her doctoral thesis discussed depositions of monarchs in England, Scotland, Sweden, and Denmark-Norway and is forthcoming as *Deposing Monarchs: Domestic Conflict and State Formation, 1500–1700* (Routledge). Her publications include several edited volumes on cultural history and monarchical studies, and book chapters on the history of deposition and political thought.

Elena Teibenbacher is a PhD candidate at Karl-Franzens University Graz, Austria. She has previously studied history and international relations at Sciences-Po Paris and the Diplomatic Academy of Vienna. Elena specialises in cultural history with a focus on early modern Russia. For her thesis she is researching the different cultural influences on Moscow that contributed to its symbolic development as the centre of an emerging empire. Elena is also working on more upcoming publications on Catherine II and her role in Russian cultural history.

Lynsey Wood has just obtained her PhD from Lancaster University examining the place of women in the line of royal succession in the Tudor and early Jacobean periods. She is currently an associate lecturer at Manchester Metropolitan University, where she teaches undergraduate courses on the medieval and early modern world and women in power in early modern Europe.

INTRODUCTION

Ana Maria S. A. Rodrigues, Manuela Santos Silva, and Jonathan Spangler

In the broad canvas of the history of monarchy, there is one constant: royal dynasties rise to power, they weaken and fall, and others replace them. Dynastic change must be legitimised to secure the new regime, but historically this has been done through a variety of means. This volume brings together scholars from across Europe and beyond to examine the strategies for change and legitimacy in monarchies in the medieval and early modern eras. Particular themes include the roles played by royal women in strengthening dynastic rule, the uses of the arts for representational and propaganda purposes, and the place of religion or popular will in determining the outcomes of dynastic change. Through a broadly comparative approach, this volume allows us to examine the mechanisms employed as well as both theoretical and practical approaches to monarchical legitimisation from a variety of perspectives.

The central question is: when faced with dynastic crises of various kinds, from lack of a male heir to unfitness for rule of a reigning monarch, how do monarchical families react, adjust, or strategise? Once a dynasty has obtained power, how do they then legitimise their rule? What methods are used? And what further hurdles could remain to be overcome, namely issues of gender, religion, or foreignness? The essays included in this volume have been selected from papers that were presented at a conference of the same name held in Lisbon in 2015.[1] They represent a unique blend of new research currently being conducted by both emerging and seasoned scholars and ranging in focus across Europe and beyond, and from the tenth to the eighteenth centuries, from the Ottonian monarchy to regimes in the Age of Enlightenment.

Specialists of monarchy in the medieval and early modern periods would readily agree that the central-most concern of any monarch is dynasticism.[2] Whether this concern is manifest as a desire for glory and conquest, expressing religious authority, or establishing a historical legacy, all monarchs focus a disproportionate amount of their energies in ensuring the security of their family, their dynasty. Even the most "absolute" of monarchs, those who in theory ruled completely alone, are now seen as subject to the same drive, to preserve and pass on what they have to the next generation.[3] In this light, recent scholarship has therefore focused on the means employed for transmitting dynastic power from generation to generation, including, notably, through the agency of royal women.[4] This collection, then, aims to turn this investigation on its head to analyse situations in which normal patterns of succession were disrupted and dynasticism faced threats or even failed outright. The volume looks at periods of weakness—minorities, regencies, civil wars—to see how dynasties dealt with them (or did not), but also at succeeding periods when new dynasties sought to legitimise and consolidate their rule through various means. This final aspect of legitimacy, the legal tools used, brings in some very interesting questions on the relationship between monarchy, dynasty, and "the people", in that many unstable dynasties turned to "election" of some form or another in order to consolidate their hold on power, as seen in the medieval Iberian monarchies—or in some cases, it was the reverse, and the wider elites maintained a practice of elective monarchy to *prevent* the consolidation of dynastic power, as in Poland-Lithuania.[5]

The case studies presented here are not solely focused on Western Europe, as in many collections, but include chapters on Orthodox monarchy in Byzantium and Russia and on an Islamic regime in Morocco. Where Islamic and Christian cultures collided in the early medieval period was in Iberia, and there are a number of essays in this collection that focus on the kingdoms of Portugal, Castile, and Aragon, which, each in their way, struggled to determine the relationship between a warrior kingship developed in this region of conflict, family rule or dynasticism based on more clearly hereditary principals being developed elsewhere in Europe, and the popular will of those being governed. It is the latter group who were the intended audience for much of the material that is being discussed in the chapters in this volume: the artwork, the literary propaganda, the religious sanctification offered by the Church, or the legal arguments presented to public assemblies. And throughout each of these themes runs the important role of women, either as claimants to the throne or agents acting behind the throne for the interests of their husbands or sons. The volume is divided into two parts: the first includes chapters on dynastic change resulting from dethroning, delegitimising, or other succession crises; while the second examines methods for legitimising royal authority, from the visual and literary to religious and legal.

The idea of legitimacy

What is dynastic change? From a strictly definitional point of view it is the transition from one clan or kinship group (a "dynasty") to another, or in more modern terms, the shift from one family surname to another, for example Tudor to Stuart, or Oldenburg to Vasa. But this may be too simplistic: sometimes these shifts could occur within one overarching patrilineal dynasty (for example, from Valois to

Bourbon, both descended in the male line from Hugh Capet) or, more complexly, a male taking on a dynastic claim from his mother, like King Henry VII of England, who presented himself not so much as head of a new dynasty ("Tudor"), but as the legitimate continuator of the House of Lancaster, the dynasty of his predecessors as kings of England, Henry IV, Henry V, and Henry VI, or indeed the re-unifier of the feuding houses of Lancaster and York. Legitimacy was then sought for his grab for power at the Battle of Bosworth Field in 1485, either through obscuring his descent from the houses of Tudor or Beaufort, or in highlighting historical continuities by means of the commissioned works of Polydore Vergil and other historical writers.[6]

Thinking in the broadest terms for the history of monarchy and dynasticism, legitimacy is sought by a royal dynasty for two things: (1) obtaining the throne (by conquest, usurpation, acclamation by soldiers or the populace, election or confirmation by peers or popular representatives, or by hereditary succession); and (2) keeping the throne (by staying the strongest, gaining the approval of the Church or public opinion, or by defaming predecessors and rivals). As the medieval and early modern eras gave way to the modern, there were two other distinctive scenarios for obtaining or keeping thrones, which are not covered in this volume but are certainly worthy of consideration in the history of the evolution of the institution of monarchy on their own: the idea of obtaining a throne through parliamentary agreement, as happened in Britain during the "Glorious Revolution" of 1688–89 (and adjusted through the Act of Settlement, 1701), or through treaty agreements between the Great Powers, as with the House of Lorraine in 1737, which was given the Grand Duchy of Tuscany and eventual rights of succession to the entire Habsburg patrimony, in exchange for its hereditary lands which became part of France.[7]

The concept of "dynastic legitimacy" has several connotations and varies from context to context, depending in particular on the period of history in which it is applied. A writer looking at political legitimacy in the Enlightenment era in Europe measures whether legitimate authority comes from a divinely sanctioned hereditary monarchy or from the will of a sovereign people. In earlier periods such a conversation would have been meaningless, as government based on monarchy, approved by God, was seen by most to be an assumed norm. The relevant question for jurists and philosophers of the earlier period, instead, was whether this form of government should be hereditary or not; why should power and authority be transmitted from father to son, rather than simply to the next most competent leader? And if it was hereditary, what kind of inheritance system should be used? Primogeniture, agnatic seniority, tanistry, or something else altogether?[8] The premodern world was a dynastic world, and not only in Europe, as shown recently by global studies focused on this topic.[9] Dynasties thus struggled to define their legitimate place as rulers of their individual societies. But often legitimacy implied something bigger, a divine sanction. What role did the official religion of a state play in the regulating of legitimacy of its rulers?

At the most basic level, legitimacy comes from the Latin *lex*, as something being done or measured according to a law—thus a child born within the legal rejection (the chapters by Baleiras and Brady Carter). Entering into the Age of Enlightenment, we see a struggle to embed older ideas of monarchical legitimacy within emerging notions of popular sovereignty (see the chapter by Choińska-Mika and Kuras). And running through nearly all strategies of legitimacy is an involvement with religion; it is certainly interesting to see such similar approaches taken by both Christian and Islamic dynasties, in the case studies presented by Rhorchi and Mendes.

The chapters are divided into two groups: (1) dynastic change, and (2) legitimisation of rule. The first chapter, by Lynsey Wood, examines approaches taken in England over the *longue durée* to preserving stability while dynasties change—the patriline may change, but regulating the rights of women to pass on their claims to the throne preserved a sense of continuity. Wood explores shifts in attitudes towards female dynastic succession between the twelfth and the early seventeenth centuries, examining the development of a legal framework which culminated in the succession statutes introduced by Henry VIII (and revised by his children) which sought to legitimate the female contenders in sixteenth-century England. By then the unparalleled numbers of potential female heirs in England demonstrated the structural need for a female-inclusive rule of primogeniture in royal succession law. In a more focused case study, Isabel de Pina Baleiras looks at the transition between Portugal's first and second royal dynasties in 1383–85, in which the legitimate heir to the throne (a woman) was rejected and the traditional pathway of succession altered. She asks whether the use of an electoral process in proclaiming a new king by the Cortes of Coimbra was a sign of a democratic monarchy, or merely the legitimisation of a *coup d'état.* This chapter also compares this activity with the similar and chronologically contiguous case of the kingdom next door, Castile, where another dynasty founded by an illegitimate royal son (Enrique de Trastámara) was similarly legitimised. The analysis focuses in particular on the role of writers of chronicles in legitimising the successful takeovers of the Avis and Trastámara dynasties. In a parallel case study, Lledó Ruiz Domingo looks at the consolidation of the new Trastámara dynasty in the Kingdom of Aragon. After the unusual accession, involving election, of this dynasty, it was deemed necessary to re-configure an integrated vision of royal ceremonial. In order to decipher the changes that were introduced into Aragonese ritual, this chapter scrutinises coronations and funerals connected to the reign of the first king of the new dynasty, King Ferdinand I of Aragon, and in particular the ceremonial symbols and gestures used to form the royal image. The King's discourses before the Cortes also constitute a valuable source of information to uncover what kinds of propaganda manoeuvres were employed as part of his ideological programme for legitimising his dynasty.

Moving to a later period, and to northern Europe, the next three chapters examine how dynasties or leading elites could modify the hereditary system to suit the political needs of the family or of the nation. Cathleen Sarti looks at the case of the Vasa dynasty in Sweden, whose dual role, as kings of Poland, brought them greater influence but also internal divisions. In this chapter, Sarti looks at the manipulation of the public image of one Vasa prince by another, leading to a more specifically "Swedish" political culture. The deposition of King Sigismund of Sweden in 1599 was possible because his deposer, his uncle Duke Charles, had succeeded in making himself the champion of Swedish national culture while at the same time depicting Sigismund as alien. Making use of the religious conflict between Protestant Sweden and their Catholic king, as well as the practical problems brought by Sigismund's simultaneous kingship of Sweden and Poland-Lithuania, Charles succeeded in ousting Sigismund and becoming the new ruler. Charles' efforts to nationalise the Vasa dynasty and Swedish political culture was then in turn used to legitimise the change of ruler. Back across the Baltic, this deposition contributed to the ongoing debate about the usefulness of the elective process in selecting a monarch, and the pros and cons of selecting a foreign dynasty to rule over the Polish-Lithuanian Commonwealth. In their joint-authored chapter, Jolanta Choińska-Mika and Katarzyna Kuras trace the legal and theoretical arguments behind free election of kings from its start in the late sixteenth century to its last days in the eighteenth, when the practice weakened the Commonwealth to such an extent that it ultimately led to its dismemberment. In particular, the chapter examines the way Polish-Lithuanian eighteenth-century elective monarchs were regarded by their subjects due to a combination of factors, including the bald-faced military intervention in the election procedure by foreign powers and the attempts to introduce Enlightenment ideas into the notions of governance and monarchical rule. Looking in almost the opposite direction, the House of Hanover in the opening years of the eighteenth century were keen to stress that they were *not* a new dynasty, as they approached the succession to the throne of Great Britain, but had an ancient lineage and indeed ancient ties with England. In her chapter, Charlotte Backerra analyses the preparations laid down to ensure a smooth transition of dynasty from Stuart to Hanover. The first Hanoverians, the Electress Sophia, kings George I and George II, and the latter's wife Caroline, adopted English traditions in their representation of themselves as defenders of the Protestant faith, in celebrating coronations and other ceremonies according to older examples, and bowed to national culture with their acceptance of political rules established in England and the prevalent concepts of the ancient liberties of the people. The new (old) dynasty accepting British national culture played a major part in its success in resisting forces of Jacobitism, isolationism, and the rejection of a foreign ruling family.

Back in southern Europe, the Italian Peninsula in the eighteenth century witnessed several changes of dynasty, as the Habsburgs and Bourbons struggled to maintain the balance of power in the Mediterranean following the dismemberment of the ascendency of the Spanish Habsburgs after the War of Spanish Succession. In her chapter, Cinzia Recca looks in particular at the methods employed by the Spanish Bourbons to legitimise their rule in the Kingdom of Naples, at first successfully bringing Italy back into the orbit of Spanish influence at the expense of the Austrian Habsburgs, but facing dynastic reversal following the marriage of King Ferdinand IV of Naples with Archduchess Maria Carolina of Austria in 1768. In a curious blending of dynastic practice, Recca demonstrates how the legitimacy of the Neapolitan Bourbons was ironically solidified through the rule of a Habsburg consort and the return of Naples into the sphere of Austrian influence. In the end, this chapter helps us see that often, though the dynasty may change in name, much remains the same in practice.

The second half of this collection of essays focuses less on change and more on "staying power"—how did monarchs maintain legitimacy in times of dynastic stress? These chapters examine this question by looking at a variety of tools of dynastic strategy: the uses of visual or literary culture, and the importance of gender and religion. The first chapter, by Alexandra Karagianni, looks at the interesting combination of visual means and religious feeling in erasing the memory of a violent takeover from one Byzantine dynasty to another. Karagianni examines six prophetic dreams connected to the accession of Emperor Basil I the Macedonian in the ninth century, as narrated in two key sources from later centuries: the *Vita Basilii* and the manuscript of *Ioannis Skylitzes*. The chapter investigates how a prophetic or symbolic dream (or *chrimatismos*) was used to legitimise the actions of the simple peasant Basil and gave him the extraordinary chance to usurp the imperial throne. In a similar way, English kings in the fifteenth century re-packaged brutal usurpations through honouring (or dishonouring) their predecessors in funeral rites. Anna M. Duch's chapter looks at the manner in which King Edward IV, of the House of York, referred to Henry VI and his forebears of the House of Lancaster as "kings by fact, not by law" at his funeral in 1471. Subsequently, Richard III made an effort to reconcile himself with the legacy of his house's former enemy, Henry VI, by reburying him at Windsor. And yet, in shifting back from the House of York to the House of Lancaster (aka Tudor), after his victory at Bosworth Field in 1485, Henry VII declared Richard III and his reign invalid, a status demotion confirmed in Richard's rather un-kingly burial in a modest friary in Leicester. Because of these shifts in power, the reputations (and physical bodies) of Henry VI and Richard III underwent changes in status which affected their funerals and later reburials. To fully contextualise these changes in status, and their uses in legitimising newly established rulers, Duch compares these cases to other royal exequies in the House of Plantagenet, particularly those of Edward II and Richard II, two other humbled kings, later rehabilitated in death.

Another approach to making use of religious ceremonial to erase the past and create a more positive reputation for a ruling dynasty is taken in the chapter by Paula Almeida Mendes. Against the backdrop of the context of the Portuguese Restoration of 1640 and the difficulties that the newly inaugurated dynasty of Bragança faced in obtaining legitimacy and recognition from the wider European community in the second half of the seventeenth century, this chapter draws attention to the way in which the dynasty promoted an exaltation of "holiness" in some of its members (Prince Teodósio, Princess Joana), or at least of their "virtues" (Queen Luísa de Gusmão; Princess Catarina, later queen of England; Princess Isabel Luisa Josefa). This policy was taken to such an extent as a strategy to defend the legitimacy of the dynasty that it created the impression of an "illustrious" royal family, one that was able to "generate saints". The parallel case is seen in the study by Fatima Rhorchi of a dynasty descended from and consisting of living saints, in the Alawi dynasty in the Sultanate of Morocco in the same century. This chapter demonstrates how Sultan Moulay Ismail, in the face of rebellion by disenfranchised relatives, legitimised his rule and imposed his authority through several means, both religious and political. He promoted Sharifism, the traditional right to rule based on descent from the Prophet. He also strengthened his alliances with some of the mountain tribes in the countryside, and strengthened the Abid Alboukhari, or Black Slaves Army. Nevertheless, his reliance on force proved unsustainable, and the death of Moulay Ismail resulted in a new period of internal strife in Morocco. The problem of Alawi legitimacy would not be solved until the enthronement of his grandson, Sidi Mohamed Ibn Abdellah, who rebuilt Alawi dynastic power on new principles, based on religious ties plus economic power, not force.

As another alternative to force, the final three chapters look at the roles assumed by women in ruling dynasties from various aspects, successfully and unsuccessfully. By nature and social custom, royal women were discouraged from the use of force in maintaining order—they therefore looked for other means. Penelope Nash examines the role of Ottonian women in Germany across the tenth century, as they guided the dynasty through unstable times brought on by periods of minority. In 1024, 100 years after Henry I's election as king, the fifth and last member of the Ottonian dynasty, Emperor Henry II, died without issue, and the succession passed to a new line, whose members came to be known as the Salians. Nash explains how historians have usually depicted the Ottonian dynasty as one that progressed from an uncertain beginning to one of relative stability, attributed primarily to the efforts of its male leaders, and proposes a different reason for this stability. She claims that the ruling women, as regents, mothers, wives, and sisters, maintained stability through political agency and as negotiators rather than warmongers, by looking in particular at three women: Empress Adelheid, Empress Theophanu, and Abbess Mathilda of Quedlinburg.

Several centuries later, another queen regent, Mariana of Austria, widow of Philip IV of Spain, faced similar problems. In her chapter, Caitlin Brady Carter considers the debate between male and female rule, and intellectual versus emotional leadership, as depicted in a work of theatre from the period. This chapter considers the struggle to control the Regency of King Carlos II between his mother, Mariana, and his illegitimate half-brother, Don Juan José, as it was manifested in court performances of a play by Pedro Calderón de la Barca, *La estatua de Prometeo*, written in the early 1670s. This play presents not only a parallel to the actual struggles for power in the Spanish court, but a critique of the young king's weaknesses as well. Such theatrical performances as *La estatua de Prometeo* not only provide us with insight into court culture, but can be used as a way to approach and understand the politics surrounding Mariana and Don Juan José's rival claims to legitimacy of their claims to hold power. Taking this debate one step further, the final chapter, by Elena Teibenbacher, looks at the justifications put forward by

Catherine II of Russia for her usurpation of the throne from her husband in 1762, notably by arguing that power should be legitimately held by those best suited to wield it. This chapter contrasts the actions of Catherine as a monarch with her (self-)portrayal as an enlightened thinker, exploring the discrepancies between the two by examining the importance of legitimacy in Catherine's life and politics. Having overthrown her husband Peter III without any dynastic claim to the throne herself, she needed to prove her legitimacy in other ways. Catherine II did not want to enter history as a usurper but as a saviour. Yet contradictory positions remain: she is seen as ruling as an autocratic sovereign rather than an "enlightened" reformer, failing to introduce constitutional and democratic changes. Was this because she believed power to be her legitimate right as the most capable, as opposed to strictly hereditary, leader? Did she make use of the theories of the Enlightenment to defend her legitimacy while never really intending to actually apply them?

Towards the end of Catherine of Russia's reign, all of these questions, and all of those examined across this collection of chapters, would be re-examined in the wake of the French Revolution. Was monarchy intended to lead and serve the people, or to serve the dynasty which occupied its throne? Questions of elective monarchy, religious legitimacy, the position of women, and the uses of history and the arts in maintaining the image of monarchy, all returned to the floor of debate, and would do so repeatedly across the nineteenth century, as monarchies were removed then restored, or modified by constitutional reforms (also made and unmade), until the final curtain fell on many European monarchies altogether following the end of the First World War. Yet still today, those monarchies that survive make use of strategies of legitimisation to connect themselves with the past—whether through the change of dynastic name (for example, from Saxe-Coburg to Windsor in the United Kingdom), the maintenance of a dynastic name despite female succession (as in the Netherlands or in Luxembourg), or through the close identification of a dynasty with a historical continuity (as in Japan) or with religious faith (as in Saudi Arabia). Debates about gender are central in discussions about the relevance—a new word to indicate legitimacy—of monarchy in the modern era: most twenty-first-century European monarchies have now changed succession laws to allow for a monarch to be succeeded by an eldest child, regardless of gender ("absolute primogeniture")—led by the liberal Scandinavian countries, but now also poised to be changed in more conservative Catholic countries like Spain. Narrative histories and plays continue to be written and performed that maintain the legitimacy of past dynasties, even in countries like France where the monarchy is long abolished, notably in cultivating the memory of Napoleon as emperor of the French, or Austria, where the cult of "Sisi", the Empress Elizabeth, is a mainstay of tourism. Religious revivals continue to stress the legitimacy of monarchical rule in the eyes of God, as in contemporary Russia, where the recently canonised Nicholas II and his family attracts increasing devotion, or in Serbia, where the current royal family in waiting represents for many a living link to a more spiritual past.

Notes

1 Kings and Queens 4, "Dynastic Change and Legitimacy", Faculty of Arts and Humanities, University of Lisbon, 23–27 June 2015.
2 Some useful examples in English include Paula Sutter Fichtner, *The Habsburg Empire: From Dynasticism to Multinationalism* (Malabar: Krieger, 1997); Pamela Ritchie, *Dynasticism and Diplomacy: The Political Career of Marie de Guise in Scotland, 1548–1560* (East Linton: Tuckwell Press, 2002); Matthew Vester, *Renaissance Dynasticism and Apanage Politics: Jacques de Savoie-Nemours 1531–1585* (Kirksville: Truman State University Press, 2012); or, more recently, Catriona Murray, *Imaging Stuart Family Politics: Dynastic Crisis and Continuity* (Burlington: Ashgate, 2016). At a broader level, inclusive of the aristocracy as well as royalty, see Liesbeth Geevers and Mirella Marini, eds, *Dynastic Identity in Early Modern Europe: Rulers, Aristocrats and the Formation of Identities* (Farnham: Ashgate, 2015).
3 See for example, Matthieu Lahaye, "Heir Obedience, Heir Disobedience: Two Generations of Dauphins for Louis XIV", *The Court Historian* 19, 2 (2014): 129–44.
4 Most recently, Elena Woodacre and Carey Fleiner, eds, *Royal Mothers and their Ruling Children: Wielding Political Authority from Antiquity to the Early Modern Era* (Basingstoke: Palgrave Macmillan, 2015); and Helen Watanabe-O'Kelly and Adam Morton, eds, *Queens Consort, Cultural Transfer and European Politics, c. 1500–1800* (Abingdon: Routledge, 2016).
5 See chapters in this volume by Isabel de Pina Baleiras and Lledó Ruiz Domingo for Iberia, and that of Jolanta Choińska-Mika and Katarzyna Kuras for Poland-Lithuania.
6 C. S. L. Davies, "Tudor: What's in a Name?" *History* 97, 325 (2012): 24–42, esp. 34–35.
7 See Howard Nenner, *The Right to be King: The Succession to the Crown of England, 1603–1714* (Basingstoke: Macmillan, 1995); and Hubert Collin, "Cas de conscience dynastique, ambition personelle et raison d'Etat: Pourquoi le duc François III dut se laisser arracher la Lorraine et l'échanger contre la Toscane", in *Il Granducato di Toscana e i Lorena nel secolo XVIII*, Alessandra Contini and Maria Grazia Parri, eds (Florence: Olschki, 1999), 35–70.
8 For definitions of these types of succession patterns, see Nenner, *The Right to be King*, "Introduction"; or Jeroen Diundam, *Dynasties: A Global History of Power, 1300–1800* (Cambridge: Cambridge University Press, 2016), chapter 2: "Dynasty: Reproduction and Succession".
9 Duindam, *Dynasties*; Jeroen Duindam, Tülay Artans, and Metin Kunt, eds, *Royal Courts in Dynastic States and Empires: A Global Perspective* (Leiden and Boston, MA: Brill, 2011); W. M. Spellman, *Monarchies 1000–2000* (London: Reaktion, 2001).
10 See for example, Sara McDougall, *Royal Bastards: The Birth of Illegitimacy, 800–1230* (Oxford: Oxford University Press, 2017); and Matthew Gerber, *Bastards: Politics, Family, and Law in Early Modern France* (Oxford: Oxford University Press, 2012). Or more specifically: Chris Given-Wilson, "Legitimation, Designation and Succession to the Throne in Fourteenth-Century England", in *Building Legitimacy: Political Discourses and Forms of Legitimation in Medieval Societies*, Isabel Alfonso, Hugh Kennedy, and Julio Escalona, eds (Leiden: Brill, 2004), 89–105.
11 See Deborah Baumgold, *Contract Theory in Historical Context: Essays on Grotius, Hobbes, and Locke* (Leiden: Brill, 2010); and for the later period, H.W. Blom, Luisa Simonutti, and John Christian Laursen, eds, *Monarchisms in the Age of Enlightenment: Liberty, Patriotism, and the Common Good* (Toronto: University of Toronto Press, 2007).
12 See Chapter 1 by Lynsey Wood in this volume for full citations.
13 Isabel Alfonso, Hugh Kennedy, and Julio Escalona, eds, *Building Legitimacy: Political Discourses and Forms of Legitimation in Medieval Societies* (Leiden: Brill, 2004).
14 Many of these themes are pursued in the recent volume of essays, *The Routledge History of Monarchy*, edited by Elena Woodacre, Lucinda H. S. Dean, Chris Jones, Zita Rohr, and Russell Martin (Abingdon: Routledge, 2019).
15 1 Samuel 8.
16 1 Samuel 11.
17 Israel Finkelstein, "The Last Labayu: King Saul and the Expansion of the First North Israelite Territorial Entity", in *Essays on Ancient Israel in its Near Eastern Context: A Tribute*

to Nadav Na'aman, Yairah Amit, Ehud Ben Zvi, Israel Finkelstein, et al., eds (Winona Lake: Eisenbrauns, 2006), 171ff.

18 1 Samuel 13 to 2 Samuel 5.

19 A term first used in 1 Timothy 6:14–15.

20 Matthew 1:1–17; Luke 3:23–38.

21 Barbara Sivertsen, "New Testament Genealogies and the Families of Mary and Joseph", *Biblical Theology Bulletin* 35, 2 (2005): 43–50.

22 Hugh Lindsay, *Adoption in the Roman World* (Cambridge: Cambridge University Press, 2009), especially chapter 16, "Political Adoption in the Early Empire at Rome, Pompeii and Ostia: The Imperial Family". Notable artificially constructed imperial dynasties include the Julio-Claudians or the Nerva-Antonines.

23 John Julius Norwich, *Byzantium: The Early Centuries* (London: Penguin, 1990), 334–37; Jonathan Stumpf notes that *rhinotomy* (another word for *rhinokopia*) had existed for centuries, used by the Egyptians to punish corrupt judges, and the ancient Indians, Romans, and Arabs for adultery: "On the Mutilation and Blinding of Byzantine Emperors from the Reign of Heraclius I until the Fall of Constantinople", *Journal of Ancient History and Archaeology* 4, 3 (2017): 46–54 (47).

24 C. van Arendonk and W. A. Graham, "Sharīf", in *The Encyclopaedia of Islam*, P. Bearman, Th. Bianquis, et al., eds. 2nd edn. Leiden: Brill Online, 2012, http://dx.doi.org/10.1163/1573-3912_islam_COM_1041 [accessed 20 November 2018].

25 Jenny M. Jochens, "The Politics of Reproduction: Medieval Norwegian Kingship", *American Historical Review* 92, 2 (1987): 327–49.

26 Ian Whitaker, "Regal Succession Among the Dálriata", *Ethnohistory* 23, 4 (1976): 343–63.

27 Paul Fouracre, "Conflict, Power and Legitimation in Francia in the Late Seventh and Eighth Centuries", in Alfonso, Kennedy, and Escalona, eds, *Building Legitimacy*, 3–26 (esp. 4–5).

28 Ian Wood, *The Merovingian Kingdoms 450–751* (London and New York: Longman, 1994), 55–60.

29 There is an ongoing discussion on the meaning of the Merovingian kings' hair: Maximilian Diesenberger, "Hair, Sacrality and Symbolic Capital in the Frankish Kingdoms", in R. Corradini, M. Diesenberger, and H. Reimitz, eds, *The Construction of Communities in the Early Middle Ages: Texts, Resources and Artifacts* (Leiden: Brill, 2003), 173–212; Régine Le Jan, "La sacralité de la royauté mérovingienne", *Annales. Histoire, Sciences Sociales* 58, 6 (2003): 1217–1241; Eduardo Fabbro, "Conspicuously by Their Absence: Long-Haired Kings, Symbolic Capital, Sacred Kingship and Other Contemporary Myths", *Signum* 13, 1 (2012): 22–45.

30 Bernard Dumézil, "Ruptures dynastiques dans les royaumes barbares", in Flocel Sabaté i Curull and Maite Pedrol, eds, *Ruptura i legitimació dinàstica a l'Edat Mitjana* (Lleida: Pagès, 2015), 41–58 (56).

31 Régine Le Jan, *Famille et pouvoir dans le monde franc* (Paris: Publications de la Sorbonne, 1995), 202.

32 See Bernd Kannowski, "The Impact of Lineage and Family Connections on Succession in Medieval Germany's Elective Kingdom"; and Corinne Péneau, "La succession royale dans la royaume de Suède, entre coutume héréditaire et loi élective (XIIIe-XIVe siècles)", both in *Making and Breaking the Rules: Succession in Medieval Europe, c.1000–c.1600*, Frédérique Lachaud and Michael Penman, eds (Turnhout: Brepols, 2008).

33 See Andrew W. Lewis, *Royal Succession in Capetian France: Studies in Familial Order and the State* (Cambridge: Harvard University Press, 1981).

34 Craig Taylor, "The Salic Law, French Queenship, and the Defense of Women in the Late Middle Ages", *French Historical Studies* 29, 4 (2006): 543–64.

35 Mark Cruse, "The Louvre of Charles V: Legitimacy, Renewal, and Royal Presence in Fourteenth-Century Paris", *L'Esprit Créateur* 54, 2 (2014): 19–32.

36 Robert Knecht, *The Valois: Kings of France, 1328–1589* (London: Hambledon & London, 2004), 28–29.

37 Cruse, "The Louvre of Charles V", 30–31.
38 Paul Kléber Monod, *The Power of Kings: Monarchy and Religion in Europe 1589–1715* (New Haven and London: Yale University Press, 1999); Nicholas Henshall, *The Zenith of European Monarchy and its Elites: The Politics of Culture, 1650–1750* (Basingstoke: Palgrave Macmillan, 2010).
39 See chapters in this volume by Teibenbacher, Choińska-Mika/Kuras, Backerra, and Recca.
40 This theme is ripe for comparative study. In a random sampling of academic databases for relevant articles with the words "royal" and "legitimacy" in their titles, a number of intriguing titles emerged; for example: Joanna Wolfarth, "Lineage and Legitimacy: Exploring Royal-Familial Visual Configurations in Cambodia", *Trans-Asia Photography Review* 8, 1 (2017); or Ernest Tucker, "Explaining Nadir Shah: Kingship and Royal Legitimacy in Muhammad Kazim Marvi's *Tarikh-i 'Alam-ara-yi Nadiri*", *Iranian Studies* 26, 1–2 (1993): 95–117.

Bibliography

Alfonso, Isabel, Hugh Kennedy, and Julio Escalona, eds, *Building Legitimacy: Political Discourses and Forms of Legitimation in Medieval Societies*. Leiden: Brill, 2004.

Baumgold, Deborah. *Contract Theory in Historical Context: Essays on Grotius, Hobbes, and Locke*. Leiden: Brill, 2010.

Blom, H. W., Luisa Simonutti, and John Christian Laursen, eds. *Monarchisms in the Age of Enlightenment: Liberty, Patriotism, and the Common Good*. Toronto: University of Toronto Press, 2007.

Collin, Hubert. "Cas de conscience dynastique, ambition personelle et raison d'Etat: Pourquoi le duc François III dut se laisser arracher la Lorraine et l'échanger contre la Toscane". In *Il Granducato di Toscana e i Lorena nel secolo XVIII*, edited by Alessandra Contini and Maria Grazia Parri, 35–70. Florence: Olschki, 1999.

Cruse, Mark. "The Louvre of Charles V: Legitimacy, Renewal, and Royal Presence in Fourteenth-Century Paris". *L'Esprit Créateur* 54, 2 (2014): 19–32.

Davies, C. S. L. "Tudor: What's in a Name?" *History* 97, 325 (2012): 24–42.

Diesenberger, Maximilian. "Hair, Sacrality and Symbolic Capital in the Frankish Kingdoms". In *The Construction of Communities in the Early Middle Ages: Texts, Resources and Artifacts*, edited by R. Corradini, M. Diesenberger, and H. Reimitz, 173–212. Leiden: Brill, 2003.

Duindam, Jeroen, Tülay Artans, and Metin Kunt, eds. *Royal Courts in Dynastic States and Empires: A Global Perspective*. Leiden and Boston: Brill, 2011.

Duindam, Jeroen. *Dynasties: A Global History of Power, 1300–1800*. Cambridge: Cambridge University Press, 2016.

Dumézil, Bernard. "Ruptures dynastiques dans les royaumes barbares". In *Ruptura i legitimació dinástica a l'Edat Mitjana*, edited by Flocel Sabaté i Curull and Maite Pedrol, 41–58. Lleida: Pagès, 2015.

Fabbro, Eduardo. "Conspicuously by Their Absence: Long-Haired Kings, Symbolic Capital, Sacred Kingship and Other Contemporary Myths". *Signum* 13, 1 (2012): 22–45.

Fichtner, Paula Sutter. *The Habsburg Empire: From Dynasticism to Multinationalism*. Malabar: Krieger, 1997.

Finkelstein, Israel. "The Last Labayu: King Saul and the Expansion of the First North Israelite Territorial Entity". In *Essays on Ancient Israel in its Near Eastern Context: A Tribute to Nadav Na'aman*, edited by Yairah Amit, Ehud Ben Zvi, Israel Finkelstein, et al., 171–87. Winona Lake: Eisenbrauns, 2006.

Fouracre, Paul. "Conflict, Power and Legitimation in Francia in the Late Seventh and Eighth Centuries". In *Building Legitimacy: Political Discourses and Forms of Legitimation in Medieval Societies*, edited by Alfonso, Isabel, Hugh Kennedy, and Julio Escalona, 3–26. Leiden: Brill, 2004.

Geevers, Liesbeth, and Mirella Marini, eds. *Dynastic Identity in Early Modern Europe: Rulers, Aristocrats and the Formation of Identities*. Farnham: Ashgate, 2015.

Gerber, Matthew. *Bastards: Politics, Family, and Law in Early Modern France*. Oxford: Oxford University Press, 2012.

Given-Wilson, Chris. "Legitimation, Designation and Succession to the Throne in Fourteenth-Century England". In *Building Legitimacy: Political Discourses and Forms of Legitimation in Medieval Societies*, edited by Alfonso, Isabel, Hugh Kennedy, and Julio Escalona, 89–105. Leiden: Brill, 2004.

Henshall, Nicholas. *The Zenith of European Monarchy and its Elites: The Politics of Culture, 1650–1750*. Basingstoke: Palgrave Macmillan, 2010.

Jochens, Jenny M. "The Politics of Reproduction: Medieval Norwegian Kingship". *American Historical Review* 92, 2 (1987): 327–49.

Kannowski, Bernd. "The Impact of Lineage and Family Connections on Succession in Medieval Germany's Elective Kingdom". In *Making and Breaking the Rules: Succession in Medieval Europe, c.1000–c.1600*, edited by Frédérique Lachaud and Michael Penman, 13–22. Turnhout: Brepols, 2008.

Knecht, Robert. *The Valois: Kings of France, 1328–1589*. London: Hambledon & London, 2004.

Lahaye, Matthieu. "Heir Obedience, Heir Disobedience: Two Generations of Dauphins for Louis XIV". *Court Historian* 19, 2 (2014): 129–44.

Le Jan, Régine. *Famille et pouvoir dans le monde franc*. Paris: Publications de la Sorbonne, 1995.

Le Jan, Régine. "La sacralité de la royauté mérovingienne". *Annales. Histoire, Sciences Sociales* 58, 6 (2003): 1217–41.

Lewis, Andrew W. *Royal Succession in Capetian France: Studies in Familial Order and the State*. Cambridge: Harvard University Press, 1981.

Lindsay, Hugh. *Adoption in the Roman World*. Cambridge: Cambridge University Press, 2009.

McDougall, Sara. *Royal Bastards: The Birth of Illegitimacy, 800–1230*. Oxford: Oxford University Press, 2017.

Monod, Paul Kléber. *The Power of Kings: Monarchy and Religion in Europe 1589–1715*. New Haven and London: Yale University Press, 1999.

Murray, Catriona. *Imaging Stuart Family Politics: Dynastic Crisis and Continuity*. Burlington: Ashgate, 2016.

Nenner, Howard. *The Right to be King: The Succession to the Crown of England, 1603–1714*. Basingstoke: Macmillan, 1995.

Norwich, John Julius. *Byzantium: The Early Centuries*. London: Penguin, 1990.

Péneau, Corinne. "La succession royale dans la royaume de Suède, entre coutume héréditaire et loi élective (XIIIe-XIVe siècles)". In *Making and Breaking the Rules: Succession in Medieval Europe, c.1000–c.1600*, edited by Frédérique Lachaud and Michael Penman, 23–42. Turnhout: Brepols, 2008.

Ritchie, Pamela. *Dynasticism and Diplomacy: The Political Career of Marie de Guise in Scotland, 1548–1560*. East Linton: Tuckwell Press, 2002.

Sivertsen, Barbara. "New Testament Genealogies and the Families of Mary and Joseph". *Biblical Theology Bulletin* 35, 2 (2005): 43–50.

Spellman, W. M. *Monarchies 1000–2000*. London: Reaktion, 2001.

Stumpf, Jonathan. "On the Mutilation and Blinding of Byzantine Emperors from the Reign of Heraclius I until the Fall of Constantinople". *Journal of Ancient History and Archaeology* 4, 3 (2017): 46–54.

Taylor, Craig. "The Salic Law, French Queenship, and the Defense of Women in the Late Middle Ages". *French Historical Studies* 29, 4 (2006): 543–64.

Tucker, Ernest. "Explaining Nadir Shah: Kingship and Royal Legitimacy in Muhammad Kazim Marvi's *Tarikh-i 'Alam-ara-yi Nadiri*". *Iranian Studies* 26, 1–2 (1993): 95–117.

Van Arendonk, C., and W. A. Graham. "Sharīf". In *The Encyclopaedia of Islam*, edited by P. Bearman, Th. Bianquis, et al., n.p. 2nd edn. Leiden: Brill Online, 2012, http://dx.doi.org/10.1163/1573-3912_islam_COM_1041 [accessed 20 November 2018].

Vester, Matthew. *Renaissance Dynasticism and Apanage Politics: Jacques de Savoie-Nemours 1531–1585*. Kirksville: Truman State University Press, 2012.

Watanabe-O'Kelly, Helen, and Adam Morton, eds. *Queens Consort, Cultural Transfer and European Politics, c.1500–1800*. Abingdon: Routledge, 2016.

Whitaker, Ian. "Regal Succession Among the Dálriata", *Ethnohistory* 23, 4 (1976): 343–63.

Wolfarth, Joanna. "Lineage and Legitimacy: Exploring Royal-Familial Visual Configurations in Cambodia". *Trans-Asia Photography Review* 8, 1 (2017), n.p.

Wood, Ian. *The Merovingian Kingdoms 450–751*. London and New York: Longman, 1994.

Woodacre, Elena, and Carey Fleiner, eds. *Royal Mothers and their Ruling Children: Wielding Political Authority from Antiquity to the Early Modern Era*. Basingstoke: Palgrave Macmillan, 2015.

Woodacre, Elena, Lucinda H. S. Dean, Chris Jones, Zita Rohr, and Russell Martin, eds. *The Routledge History of Monarchy*. Abingdon: Routledge, 2019.

PART I

Dynastic change

1

"THE VERY NEXT BLOOD OF THE KING"

The rules governing female succession to the throne in English history

Lynsey Wood

It is one of the great ironies of history that Henry VIII's desperate quest for a son led both Crown and Parliament to recognise the right of women to succeed to the English throne. In the past fifty years historians including Mortimer Levine and Eric Ives have investigated what they called Tudor "dynastic problems": the complications of English law and custom that led to the fifteenth-century Wars of the Roses, and were later exacerbated by Henry VIII's efforts to confirm the monarch's ecclesiastical supremacy and to delineate a clear line of succession.[1] One of these key "dynastic problems" was the possibility that the crown might devolve upon a woman. For over four centuries the English throne had been an exclusively male preserve, with the exception of the contested lordship of Matilda in the twelfth century. There were nevertheless several moments in English history when Crown and Parliament addressed the ability of a woman to transmit a dynastic claim to her children or even succeed to the throne in her own right.

Sharon Jansen, in her study of female rulers in early modern Europe, recognised the need for scholars to redraw the lines of power in this period. Part of this proposed "counter-narrative" included restoring women to dynastic trees from which they had often been excluded.[2] This chapter outlines the rules governing female succession to the English throne between the twelfth and early seventeenth centuries. Much like their male relatives, the claims of royal women were addressed through a series of precedents and ad hoc solutions which were invoked, adapted, or even ignored when it was deemed politically expedient. Although this topic has started to receive attention from historians of female kingship, this chapter seeks to expand on this area of enquiry and detail a number of key moments when the dynastic potential of women was recognised by the wider political community of England.[3] More specifically, it will trace the historical and legal significance of a series of precedents, crown entails, and parliamentary statutes that anticipated, enabled, and even undermined the advent of female rule in the sixteenth century.

The twelfth-century example of Matilda

Ruling queens were already a feature of the political landscape of Western Europe before the sixteenth century. Women had succeeded to the throne after the failure of the male line in a number of medieval kingdoms, including León-Castile, Aragon, Sicily, Navarre, Scotland, Naples, Denmark, Norway, Sweden, Hungary, and Poland. Royal heiresses also challenged rivals for the throne, without success, in kingdoms such as Portugal, Mallorca, and Bohemia before the early modern period.[4] The mechanisms of royal succession varied immensely between medieval kingdoms. In Castile, royal succession was governed by *Las Siete Partidas* or "The Seven Divisions", a set of laws that acknowledged the right of women to succeed to the throne upon the failure of the direct male line.[5] This was not the case in France, where royal succession was limited to men by the Salic Law, an archaic legal code revived in the fourteenth century and used to justify the exclusion of women from the French throne. Although this law was based upon a fabrication, the end result was that male primogeniture was upheld and women could neither inherit nor transmit a dynastic claim in France.[6] There was no such codified law of succession in medieval England. Instead the right of a woman to claim the throne was addressed only when male primogeniture was threatened, a situation which occurred a number of times before the sixteenth century.

The problem of female succession in England was first addressed in the twelfth century through the career of Matilda.[7] Although the mechanism of royal succession varied widely in Anglo-Saxon and early Norman England, the candidate for kingship was always male and no woman before Matilda laid formal claim to regal office in her own right.[8] It was the third Norman king, Henry I, who addressed female succession for the first time. Shortly after claiming the throne, Henry had married Edith-Matilda, the daughter of Malcolm III of Scotland. Together they had two children, Matilda and William. Two years after his wife's death in May 1118, the King suffered another loss when his son was drowned in the disaster of the White Ship. Henry's second marriage also remained childless. The King therefore designated his daughter Matilda as heir to the kingdom in early 1127. In making this choice Henry passed over his bastard son Robert, earl of Gloucester, as well as his nephews Theobald and Stephen, the sons of his sister, Adela of Blois, and thwarted the ambitions of his dynastic rival William Clito, son of his elder brother, Robert Curthose.[9] The King evidently came to this decision "after deliberating long and deeply".[10] By choosing Matilda as his successor, Henry believed that a legitimate daughter should inherit the throne upon the failure of the direct male line, a decision which reflected changing attitudes towards bastardy in the Anglo-Norman ruling house.[11]

There were no fixed rules governing succession to the English throne in the twelfth century. In order to settle the kingdom upon his daughter, Henry compelled the clergy and nobility to swear oaths of fealty "to defend her right to the crown of England".[12] Similar oaths had also been sworn to his late son in separate ceremonies at the English and Norman courts, but for his daughter Henry summoned one great court at Windsor, which adjourned to Westminster in January 1127 for the oath-taking.[13] This oath of fealty was taken by the clergy and the laity, including Matilda's cousin, Stephen, and her half-brother, Gloucester.[14] The chronicler William of Malmesbury was one of several writers favourable to Matilda's cause. His account of this oath-taking included a lengthy declaration by Henry outlining his daughter's descent from Norman kings through her father and Anglo-Saxon kings through her mother. It was therefore Matilda "in whom alone lay the legitimate succession".[15] Matilda's position as heir was nevertheless dependent on the King having no further legitimate sons to displace her, demonstrating that female inheritance of the throne was subject to certain conditions.

The importance of the oaths that settled the crown upon Matilda should not be underestimated, for they constituted a legal position from which Matilda challenged her cousin, Stephen, who usurped the English throne after her father's death in December 1135. Matilda's supporters argued that by seizing the crown and disregarding these oaths, Stephen was guilty of perjury and was consequently unfit to rule.[16] The anonymous author of the *Gesta Stephani*, who was hostile to Matilda's cause, tells us that Stephen's supporters disregarded their oaths because they had been made under duress and even claimed that the late king had released the barons from their oaths on his deathbed.[17] According to William of Malmesbury, the bishop of Salisbury maintained that he and others had "sworn only on condition that the king should not give his daughter in marriage to anyone outside the kingdom" without consulting his chief men.[18] Malmesbury nevertheless reports that those who swore fealty to Matilda were required to do so on two separate occasions: in 1127, at her father's court at Westminster, and in 1131, after her marriage to Geoffrey of Anjou.[19]

Matilda's right to inherit the throne was fiercely debated by those on either side of this dynastic conflict. In early 1139 Matilda appealed to the papal curia. Her case was presented by Ulger, bishop of Angers, who argued that the throne rightfully belonged to Matilda by hereditary right and the oaths sworn to her by the leading men of the realm. Arnulf of Lisieux, replying on behalf of Stephen, resorted to the charge that the marriage of Matilda's parents was invalid and that she was therefore illegitimate.[20] Although Innocent II did not withdraw his support from Stephen, this appeal established the disputed nature of the English succession. Others who were loyal to Matilda, such as Brian fitz Count, emphasised the righteousness of her cause. In a letter to the bishop of Winchester, Brian revealed his high regard for the oaths of fealty he had taken to Matilda.[21] Brian also wrote a manifesto in support of Matilda's claim which he sent to Gilbert Foliot, abbot of Gloucester. Foliot agreed with Brian's conclusions and detailed aspects of divine, natural, and human law supporting a woman's right to receive her lawful inheritance, including the biblical example of the daughters of Zelophehad, who were recognised as their father's heirs in the absence of a son.[22] Altogether this series of letters and appeals represents the earliest debate concerning female succession to the English throne.

The position of Matilda's husband also raised doubts regarding the nature of her inheritance. In June 1128 she was married to Geoffrey of Anjou, with whom she had three sons. Matilda's position as heir was greatly enhanced by the birth of male issue, but her marriage to Geoffrey proved controversial. The bishop of Salisbury apparently complained that only a handful of men at Henry I's court had been aware that this marriage would take place.[23] The Worcester chronicler also tells us that the barons viewed Geoffrey as an alien who would seek to reign over them, in light of long-running hostilities between the ruling houses of Normandy and Anjou.[24] These anxieties concerning Geoffrey's role had their basis in contemporary practice, for under common law a woman's inheritance to title and possessions was transferred to her husband upon marriage. It is clear that uncertainty surrounding female succession extended not only to a woman's ability to inherit the English throne in her own right, but also to the position of her husband.

Matilda's moment of triumph came in early 1141, when Stephen was captured and imprisoned at Bristol Castle. A church council was summoned at Winchester and the assembled bishops and magnates recognised Matilda's hereditary right and elected her as *domina Anglorum*, or "Lady of the English".[25] Charles Beem notes that the basis of Matilda's authority in this period was threefold, consisting of the oaths given during her father's lifetime, the theory of a female-inclusive rule of primogeniture, and God's blessing as revealed though successful conquest.[26] Matilda's new title was probably intended as an anticipatory measure before she could be crowned and anointed as queen.[27] But Matilda's coronation never took place, for in June 1141 her forces were driven from London. Further difficulties arose when the earl of Gloucester was captured, and Matilda was forced to agree to an exchange of royal prisoners. Matilda's brief acceptance by the leading men of the realm raised questions concerning not only the elective nature of kingship in this period, but also the extent to which a woman could be recognised as ruler in a military feudal society.

By the late 1140s the conflict with Stephen had settled into a prolonged stalemate, and Matilda supported the cause of her eldest son Henry to claim the inheritance that had been denied to her. Almost fifteen years of civil war was brought to an end with the Treaty of Winchester in November 1153. By the terms of this agreement Stephen was to remain king and Henry would succeed him on the throne after his death. Stephen therefore agreed to prefer Henry over his own surviving son, William.[28] Lois Huneycutt argues that Matilda was not rejected by the feudal nobility of England primarily because of her sex.[29] Instead, the protracted hostilities of this period meant that she was unable to successfully claim the throne in her own right and later concentrated on advancing the cause of her son. Henry II succeeded to the throne in October 1154 and became the second English king, after Stephen himself, to trace his descent through the female line.[30] Matilda's failure in the twelfth century to claim the throne in her own right demonstrates that a growing preference for the hereditary principle to determine the English succession did not lead to the establishment of a female-inclusive rule of primogeniture.

The problem of female succession in later medieval England

The possibility of a woman transmitting a claim to the throne greatly complicated the politics of medieval England. Although Henry II had his eldest son crowned during his lifetime, the young Henry predeceased his father and the throne passed instead to the King's second surviving son Richard (the "Lionheart").[31] Richard I died in April 1199 without legitimate issue. The principle of representation—whereby the son of an elder brother represented his father's claim and took precedence over his uncle—was rejected on this occasion and Richard was succeeded by his brother John, passing over the claim of his twelve-year-old nephew Arthur, duke of Brittany, the posthumous son of John's elder brother, Geoffrey. In order to prevent any challenge to his throne, King John had his young nephew imprisoned and presumably murdered in April 1203.[32] Arthur's sister Eleanor of Brittany was also kept an effective state prisoner. She died unmarried and without issue in August 1241.[33] Although Eleanor's claim to the throne was not ultimately advanced, her dynastic potential was recognised after her death by a number of chroniclers. For example, the *Lanercost Chronicle* included a fanciful tale in which John's son and successor, Henry III, doubted his right to the crown and resigned it to Eleanor, who kept it for three days and then voluntarily gave up her rights to Henry's son, the future Edward I.[34] John and Henry III's actions in controlling Eleanor's reproductive potential demonstrated that advancing a dynastic claim through a woman was a recognised threat to the line of English succession.[35]

The question of a woman inheriting the English throne in her own right was addressed again at the close of the thirteenth century. After the death of three of his sons, Edward I called a gathering at Amesbury in April 1290. Here the King announced that the throne would descend to his surviving son Edward of Carnarvon (later Edward II), followed by the prince's children whether male or female. If Carnarvon predeceased his father without issue and Edward I had no further sons (or those sons had no issue) then the throne would descend to Eleanor, the King's eldest daughter, and her children. Failing Eleanor's issue then the throne would pass to the King's next daughter, Joan, and so on in turn "from daughter to daughter, and from heir to heir".[36] Edward I had five surviving daughters at this time, including Margaret, Mary, and Elizabeth, and the terms of Edward's settlement reveal his concern that the rule of primogeniture should apply amongst both sons and daughters, eliminating the possibility of the kingdom being divided amongst co-heiresses like a barony.[37] As well as recognising a woman's right to inherit on the failure of the direct male line, Edward I's crown entail also established that the principle of representation was a valid method of settling the succession whether the heir was male or female. Edward reinforced his crown entail with a series of strategic marriages. Margaret was married in July 1290 to the future John II, duke of Brabant, whilst her older sister Eleanor was married by proxy in August 1290 to Alfonso III, king of Aragon.[38] Joan was also married to Gilbert de Clare, earl of Gloucester, who was required to swear an oath upholding this settlement; it is only from the charter which Gloucester issued that day that the terms of this entail are known to historians.[39]

Although this arrangement was reminiscent of Henry I's crown entail in the twelfth century, there was another precedent which probably influenced Edward I's decision to recognise the inheritance rights of his daughters and grand-daughters. In February 1284 a similar gathering had been called at Scone by Alexander III to secure the Scottish succession after the death of his last surviving child. Alexander required his magnates to swear an oath to accept his infant grand-daughter Margaret, "the Maid of Norway" as his heir, and she was recognised as "Lady of Scotland" after the King's death in March 1286. Scotland was ruled by a council of Guardians during her minority, but Margaret would not become queen until she was crowned at Scone. In anticipation of her arrival from Norway, negotiations took place for a marriage between Margaret and Edward of Carnarvon. But this union never took place, for Margaret died on her journey to Scotland in September 1290, aged only seven.[40] Margaret's recognition as heir to the Scottish throne offered another precedent for Edward I's entail of 1290, which demonstrated that in England a female-inclusive rule of primogeniture was again regarded as a viable option in a period of dynastic uncertainty. Like other kingdoms such as Scotland and France, the rules of succession in England were subject to change when political and dynastic circumstances dictated.

It is possible that Edward III was aware of the provisions set down by his grandfather when he drew up his own crown entail around October 1376.[41] Edward III's entail established his nine-year-old grandson Richard (later Richard II) as his successor, affirming the principle of representation in the case of a male heir. Richard's father was Edward of Woodstock ("the Black Prince"), the eldest son of Edward III, who had predeceased his father, dying in June 1376. This entail nevertheless excluded the King's second child Isabella, countess of Bedford, and her own daughters, Marie and Philippa. Instead, if Richard died without sons then the throne would descend in turn to his three surviving uncles—John of Gaunt, duke of Lancaster; Edmund of Langley, duke of York; and Thomas of Woodstock, duke of Gloucester—and their male issue. Edward III also passed over his grand-daughter Philippa and her children, including her son, Roger Mortimer.[42] Philippa was the only child of Lionel, duke of Clarence, the second surviving son of Edward III, who had predeceased his father in 1368. Edward III's entail therefore ruled that women could neither inherit nor transmit a claim to the throne to their children, much like the Salic Law that had been introduced in France.[43]

Edward III's decision to limit the crown in this manner appears to have been a response to anxieties about the succession in light of his own failing health. The chronicler Thomas Walsingham claimed that Gaunt had petitioned Parliament to "make a law on the pattern of the French that no woman be heir to the kingdom".[44] Indeed, it is even possible that Edward had contemplated excluding the female line as early as 1368.[45] In the fifteenth century Sir John Fortescue alleged that shortly after Clarence's death, Edward III had entailed the crown upon his male heirs, and that the King's daughters had come into Parliament "in there mantels of estate embroidred with the armes of Englande" and publicly renounced any claim to the throne.[46] Edward had one surviving daughter at this time, Isabella, and Michael Bennett suggests that if this ceremony had taken place then it might have included the King's grand-daughter, Philippa.[47] Concerns over the husband of a female claimant might have also influenced Edward III's male-exclusive entail, for Thomas Walsingham tells us that Philippa's husband, Edmund Mortimer, earl of March, had expectations concerning his wife's title.[48] Following the accession of Richard II in June 1377, the Mortimer claim continued to draw support, but it is difficult to ascertain Richard's exact intentions for the succession or even the degree to which Edward III's entail was known to contemporaries.[49]

Although historical memory of Edward III's crown entail remains unclear, its provisions were partly fulfilled when Henry IV, the eldest surviving son of John of Gaunt, usurped the throne from Richard II in 1399. Henry secured parliamentary recognition of his own entail in February 1404, vesting the crown upon his sons—Henry, Thomas, John, and Humphrey—and their issue, male or female, in order of seniority.[50] At the request of the Commons the King issued a charter in June 1406 that instead limited the succession to his sons and their male heirs only.[51] A series of rebellions in support of the Mortimer claim possibly led to Henry's decision to affirm the principle of descent in the male line.[52] This new entail of the crown was nevertheless repealed at the petition of the Commons in December 1406, and the 1404 settlement was reinstated and given statutory form.[53] Although this settlement recognised the succession rights of Henry IV's grand-daughters, it excluded the King's daughters Blanche and Philippa, who both married into other ruling houses.[54] Several motivations for this reversal have been suggested, including wider concerns about the implications of adopting the Salic Law in England.[55] It was noted that in excluding the female sex, the June 1406 settlement "greatly restricted that which they by no means intended to diminish but rather to increase".[56]

The ability of a woman to transmit a dynastic claim became a matter of critical importance during the reign of Henry VI. Although the House of Lancaster had successfully asserted its right through military prowess, the sudden death of Henry V in August 1422 meant that the throne passed to his nine-month-old son. Henry VI's troubled reign marks the beginning of the Wars of the Roses (1455–87), a series of dynastic conflicts between adherents of the Lancastrian and Yorkist claims to the throne. Henry VI's title was challenged by Richard, duke of York, who walked into the Parliament chamber at Westminster in October 1460 and advanced his own claim by placing a hand upon the empty throne. Three weeks later Parliament passed the Act of Accord, which ruled that York would inherit the throne after Henry's death, passing over the King's only child, Edward, Prince of Wales.[57] York derived a claim to the throne from his father, Richard Conisburgh, earl of Cambridge, the son of Edmund of Langley, but the senior hereditary claim York asserted was through his mother, Anne Mortimer, by virtue of her descent from Lionel, duke of Clarence.[58] The Act of Accord therefore established that the English throne could be inherited through a woman, confirming by parliamentary statute the same hereditary principle that had supported the accessions of Stephen and Henry II in the twelfth century. York was killed in battle shortly after his recognition as heir to the throne, but his son Edward asserted his own claim and defeated the Lancastrian army at the Battle of Towton in March 1461.

The validity of Edward IV's title was fiercely disputed by a number of Lancastrian adherents including Sir John Fortescue, Chief Justice of the Bench under Henry

VI. Fortescue wrote a series of polemical works challenging the legitimacy of the House of York. In his works, Fortescue argued that women could neither inherit nor transmit a claim to the English throne, dismissing the example of Matilda and stating that Henry II had succeeded Stephen by election of the people. The Treaty of Winchester had instead established that the crown should pass through the male line in perpetuity for it was "contrary to the laws and customs of England" that anyone should claim the throne through a woman.[59] Fortescue also warned that a royal heiress might make an unsuitable marriage, and that the kingdom itself would be divided between co-heiresses if the king had more than one daughter. For good measure, Fortescue even questioned the legitimacy of Philippa of Clarence and therefore the entire basis of the House of York's superior claim to the throne.[60] Fortescue was later obliged to refute these earlier writings against female inheritance in order to be restored to royal favour, demonstrating that such arguments were as opportunistic as they were flexible.[61]

Female succession claims accompanied another reversal of dynastic fortunes in the late fifteenth century. Edward IV died in April 1483 and was succeeded by his twelve-year-old son, Edward V. The new king was quickly usurped by his uncle, Richard III, and Edward and his brother Richard vanished behind the walls of the Tower in the summer of 1483. Their disappearance meant that if female succession was to be upheld, Edward IV's claims now descended to his surviving daughters Elizabeth, Cecily, Anne, Katherine, and Bridget.[62] Their significance as potential claimants to the throne was well recognised by contemporaries. The continuator of the *Crowland Chronicle* mentions rumours of a plan to smuggle the Yorkist princesses overseas and so ensure that "the kingdom might someday return to the rightful heirs".[63] Richard III, in order to legitimate his title, caused Parliament to pass a statute known as *Titulus Regius*, which ruled that Edward IV's children were illegitimate. Richard also argued that the attainder of his elder brother George, duke of Clarence, barred Clarence's young children, Margaret and Edward, from the succession.[64] In the event, however, it was Henry Tudor, earl of Richmond, who emerged as the main rival for Richard's crown. Henry's royal claim came from his mother, Lady Margaret Beaufort, who was a descendant of John of Gaunt. The Beauforts were the product of Gaunt's union with his mistress Katherine Swynford, who later became his third wife. Gaunt and Katherine's children had been legitimated by Richard II through letters patent in 1397, but a clause (*excepta dignitate regali*) was inserted into this patent after its confirmation by Henry IV in 1407, demonstrating that they were not viewed as candidates for the throne.[65]

Like her ancestor Matilda in the twelfth century, Margaret Beaufort dedicated her efforts to ensuring that her son would one day succeed to the throne. In order to strengthen Yorkist support for his cause, Henry Tudor swore an oath to marry Elizabeth of York at Rennes Cathedral in December 1483.[66] Marriage to Elizabeth was clearly recognised as a method of consolidating an existing claim to the throne, and after Richard III was widowed in March 1485 he was forced to deny rumours that he planned to marry his niece in order to strengthen his position.[67] Henry ultimately defeated Richard at the Battle of Bosworth Field in August 1485 and was crowned as the first king of the Tudor dynasty. Although his first Parliament simply confirmed Henry VII's royal title, the new king claimed the throne by conquest, his election by the nobility, and his recognition by Parliament, as well as his descent from Edward III.[68] His promised marriage to Elizabeth in January 1486 united the claims of these formerly warring houses and allowed Henry to consolidate Yorkist support for his rule. Before this marriage was accomplished, however, it was necessary for Henry to repeal *Titulus Regius*, which had bastardised Elizabeth and her siblings.[69] It was therefore claims descending from the female line of the Houses of Lancaster and York that supported the establishment of the Tudor dynasty, but England did not yet recognise the right of a woman to claim the throne in her own right.

The law of female succession in Tudor England

The question of whether a woman might wear the English crown was finally answered in the mid-sixteenth century. The necessary legal framework was introduced during the reign of Henry VIII, the second king of the Tudor dynasty. Henry's eldest daughter Mary was born in February 1516, the only surviving child of Henry and his first wife Katherine of Aragon. Although Mary was effectively heiress presumptive for the first seventeen years of her life, her father desperately hoped for a male heir to succeed him.[70] Henry eventually secured an annulment of his marriage to Queen Katherine, but not before marrying his pregnant mistress, Anne Boleyn, who gave birth in September 1533 to a daughter named Elizabeth. Like Sir John Fortescue in the fifteenth century, Tudor commentators were familiar with the stories of Matilda in the medieval chronicles, but had limited understanding of the rules governing royal succession before the emergence of a settled parliamentary tradition.[71] In order to effectively provide for the succession during his lifetime, Henry VIII was therefore compelled to address the claims of his daughters to ensure that he might leave his crown to a suitable heir.

Female succession to the English throne was established in this period through a series of parliamentary statutes. The First Succession Act of 1534 ruled that the marriage between Henry and Katherine of Aragon was invalid. This act instead vested the crown upon the children of Henry and Anne Boleyn, establishing their daughter Elizabeth as heiress presumptive in the absence of a son. This act also ruled that for want of male issue the crown should pass to Henry and Anne's daughters "one after another, by course of inheritance, according to their ages, as the crown of England has been accustomed, and ought to go, in cases where there be heirs female to the same". This act was silent, however, on Mary's exact status.[72] In contrast, the Second Succession Act of 1536 set aside the terms of the first, confirming that the marriage between Henry and Anne Boleyn was invalid and ruling that both Mary and Elizabeth were illegitimate and therefore unable to inherit the throne. The crown would instead descend to the King's male or female issue by his recent marriage to Jane Seymour or any future wife. This act also ruled that if any of the King's heirs attempted to interrupt the rightful order of succession then they would forfeit their right to the throne. Female inheritance was again subject to certain conditions, but Henry VIII was also granted the unprecedented power to nominate his own heir by letters patent or his last will if he failed to produce any lawful issue.[73]

Henry VIII further consolidated his settlement of the crown in the final years of his reign. The Third Succession Act of 1544 restored Mary and Elizabeth to the line of succession after their brother Edward, born in October 1537, and any further lawful issue the King might have. Mary and Elizabeth nevertheless remained illegitimate.[74] Henry's last will of 1546 confirmed the right of his daughters to succeed to the throne but only on condition that their marriages were approved by their brother's Privy Council. If each failed to meet these conditions, their claims to the throne would be forfeit. The inclusion of this matrimonial provision revealed that the prospect of a royal heiress ruling unaided by a husband had not yet been considered.[75] If both Mary and Elizabeth failed to qualify then next in the line of succession were the female heirs of their Suffolk cousins, Lady Frances Grey and Lady Eleanor Clifford, the daughters of Henry's younger sister, Mary Tudor. This was in preference to their Scottish cousins, descended from Henry's elder sister, Margaret Tudor.[76]

The demands of the rebels during the Pilgrimage of Grace in 1536 provides a glimpse into popular feeling towards this series of succession acts. Robert Aske, the leader of this revolt, demanded that the "statute of illegitimacy" (the act of 1534) be repealed and the act of 1536 amended so that the heir apparent would be clearly named, or else that the succession would come as it had before "to the very next blood of the King": namely, his eldest daughter, Mary.[77] Aske's demands revealed the strength of popular feeling towards the hereditary principle in deciding the succession, and a daughter's right to claim her father's inheritance. The importance of the Henrician succession statutes is obvious, for they allowed a woman to claim the English throne in her own right. Eric Ives nevertheless points out that this last series of acts allowed Mary and Elizabeth to succeed to the throne as nominees but not to inherit it.[78] This distinction was crucial, for it meant that although these succession acts allowed a woman to claim regal office for the first time, both Mary and Elizabeth held a parliamentary title to the throne.

After Henry VIII's death there was one last attempt to divert the crown towards a male heir before a woman finally claimed the English throne in her own right. The third Tudor king, Edward VI, alongside his chief minister, John Dudley, duke of Northumberland, attempted to change his father's settlement with Edward's "devise" for the succession, barring Mary and Elizabeth from the throne and preferring the claims of the King's Suffolk cousins instead. This devise was issued as letters patent in June 1553, but Edward did not live long enough to have these changes ratified by Parliament. Historians have also debated whether the fifteen-year-old Edward had the same power as his father to nominate an heir;[79] Mary and Elizabeth had been reinstated into the line of succession by statute law, and only statute law could remove them once again.[80] Faced with a pool of English-born candidates in the direct line who were all female, the young king responded first by diverting the succession to a hypothetical male heir. However, when it became obvious that no male heir would be born in his lifetime, Edward amended his devise and raised his married cousin, Lady Jane Grey, to the throne in her own right. This arrangement would redirect the crown to the Protestant Jane with the view of producing a male heir as soon as possible.[81] Jane's sisters, Katherine and Mary, would then succeed in turn if each failed to produce a male heir of their own, but this same rule did not apply to their mother Frances or to their aunt Eleanor's daughter, Margaret Clifford, neither of whom would succeed themselves, but who would merely transmit their claim to further male issue.

This new line of succession was confirmed in Queen Jane's accession proclamation, which was promulgated after Edward's death in July 1553. Mary and Elizabeth's exclusion from this settlement was justified because of their illegitimacy, but it was also feared that if either became queen and took a foreign husband, then, having the throne in his hands, he would bring about "the utter subversion of the common weale". In contrast, the King's Suffolk cousins were "naturally borne here within the realme", differentiating them from their Scottish relations.[82] Jane and her sister Katherine were also safely married to Englishmen.[83] Those who installed Jane upon the throne were also concerned to safeguard their own positions and ensure that Edward's Protestant settlement would not be overturned after his death by the Catholic Mary.

Mary I led a popular uprising and took the throne in July 1553 in spite of the provisions of her brother's entail, asserting her hereditary right as "the most excellent princess Mary, elder daughter of King Henry VIII and sister to King Edward VI".[84] The first Tudor queen's accession proclamation made no mention of Jane's brief ascendancy but stated simply that the crown of England did "most rightfully and lawfully belong" to her.[85] Mary officially remained illegitimate until her first Parliament repealed the 1534 succession act which had invalidated her parents' marriage, and voided that part of the 1536 succession act which had legally bastardised her.[86] Mary nevertheless ensured that Parliament confirmed her title only after she had been crowned and anointed.[87] Fears concerning a foreign husband were raised again when Mary announced her intention to marry Prince Philip of Spain soon after her accession.[88] Mary wished to name her successor as part of the marriage treaty with Philip "in order to avoid the troubles and disputes" that might ensue if she died without an heir. The three main candidates for the throne were her cousins Mary, Queen of Scots, and Lady Frances Grey, as well as her sister Elizabeth. Mary did not wish Elizabeth to succeed her for a number of reasons, including her bastardy. Instead Mary believed that her Catholic cousin Lady Margaret Douglas was "the person best suited to succeed".[89]

Although Mary did not nominate a successor during her reign, she appears to have had the chancery enrolment of her father's will destroyed, which ruled that she needed the consent of a majority of her brother's councillors before she could take a husband.[90] Mary's marriage to Philip of Spain took place in July 1554. The marriage treaty confirmed that Mary would remain sole queen and that Philip

48 Thompson, ed., *Chronicon Angliae*, 93.
49 See Chris Given-Wilson, "Legitimation, Designation and Succession to the Throne in Fourteenth-Century England", in *Building Legitimacy: Political Discourses and Forms of Legitimation in Medieval Societies*, eds Isabel Alfonso, Hugh Kennedy and Julio Escalona (Leiden: Brill, 2004), 89–105.
50 Alexander Luders et al., eds, *The Statutes of the Realm*, vol. 2 (London: Dawsons of Pall Mall, 1810–28), 151; Bennett, "Edward III's Entail", 600.
51 Chris Given-Wilson et al., eds, *Parliament Rolls of Medieval England*, vol. 8 (London: Boydell Press, 2005), 341–47.
52 Bennett, "Edward III's Entail", 600.
53 Given-Wilson et al., *Parliament Rolls*, vol. 8, 354–61.
54 Blanche married the future Louis III, Elector Palatine, in July 1402. Her sister Philippa married Eric of Pomerania in October 1406. During Edward III's reign a statute had confirmed that children of the kings of England born overseas might inherit the throne if their parents were in allegiance to the king at the time of their birth. It was not clear, however, whether this ruling applied to further royal descendants. See Given-Wilson et al., *Parliament Rolls*, vol. 5, 22; Levine, *Tudor Dynastic Problems*, 110–11.
55 Bennett, "Edward III's Entail", 600; Given-Wilson, "Legitimation", 103, n. 27.
56 Given-Wilson et al., *Parliament Rolls*, vol. 8, 354–61.
57 Given-Wilson et al., *Parliament Rolls*, vol. 12, 516–25.
58 For a recent study of the Wars of the Roses, see Michael Hicks, *The Wars of the Roses, 1455–1485* (London: Bloomsbury, 2014).
59 Fortescue, *Works*, vol. 1, 511–12.
60 Fortescue, *Works*, vol. 1, 498–99 and 517.
61 Paul E. Gill, "Politics and Propaganda in Fifteenth-Century England: The Polemical Writings of Sir John Fortescue", *Speculum* 46 (1971): 333–47.
62 Bridget of York later became a nun.
63 Nicholas Pronay and John Cox, eds, *The Crowland Chronicle Continuations, 1459–1486* (London: Richard III and Yorkist History Trust, 1986), 163.
64 Given-Wilson et al., eds, *Parliament Rolls*, vol. 15, 13–18. Both Margaret and Edward were executed during the reigns of the Tudors. Richard III's son Edward died in April 1484. The King's nearest adult male heir was his nephew John de la Pole, earl of Lincoln, the son of Elizabeth, duchess of Suffolk. Historians disagree whether Lincoln was publicly recognised as heir to the throne. See Charles Ross, *Richard III* (London: Yale University Press, 1981), 158.
65 Given-Wilson et al., eds, *Parliament Rolls*, vol. 7, 322–23; Michael K. Jones and Malcolm G. Underwood, *The King's Mother: Lady Margaret Beaufort, Countess of Richmond and Derby* (Cambridge: Cambridge University Press, 1993), 24. See also Joanna L. Chamberlayne, "Crowns and Virgins: Queenmaking during the Wars of the Roses", in *Young Medieval Women*, eds Katherine J. Lewis, Noël James Menuge, and Kim M. Phillips (Stroud: Sutton, 1999), 59–60.
66 Pronay and Cox, *Crowland Chronicle*, 171.
67 Pronay and Cox, *Crowland Chronicle*, 175, 177.
68 Given-Wilson et al., eds, *Parliament Rolls*, vol. 15, 97; P. L. Hughes and J. F. Larkin, eds, *Tudor Royal Proclamations*, vol. 1 (London: Yale University Press, 1964–69), 6.
69 Given-Wilson et al., eds, *Parliament Rolls*, vol. 15, 133–34. Henry also ordered all copies of this statute to be destroyed.
70 See Charles Beem, "Princess of Wales? Mary Tudor and the History of English Heirs to the Throne", in *The Birth of a Queen: Essays on the Quincentenary of Mary I*, eds Sarah Duncan and Valerie Schutte (Basingstoke: Palgrave Macmillan, 2016), 13–30.
71 Chibnall, *Empress Matilda*, 200.
72 Luders et al., *Statutes*, vol. 3, 471–74.
73 Luders et al., *Statutes*, vol. 3, 655–62.
74 Luders et al., *Statutes*, vol. 3, 955–58.

75 Beem, *Lioness Roared*, 71–72.
76 James Gairdner et al., eds, *Letters and Papers, Foreign and Domestic, Henry VIII,* vol. 11, ii (London: His Majesty's Stationery Office, 1864–1920), 634. Mary's husband was Charles Brandon, duke of Suffolk, from whom this line derives its name.
77 Levine, *Tudor Dynastic Problems*, 68, 157.
78 Ives, "Tudor Dynastic Problems Revisited", 255.
79 Paulina Kewes, "The 1553 Succession Crisis Reconsidered", *Historical Research* 90 (2017): 465–85.
80 Beem, *Lioness Roared*, 74.
81 Beem, *Lioness Roared*, 74.
82 *Tudor Proclamations: Facsimiles of Proclamations of Henry VII, Henry VIII, Edward VI, and Philip and Mary, now in the Library of the Society of Antiquaries of London* (Oxford: Horace Hart, 1897), 86–87.
83 The Grey sisters were married in May 1553. Jane wed Guildford Dudley, son of the duke of Northumberland, whilst her younger sister Katherine wed Henry Herbert, son of the earl of Pembroke. Jane and Guildford were executed in February 1554, whilst Katherine's marriage to Herbert was annulled. She later married Edward Seymour, earl of Hertford.
84 Linda Porter, *Mary Tudor: The First Queen* (London: Portrait, 2007), 208–09.
85 Hughes and Larkin, eds, *Tudor Royal Proclamations*, vol. 2, 3.
86 Mortimer Levine, "Henry VIII's Use of His Spiritual and Temporal Jurisdictions in His Great Causes of Matrimony, Legitimacy, and Succession", *Historical Journal* 10 (1967): 9.
87 Mortimer Levine, "A Parliamentary Title to the Crown in Tudor England", *Huntingdon Library Quarterly* 25, 2 (1962): 126.
88 For discussion of Mary and Philip's marriage, see Judith M. Richards, "Mary Tudor as 'Sole Quene'? Gendering Tudor Monarchy", *Historical Journal* 40 (1997): 895–924; Glyn Redworth, "'Matters Impertinent to Women': Male and Female Monarchy under Philip and Mary", *English Historical Review* 112 (1997): 597–613; and Alexander Samson, "Changing Places: The Marriage and Royal Entry of Philip, Prince of Austria and Mary Tudor, July–August 1554", *Sixteenth Century Journal* 36 (2005): 761–84.
89 G. A. Bergenroth, et al., eds, *Calendar of State Papers, Spain*, vol. 11 (London: His Majesty's Stationery Office, 1862–1954), 393. Mary, Queen of Scots was the grand-daughter of Margaret Tudor by her marriage to James IV of Scotland, whilst Lady Margaret Douglas was the daughter of Margaret Tudor by her second marriage to Archibald Douglas, earl of Angus.
90 Levine, *Tudor Dynastic Problems*, 91.
91 Luders et al., *Statutes*, vol. 4, i, 222–26.
92 J. R. Tanner, ed., *Tudor Constitutional Documents, A.D. 1485–1603: With An Historical Commentary* (Cambridge: Cambridge University Press, 1930), 123.
93 Tanner, *Tudor Constitutional Documents*, 410.
94 J. M. Stone, *Mary I: Queen of England* (London: Sands & Co, 1901), 507–17.
95 Stone, *Mary I,* 507–19.
96 Hughes and Larkin, *Tudor Royal Proclamations*, vol. 2, 99.
97 Luders et al., *Statutes*, vol. 4, i, 358–59.
98 Elizabeth's first Parliament did, however, pass an act declaring that the Queen was "enhabled in bloode" and inheritable to her mother Anne Boleyn. See Luders et al., *Statutes*, vol. 4, i, 397; and Mary Hill Cole, "The Half-Blood Princes: Mary I, Elizabeth I, and Their Strategies of Legitimation", in *Birth of a Queen*, eds Duncan and Schutte, 82–83.
99 This included Lady Arbella Stuart, grand-daughter of Margaret Douglas, and ladies Anne, Frances, and Elizabeth Stanley, the grand-daughters of Margaret Clifford. For the Elizabethan succession debate, see Mortimer Levine, *The Early Elizabethan Succession Question, 1558–1568* (Stanford: Stanford University Press, 1966); Susan Doran and

Paulina Kewes, eds, *Doubtful and Dangerous: The Question of Succession in Late Elizabethan England* (Manchester: Manchester University Press, 2014).

100 Howard Nenner, *The Right to be King: The Succession to the Crown of England, 1603–1714* (Basingstoke: Palgrave Macmillan, 1995), 14.

101 Luders et al., *Statutes*, vol. 4, i, 704–05.

102 See Amanda Shephard, *Gender and Authority in Sixteenth-Century England: The Knox Debate* (Keele: Ryburn, 1995); Sharon L. Jansen, *Debating Women, Politics and Power in Early Modern Europe* (Basingstoke: Palgrave Macmillan, 2008).

103 Luders et al., *Statutes*, vol. 4, ii, 1017–18.

Bibliography

Primary sources

Bergenroth, G. A., et al., eds. *Calendar of State Papers, Spain*. 13 vols. London: His Majesty's Stationery Office, 1862–1954.

Brooke, C. N. L, ed. *The Letters and Charters of Gilbert Foliot*. Cambridge: Cambridge University Press, 1967.

Chibnall, Marjorie, ed. *The Historia Pontificalis of John of Salisbury*. Oxford: Clarendon Press, 1986.

Douglas, David C., and George W. Greenway, eds. *English Historical Documents, 1042–1189*. 13 vols. London: Eyre & Spottiswoode, 1953.

Forester, Thomas, trans. *The Chronicle of Florence of Worcester*. London: H. G. Bohn, 1854.

Fortescue, Thomas Lord Clermont, comp. *The Works of Sir John Fortescue*. 2 vols. London: self-published, 1869.

Gairdner, James, et al., eds. *Letters and Papers, Foreign and Domestic, Henry VIII*. 21 vols. London: His Majesty's Stationery Office, 1864–1920.

Given-Wilson, Chris, Paul Brand, Seymour Phillips, Mark Ormrod, Geoffrey Martin, Anne Curry, and Rosemary Horrox, eds. *Parliament Rolls of Medieval England*. 16 vols. London: Boydell Press, 2005.

Hughes, P. L., and J. F. Larkin, eds. *Tudor Royal Proclamations*. 3 vols. London: Yale University Press, 1964–69.

Luders, Alexander et al., eds. *The Statutes of the Realm*. 11 vols. London: Dawsons of Pall Mall, 1810–28.

Malmesbury, William of. *Historia Novella: The Contemporary History*. Edited by Edmund King and translated by K. R. Potter. Oxford: Clarendon Press, 1998.

Potter, K. R., ed. and trans., and R. H. C. Davis. *Gesta Stephani*. Oxford: Clarendon Press, 1976.

Pronay, Nicholas, and John Cox, eds. *The Crowland Chronicle Continuations, 1459–1486*. London: Richard III and Yorkist History Trust, 1986.

Rymer, Thomas, ed. *Foedera*. 4 vols. London, 1816–69.

Stevenson, Joseph, ed. *Chronicon de Lanercost, 1201–1346*. Edinburgh: Impressum, 1839.

Tanner, J. R., ed. *Tudor Constitutional Documents, A.D. 1485–1603: With An Historical Commentary*. Cambridge: Cambridge University Press, 1930.

Thompson, Edward Maunde, ed. *Chronicon Angliae, 1328–1388*. London: Roll Series, 1874.

Tudor Proclamations: Facsimiles of Proclamations of Henry VII, Henry VIII, Edward VI, and Philip and Mary, now in the Library of the Society of Antiquaries of London. Oxford: Horace Hart, 1897.

Secondary sources

Alsop, J. D. "The Act for the Queen's Regal Power, 1554". *Parliamentary History* 13 (1994): 261–76.

Bailey, Alfred. *The Succession to the English Crown: A Historical Sketch*. London: Macmillan and Co., 1879.

Barrow, G. W. S. "A Kingdom in Crisis: Scotland and the Maid of Norway". *Scottish Historical Review* 69 (1990): 120–41.

Beem, Charles. *The Lioness Roared: The Problems of Female Rule in English History*. Basingstoke: Palgrave Macmillan, 2008.

Beem, Charles. "Princess of Wales? Mary Tudor and the History of English Heirs to the Throne". In *The Birth of a Queen: Essays on the Quincentenary of Mary I*, edited by Sarah Duncan and Valerie Schutte, 13–30. Basingstoke: Palgrave Macmillan, 2016.

Bennett, Michael. "Edward III's Entail and the Succession to the Crown, 1376–1471". *English Historical Review* 113 (1998): 580–609.

Bennett, Michael. "Henry IV, the Royal Succession and the Crisis of 1406". In *The Reign of Henry IV: Rebellion and Survival, 1403–13*, edited by Gwilym Dodd and Douglas Biggs, 9–27. York: York Medieval Press, 2008.

Castor, Helen. "Exception to the Rule: Medieval England Could Not Accept a Female Monarch". *History Today* 60 (2010): 37–43.

Chamberlayne, Joanna L. "Crowns and Virgins: Queenmaking during the Wars of the Roses". In *Young Medieval Women*, edited by Katherine J. Lewis, Noël James Menuge, and Kim M. Phillips, 47–68. Stroud: Sutton, 1999.

Chibnall, Marjorie, *The Empress Matilda: Queen Consort, Queen Mother and Lady of the English*. Oxford: Blackwell, 1991.

Cole, Mary Hill. "The Half-Blood Princes: Mary I, Elizabeth I, and Their Strategies of Legitimation". In *The Birth of a Queen: Essays on the Quincentenary of Mary I*, edited by Sarah Duncan and Valerie Schutte, 71–88. Basingstoke: Palgrave Macmillan, 2016.

Crouch, David. "Robert of Gloucester and the daughters of Zelophehad". *Journal of Medieval History* 11 (1985): 227–43.

Davis, H. W. C. "Henry of Blois and Brian Fitz-Count". *English Historical Review* 25 (1910): 297–303.

Doran, Susan, and Paulina Kewes, eds. *Doubtful and Dangerous: The Question of Succession in Late Elizabethan England*. Manchester: Manchester University Press, 2014.

Duncan, A. A. M. "Margaret [the Maid of Norway] (1282/3–1290)". *Oxford Dictionary of National Biography* (2004). Accessed May 28, 2017. doi:10.1093/ref:odnb/18048.

Dunham, Jr., William Huse, and Charles T. Wood. "The Right to Rule in England: Depositions and the Kingdom's Authority, 1327–1485". *American Historical Review* 81 (1976): 738–61.

Gill, Paul E. "Politics and Propaganda in Fifteenth-Century England: The Polemical Writings of Sir John Fortescue". *Speculum* 46 (1971): 333–47.

Given-Wilson, Chris. "Richard II, Edward II, and the Lancastrian Inheritance". *English Historical Review* 109 (1994): 553–71.

Given-Wilson, Chris. "Legitimation, Designation and Succession to the Throne in Fourteenth-Century England". In *Building Legitimacy: Political Discourses and Forms of Legitimation in Medieval Societies*, edited by Isabel Alfonso, Hugh Kennedy, and Julio Escalona, 89–105. Leiden: Brill, 2004.

Given-Wilson, Chris, and Alice Curteis, *The Royal Bastards of Medieval England*. London: Routledge & Kegan Paul, 1984.

Griffiths, R. A. "The Sense of Dynasty in the Reign of Henry VI". In *Patronage, Pedigree and Power in Later Medieval England*, edited by Charles Ross, 13–36. Gloucester: Alan Sutton, 1979.

Hanley, Catherine. *Louis: The French Prince Who Invaded England*. London: Yale University Press, 2016.

Hanley, Sarah. "Identity Politics and Rulership in France: Female Political Place and the Fraudulent Salic Law in Christine de Pizan". In *Changing Identities in Early Modern France*, edited by Michael Wolfe, 78–94. Durham: Duke University Press, 1997.

Helmholz, R. H. "The Sons of Edward IV: A Canonical Assessment of the Claim that They Were Illegitimate". In *Richard III: Loyalty, Lordship and Law*, edited by P. W. Hammond, 91–103. London: Richard III and Yorkist History Trust, 1986.

Hicks, Michael. *The Wars of the Roses, 1455–1485*. London: Bloomsbury, 2014.

Hollister, C. Warren. "The Anglo-Norman Succession Debate of 1126: Prelude to Stephen's Anarchy". *Journal of Medieval History* 1 (1975): 19–41.

Hollister, C. Warren. *Henry I*. London: Yale University Press, 2001.

Holt, J. C. "The *Casus Regis*: The Law and Politics of Succession in the Plantagenet Dominions, 1185–1247". In *Law in Medieval Life and Thought*, edited by Edward B. King and Susan J. Ridyard, 21–41. Sewanee: University of the South, 1990.

Holt, J. C. "King John and Arthur of Brittany". *Nottingham Medieval Studies* 44 (2000): 82–103.

Holt, J. C. "The *Casus Regis* Reconsidered". *Haskins Society Journal* 10 (2001): 163–82.

Huneycutt, Lois L. "Female Succession and the Language of Power in the Writings of Twelfth-Century Churchmen". In *Medieval Queenship*, edited by John Carmi Parsons, 189–201. Stroud: Sutton, 1998.

Ives, Eric. "Tudor Dynastic Problems Revisited". *Historical Research* 81 (2008): 255–79.

Ives, Eric. *Lady Jane Grey: A Tudor Mystery*. Oxford: Wiley-Blackwell, 2011.

Jansen, Sharon L. *The Monstrous Regiment of Women: Female Rulers in Early Modern Europe*. Basingstoke: Palgrave Macmillan, 2002.

Jansen, Sharon L. *Debating Women, Politics and Power in Early Modern Europe*. Basingstoke: Palgrave Macmillan, 2008.

Jones, Michael. "Eleanor, Suo Jure Duchess of Brittany (1182x4–1241)". *Oxford Dictionary of National Biography* (2008). Accessed May 28, 2017. doi:10.1093/ref:odnb/46702.

Jones, Michael K., and Malcolm G. Underwood. *The King's Mother: Lady Margaret Beaufort, Countess of Richmond and Derby*. Cambridge: Cambridge University Press, 1993.

Kekewich, Margaret L. ""Thou shalt be under the power of the man": Sir John Fortescue and the Yorkist Succession". *Nottingham Medieval Studies* 42 (1998): 188–230.

Kewes, Paulina. "The 1553 Succession Crisis Reconsidered". *Historical Research* 90 (2017): 465–85.

Levine, Mortimer. "A Parliamentary Title to the Crown in Tudor England". *Huntingdon Library Quarterly* 25 (1962): 121–27.

Levine, Mortimer. "The Last Will and Testament of Henry VIII: A Reappraisal Appraised". *Historian* 26 (1964): 471–85.

Levine, Mortimer. *The Early Elizabethan Succession Question, 1558–1568*. Stanford: Stanford University Press, 1966.

Levine, Mortimer. "Henry VIII's Use of His Spiritual and Temporal Jurisdictions in His Great Causes of Matrimony, Legitimacy, and Succession". *Historical Journal* 10 (1967): 3–10.

Levine, Mortimer. *Tudor Dynastic Problems, 1460–1571*. London: Allen and Unwin, 1973.

Lewis, Andrew W. "Anticipatory Association of the Heir in Early Capetian France". *American Historical Review* 83 (1978): 906–27.

Litzen, Veikko. *A War of Roses and Lilies: The Theme of Succession in Sir John Fortescue's Works.* Helsinki: Suomalainen Tiedeakatemia, 1971.

Lyon, Ann. "The Place of Women in European Royal Succession in the Middle Ages". *Liverpool Law Review* 27 (2006): 361–93.

Matthew, Donald. *King Stephen.* London: Hambledon Continuum, 2002.

McNiven, Peter. "Legitimacy and Consent: Henry IV and the Lancastrian Title, 1399–1406". *Mediaeval Studies* 44 (1982): 470–88.

Monter, William. *The Rise of Female Kings in Europe, 1300–1800.* London: Yale University Press, 2012.

Nenner, Howard. *The Right to be King: The Succession to the Crown of England, 1603–1714.* Basingstoke: Palgrave Macmillan, 1995.

Parks, Annette P. "Rescuing the Maidens from the Tower: Recovering the Stories of Two Female Political Hostages". In *Feud, Violence and Practice: Essays in Medieval Studies in Honor of Stephen D. White*, edited by Belle S. Tuten and Tracey L. Billado, 279–91. Aldershot: Ashgate, 2010.

Patourel, John Le. "The Norman Succession, 996–1135". *English Historical Review* 86 (1971): 225–50.

Porter, Linda. *Mary Tudor: The First Queen.* London: Portrait, 2007.

Redworth, Glyn. "'Matters Impertinent to Women': Male and Female Monarchy under Philip and Mary". *English Historical Review* 112 (1997): 597–613.

Richards, Judith M. "Mary Tudor as 'Sole Quene'? Gendering Tudor Monarchy". *Historical Journal* 40 (1997): 895–924.

Richards, Judith M. "Gender Difference and Tudor Monarchy: The Significance of Queen Mary I". *Parergon* 21 (2004): 27–46.

Ross, Charles. "Rumour, Propaganda and Popular Opinion During the Wars of the Roses". In *Patronage, the Crown and the Provinces in Later Medieval England*, edited by R. A. Griffiths, 15–32. Gloucester: Alan Sutton, 1981.

Ross, Charles, *Richard III.* London: Yale University Press, 1981.

Samson, Alexander. "Changing Places: The Marriage and Royal Entry of Philip, Prince of Austria and Mary Tudor, July–August 1554". *Sixteenth Century Journal* 36 (2005): 761–84.

Seabourne, Gwen. "Eleanor of Brittany and Her Treatment by King John and Henry III". *Nottingham Medieval Studies* 51 (2007): 73–110.

Searle, Eleanor. "Women and the Legitimization of Succession at the Norman Conquest". *Anglo-Norman Studies* 3 (1981): 159–70.

Shephard, Amanda. *Gender and Authority in Sixteenth-Century England: The Knox Debate.* Keele: Ryburn, 1995.

Stafford, Pauline. "The Portrayal of Royal Women in England, Mid-Tenth to Mid-Twelfth Centuries". In *Medieval Queenship*, edited by John Carmi Parsons, 143–67. Stroud: Sutton, 1993.

Stone, J. M. *Mary I: Queen of England.* London: Sands & Co, 1901.

Strohm, Paul. *England's Empty Throne: Usurpation and the Language of Legitimation, 1399–1422.* London: Yale University Press, 1998.

Taylor, Craig. "Sir John Fortescue and the French Polemical Treatises of the Hundred Years War". *English Historical Review* 114 (1999): 112–29.

Taylor, Craig. "Edward III and the Plantagenet Claim to the French Throne". In *The Age of Edward III*, edited by J. S. Bothwell, 155–69. York: York Medieval Press, 2001.

Taylor, Craig. "The Salic Law and the Valois Succession to the French Crown". *French History* 15 (2001): 358–77.

Taylor, Craig. "The Salic Law, French Queenship, and the Defense of Women in the Late Middle Ages". *French Historical Studies* 29 (2006): 543–64.

Tolhurst, Fiona. *Geoffrey of Monmouth and the Translation of Female Kingship*. Basingstoke: Palgrave Macmillan, 2013.

Warren, Wilfred Lewis. *Henry II*. California: University of California Press, 1973.

Weir, Alison. *Britain's Royal Families: The Complete Genealogy*. London: Vintage, 2008.

Whitelock, Anna, "'A queen, and by the same title, a king also': Mary I, Queen-in-Parliament". In *The Birth of a Queen: Essays on the Quincentenary of Mary I*, edited by Sarah Duncan and Valerie Schutte, 89–112. Basingstoke: Palgrave Macmillan, 2016.

Wolf, Armin. "Reigning Queens in Medieval Europe: When, Where, and Why". In *Medieval Queenship*, edited by John Carmi Parsons, 169–88. Stroud: Sutton, 1998.

Wood, Charles T. "The First Two Queens Elizabeth, 1464–1503". In *Women and Sovereignty*, edited by Louise Olga Fradenburg, 121–31. Edinburgh: Edinburgh University Press, 1992.

2

PORTUGAL, 1385

A people's choice or *coup d'état*?

Isabel de Pina Baleiras

This chapter takes a fresh look at the political and social processes that in 1385 led João, Master of the Military Order of Avis, to the throne of Portugal via the method of acclamation at the assembly of the Cortes at Coimbra. João (1357–1433) was the son of King Pedro I of Portugal, though born out of wedlock and therefore an illegitimate brother of King Fernando, who died in October 1383. After two years of social rebellion and war, the Master of Avis managed to overtake the claims of his niece, Beatriz, daughter of King Fernando and Queen Leonor Teles, and heiress of the throne, to become King João I of Portugal. How did that happen? Traditional sources assert that he was elevated to the throne through an electoral process at the Cortes (the Portuguese political body made up of representatives of the clergy, the nobility, and the commoners), but was he elected? Or acclaimed? Or both? Were there other candidates? Was it a democratic process or a *coup d'état*, or can we say it was a mixture of both?

For a helpful comparison, we can look to contemporary events in Castile, where the bastard son of Alfonso XI, Enrique of Trastámara, killed his brother, the legitimate King Pedro I, to become King Enrique II. In historical hindsight, we know that both João I of Portugal and Enrique II of Castile gave birth to new dynasties, Avis and Trastámara, but at the time, the legitimacy of their rule continued to be disputed by means of armed conflict, with nobles circulating between various kingdoms, offering their services to different kings, sometimes back and forth in rapid succession, according to the context of the war and their own personal interests. An analysis of some of these trans-national movements by the elites of the Iberian monarchies also helps us understand the forces that were at work in forging and maintaining new reigns and new reigning dynasties.

Diogo Lopes Pacheco is a paradigmatic example. A nobleman who first served King Pedro I of Portugal, he later clashed with his policies and fled to Castile; and although he was later pardoned and returned to Portugal, serving King

The regency of Queen Leonor Teles

Despite these assurances about the succession to the throne, as events unfolded, nothing happened as King Fernando wished. After his death on 22 October 1383, Leonor Teles took over the regency in the name of her daughter Beatriz, and received the citizens of Lisbon, who came to her demanding changes in the government of the realm: in a clear criticism of King Fernando's reign, marked by wars, death, and destruction, they asked her to appoint only Portuguese officers, and to constitute her Council with citizens from Lisbon and other cities, alongside nobles and clerics. The Queen Regent agreed to respect these suggestions.[20]

But in spite of these harmonious beginnings, matters became complicated when the Regent ordered the acclamation of Beatriz as the new queen of Portugal. This practice originated in early Visigothic monarchy in the Iberian Peninsula and continued to be observed in the early centuries of the Portuguese monarchy; it consisted of acclaiming the new king as soon as the defunct king passed away.[21] Leonor Teles was therefore adhering to traditional practice, and respecting the terms of the Treaty of Salvaterra de Magos. Nevertheless, Beatriz's rights were soon contested. In Lisbon, the people rejected Beatriz because she was married to the king of Castile, and they did not want to be ruled by Castilians, who were often compared to Moors because both were seen as enemies of Portuguese independence: "Now Portugal is sold by donation, after so many heads and so much blood had been spent to conquer it from the Moors."[22] But while the people rejected Beatriz without presenting any solution, the noble Álvaro Peres de Castro suggested "whosoever deserves the kingdom will take it".[23] The chronicler Fernão Lopes clarifies that Castro was suggesting his two nephews, the princes João and Dinis, sons of King Pedro I and Inês de Castro, both still living in Castile. In Santarém, a similar scenario occurred: the people contested the acclamation of Beatriz, without presenting solutions, but in the *Chronicle of D. Fernando* an old woman again suggested Prince João.[24] In Elvas, the contestation against Beatriz was repeated, but this time a local nobleman, Gil Fernandes, shouted simply "Portugal" as the solution.[25]

The *Chronicle* ends without naming the Master of Avis as a possible candidate to the throne. Until now, only his brothers João and Dinis were mentioned. In fact, already during the marriage negotiations for Beatriz, Juan I of Castile had warned King Fernando and Queen Leonor Teles that Prince João was very popular and would surely be preferred as king after Fernando instead of Beatriz. Perhaps because of this, Juan I ordered João's arrest in Castile as soon as he heard of the death of his father-in-law and ally.[26]

The Master of Avis

When Lopes' *Chronicle of D. João I* begins, prominent nobles and citizens of Lisbon—notably Álvaro Pais, chancellor of the late King[27]—conspire against the Regent's chief advisor, the Galician nobleman Juan Fernández de Andeiro, who had represented Portugal in negotiating the Treaty of Salvaterra de Magos. Andeiro had close contacts in both Castile and England and exercised a strong influence with the Regent. The nobility and citizens of Lisbon felt Andeiro's influence did not give them space for their own goals and ambitions, and there were also rumours that he had been Leonor's lover, possibly even the true father of Beatriz. So they tried to convince the Master of Avis—the only brother of King Fernando still living in Portugal—to murder him. Avis hesitated, fearing the reactions of the Regent and King Juan I, but Álvaro Pais promised him that he would have the support of the people of Lisbon. Avis finally consented and Pais commented that now he could see clearly "the difference between the sons of kings and the sons of other men".[28] From that moment it seems the idea of the Master of Avis becoming king was born, as pointed out by the historian Margarida Garcez Ventura.[29]

The murder of Andeiro by the Master of Avis occurred in the palace of the Regent in Lisbon (where Leonor Teles was living) on 6 December 1383.[30] As promised, the people of Lisbon rushed to the palace when they heard Álvaro Pais and others shouting that the Master was in danger of being killed. According to the *Chronicle*, they cried: "Let us run to the Master, friends, let us run to the Master, because he is the son of King Dom Pedro [. . .] let us approach the Master whom they want to kill without reason." The people only calmed down when the Master appeared at a window.[31]

Fernão Lopes compared Lisbon to a widow and the Master of Avis to the new husband (king) she should acquire to preserve her safety and reputation.[32] Lisbon was represented as the Kingdom as a whole, and so according to the myth being constructed by the chronicler of the Master of Avis, step by step, he was already king in all but name. Indeed a sense of predestination that the Master would become king had begun early, even during his father's lifetime: in the *Chronicle of D. Pedro I*, Lopes reports a prophecy that this king heard several times about the ascension of a son named "João" to a very high position. He also dreamed once that the whole kingdom was collapsing in flames, and his son "João" was the one who saved it. King Pedro did not know which of his two sons named João was designated by this prophecy and the dream, but in spite of preferring the Infante João of Portugal, he had accepted whichever would be the choice of God.[33]

After the murder of Andeiro, other murders occurred, such as the bishop of Lisbon, who was killed by the people because he was Castilian and a loyal servant of the Regent. Violence took hold, such as the assault on the homes of rich Jews. People said the Jews had served King Fernando and that their fortunes should now finance the cause of the Master. By that time, the Master of Avis was already perceived as king by the people, who felt that Prince João could not be king because he was under arrest in Castile and sooner or later would be killed. The Master of Avis therefore was the logical alternative: he was the only male member of the royal house living in the Kingdom, and was the son of King Pedro, "as much as the other [João]".[34] The Master of Avis ordered, in the name of the Regent, a stop to the assaults on Jewish homes, but the city officials issued this order in the name of the Master himself, and the people obeyed, and suggested again that they should "have this man as their lord, and acclaim him as king".[35]

Observing these events, Leonor Teles feared for her life, and decided to leave Lisbon and take refuge in her own village of Alenquer, looking for security and support. The Master of Avis on his part feared possible revenge by the Regent for Andeiro's assassination, and the reaction of Juan I of Castile, to whom she had written requesting help.[36] He prepared to go to England, but once again the people of Lisbon intervened and asked him to stay. People wanted to acclaim him as regent; they offered their service and their wealth to help him protect them from their enemies, which, to them, were Leonor Teles, her supporters, and the king of Castile.[37] But the Master still hesitated until his views were changed by Friar João da Barroca. Friar Barroca was Castilian and had lived in Jerusalem, until, just before the murder of Andeiro, he had a revelation that he should come to Portugal, where he soon became well known for his saintly life and his curative powers. Barroca told the Master that he should stay in Portugal because God would take pleasure in seeing him become king—him and his children.[38] This is therefore another step in the mythic history surrounding the Master of Avis and the legitimation of his future royal dynasty.

On 13 December 1383, Juan I and Beatriz entered Portugal with a Castilian army to defend their succession rights. Nevertheless, the popular movement to promote the candidacy of the Master of Avis increased daily, and on 16 December he was finally acclaimed "ruler and defender" of Portugal by citizens and other members of the public. The Portuguese kingdom entered an unusual period, with two regents commanding its destiny: Leonor Teles, who ruled according to the law, and the Master of Avis, whose power emerged—according to the legend created by the chroniclers—from the will of the people and the citizens of Lisbon.[39] To the historian José Mattoso, the nomination of the Master as Regent was an attack on the law and all the treaties that had been signed before by King Fernando.[40]

But despite his acclaim as regent, the Master of Avis was still not convinced that he should be the leader of Portugal's fate. He believed that this mission belonged to his eldest half-brother, Prince João, imprisoned in Castile. He informed him of his intentions, but the Prince sent him the message that he was pleased with the appointment of the Master as regent, and in fact that he should be king of Portugal himself (probably hoping this would get him out of prison),[41] and he ordered his vassals to serve the Master. This episode represents another confirmation—at least according to the chroniclers—that the rise of the Master of Avis as king of Portugal pleased not only the common people but also the great magnates, namely Prince João, the main favoured candidate for the throne of Portugal thus far.

Once the Queen knew of the nomination of the Master of Avis, she decided to leave Alenquer and go to Santarém, where she hoped to find even more safety, as this was one of the strongest cities of Portugal, where she and Fernando had spent long periods.[42] When Juan I of Castile and Beatriz joined Leonor Teles in Santarém, he persuaded her to abdicate her position as regent in his favour, to ensure he could help her in recovering her honour and dignity. Leonor consented and abdicated her powers to him on 14 January 1384.[43] Her political role ended that day, and as far as it is known, she had no other political activity in Portugal.[44] Her daughter Beatriz never gave up her title of queen of Portugal, though she never actually occupied the throne.[45]

Sometime after the abdication of Leonor Teles as regent, the war between Castile and Portugal began (and would persist for the next half-century until a definitive peace was signed at Medina del Campo in 1431). The forces of the Master of Avis, with the support of Nuno Álvares Pereira, the chief commander of his military forces and later his Constable, achieved a series of victories, most notably the defence of the city of Lisbon against besieging Castilian forces. This success led to the Master of Avis being re-confirmed as regent of the Kingdom by leading nobles (such as Diogo Lopes Pacheco; Gonçalo Teles, the brother of Leonor; and Nuno Álvares Pereira, among others), by prominent citizens in Lisbon (2 October 1384) and in other cities. Four days later, on 6 October, in Lisbon, this same group swore loyalty and paid homage to the Master, kissing his hand as a sign of recognition and submission to his authority. The chronicler Fernão Lopes adds that the Master, as a royal "love child"—once again emphasising his royal affiliation—thanked the people for their support, especially the city of Lisbon.[46]

In Lopes' narrative, at this moment, in the mentality of the people, the person of the Master of Avis concentrated within itself three important competencies that would legitimise his future political action: he was the son of a king; he had managed to avenge King Fernando's honour by killing Leonor Teles' supposed lover Andeiro; and he demonstrated ability in resisting the Castilian threat.[47] In fact, as he rode through Lisbon, the people followed him as a saviour. They offered him their wealth and were willing to fight in his service until death.[48] His pathway to the throne was thus facilitated at the popular level.

The Cortes of Coimbra, 1385

Despite the strengthening of his position as ruler and defender of the Kingdom, the Master of Avis wanted to clarify in a more comprehensive and clear way his political role in the Kingdom. He summoned the national assembly or Cortes to the city of Coimbra to deal mainly with this issue. It was the first time a Cortes had been summoned by someone who was not the king. His entry into the city of Coimbra recalled the usual royal entrances of kings. In fact, many ordinary people followed him from Lisbon all the way to Coimbra, beseeching him to protect them from the enemies of the realm. In his descriptions of these events, Fernão Lopes compares the Master of Avis to Moses, both chosen by God to free their people from slavery, war, and unhappiness. In almost messianic symbolism, he has the children cry, "Portugal, Portugal for King João! In good time our king comes!"[49]

Thanks in part to the persuasive arguments of the jurist João das Regras (1357–1404), the Master was elected king of Portugal on 6 April 1385.[50] Das Regras had been a supporter of the Master of Avis' cause since its beginning and later served as his chancellor.[51] He began his oration to the Cortes by stating that the throne had been empty since King Fernando's death, and a solution was urgently needed to guarantee justice and security in the Kingdom. Then, he presented the four possible candidates: Juan I of Castile; Beatriz, daughter of King Fernando; and João and Dinis, brothers of the late King. The party that supported Beatriz and Juan I of Castile's aspirations does not seem to have been represented at this assembly or, at least, there is no evidence for it in the written chronicles. In contrast, it is clear that the princes João and Dinis could count on a degree of support from the assembled nobles.[52]

João das Regras continued by eliminating all of these candidates one by one. He started by alleging that King Juan I was a heretic and therefore incapable of succeeding because he followed the anti-pope Clement VII, and furthermore, had made war against Portugal; Beatriz was certainly illegitimate as her mother had slept with two men in the time before her birth (an indirect reference to Juan Fernández de Andeiro suspected of being Leonor Teles' lover, according to Fernão Lopes, as mentioned above). Das Regras also brought out the old argument that Leonor Teles' marriage to King Fernando had not been valid as she had been married first to a vassal, nor had they obtained the proper documentation to conclude a legal marriage.[53] Nor could João and Dinis be king as their father, King Pedro I, had never completed the process of formally legitimising their birth or his claimed marriage with their mother, Inês de Castro. Moreover, João and Dinis, like Juan I of Castile, had fought against Portugal, causing damage and destruction.[54]

Finally, João das Regras presented the Master of Avis as the better and indeed the only choice: he was King Pedro's son; he had fought bravely with his people in resisting the Castilian siege of Lisbon; he had been very generous to those who had helped him, noble or not; and he followed the true pope, Urban VI. The Master of Avis appreciated this proposal, but rejected it, due to his illegitimate birth (his father King Pedro had never married his mother Teresa Lourenço). He was also bound by the ecclesiastic vows he had taken, as head of a religious order of knighthood, the Order of Avis. Nevertheless, these were not considered insurmountable obstacles, and important Portuguese clerics offered to intercede with Urban VI to provide the necessary dispensations. Therefore the Master of Avis accepted the challenge and was acclaimed King João I of Portugal.[55]

A closer look at the Cortes of Coimbra and the enthronement of João I

We can identify the key steps that preceded and prepared the Master of Avis' election to the throne of Portugal: the murder of Juan Fernández de Andeiro and the clear support of the people for him as their lord and later as their desired king; his proclamation, twice, as ruler and defender of the Kingdom, and the support received from Prince João; his part in the defence of Lisbon under Castilian siege; his demonstration of military skill in the conquest of some Castilian towns; and his attribution of generous benefits to those who were on his side.[56] With all these victories, God seemed to be in his favour, as Fernão Lopes states in the *Chronicle of D. João I*, in constructing the mythical narrative around him. Moreover, João was seen as a friend of the true Church of Rome and a necessary champion to defeat the Castilian enemy that was allied to the anti-pope in Avignon. João's rise was supported, moreover, by the leading citizens of Lisbon such as Chancellor Álvaro Pais, who had convinced the Master of Avis to murder Andeiro and brought with him the support of the people of Lisbon due to his prestigious background,[57] and by prominent nobles like Nuno Álvares Pereira, who led the Master's armies to victory in the war against Castile.

It can be said, therefore, that the climate was favourable for choosing the Master of Avis for the throne of Portugal. It was likely that he would have been chosen anyway by his supporters (the people, citizens, jurists, some nobles and clerics), but he needed to make certain this decision was legitimised. Thus a Cortes was convened. As remarked by Maria Helena da Cruz Coelho—a leading biographer of João I—the Cortes of Coimbra was essential for legalising the decision of choosing the Master of Avis as king and to overcome the two main obstacles noted above: his previously sworn religious vows and his illegitimate birth. However, it took time to obtain the necessary dispensations from the Pope. Only in 1391 did Pope Boniface IX send these documents, releasing him from religious orders, on the assumption that João I would be faithful to Rome and would combat enemies that threatened the Church in Portugal.[58]

To fully understand this situation, it is important to consider whether or not an election of a king was a legitimate form of royal selection. The Visigoths, the former Germanic rulers in the Iberian Peninsula, based possession of the crown mostly on election or usurpation. The latter of these existed but was not desirable: seizing the throne while a king was still alive (even with the support of clerics) was clearly condemned through excommunication.[59] The Visigothic code *Fuero Juzgo*, probably written in Latin in the seventh century and first published in Castilian in the thirteenth century, prescribes that the person who would be king should have a good lineage descending from Visigothic stock; he should be noble, pious, and well mannered; and he should be elected by councils composed of bishops, prestigious nobles, and representatives of the people. But before receiving the kingdom, a king should swear that he would rule for the welfare of the people and in God's name.[60] In fact, the Visigoths, who were already influenced by the Roman culture that prevailed in the Iberian Peninsula before their invasion, believed, like them, that it was God who gave authority to the king, as well as the people for him to rule over.[61] The *Fuero Juzgo* also states that patrimony received by the king from his relatives and friends, or whatever he possessed before becoming king, should be passed on to his children and natural heirs; but whatever patrimony he conquered after becoming king could belong to whomever he designated; in other words, his successor. The code further underlines that these acquisitions should really be left to the kingdom, and that the king should not keep them for himself. The right of inheriting a throne seems to have been unknown to the Visigoths, although the king's chosen successor may well have been his son. However, this choice was always confirmed by representative councils of varying types.[62]

With time, Roman law was increasingly observed, as attested by the idea that the power of the sovereign (the emperor for the Romans, the king for the

Germanic peoples) had a divine origin and its transmission should be done through inheritance. This transmission through inheritance also stressed the Roman idea that kingdoms were considered the personal property of kings. These theories, already followed in practice, were later formalised through legal codes, such as those in *Las Siete Partidas*, a compilation of laws commissioned by King Alfonso X of Castile in the mid-thirteenth century.[63] This code explains that kings must have castles, fortresses, and harbours, because the safety of the kingdom is in their hands. They should have great power because kings receive their kingdoms through inheritance, and so after their deaths they could, and should, leave it to their heirs, unlike emperors who could not do this because they were elected.[64] However, these practices displeased the people and the Church. In fact, King Fernando was criticised in the Cortes for distributing many Portuguese crown territories to the nobles, instead of granting them from his own patrimony, as previous kings had done.[65] The Castilian Bishop of Silves, Álvaro Pais (1275?–1349), who wrote *Speculum Regum* (1341–44) as an homage to King Alfonso XI (a book intended to guide the rule of kings according to Christian precepts), also stated that kings were only the caretakers of their kingdoms, not their owners (as noted in Visigothic law[66]), and so they should refrain from making donations to the nobility as if the crown lands were theirs to distribute.[67] In fact, these changes were contentious: the transmission of the crown through inheritance probably also displeased the nobles because they lost the possibility of being chosen as kings themselves, which the Visigothic election principle had offered. Clerics, on the other hand, would have been pleased, because hereditary succession and a divine origin for kingly power sat well together, and reinforced the position of the Church within politics.[68]

The ideas from Roman and Visigothic codes persisted in the Iberian Peninsula throughout the period of Muslim domination, the Christian *Reconquista*, and the foundation of Christian kingdoms like Leon, Castile, and Portugal.[69] In Portugal, under the first royal dynasty, the crown was mostly transmitted from father to son; the successor would be sworn in and confirmed by the Cortes, which recalls the practice of the Visigothic councils, but can also be seen as a passage from the election principle to an idea of hereditary dynastic succession.[70]

The transmission of the divine power to kings could occur through different ways, according to medieval doctrine: directly from God to king, as King Fernando believed,[71] or though mediators, which could be either the pope or the people. *Fuero Juzgo* and *Las Siete Partidas* sustained different positions. According to the first code, kings were elected but needed to be sacralised by clerics, which means that *sacerdotium* (ecclesiastic power) preceded *imperium* (temporal power).[72] *Speculum Regum* also insists that bishops should be those who transmit divine power to kings through sacralisation, even though they have inherited the crown.[73] *Las Siete Partidas*, following Roman law, asserted instead that the sovereign ruler's divine power had its origin in the will of the people, even when a king ascended the throne by inheritance. Consequently a pact would be established between king and people, obliging the former to act for the good of the latter, and if he did not do so, the pact ceased and he could be rejected.[74] In a similar manner, the *Fuero*

Juzgo argued that a king should be excommunicated and removed from the throne if he ruled without dignity.[75] The pact also ceased if the crown became vacant, without any legitimate heirs of the last king. In this case, power returned to the people, giving them the right to choose a new king. This was the position sustained by João das Regras at the Cortes of Coimbra: there were several candidates, but none was legitimate.[76]

This idea of a political contract between ruler and ruled has appeared frequently in the writings of various medieval thinkers, from Marsilius of Padua to William of Ockham,[77] and was now repeated in the Portuguese context by Bishop Álvaro Pais. In fact, in spite of the sacralisation of the power of the king mentioned above, *Speculum Regum* also maintained that there was also a pact of friendship between the monarch and the multitudes to be respected; but if the king broke it through tyrannical behaviour, the people could expel him, as the Romans did to King Tarquinius Superbus.[78] Later, Infante Pedro (1392–1449), one of the sons of João I of Portugal, underlined the same idea in his *Livro da Vertuosa Benfeytoria* (1418?–1431?): should the monarchical pact be broken, the people would have the right to elect a new prince.[79] This position was not expressed by Fernão Lopes regarding the crisis of 1385; however, he did stress several times that the reign of King Fernando had been marked by wars and destruction and a new government policy was therefore desired.[80] Philosophers as far back as Aristotle had articulated the principle of a governing pact, adding that the people should only decide about general public business, leaving important political activity to distinguished citizens due to their higher social and cultural status.[81] This is precisely what João I considered when creating his government.

In the thirteenth century, Alfonso X of Castile, in the legal code *Las Siete Partidas*, enumerated four ways to acquire a kingdom legitimately and be named its king: the first was the inheritance of a kingdom by the firstborn son of a monarch or by one of his closest relatives; the second consisted of being chosen king by the community if no relatives of the deceased king survived; the third would occur by marrying a woman who was heiress of the crown; and the fourth depended on the pope's authorisation, though this only related to territories directly under papal feudal jurisdiction, such as the Kingdom of Naples.[82]

As pointed out above, medieval doctrine declared that a monarch's power had a divine origin. "Vicarios de Dios son los reyes de cada uno en su reyno" (kings are vicars of God, each in his own kingdom), affirmed Alfonso X. He explained that the king was the head, and the kingdom was the body that obeyed the head.[83] This was necessary for ensuring peace and justice. Bishop Pais also sustained that kings were essential for the care of their people and to lead them towards the Heavenly Kingdom. Monarchs were ministers of God, but their power was delivered to them through the Church, who could therefore interfere in the election of a king.[84] This point of view was expressed at the Cortes in Coimbra and increasingly dominant after the decisive victory of the forces supporting the Master of Avis over those of Juan of Castile at Aljubarrota in August 1385, signifying to the Portuguese clergy divine favour for his cause. As mentioned before, the Cortes asked the Master to accept their invitation and he initially rejected it, because of his illegitimate birth and the sacred vows he had made. But prelates promised promptly to address the Pope, in order to overcome these impediments, and so he reconsidered. The Master of Avis was then able to say that he would accept the throne only because the Pope had consented, indicating that it was God's will.[85] In fact, as Margarida Garcez Ventura notes, as expressed in the chronicle of Fernão Lopes, it was clear that the fate of the Master did not depend on men but on God alone.[86] The approval of the Church was therefore essential in the legitimisation of a king's power, and in this case was certainly relevant in supporting the Master of Avis against Beatriz, the legitimate heir.

Last but not least, the state of necessity—considering in what state the Kingdom had emerged after a series of brutal wars—superseded patterns of traditional inheritance regarding the crown. This principle justified why the Cortes had proclaimed the Master of Avis as king of Portugal before formally receiving the Pope's confirmation, as the legal scholar Marcelo Caetano underlines.[87] This principle too had already emerged in the *Partidas*, which states that everything survives in nature except man, who needs to have a regulator (a king) to protect him from injustice and war.[88] If the Master of Avis would not accept the Portuguese crown, it was reckoned, the Kingdom would likely be delivered into the hands of the Castilian heretic enemy, and chaos and perdition would follow.

Based on these three predicating factors—the will of the people inscribed in the contract between ruler and ruled, a king's divine power, and the state of emergency in a particular kingdom—the process of electing a king was legitimate, as João das Regras successfully argued before the assembled Cortes at Coimbra when proposing the Master of Avis.

But was João I's elevation to kingship based on a democratic ideal, or more simply a *coup d'état*? João das Regras centred his argumentation on the principle that there was no legitimate heir to the throne. Consequently, the throne was vacant and the Cortes had the right to choose whomever they wanted.[89] According to the jurisconsults, when a dynasty is extinguished, the rules of succession or election of the new king should be based on the principle *jure sanguinis* and not in the principle *jure hereditas*.[90] Yet, the Portuguese throne was not in fact vacant. There *was* a legitimate heir: Beatriz, the daughter of King Fernando and Queen Leonor Teles. Nevertheless, due to the particular circumstances of 1385, she was declared illegitimate at the Cortes of Coimbra, in a time when it was often easy to declare marriages illegitimate that had previously been considered legitimate (for example, it was common to make use of an absence of documents proving papal dispensation for marriages between relatives). In consequence, legitimate children of such marriages would become bastards overnight, a political strategy frequently employed in this period.[91]

In this case, Leonor Teles was undeniably married when she and Fernando initiated their physical relationship. She and her first husband, João Lourenço da Cunha, most likely had obtained papal dispensation for their marriage due to their close consanguinity. Yet King Fernando's request for an annulment of Leonor's first marriage was based on the non-existence of such a document, and the Pope consented. In 1372 Fernando and Leonor married in a "public manner", in the presence of members of the high nobility and clergy. The ceremony took place at the church of Leça do Balio, significantly, as it was the headquarters of the Military Order of the Knights Hospitaller, to whom Fernando had given several privileges, thus buying their support in the war.[92] In return, this important and prestigious religious order signalled their approval of this marriage by permitting the use of their church. The marriage was not contested by the court, except by Dinis, brother of the King.

João das Regras later asserted in his oration at Coimbra that Leonor Teles was an adulterous wife, referring to the alleged affair with Juan Fernández de Andeiro (though not mentioning his name), but it is important to underline that the chronicler Fernão Lopes is the only contemporary source who makes this accusation in a written history. Neither López de Ayala (1332–1407)—whose writings were more contemporary to Leonor Teles and was himself an eyewitness of many events[93]—nor Jean Froissart (1337–1404?)—one of the chief international chroniclers of the period—or indeed the *Chronica do Condestabre de Portugal Don Nuno Álvarez Pereira* (Chronicle of the Constable of Portugal Nuno Álvares Pereira) whose protagonist was a close companion of the Master of Avis, ever said a word on this subject. However, if we accept Lopes' version, Leonor Teles' affair with Juan Fernández de Andeiro only began around 1380, while the diplomat was in Portugal negotiating details for English military assistance for the third Fernandine War. There is no reference to this eventual love affair before that time, as pointed out by the sixteenth-century chronicler Duarte Nunes de Leão.[94] In consequence, as Beatriz was born in 1373, a year after Leonor and King Fernando's marriage, it seems safe to conclude that she was really their legitimate daughter. But, as pointed out recently by Maria José Pimenta Ferro, Leonor's beauty, strong character, and passion for power were not aligned with the medieval ideal for queen-consorts, based on moral virtues and apolitical behaviour. Furthermore, this negative image was subsequently useful to the Avis dynasty's publicity strategies for improving perceptions of legitimacy surrounding the ascension of their founder, the bastard-born João I.[95]

As many researchers have remarked, Fernão Lopes was employed by the Avis dynasty to write their history.[96] He was invited by King Duarte (João I's son) in about 1418/19 to write about his father's reign as well as about the realm in his ancestors' lifetime. He could not therefore displease his employer. It was important for João I and his descendants to legitimise their illegitimate dynasty. In order to achieve that goal, the defamation of the predecessors would be a benefit and would help validate their occupation of the throne. As a result, the people would see the Avis dynasty as redeemers of public morality and order. The new dynasty would be honest and able to free Portugal from its interminable Castilian wars.

As a point of comparison, we can see that the same scenario occurred in Castile concerning the succession of the Trastámara dynasty. These events began in 1366, when Infante Enrique of Castile, brother of Pedro I, the legitimate king, proclaimed himself as king of Castile in Burgos (1366), followed by a civil war between the two

her parents' marriage explained above, the most compelling argument in favour of her legitimacy came at the Cortes of Leiria of 1376, when Beatriz was three years old, where all of the assembled nobles, including the Master of Avis and Infante João of Portugal, recognised and swore oaths upholding Beatriz as the legitimate heir to the throne. All of the subsequent marriage contracts that her parents established for their daughter repeated that same status. When Beatriz was ten years old—at all the stages of her betrothal and marriage to King Juan I, at Salvaterra de Magos, Elvas, and Badajoz—all the main Portuguese nobles were in attendance (the Master of Avis included) and swore later, at the Cortes of Valladolid and the Cortes of Santarém, that Beatriz would be the future queen of Portugal. It seems safe to state that what happened in 1385 was a *coup d'état* because the throne was not empty, a legitimate heir did exist, and that the Master of Avis in fact discarded Beatriz's previously recognised rights to the crown.

To ask a further question, was João I really elected? The historian Alfredo Pimenta (1882–1950) stated that the Cortes of Coimbra did not elect João as king but only confirmed his right to it. Another historian, Sérgio da Sousa Pinto (1915–70), affirmed that there had been a conditional election, but Marcelo Caetano and Martim de Albuquerque, a contemporary doctor of law who studied political power in the Portuguese Renaissance, argued that it is correct to accept that there was indeed an election, as it was written in the *Auto* (the official acts) of the Cortes, and as the Master of Avis corroborated, by saying that he did not receive the crown through inheritance, but *ex novo* (as a new thing).[106] The historian Humberto Baquero Moreno also underlined this position, but remarked that this question is unclear.[107] Yet, Paulo Merêa (1889–1977), who studied the acclamation of Portuguese kings up to the fifteenth century, sustained that the word "election" does not necessarily imply an election in the usual sense, but may rather be the simple ratification of the rights of the new king, representing as such a derivation or survival of the primitive idea of choosing a king by the nation.[108]

The words "election" and "elected" (*emlliçom* and *enlegido*) were used by Fernão Lopes while reporting the choice made at the Cortes of Coimbra of the Master of Avis as king. The above-mentioned *Auto* of these Cortes also used the word "election" (*emliçom/Jnliçom/enliçom*) in recording this ceremony, and the verbs "we nominate, we choose, we take" (*nomeamos escolhemos tomamos*) to indicate that they received the Master of Avis as king.[109] Indeed, it is not clear that a formal election had been made in the modern sense, since it does not appear that they took any kind of official vote: the chronicler maintains that the magnates and the commons agreed unanimously to promote the Master of Avis to the dignity of king; but they also agreed to stop anyone else from arguing against their decision.[110] Therefore, the Master of Avis was not elected but imposed and proclaimed, and what happened at the Cortes of Coimbra cannot be described as a democratic process because the assembly silenced any opposition. We see this explicitly in the actions of the military commander, Nuno Álvares Pereira, when he threatened with violence members of the noble house of da Cunha, supporters of the alternate choice of the princes João and Dinis.[111]

One of the principles used to support the choice of the Master of Avis was his royal lineage, as son of a king. The principle of heredity was thus not excluded from this process, and was necessary to more confidently legitimise the decision. The Master of Avis' rise to the crown was exceptional in the Portuguese monarchy and was enforced by a legal argument that combined the ancient idea of the election of kings with the newer principle of hereditary succession. Yet, the need to be accepted and recognised drove King João I to support popular mediation: he convened more representative assemblies during his reign of forty-eight years than most monarchs, and his government incorporated all social groups: one prelate, two nobles, three jurists, and one urban official. In fact, King João I did just what Aristotle recommended: he created a corporative government by sharing his power with those he most trusted.[112] Regarding the egalitarian nature of his reign, Fernão Lopes wrote that King João I created a "Seventh Age" on Earth (reflecting the idea that God had created a Seventh Age in Heaven, Paradise for the eternal rest of souls), because a new world was born with him: people of low status were rewarded for their work and loyalty and received titles of nobility, giving rise to a new generation of nobles.[113] Even though this was done to better support his kingly power, Lopes claims that King João I opened a door to what, today, can be seen as a democratic distribution of political and social power by rewarding merit over birth.

João I's acclamation as king of Portugal was theoretically well supported by ancient and medieval political doctrines, as argued by João himself, his sons, and jurists like João das Regras. The support of the people for his cause reinforced clearly his position but does not erase the idea that he was risen to kingship through a *coup d'état.* In addition, painful memories of the previous reign, marked by continual wars against Castile, also helped him ascend to power. Beatriz symbolised this past and the Portuguese current enemy, the king of Castile to whom she was married. In the context of the ideas and events of 1385, she was a victim of circumstances and João I the beneficiary who learned how to manipulate them in his favour.

Notes

1 On Diogo Lopes Pacheco, see: Instituto dos Arquivos Nacionais/Torre do Tombo [henceforth IAN/TT], *Chancelaria de D. Fernando*, book 1, fols 2–2v, 66–66v; Fernão Lopes, *Crónica de D. Fernando* (Lisbon: Imprensa Nacional–Casa da Moeda, 1975), chapters [chs.] LIII, LXVI, LXX, LXXII, LXXX; and Fernão Lopes, *Crónica de D. João I*, vols. I, II (Porto: Livraria Civilização, not dated.), vol. I, chs. 116, 154; vol. II, chs. 21, 98.

2 On the Infant Dinis of Portugal: Lopes, *D. Fernando*, chs. XXXVI, LIX, LXVI, LXXI, LXVIII; Pero López de Ayala, "Crónica del Rey Don Enrique, Segundo de Castilla", in *Crónicas de los Reyes de Castilla, desde don Alfonso el Sabio, hasta los Católicos don Fernando y doña Isabel* (Madrid: Ediciones Atlas, 1953), vol. II, year 1372, chs. III, V, 41, 44; Léon Mirot, "Les mésaventures d'un prince portugais au XIVème siècle", in *Revue des Études Historiques* (Paris: Librairie Alphonse Picard et Fils, 1911), 134, 138–49. And on the Infant João of Portugal: Lopes, *D. Fernando*, chs. XXXVI, CVI, CXX; Pero López de Ayala, "Crónica del Rey Don Juan, Primero de Castilla é de Leon", in *Crónicas de los Reyes de Castilla*, vol. II, year 1381, ch. IV; year 1386, ch. IV.

3 For Juan Fernández de Andeiro, see: Lopes, *D. Fernando*, chs. XXX, CXV, CLVII–CLVIII, CLXI.
4 Lopes, *D. Fernando*, chs. LVII, LX, LXII.
5 Pero López de Ayala, "Crónica del Rey Don Pedro, fijo del Rey Don Alfonso, onceno de este nombre en Castilla", in *Crónicas de los Reyes de Castilla*, vol. I, 590–93.
6 Lopes, *D. Fernando*, chs. XXV, XXX; López de Ayala, "Rey Don Enrique", vol. II, 3.
7 In these last alliances, Fernando was no longer fighting to obtain the Castilian throne, as this was now claimed by the English Duke of Lancaster (the son of King Edward III) and his wife Constanza (daughter of the assassinated Pedro I of Castile). But Fernando continued the war, now with the aim of defeating Castile and increasing commercial relations with England. Those connections were indeed improved, as Peter Russel confirms, but Castile was not conquered. Peter Russell, "João Fernandes Andeiro at the Court of John of Lancaster, 1371–1381", in *Revista da Universidade de Coimbra* (Coimbra: Imprensa Académica, 1938), vol. XIV, 12.
8 "Contrato de casamento de João I de Castela com D. Beatriz", Archivo General de Simancas [henceforth AGS], Patronato Real [PR], leg. 47, fol. 46, in Salvador Dias Arnaut, ed., "A Crise Nacional dos Fins do século XIV, vol. I, A sucessão de D. Fernando" (PhD diss., Faculdade de Letras da Universidade de Coimbra, Instituto de Estudos Históricos Vasconcelos, 1960), doc. 26, p. 357; Lopes, *D. Fernando*, 362.
9 The five marriages planned for Beatriz were as follows: (1) Fadrique, duke of Benavente (six years old) when Beatriz was only days or months old, and again when she was three, by the Treaty of Santarém (19 March 1373); the Cortes of Leiria (24 November 1376); and the Treaty of Córdoba (9 January 1377) [see "Tractos de Casamiento entre don fadrique hijo del rey don enrrique segundo de Castilla y doña beatriz hija primogénita del rey don fernando de Portugal, ano de la hera de cesar 1414 y 15 que es del nascimiento de christo 1376 y 77", in AGS, PR, Leg. 47, fols. 1, 5, 9, in Arnaut, ed., "Crise Nacional", doc. 1; López de Ayala, "Crónica Rey Enrique", vol. II, 17; and Lopes, *D. Fernando*, ch. XCVI]; (2) Prince Enrique of Castile (seven months), when Beatriz was seven years old, by the Treaty of Portalegre (21 May 1380) [Lopes, *D. Fernando*, chs. CX–CXII; "Trauto de casamento fecto antre elRey dom fernamdo Rey destes Regnos da portogal E elRey dom Ioham Rey de Castela com o Ifamte dom amrrique filho do dito senhor Rey dom Ihom de castela E a Ifante dona briatiz filha do dito senhor Rey dom fernamdo Rey de portogal", in IAN/TT, gav. 17, m. 6, no 11, in Arnaut, ed., "Crise Nacional", doc. 8]; (3) Prince Edward of England (six years old) when Beatriz was eight, agreed in Estremoz (15 July 1380), with a betrothal in Braga (19 August 1381) [Lopes, *D. Fernando*, chs. CXV, CXXVIII, CXXX]; (4) Prince Fernando of Castile (two years old) and Beatriz (age nine) by the Treaty of Badajoz (10 August 1382) [Lopes, *D. Fernando*, chs. CLIV, CLV]; and (5) King Juan I of Castile (around thirty years old) and Beatriz (age ten) by the Treaty of Pinto (9 December 1382), and the Treaty of Salvaterra de Magos (2 April 1383), with a betrothal in Salvaterra de Magos (30 April 1383), another in Elvas (14 May 1383), and a wedding in Badajoz (17 May 1383) [Lopes, *D. Fernando*, ch. CLVII; AGS, PR, leg. 47, fols 17, 46, in Arnaut, ed., "Crise Nacional", docs. 23, 26].
10 Lopes, *D. Fernando*, chs. LXXXIII, XCVI.
11 IAN/TT, *Chancelaria de D. Fernando*, book 1, fols 189v–190v.
12 IAN/TT, *Gaveta 3*, m. 4, no 5, in João António Mendes Neves, ed., "A 'Formosa Chancelaria': Estudo dos originais da Chancelaria de D. Fernando (1367–1383)" (Master's thesis, Faculdade de Letras da Universidade de Coimbra, 2005), 310–13.
13 "Testamento de D. Fernando", in Biblioteca Pública e Arquivo Distrital de Évora, cód. CIX/2-2, no 9, in Arnaut, ed., "Crise Nacional", doc. 7, pp. 291–95.
14 IAN/TT, *Chancelaria de D. Fernando*, book 2, fols 27r, 39v, 50r–v, 87r–v, 91r, 103v–104r; book 1, fol. 89r.
15 IAN/TT, *Chancelaria de D. Fernando*, book 1, fols 185r–185v; book 2, fols. 53r–53v.
16 IAN/TT, *Chancelaria de D. Fernando*, book 1, fol. 183v; IAN/TT, *Chancelaria de D. Dinis*, book 3, fols 31v–32r.

17 López de Ayala, "Rey Don Juan", vol. II, ch. 4, p. 78; Lopes, *D. Fernando*, ch. CLVII.
18 "Contrato de casamento", in Arnaut, ed., "Crise Nacional", 360–62; López de Ayala, "Rey Don Juan", vol. II, 83–84; Lopes, *D. Fernando*, 554.
19 "Contrato de casamento", in Arnaut, ed., "Crise Nacional", 382–86.
20 Lopes, *D. Fernando*, chs. CLXXIII–CLXXIV.
21 *Fuero Juzgo en latín y castellano* (Madrid: Real Academia Española, 1815), "El Primero Titolo", p. III.
22 "Agora se vende Portogall doado, que tantas cabeças e sangue custou a gaanhar quando foi filhado aos mouros", Lopes, *D. Fernando*, ch. CLXXV.
23 "Arreall, arreall, cujo for o regno leva-llo-á", in Lopes, *D. Fernando*, ch. CLXXV. Margarida Garcez Ventura, *O Messias de Lisboa: Um Estudo de Mitologia Política (1383–1415)* (Lisboa: Edições Cosmos, 1992), 15–16.
24 Lopes, *D. Fernando*, ch. CLXXVI.
25 Lopes, *D. Fernando*, ch. CLXXVII.
26 "Testamento del Rey Don Juan el Primero" (King Juan I of Castile), in Pero López de Ayala, "Crónica del Rey Don Enrique, Tercero de Castilla é de León", in *Crónicas de los Reyes de Castilla*, vol. II, 193; Lopes, *D. João I*, vol. I, ch. LIII.
27 Lopes, *D. João I*, vol. I, chs. V–VI.
28 "Hora vejo eu, filho, Senhor, a deference que ha dos filhos dos Reis aos outros homes", in Lopes, *D. João I*, vol. I, chs. VI, VIII.
29 Ventura, *O Messias de Lisboa*, 19.
30 Lopes, *D. João I*, vol. I, ch. IX.
31 "Acorramos ao Meestre, amigos, acorramos ao Meestre, ca filho he delRei dom Pedro [. . .] acorramos ao Mestre que matam sem por que", in Lopes, *D. João I*, vol. I, ch. XI.
32 "e assi como viuva que rei nom tiinha, e como sse lhe este ficara em logo de marido [. . .]", in Lopes, *D. João I*, vol. I, ch. XI.
33 Fernão Lopes, *Crónica de D. Pedro I* (Porto: Livraria Civilização, 1965), ch. XLIII.
34 "salvo ho Meestre dAvis que era filho delRei dom Pedro come o outro, e que este tomassem por seu rrei e senhor", in Lopes, *D. João I*, vol. I, ch. XIV.
35 "Tomemos este homem por senhor, e alçemollo por rei", in Lopes, *D. João I*, vol. I, ch. XIV.
36 Lopes, *D. João I*, vol. I, chs. XVI, XVIII.
37 Lopes, *D. João I*, vol. I, chs. XIX–XX.
38 Lopes, *D. João I*, vol. I, chs. XXIII–XXIV.
39 Luís de Sousa Rebelo, *A Concepção de Poder em Fernão Lopes* (n.p., Livros Horizonte, 1983), 25.
40 José Mattoso, ed., *História de Portugal, A Monarquia Feudal*, vol. 2 (Lisbon: Editorial Estampa, 1993), 495.
41 Lopes, *D. João I*, vol. I, ch. XXVIII.
42 Lopes, *D. João I*, vol. I, chs. XXIX–XXX.
43 Lopes, *D. João I*, vol. I, chs. LXI, LXV; López de Ayala, "Rey Don Juan", vol. II, ch. 1, p. 88.
44 Antero de Figueiredo, *Leonor Teles "flor de Altura"* (Lisbon: Livraria Bertrand, 1936), 359. For more information about the end of her life in Castile, see Isabel de Pina Baleiras, *Leonor Teles, uma rainha inesperada* (Lisbon: Círculo de Leitores, 2012), 327–46. Leonor Teles died sometime between 1403, when she and her daughter Beatriz sent some jewels to the Castilian Convent of Santa Clara de Rapariegos, and 1410, when Prince Fernando of Antequera received revenue from estates in Castile that had belonged to Leonor Teles, indicating that she was now deceased. César Olivera Serrano, "Las secuelas religiosas de un conflicto dinástico: portugueses en Castill el siglo XV", in Isabel Beceiro Pita, ed., *Poder Piedad y Devoción, Castilla y su entorno. Siglos XII-XV* (Madrid: Sílex ediciones, n.p., 2014), 172; Baleiras, *Leonor Teles*, 345–46.
45 César Olivera Serrano, *Beatriz de Portugal, la pugna dinástica Avís-Trastámara* (Santiago de Compostela: Consejo Superior de Investigaciones científicas Xunta de Galicia / Instituto de Estúdios Gallegos "Padre Sarmiento", 2005), 124.

46 Lopes, *D. João I*, vol. I, chs. CLIII–CLIV.
47 Ventura, *O Messias de Lisboa*, 29.
48 Lopes, *D. João I*, vol. I, ch. XX.
49 Lopes, *D. João I*, vol. I, chs. CLXXX–CLXXXI; Ventura, *O Messias de Lisboa*, 73.
50 Lopes, *D. João I*, vol. I, ch. CXCII.
51 Lopes, *D. Fernando*, ch. CLVI; Marcelo Caetano, *História do Direito Português, Fontes-Direito Público (1140–1495)*, 3rd edn (Lisbon/São Paulo: editorial Verbo, 1992), 452; Padre António Brásio, "As 'razões' de João das Regras nas Cortes of Coimbra", in Separata da Revista *Lusitania Sacra* (Lisbon: União Gráfica, 1958), vol. III, 6–7.
52 Caetano, *Direito Português*, 448.
53 Lopes, *D. João I*, vol. I, chs. CLXXXIV–CLXXXV.
54 Lopes, *D. João I*, vol. I, chs. CLXXXIII–CXCII.
55 Lopes, *D. João I*, vol. I, chs. CXCI–CXCII.
56 Lopes, *D. João I*, vol. I, ch. CLXXVIII
57 Lopes, *D. João I*, vol. I, chs. V–VI, VIII, XI, XXIV–XXV, XXVII.
58 Maria Helena da Cruz Coelho, *D. João I* (Rio de Mouro: Círculo de Leitores, 2005), 67, 69.
59 *Fuero Juzgo*, "El Primero Titolo", pp. III, IX.
60 *Fuero Juzgo*, "El Primero Titolo", pp. VIII, III.
61 See also Marcelo Caetano, "Subsídios para a história das Cortes Medievais portuguesas", in separata da *Bracara Augusta*, vols. XIV–XV, nos 1–2 (49–50) (Braga: Cruz & Cª Lda, 1963), 25.
62 *Fuero Juzgo*, "El Primero Titolo", pp. III, V–VI; Henrique da Gama Barros, *História da Administração Pública em Portugal nos séculos XII a XV* (Lisbon: Imprensa Nacional, 1885), vol. I, 626, 628–29.
63 Alfonso X El Sabio, *Las Siete Partidas*, www.biblioteca.org.ar/libros/130949.pdf, Segunda partida, tít. 1, Laws 1, 5, 6, 8, 9; Barros, *História da Administração Pública em Portugal*, vol. I, 632.
64 *Las Siete Partidas*, Segunda partida, tít. 1, Laws 3, 8.
65 *Cortes Portuguesas, Reinado de D. Fernando (1367–1383)*, vols I–II (Lisbon: Instituto Nacional de Investigação Científica, Centro de Estudos Históricos da Universidade Nova de Lisboa, 1990), Cortes de Lisboa de 1371, vol. I, art. 43, p. 35.
66 *Fuero Juzgo*, "El Primero Titolo", pp. II–III, VI.
67 "Efectivamente, os reis não são proprietários, mas defensores, administradores, e aumentadores do reino. [...] Ao rei pertence o poder de todas as coisas, e a sua defesa e governação; a cada indivíduo, a propriedade." ("Indeed, kings are not proprietors, but defenders, administrators, and enrichers of the realm. [...] To the king belongs the power of all things, and its defence and governance; to each person, his own property"). Frei Álvaro Pais, *Espelho dos Reis* (*Speculum Regum*) (Lisbon: Instituto de Alta Cultura, Centro de Estudos de Psicologia e de História da Filosofia anexo à Faculdade de Letras da Universidade de Lisboa, 1955), vol. I, 245.
68 Barros, *História da Administração Pública em Portugal*, vol. I, 629–30.
69 Barros, *História da Administração Pública em Portugal*, vol. I, 1–2, 40–41.
70 Barros, *História da Administração Pública em Portugal*, vol. I, 637.
71 See *Ordenações Afonsinas* (Lisbon: Fundação Calouste Gulbenkian, 1998), book 1, tit. 60; book II, tit. 63, 394–95, 404. Marcelo Caetano sustains that Portuguese kings Dinis, Afonso IV, and Fernando thought that God had given them the power to rule, and they were only accountable to Him. Caetano, *Direito Português*, 297.
72 *Fuero Juzgo*, "El Primero Titolo", p. III.
73 Pais, *Espelho dos Reis*, vol. I, 41–43, 109, 119–21.
74 Alfonso X, *Siete Partidas*, Segunda partida, tít. 1, Laws 1, 2, 9; António Manuel Hespanha, *História das Instituições. Épocas medieval e moderna* (Coimbra: Livraria Almedina, 1982), 302–94; Caetano, *Direito Português*, 472; Coelho, *D. João I*, 65–66.
75 *Fuero Juzgo*, "El Primero Titolo", pp. III, VII.

76 The historian António Manuel Hespanha and the jurist Marcelo Caetano agree that the rise of the Master of Avis at the Cortes of 1385 corresponded to the theory of popular sovereignty. Hespanha, *História das Instituições*, 308; Caetano, *Direito Português*, 472.
77 Isabel Banond, *História das Ideias Políticas* (Cascais: Princípia Editora, 2014), 40–41.
78 Pais, *Espelho dos Reis*, vol. I, 175, 177.
79 Banond, *Ideias Políticas*, 46; Infante Dom Pedro, Frei João Verba, *Livro da Vertuosa Benfeytoria* (Coimbra: Biblioteca Geral da Universidade de Coimbra, 1994), Livro II, cap. XVI, p. 103.
80 Lopes, *D. Fernando*, chs. CLXXII–CLXXIII.
81 Aristotle, *A Política* (no publication place: Círculo de Leitores, 1975), 127.
82 Alfonso X, *Siete Partidas*, Segunda partida, tít. 1, Law 9.
83 Alfonso X, *Siete Partidas*, Segunda partida, tít. 1, Law 5.
84 Pais, *Espelho dos Reis*, vol. I, 119–20, 123, 147, 227, 229.
85 Coelho, *D. João I*, 67.
86 Ventura, *O Messias de Lisboa*, 18.
87 Marcelo Caetano, *A crise nacional 1383–1385, subsídios para o seu estudo* (Lisbon/São Paulo: editorial Verbo, 1985), 33.
88 Alfonso X, *Siete Partidas*, Segunda partida, tít. 1, Law 7.
89 Caetano, *A crise nacional de 1383–1385*, 30. See also Martim de Albuquerque, *O poder político no Renascimento Português*, 2nd edn (Lisbon: Verbo-Babel editor, 2012), 39.
90 Paulo Merêa, *O Poder Real e as Cortes: Lições feitas na Faculdade de Direito de Coimbra aos alunos de "História do Direito Português" no ano lectivo de 1922–1923* (Coimbra: Coimbra Editora, 1923), 16.
91 Olivera Serrano, *Beatriz de Portugal*, 38.
92 Before Leonor and Fernando's marriage, the King gave several privileges to the Order, or to its headmaster Álvaro Gonçalves, such as those found in IAN/TT, *Chancelaria de D. Fernando*, book 1, fols 36v (1367); 28v–29 (1368); and 104v (3 May 1372). After the marriage, the King continued to offer gifts: IAN/TT, *Chancelaria de D. Fernando*, book 1, fols 159–69 (1374–1375); and 164r–164v. (1375).
93 Baleiras, *Leonor Teles*, 23.
94 Duarte Nunes de Leão, "Chronica del Rey D. Fernando, dos reys de Portugal o IX", in *Crónicas dos reis de Portugal* (Porto: Lello e irmãos Editores, 1975), 411.
95 Maria José Ferro Tavares, *Fernando e Leonor: um reinado (mal)dito* (Lisbon: Chiado Editora, 2013), 21–22, 443.
96 Baleiras, *Leonor Teles*, 21. Concerning Fernão Lopes' partiality towards the Avis dynasty, see: Horácio Ferreira Alves, *Dois Caluniados (D. Fernando e Leonor Teles)* (Lisbon: Livraria Clássica Editora, 1927), 28–32; Teresa Amado, *Fernão Lopes, contador de História, sobre a Crónica de D. João I* (Lisbon: Editorial Estampa, 1991), 31, 52; Manuel Marques Duarte, *Leonor Teles, ensaio biográfico* (Porto: Campo das Letras, 2002), chs. I–II; and Ana Paula Sousa, "Leonor Teles. 'Huma maa molher'?" (Master's thesis, Faculdade de Letras da Universidade do Porto, 2004), 4–14.
97 López de Ayala, "Rey Don Pedro", 555–56.
98 IAN/TT, *Chancelaria de D. Fernando*, book 1, fols 132, 163r–163v; book 2, fols 67, 90, 91v.
99 Julio Valdeón Baruque, *Enrique II, 1366–1379* (Palencia: Diputación Provincial de Palencia, Editorial La Olmeda, 1996), 79–80.
100 Valdeón Baruque, *Enrique II*, 92–93.
101 Olivera Serrano, *Beatriz de Portugal*, 345.
102 Olivera Serrano, *Beatriz de Portugal*, 32.
103 "Contrato de casamento", in Arnaut, ed., "Crise Nacional", 372; Olivera Serrano, *Beatriz de Portugal*, 85.
104 The historian José Manuel Nieto Soria stated that in the late Middle Ages political and religious propaganda remained united, constituting an essential ideological base of the king's power: *Fundamentos ideológicos del poder real en Castilla (siglos XIII-XVI)* (Madrid: Eudema, 1988), 43.

105 Pais, *Espelho dos Reis*, vol. I, 127, 175, 177, 131.
106 Caetano, *Direito Português*, 472; Albuquerque, *O poder político*, 39–41.
107 Humberto Baquero Moreno, "Estado, Nobreza e Senhorios", in *A Génese do Estado Moderno no Portugal Tardo-Medievo (séculos XIII-XV)*, eds. Maria Helena da Cruz Coelho and Armando Luís de Carvalho Homem (Lisbon: Universidade Autónoma de Lisboa, 1999), 257.
108 Election "não implica necessariamente uma eleição no sentido habitual, podendo ser antes a simples ratificação dos direitos do novo rei, e representando como tal uma derivação ou sobrevivência da primitiva escolha do rei pela nação." In Paulo Merêa, "Sobre a aclamação dos nossos reis", Separata da *Revista Portuguesa de História*, vol. X (Coimbra: Faculdade de Letras da Universidade de Coimbra, 1962), 8. See also Albuquerque, *O poder político*, 107–08.
109 "Auto da eleição de D. João I – Coimbra, 1385, abril, 6", in Marcelo Caetano, ed., "As Cortes de 1385", in Separata da *Revista Portuguesa de História*, vol. V (Coimbra: Faculdade de Letras da Universidade de Coimbra, Instituto de Estudos Históricos Vasconcelos, 1951), 70–71.
110 Lopes, *D. João I*, vol. I, 421, 422.
111 Lopes, *D. João I*, vol. I, chs. CLXXXVIII, CXCI.
112 Aristotle, *A Política*, 152.
113 Lopes, *D. João I*, vol. I, ch. CLXIII.

Bibliography

Primary sources

Alfonso X El Sabio. *Las Siete Partidas*. (www.biblioteca.org.ar/libros/130949.pdf), Segunda Partida.

Aristotle. *A Política*. No publication place: Círculo de Leitores, 1975.

"Auto da eleição de D. João I – Coimbra, 1385, abril, 6". Ed. by Marcelo Caetano, "As Cortes de 1385". In reprint of *Revista Portuguesa de História*, vol. V, Coimbra: Faculdade de Letras da Universidade de Coimbra, Instituto de Estudos Históricos Vasconcelos, 1951, 66–73.

"Contrato de casamento de João I de Castela com D. Beatriz". Ed. by Salvador Dias Arnaut, *A Crise Nacional dos Fins do século XIV, I, A sucessão de D. Fernando*, doc. 26, 360–62. PhD diss., Faculdade de Letras da Universidade de Coimbra, Instituto de Estudos Históricos Vasconcelos, 1960.

Cortes Portuguesas, Reinado de D. Fernando (1367–1383). Vols I–II. Lisbon: Instituto Nacional de Investigação Científica, Centro de Estudos Históricos da Universidade Nova de Lisboa, 1990, Cortes de Lisboa de 1371, vol. I, art. 43, 35.

Forez, Fr. Enrique. *Memorias de las Reynas Catholicas*. Vol. II, Madrid: António Marin, 1761, 693.

Fuero Juzgo, en latín y castellano. Madrid: Real Academia Española, 1815. Titulo I.

Instituto dos Arquivos Nacionais/Torre do Tombo. *Chancelaria de D. Dinis*, book 3, folios 31v–32r.

Instituto dos Arquivos Nacionais/Torre do Tombo. *Chancelaria de D. Fernando*, book 1, folios 89r, 132, 163r–163v, 183v, 185r–185v, 189v–190v; book 2, folios 27r, 39v, 50r–v, 53r–53v, 67r, 90r, 91v, 87r–v, 91r, 103v–104r.

Leão, Duarte Nunes de. "Chronica del Rey D. Fernando, dos reys de Portugal o IX". In *Crónicas dos reis de Portugal*, 411. Porto: Lello e irmãos Editores, 1975.

Lopes, Fernão. *Crónica de D. João I*. Vols. I, II. Porto: Livraria Civilização, not dated.

Lopes, Fernão. *Crónica de D. Pedro I.* Porto: Livraria Civilização, 1965.

Lopes, Fernão. *Crónica de D. Fernando.* Lisbon: Imprensa Nacional/Casa da Moeda, 1975.

López de Ayala, Pero. "Crónica del Rey Don Enrique, Segundo de Castilla". In *Crónicas de los Reyes de Castilla, Desde don Alfonso el Sabio, hasta los Católicos don Fernando y doña Isabel.* Vol. II, 1–64. Madrid: Ediciones Atlas, 1953.

López de Ayala, Pero. "Crónica del Rey Don Juan, Primero de Castilla é de Leon". In *Crónicas de los Reyes de Castilla, Desde don Alfonso el Sabio, hasta los Católicos don Fernando y doña Isabel.* Vol. II, 65–159. Madrid: Ediciones Atlas, 1953.

López de Ayala, Pero. "Crónica del Rey Don Pedro, fijo del Rey Don Alfonso, onceno de este nombre en Castilla". In *Crónicas de los Reyes de Castilla, Desde don Alfonso el Sabio, hasta los Católicos don Fernando y doña Isabel.* Vol. I, 401–629. Madrid: Ediciones Atlas, 1953.

Ordenações Afonsinas. Lisbon: Fundação Calouste Gulbenkian, 1998, book 1, tit. 60; book 2, tit. 63.

Pais, Frei Álvaro. *Espelho dos Reis.* Vol. I. Lisbon: Instituto de Alta Cultura, Centro de Estudos de Psicologia e de História da Filosofia, Faculdade de Letras da Universidade de Lisboa, 1955.

Pedro, Infante Dom; Verba, Frei João. *Livro da Vertuosa Benfeytoria.* Ed. by Adelino de Almeida Calado, book II, chapter XVI, 103. Coimbra: Biblioteca Geral da Universidade de Coimbra, 1994.

"Testamento de D. Fernando". In Biblioteca Pública e Arquivo Distrital de Évora, cód. CIX/2–2, no 9. Ed. by Salvador Dias Arnaut, *A Crise Nacional dos Fins do século XIV, I, A sucessão de D.Fernando,* doc. 7, 291–95. PhD diss., Faculdade de Letras da Universidade de Coimbra, Instituto de Estudos Históricos Vasconcelos, 1960.

"Testamento del Rey Don Juan el Primero". In Pero López de Ayala, *Crónica del Rey Don Enrique, Tercero de Castilla é de León.* In *Crónicas de los Reyes de Castilla, Desde don Alfonso el Sabio, hasta los Católicos don Fernando y doña Isabel,* vol. II, 186–94. Madrid: Ediciones Atlas, 1953.

Secondary sources

Albuquerque, Martim. *O poder político no Renascimento Português.* 2nd edn, Lisbon: Verbo-Babel editor, 2012.

Alves, Horácio Ferreira. *Dois Caluniados (D. Fernando e Leonor Teles).* Lisbon: Livraria Clássica Editora, 1927.

Amado, Teresa. *Fernão Lopes, contador de História, sobre a Crónica de D. João I.* Lisbon: Editorial Estampa, 1991.

Baleiras, Isabel de Pina. *Leonor Teles, uma rainha inesperada.* Lisbon: Círculo de Leitores, 2012.

Banond, Isabel. *História das Ideias Políticas.* Cascais: Princípia Editora, 2014.

Barros, Henrique da Gama. *História da Administração Pública em Portugal nos séculos XII a XV.* Vol. I. Lisbon: Imprensa Nacional, 1885.

Brásio, Padre António. "As 'razões' de João das Regras nas Cortes of Coimbra". In Separata da Revista *Lusitania Sacra,* vol. III, 6–7. Lisbon: União Gráfica, 1958.

Caetano, Marcelo. "Subsídios para a história das Cortes Medievais portuguesas". In separata da *Bracara Augusta,* vols XIV–XV, nos 1–2. Braga: Cruz & Cª Lda, 1963.

Caetano, Marcelo. *A crise nacional de 1383–1385, subsídios para o seu estudo.* Lisbon /São Paulo: editorial Verbo, 1985.

Caetano, Marcelo. *História do Direito Português. Fontes-Direito Público (1140–1495),* 3rd edn. Lisbon/São Paulo: editorial Verbo, 1992.

Coelho, Maria Helena da Cruz. *D. João I.* Rio de Mouro: Círculo de Leitores, 2005.

Duarte, Manuel Marques. *Leonor Teles, ensaio biográfico*. Porto: Campo das Letras, 2002.
Figueiredo, Antero de. *Leonor Teles "flor de Altura"*. Lisbon: Livraria Bertrand, 1936.
Hespanha, António Manuel. *História das Instituições. Épocas medieval e moderna*. Coimbra: Livraria Almedina, 1982.
Mattoso, José, ed. *História de Portugal, A Monarquia Feudal*. Lisbon: Editorial Estampa, 1993, vol. 2.
Merêa, Paulo. *O Poder Real e as Cortes: Lições feitas na Faculdade de Direito de Coimbra aos alunos de "História do Direito Português" no ano lectivo de 1922–1923*. Coimbra: Coimbra Editora, Lda, 1923.
Merêa, Paulo. "Sobre a aclamação dos nossos reis". In Separata da *Revista Portuguesa de História*. Vol. X, 5–11. Coimbra: Faculdade de Letras da Universidade de Coimbra,1962.
Mirot, Léon. "Les mésaventures d'un prince portugais au XIVème siècle". In *Revue des Études Historiques*, 129–50. Paris: Librairie Alphonse Picard et Fils, 1911.
Moreno, Humberto Baquero. "Estado, Nobreza e Senhorios". In Maria Helena da Cruz Coelho and Armando Luís de Carvalho Homem, eds, *A Génese do Estado Moderno no Portugal Tardo-Medievo (séculos XIII-XV)*, 257–67. Cycle of conferences organised by Universidade Autónoma de Lisboa in the school year 1996–97, Lisbon: Universidade Autónoma de Lisboa, 1999.
Neves, João António Mendes. "A 'Formosa Chancelaria' – Estudo dos originais da Chancelaria de D. Fernando (1367–1383)". Master's thesis, Faculdade de Letras da Universidade de Coimbra, 2005.
Nieto Soria, José Manuel. *Fundamentos ideológicos del poder real en Castilla (siglos XIII–XVI)*. Madrid: Eudema, 1988.
Olivera Serrano, César. "Beatriz de Portugal, la pugna dinástica Avís-Trastámara". PhD diss., Santiago de Compostela: Consejo Superior de Investigaciones científicas Xunta de Galicia / Instituto de Estúdios Gallegos "Padre Sarmiento", 2005.
Olivera Serrano, César. "Las secuelas religiosas de un conflicto dinástico: portugueses en Castill el siglo XV". In Isabel Beceiro Pita, ed., *Poder Piedad y Devoción, Castilla y su entorno. Siglos XII-XV*, 161–87. Madrid: Sílex ediciones, 2014.
Rebelo, Luís de Sousa. *A Concepção de Poder em Fernão Lopes*. n.p., Livros Horizonte, 1983.
Russell, Peter. "João Fernandes Andeiro, at the Court of John of Lancaster, 1371–1381". In *Revista da Universidade de Coimbra*, vol. XIV, 5–15. Coimbra: Imprensa Académica, 1938.
Sousa, Ana Paula, "Leonor Teles. 'Huma maa molher'?" Master's thesis, Faculdade de Letras da Universidade do Porto, 2004.
Tavares, Maria José Ferro. *Fernando e Leonor: um reinado (mal)dito*. Lisbon: Maria José Ferro Tavares e Chiado Editora, 2013.
Valdeón Baruque, Julio. *Enrique II, 1366–1379*. Palencia: Diputación Provincial de Palencia, Editorial La Olmeda, 1996.
Ventura, Margarida Garcez. *O Messias de Lisboa: Um Estudo de Mitologia Política (1383–1415)*. Lisbon: Edições Cosmos, 1992.

3

FROM ELECTION TO CONSOLIDATION

The strategies of legitimacy of the Trastámara dynasty in the Crown of Aragon

Lledó Ruiz Domingo

When King Martin I (1396–1410) passed away without leaving any heirs, none of the candidates to the throne of the Crown of Aragon were legitimate. Although each candidate claimed rights of kinship with the late King Martin, none were linked directly to him and as such none were direct heirs to the Crown. This chapter will explain how, during the two years from the death of King Martin until the election of the new monarch Ferdinand I (1412–16) and throughout his reign, the Trastámara dynasty deployed a communication strategy based on propaganda to guarantee his election as king and, later, to consolidate his government and the hold of his dynasty on the throne. In this sense, we are looking at the creation of a multifaceted and simultaneous process of legitimation that evolved over the years depending on the needs of the dynasty.

Thus, in the years 1410–58, we can distinguish three different periods established in the process of legitimisation:

1. 1410–12 – legitimisation of Ferdinand of Trastámara (future Ferdinand I of Aragon) as a candidate for the throne
2. 1412–16 – consolidation of Ferdinand I as a monarch
3. 1416–58 – consolidation and evolution of the legitimising process during the reign of Alfonso V

In order to achieve the defined objective of each period, the Trastámara developed arguments to be communicated politically to Aragonese society through practical mechanisms of diffusion and display of political culture. Thus, following this approach, we will analyse Alfonso V's (1416–58) process of legitimising his accession to the Crown of Aragon moving further into the fifteenth century.

he would have a political representative to speak on his behalf at all times. From 1410 on, we have Fernán Gutiérrez de Vega, Ferdinand's *repostero mayor* (chief keeper of the household), and Juan González de Acevedo defending Ferdinand and his cause in Catalonia.[14] They relentlessly tried to justify the need for pacification in the kingdoms of Valencia and Aragon with the use of Castilian troops and to prevent the interference of James of Urgell and his allies in the meetings of the estates of the realm. Similarly, Ferdinand sent Diego Gómez de Fuensalida, abbot of Valladolid and chief chaplain of his household, and García López de Sesé to the Kingdom of Aragon. These diplomats informed the Aragonese parliamentarians of the deals between James of Urgell and the sultan of Granada, while reminding the delegates of Ferdinand's reputation as a Christian general, expert in the fight against the infidels.[15] At the same time, Diego Fernández de Vadillo, Ferdinand's secretary, was sent to the Kingdom of Valencia. As has been demonstrated by Rafael Narbona Vizcaíno, Ferdinand, with this emissary's help, was able to leverage the differences between the noble families in the Kingdom of Valencia who had been at war for decades, obtaining the support of many of them, in particular the Centelles family, rivals of the Vilaragut family, and the governor-general of the Kingdom, Arnau Guillem Ballera, who were all supporters of James of Urgell.[16] When the antagonism between the factions in these kingdoms seemed about to explode into a military conflict, Ferdinand sent a large contingent of troops from Castile, allowing his supporters to be prepared in case of a battle against James of Urgell. And indeed, the dispute between the supporters of James and Ferdinand did result in a military confrontation, in February 1412, at Sagunto, near the city of Valencia, which resulted in a victory for the troops supporting the Trastámara candidate. This military victory was fundamental in Ferdinand's efforts to secure the Aragonese throne.[17]

The final part of his legitimising strategy was based on economic resources. Complementing his image as a ruler and a military expert, Ferdinand also used the financial resources at his disposal, proceeding from his lordly estates, to buy favour, bestow gifts, and promise positions in the royal administration.[18] For example, the count of Pallars had at first supported Louis of Naples, because Violant of Bar had promised to grant him the towns of Berga and Bergadà, but his alliance did not prosper because of Ferdinand's counter-offer of 10,000 florins for the Count's support.[19] With all this, Ferdinand managed to attract a much greater number of supporters to his cause than he had originally been able to call upon.

Thanks to this strategy of legitimisation and the important military victory in the Kingdom of Valencia, it was decided in 1412, after two years of conflict, to convene representatives from each of the three kingdoms (three from Aragon, three from Valencia, and three from Catalonia) in Caspe to decide which of the two candidates would be elected as the new monarch. Ferdinand presented his credentials and a vote was held whereby James of Urgell secured three votes and Ferdinand secured six. Thus Ferdinand was declared the new king of the Crown of Aragon. This result was officially sanctioned on 29 June 1412, only four months after the military victory over James of Urgell at Sagunto.

1412–16: consolidation and legitimisation of the Trastámara dynasty in Aragon

As we have seen, the arrival of this new dynasty happened after a break in the dynastic continuity and was obtained by means of a military confrontation and the creation of a social division, since part of Aragonese society considered James of Urgell to be more legitimate than the Castilian prince. Due to this, it was necessary to make a greater effort in disseminating propaganda, and legitimisation was still required to preserve and consolidate hold on the throne. This was necessary to ensure that upon Ferdinand's death, his son and successor Alfonso would assume the throne.

Ferdinand I set out to legitimise himself, and legitimise his dynasty on the throne of Aragon. The Trastámara dynasty was not inexperienced in this, and we can see many similarities between the legitimist display of Ferdinand with that of Henry II when he arrived in Castile in 1369 with his dynasty, after the death of his half-brother and the ensuing civil war.[20] For this reason, he launched the other initiatives we have mentioned (recognising the support of the kingdoms, showing political continuity, and exalting his own political success) with the same objective: to legitimise the new dynasty by combining tradition with change. This was made possible through the use of propaganda and parliamentary representation, expressing the changes brought by the Trastámara and the traditions of the Crown of Aragon. This process was multifaceted and combined the criminalisation of the opposition, verbal communication (such as speeches made by the King in the parliaments), and non-verbal communication (the most significant ceremonies such as royal entries in the cities or the coronation ceremony), with the use of the prerogatives of royal government and management of the monarchy. We can look at each of these tactics individually.

Making the opposition illegal

Although Ferdinand had been chosen by the majority of the delegates of the three kingdoms in Caspe, the opponents of the new king and supporters of the other candidate, James of Urgell, did not give up in their attempts to place him on the throne.[21]

In March 1413, James of Urgell and his supporters (including Antonio de Luna and Pedro Ximénez de Urrea) initiated a rebellion against the Trastámara king. They hired mercenaries to try to invade parts of Aragon where Ferdinand I was. The King was even warned by the *Notario* of the city of Zaragoza that very influential people from the Kingdom of Aragon were beginning to support James of Urgell.[22] Yet a real revolt was about to start not in Aragon but in the Kingdom of Valencia, so he had to cancel his visit to Zaragoza and travel immediately to Valencia to defend the Kingdom in person because popular support for the count of Urgell was increasing every day. Support for the rebellion grew notably in villages in Valencia, such as Castellón, Vilareal, his expected political future was not to be king of the Crown of Aragon but to participate in Castilian and Navarrese affairs.[42] Ferdinand I was training the future king of the Crown of Aragon and chose as his closest collaborators people from these regions to avoid any problems in Alfonso's succession, ensuring the continuation of his dynasty on that throne.

With these four mechanisms of legitimisation, Ferdinand I achieved his goal for this period: to consolidate the throne in his dynasty and also to leave it as a legacy.

1416–58: extending the legitimisation strategy

After the premature death of King Ferdinand I in 1416, the Trastámara dynasty had to double its efforts to ensure that its second monarch assumed the throne peacefully, creating a situation whereby the little opposition that remained could not negatively impact on the consolidation of his position in the Crown of Aragon. To this end, Alfonso V had to maintain an image of continuity with his father and predecessor in the same three aspects previously explored: verbal propaganda, non-verbal communication transmitted through his personal image, and concessions to the political class of the kingdoms. Nevertheless, Alfonso V also needed to bring to an end part of the strategy of legitimisation initiated by his father and to evolve.

Firstly, Alfonso "the Magnanimous" gave special attention to aspects related to the ceremonies of the monarchy and the projection of a personal image and, at the same time, the continuation of the Trastámara dynasty in the Crown of Aragon through the use of objects and symbols. His strategy of non-verbal communication evolved over time, attending to political situations as they arose. In the early years, his attire and ornaments were marked by emblems, keeping with those traditionally used by the Crown of Aragon, especially those used by his father as the first Trastámara monarch. An example of these ornaments is the use of the vase with lilies, an emblem introduced by his father as a personal symbol that Alfonso used on his clothes from his very first public appearances as monarch.[43] Other examples would be the jewels engraved with his own emblems: *siti perillós* (the burning throne), the millet, and the open book.[44] Later, when Alfonso embarked on his conquest of Naples in 1420, his clothing, luxurious objects, and personal adornments would change and be marked by the desire of the monarch to be seen as an Italian prince, employing the fashions of the Italian peninsula. That can be seen in the jewellery made by his silversmiths, Guido Antoni and Giovanni of Pisa, both of them Italians, or in the portraits on coins in which the King appears with an Italian hairstyle.[45]

As for verbal communication, King Alfonso V's speeches in the Estates were characterised by their simplicity and brevity and focused on the need for common good and good governance as a basis for stability in the kingdoms. In addition, Alfonso's speeches highlighted the memory of the monarch from whom he descended, thus legitimising Ferdinand I's election in Caspe, and expressed the deep esteem that he professed for his subjects, whom he ruled, as he underlined, with the help of God.[46]

Similarly, during the early years of his reign, Alfonso V continued to adopt legislative measures designed to compensate the Crown realms, granting petitions that had been repeatedly requested but had not thus far been obtained. In this sense, the institutional sphere was the preferred method of granting these petitions by creating separate institutions in each of the kingdoms. An important example would be the definitive institutionalisation of the *Generalitat* in each kingdom. The *Generalitat* was an institution created in 1362 by Pedro IV to manage the "donations" granted to the Crown by the Estates General through a commission of two representatives from each of the three estates of the realm. When the Estates General were not meeting, these donations were still being collected and the king decided to create the *Generalitat* to manage them. At that time, the king created a *Generalitat* for all the kingdoms under his government, but the kingdoms protested to ensure they each had their own *Generalitat*.[47] In the case of the Kingdom of Valencia, Alfonso agreed to the creation of the *Generalitat* in 1418.[48] Years later, in 1436, he would concede to grant the same to the Kingdom of Aragon. There were thus three governments, one for Catalonia, one for Valencia, and one for Aragon. Another example would be the creation of a royal archive, distinct from those located in Barcelona, Valencia, and Aragon, to store information and royal documentation relating to each of these kingdoms.[49]

These acts evolved when the political efforts of the monarch changed direction to focus on his aspirations to obtain the throne of Naples. From that moment, the monarch would employ rhetoric that would connect him not only with his father but also with his predecessors as monarchs of the Crown of Aragon, who since the thirteenth century had cast their expansionist eyes on the flourishing Mediterranean, especially in southern Italy. From that moment, the imprint of Alfonso as an Italian prince would be fundamental in not only his image but also his legitimisation strategies. So much so that when he succeeded in these ambitions, he decided to remain in Naples, constituting a very refined Renaissance court.[50]

But even after conquering the Kingdom of Naples and succeeding in extending the dominion of the Crown of Aragon in the Mediterranean, Alfonso did not cease in his attempt to legitimise his dynasty, to the point that, years later, he sponsored the writing of an account of his father's reign by the famous Italian humanist Lorenzo Valla.[51]

Conclusion

The arrival of the Trastámara dynasty onto the throne of the Crown of Aragon was an act disputed by part of the political society in that composite state. For this reason, in the early years of his reign, the new monarch Ferdinand I had to use propaganda and political communication to convey a message to legitimise himself as king of these lands. To achieve their objectives, the Trastámara deployed political arguments very similar to those used when they first ascended to royal power in neighbouring Castile. With these arguments, Ferdinand of Trastámara managed to convey a consolidated vision of his hereditary rights and his capacity as a ruler.

Thus, a political message of legitimacy was articulated in a dynasty that had reached the throne after two years of intrigue and a battle in the Kingdom of Valencia. As can be seen, this strategy was also flexible because eventually the Trastámara kings modified it and included new forms of legitimacy, such as legitimacy by conquest (in Naples), among others, without forgetting the need to continue the legitimising process regarding the origins of the dynasty in the recently acquired Crown of Aragon. By this multifaceted and simultaneous strategy, Ferdinand I succeeded in making the succession process effective, continued and augmented by Alfonso V, and the Trastámara dynasty would effectively control the Crown of Aragon for 100 years until the death of Ferdinand II in 1516.

Notes

1 In 1369, after a civil war against his half-brother, Henry II was crowned king of Castile. From that time on, the Castilian royal family would be known as the House of Trastámara, because of a title that Henry II himself had received from his father, King Alfonso XI: the county of Trastámara in Galicia.

2 Ferran Soldevila, *Compromiso de Caspe, resposta al Sr. Menéndez Pidal* (Barcelona: Dalmau, 1965). The Crown of Aragon was a confederation of territories united under the rule of the kings of Aragon from 1164 to 1715. Its origin was the result of the marriage between Ramon Berenguer IV, count of Barcelona, and Petronilla, queen of Aragon. In 1410, when King Martin I died, the Crown of Aragon was formed by Aragon, Catalonia, Valencia, Mallorca and its islands, the island kingdom of Sicily, plus Corsica, Sardinia, and the counties of Roussillon and Cerdanya.

3 Archivo de la Corona de Aragón [hereafter ACA], Procesos Cort de Tortosa 17, fol. 1037. See also Carlos López Rodríguez, "Las últimas voluntades del rey Martín I el Humano (30 y 31 de mayo de 1410)", *Aragón en la Edad Media* 26 (2013): 235–38.

4 The Cortes was the political institution for the whole of the Crown of Aragon. Its function was to unite the estates of the realm and the king to jointly pass laws. However, a meeting of the estates of the realm without the king could not be considered an assembly of the Estates General, but a parliament. Thus, in the period between 1410 and 1412, between the death of Martin I and the election of Fernando de Trastámara, the meetings held by the estates of the realm to choose the king were parliaments and not cortes.

5 Beatriz Canellas Adoz, "Actas de los Parlamentos de Cataluña y Aragón tras la muerte de Martín el Humano y del Compromiso de Caspe y elección de Fernando de Antequera", in *La Corona de Aragón en el Centro de su historia*, ed. Ángel Sesma Múñoz (Zaragoza: Actas del Gobierno de Aragón, 2010), 11–40. López Rodríguez, "Las últimas voluntades", 239–48.

6 Flocel Sabaté, "El Compromís de Casp", in *Història de la Corona d'Aragó*, ed. Ernest Belenguer (Barcelona: Edicions 62, 2007), 290–92.

7 ACA, Real Cancillería, Registro 2055, fols 57–58. See also Francisca Vendrell Gallostra, *Violante de Bar y el Compromiso de Caspe* (Barcelona: Real Academia de Buenas Letras, 1992).

8 Fernando de Trastámara was regent of Castile with Queen Catherine of Lancaster from 1406, the year of the death of his brother, King Henry III. The heir, John II, was still a minor and a regency was decreed between Fernando, his uncle, and Queen Catherine, his mother. Fernando would be regent of Castile until his death in 1416. See Ana Echevarría Arsuaga, *Catalina de Lancaster reina regente de Castilla (1372–1418)* (Hondarribia: Editorial Nerea, 2002), 93–94.

9 Santiago González Sánchez, *Los recursos militares de la monarquía castellana a comienzos del siglo XV: las campañas granadinas del Infante don Fernando: Setenil y Antequera (1407–1410)* (Madrid: Marcial Pons, 2016).

10 Víctor Muñoz Gomez, "La candidatura al trono del infante Fernando de Antequera y la intervención castellana en la Corona de Aragón durante el Interregno", in *Martí l'Humà, el darrer rei de la dinastia de Barcelona (1396–1410). L'Interregne i el Compromís de Casp*, ed. Maria Teresa Ferrer i Mallol (Barcelona: Institut d'Estudis Catalans, 2015), 868.
11 Muñoz Gomez, "La candidatura al trono", 872.
12 ACA, Procesos de Corts, Tomo 16, fol. 723. See also Próspero Bofarull y Mascarós, *Procesos de las antiguas cortes y Parlamentos de Cataluña, Aragón y Valencia*, vol. II (Barcelona: Imprenta del Archivo de la Corona de Aragón, 1847), 139–41.
13 José Manuel Nieto Soria, "Fernando de Antequera, regente de Castilla", in *La Corona de Aragón en el Centro de su historia*, 293–314.
14 ACA, Procesos de Corts, Tomo 17, fols 1076–77.
15 ACA, Procesos de Corts, Tomo 18, fol. 1163r–v. See Muñoz Gomez, "La candidatura al trono", 877.
16 Rafael Narbona Vizcaíno, "Las élites políticas valencianas durante el Interregno y el Compromiso de Caspe", in *La Corona de Aragón en el Centro de su historia*, 212.
17 Narbona Vizcaíno, "Las élites políticas valencianas", 230.
18 Muñoz Gomez, "La candidatura al trono", 874.
19 Lluís Domènech i Montaner, *La inquinitat de Casp i la fi del Comtat d'Urgell: Estudi històrico-polític* (Barcelona: Verdaguer, 1930), 122.
20 Covadonga Valdaliso, "Discursos de legitimación de la dinastía Trastámara (1366–1388)", in *Ruptura i legitimació dinàstica a l'Edat Mitjana*, eds Flocel Sabaté and Maite Pedrol (Lleida: Pagès editors, 2015), 127–42.
21 Diego Monfar y Sors, *Historia de los condes de Urgel* (Barcelona: Editorial José Eusebio Monfort, 1853), 466; Jesús Mestre i Godes, *El Compromís de Casp. Un moment decisiu en la història de Catalunya* (Barcelona: Edicions 62, 1999), 212–22.
22 Próspero de Bofarull, *Proceso contra el último conde de Urgel y su familia* (Barcelona: Imprenta del Archivo de la Corona de Aragón, 1868).
23 Andrés Giménez Soler, *Don Jaime de Aragón, último conde de Urgel* (Barcelona: Real Academia de Buenas Letras 1901), 184–85; ACA, R. 2383, fol. 58v.
24 "E, fahent tenir bones spies sobre les dites coses, aquells que trobarets culpables castigats per tal forma que a ells sia pena e càstich, e altres terror e eximpli. E axí mateix, aquells qui conexerets o sentirets ésser sospitosos a la bona custòdia de les dites viles, prenets e presos axí tenits tro de nós hajats altre manament contrari." Quoted in Giménez, *Don Jaime de Aragón*, 183. See also ACA, R. 2383, fol. 55v.
25 Santiago Sobrequés i Vidal, *Els Barons de Catalunya* (Barcelona: Vicens-Vives, 1957), 150.
26 The estates of the realm consisted of the clergy, the nobility and the representatives of the chief cities; they met together as the Estates with the monarch to carry out legislative activity.
27 Josep Maria Mas i Solench, *Les corts a la Corona catalano-aragonesa* (Barcelona: Rafael Dalmau, 1995).
28 Suzane Cawsey, *Reialesa i propaganda: l'eloqüència reial ca. 1200–1450* (Valencia: Publicacions Universitat de València, 2008).
29 "nós, liberalment e no obviant d'alguna fretura, puscam entendre en la ministració de la justícia e pacífic e bon regiment e estament d'aquest principat e dels altres nostres regnes e terres; per forma que d'açò que ens ha comanat, bon compte pixam retre a nostre senyor Déus, e nostra cosa pública sia conservasa en pau, tranquilitat e repòs", quoted in Lledó Ruiz Domingo and Elena Navarro Olmos, "Los discursos de la guerra, la propaganda regia frente a los conflictos bélicos en la Corona de Aragón", *Roda da Fortuna* 1/1 (2014): 101.
30 Quoted in Ricard Albert, ed., *Parlaments a les Corts catalanes* (Barcelona: Nostres Clàssics, 1988), 124–25. "Nós som vinguts ací e havem fet congregar a vosaltres, representadors aquest Principat de Catalunya, per denunciarvos com, per lo càrrec que tenim de la tutela del señor rei de Castella, nostre car Nebot, e regiment del seu regne, a nós convé anar [...] E abans de partir entenem, ab la gràcia de Déu, fer e concloure algunes coses en la present cort, concernents servei de Déu e nostre benefici, del dit principat e de la cosa

pública d'aquell [. . .] Bé sabets, emperò, com aprés que som venguts en aquests nostres regnes, nos fonc necessari, per inclinar la reinicosa audacia de don Jaime d'Urgel (qui aberrant de la via dels altres nostres vassalls e feels sotmesos, recusava venir prestarnos la feeltat que era tengut) portar molts càrrecs e messions molts grans, venint ab alguns assats opulent nombre de gent d'armes vers lo dit Jaime a la ciutat de Lleida, on, presents moltes e notables persones, nos féu e prestà sagradament de feeltat així com los altres nostres lleialtats vassalls havien fet. E per avant, continuant e afigint en son mal e damnat principi divulgà e mostrà en obert sa damnada rebellió, metent gent d'armes estrangeres per damnificar e ocupar nostres regnes e terres, e en moltes maneres constituintse públicament nostre enemic; per la qual raó anam personalment sobre Balaguer, on tenem sitiat lo dit don Jaime [. . .] per tres mesos. En lo qual siti molt virtuosament, alta e notable, lo dit principat així com aquell qe nós havem en gran singular reputació, nós servà. [. . .] E estant en lo dit siti convocam lo Princeps namque [. . .] E ultra les dites quantitats [. . .] per la recuperació de Sardenya, cerca la qual els nostres precedessors han treballat e disposat sos vassalls a diversos perills e damnatges [. . .] E com per les dites raons, no puscam bonament cumplir les dites obligacions [. . .] vos pregam que les dites obligacions per nós fetes dels dits vuitanta dos mil florins nos dissolvats e cancellets."

31 Winfried Künchler, *Les finances de la Corona d'Aragó al segle XV* (Valencia: Alfons el Magnànim, 1997).

32 Ruiz and Navarro, "Los discursos de la guerra", 98.

33 Cawsey, *Reialesa i propaganda*, 215.

34 Juan Fernando Utrilla, "La coronación de los reyes de Aragón", *Revista de Aragón* 374 (2013): 38–44; Núria Silleras, "Creada a su imagen y semejanza: la coronación de la Reina de Aragón según las ordenaciones de Pedro el Ceremonioso", *Lusitania Sacra* 29 (2015): 31–49; José Manuel Nieto Soria, "La coronación del rey: los símbolos y la naturaleza de su poder", in *Alfonso X y su época. El siglo del rey sabio*, ed. Miguel Rodríguez (Barcelona: Carroggio, 2001), 127–52; Bonifacio Palacios Martín, *Ordenación y ceremonial de la coronación de los reyes de Aragón* (Valencia: Scriptorium, 1994).

35 Miquel Raufast, "¿Un mismo ceremonial para dos dinastías?: las entradas reales de Martín el Humano (1397) y Fernando I (1412) en Barcelona", *En la España Medieval* 30 (2007): 91–129.

36 Antonio Duran Gudiol, "El rito de la coronación del rey en Aragón", *Argensola: Revista de Ciencias Sociales del Instituto de Estudios Altoaragoneses* 103 (1989): 17–40. And quote from Jerónimo Zurita, *Anales de Aragón*, vol. 5, ed. Ángel Canellas (Zaragoza: Institución Fernando el Católico, 1984), 384.

37 Roser Salicrú, "La coronació de Ferran d'Antequera: l'organització i els preparatius de la festa", *Anuario de Estudios Medievales* 25/2 (1995): 706.

38 José Camarena Mahiques, *Tratado de paz entre Aragón y Génova en 1413* (Valencia: Instituto Valenciano de Estudios Históricos, 1952), 91–145.

39 Isabel Sánchez de Movellán Torent, *La diputació del General de Catalunya 1413–1479* (Barcelona: Institut d'Estudis Catalans, 2004), 129.

40 Narbona Vizcaíno, "Las élites políticas valencianas", 232.

41 Víctor Múñoz Gomez, "Una aproximación a la presencia castellana en el gobierno de la Corona de Aragón durante el reinado de Fernando I", in *El compromiso de Caspe cambios dinásticos y constitucionalismo en la Corona de Aragón* (Zaragoza: Obra social Ibercaja, 2013), 556.

42 However, King Alfonso and his wife, Queen Maria of Castile, were never able to have children, so the King's successor ultimately would be his brother John.

43 Gemma Capilla Aledón, "El poder representado: Alfonso V el Magnánimo (1416–1458)" (PhD diss., Universitat de València, 2014), 93–95.

44 Joan Domenge Mesquita, "Las joyas emblemáticas de Alfonso el Magnánimo", *Anales de Historia del Arte* 24 (2014): 99–117.

45 Juan Vicente Garcia Marsilla, "Vestir el poder. Indumentaria e imagen en las cortes de Alfonso el Magnánimo y María de Castilla", *Res publica* 18 (2007): 368.

46 Jose Antonio Alabau and Raquel Madrid, "'Que Déus ne serà servit e vosaltres e tots nostres sotsmeses ne serets ben regits e governats'. Las proposiciones reales a las cortes valencianas durante el reinado de Alfonso el Magnánimo", *Saitabi* 64–65 (2014–15), 101–13.
47 Ernest Belenguer, *Vida i regnat de Pere el Cerimoniós 1319–1387* (Lleida: Pagès, 2015), 186–87.
48 Rosa Muñoz Pomer, *Orígenes de la Generalidad Valenciana* (Valencia: Conselleria de Cultura, Educació i Ciència, 1987), 29.
49 Rosa Muñoz Pomer, "Siguiendo las huellas de las cortes de 1419", *Saitabi* 59 (2009): 137–60.
50 Alan Ryder, *Alfonso el Magnánimo rey de Aragón, Nápoles y Sicilia 1396–1458* (Valencia: Alfons el Magnànim, 1992), 170–89.
51 Santiago López Moreda, "El modelo de Princeps en la obra de Lorenzo Valla", *Excerpta Philologica* 10–12 (2000–02), 301–18.

Bibliography

Alabau, José A., and Madrid, Raquel. "'Que Déus ne serà servit e vosaltres e tots nostres sotsmeses ne serets ben regits e governats'. Las proposiciones reales a las cortes valencianas durante el reinado de Alfonso el Magnánimo". *Saitabi* 64–65 (2014–15): 101–13.

Albert, Ricard, ed. *Parlaments a les Corts catalanes*. Barcelona: Nostres Clàssics, 1988.

Belenguer, Ernest. *Vida i regnat de Pere el Cerimoniós 1319–1387*. Lleida: Pagès, 2015.

Bofarull y Mascarós, Próspero de. *Procesos de las antiguas cortes y Parlamentos de Cataluña, Aragón y Valencia*, Tomo II. Barcelona: Imprenta del Archivo de la Corona de Aragón, 1847.

Bofarull y Mascarós, Próspero de. *Proceso contra el último conde de Urgel y su familia*. Barcelona: Imprenta del Archivo de la Corona de Aragón, 1868.

Camarena Mahiques, José. *Tratado de paz entre Aragón y Génova en 1413*. Valencia: Instituto Valenciano de Estudios Históricos, 1952.

Canellas Adoz, Beatriz. "Actas de los Parlamentos de Cataluña y Aragón tras la muerte de Martín el Humano y del Compromiso de Caspe y elección de Fernando de Antequera". In *La Corona de Aragón en el Centro de su historia*, edited by Ángel Sesma Múñoz, 11–40. Zaragoza: Actas del Gobierno de Aragón, 2010.

Capilla Aledón, Gemma. "El poder representado: Alfonso V el Magnánimo (1416–1458)" (PhD diss., Universitat de València, 2014).

Cawsey, Suzane. *Reialesa i propaganda: l'eloqüència reial ca. 1200–1450*. Valencia: Publicacions Universitat de València, 2008.

Domènech i Montaner, Lluís. *La inquinitat de Casp i la fi del Comtat d'Urgell: Estudi històrico-polític*. Barcelona: Verdaguer, 1930.

Domenge Mesquita, Joan. "Las joyas emblemáticas de Alfonso el Magnánimo". *Anales de Historia del Arte* 24 (2014): 99–117.

Duran Gudiol, Antonio. "El rito de la coronación del rey en Aragón". *Argensola: Revista de Ciencias Sociales del Instituto de Estudios Altoaragoneses* 103 (1989): 17–40.

Echevarría Arsuaga, Ana. *Catalina de Lancaster reina regente de Castilla (1372–1418)*. Hondarribia: Editorial Nerea, 2002.

Garcia Marsilla, Juan Vicente, "Vestir el poder. Indumentaria e imagen en las cortes de Alfonso el Magnánimo y María de Castilla," *Res publica* 18 (2007): 353–73.

Giménez Soler, Andrés. *Don Jaime de Aragón, último conde de Urgel*. Barcelona: Real Academia de Buenas Letras, 1901.

González Sánchez, Santiago. *Los recursos militares de la monarquía castellana a comienzos del siglo XV: las campañas granadinas del Infante don Fernando: Setenil y Antequera (1407–1410)*. Madrid: Marcial Pons, 2016.

Künchler, Winfried. *Les finances de la Corona d'Aragó al segle XV*. Valencia: Alfons el Magnànim, 1997.

López Moreda, Santiago. "El modelo de Princeps en la obra de Lorenzo Valla". *Excerpta Philologica* 10–12 (2000–02): 301–18.

López Rodríguez, Carlos. "Las últimas voluntades del rey Martín I el Humano (30 y 31 de mayo de 1410)". *Aragón en la Edad Media* 26 (2013): 225–68.

Mas i Solench, Josep Maria. *Les corts a la Corona catalano-aragonesa*. Barcelona: Rafael Dalmau, 1995.

Mestre i Godes, Jesús. *El Compromís de Casp. Un moment decisiu en la història de Catalunya*. Barcelona: Edicions 62, 1999.

Monfar y Sors, Diego. *Historia de los condes de Urgel*. Barcelona: Editorial José Eusebio Monfort, 1853.

Muñoz Gomez, Víctor. "La candidatura al trono del infante Fernando de Antequera y la intervención castellana en la Corona de Aragón durante el Interregno". In *Martí l'Humà, el darrer rei de la dinastia de Barcelona (1396–1410). L'Interregne i el Compromís de Casp*, edited by Maria Teresa Ferrer i Mallol, 867–97. Barcelona, Institut d'Estudis Catalans, 2015.

Muñoz Gomez, Víctor. "Una aproximación a la presencia castellana en el gobierno de la Corona de Aragón durante el reinado de Fernando I". In *El compromiso de Caspe cambios dinásticos y constitucionalismo en la Corona de Aragón*, edited by María Isabel Falcón Pérez, 548–59. Zaragoza: Obra social Ibercaja, 2013.

Muñoz Pomer, Rosa. "Siguiendo las huellas de las cortes de 1419". *Saitabi* 59 (2009): 137–60.

Muñoz Pomer, Rosa. *Orígenes de la Generalidad Valenciana*. Valencia: Conselleria de Cultura, Educació i Ciència, 1987.

Narbona Vizcaíno, Rafael. "Las élites políticas valencianas durante el Interregno y el Compromiso de Caspe". In *La Corona de Aragón en el Centro de su historia*, edited by Ángel Sesma Múñoz, 191–230. Zaragoza: Actas del Gobierno de Aragón, 2010.

Nieto Soria, José Manuel. "La coronación del rey: los símbolos y la naturaleza de su poder". In *Alfonso X y su época. El siglo del rey sabio*, edited by Miguel Rodríguez, 127–52. Barcelona: Carroggio, 2001.

Nieto Soria, José Manuel. "Fernando de Antequera, regente de Castilla". In *La Corona de Aragón en el Centro de su historia*, edited by Ángel Sesma Múñoz, 293–314. Zaragoza: Actas del Gobierno de Aragón, 2010.

Palacios Martín, Bonifacio. *Ordenación y ceremonial de la coronación de los reyes de Aragón*. Valencia: Scriptorium, 1994.

Raufast, Miquel. "¿Un mismo ceremonial para dos dinastías?: las entradas reales de Martín el Humano (1397) y Fernando I (1412) en Barcelona". *En la España Medieval* 30 (2007): 91–129.

Ryder, Alan. *Alfonso el Magnánimo rey de Aragón, Nápoles y Sicilia 1396–1458*. Valencia: Alfons el Magnànim, 1992.

Ruiz Domingo, Lledó, and Navarro Olmos, Elena. "Los discursos de la guerra, la propaganda regia frente a los conflictos bélicos en la Corona de Aragón". *Roda da Fortuna* 1/1 (2014): 90–112.

Sabaté, Flocel. "El Compromís de Casp". In *Història de la Corona d'Aragó*, directed by Ernest Belenguer, 287–304. Barcelona: Edicions 62, 2007.

Salicrú, Roser. "La coronació de Ferran d'Antequera: l'organització i els preparatius de la festa". *Anuario de Estudios Medievales* 25/2 (1995): 699–758.

Sánchez de Movellán Torent, Isabel. *La diputació del General de Catalunya 1413–1479*. Barcelona: Institut d'Estudis Catalans, 2004.

Silleras, Núria. "Creada a su imagen y semejanza: la coronación de la Reina de Aragón según las ordenaciones de Pedro el Ceremonioso," *Lusitania Sacra* 29 (2015): 31–49.

Sobrequés i Vidal, Santiago. *Els Barons de Catalunya.* Barcelona: Vicens-Vives, 1957.

Soldevila, Ferran. *Compromiso de Caspe, resposta al Sr. Menéndez Pidal.* Barcelona: Dalmau, 1965.

Utrilla, Juan Fernando. "La coronación de los reyes de Aragón". *Revista de Aragón,* 374 (2013): 38–44.

Valdaliso, Covadonga. "Discursos de legitimación de la dinastía Trastámara (1366–1388)". In *Ruptura i legitimació dinàstica a l'Edat Mitjana,* edited by Flocel Sabaté and Maite Pedrol, 127–42. Lleida: Pagès editors, 2015.

Vendrell Gallostra, Francisca. *Violante de Bar y el Compromiso de Caspe.* Barcelona: Real Academia de Buenas Letras, 1992.

Zurita, Jerónimo. *Anales de Aragón,* vol. 5, ed. Ángel Canellas. Zaragoza: Institución Fernando el Católico, 1984.

Schleswig-Holstein) in 1500, and was exposed in front of the Swedish council for making anti-Swedish treaties with Russia, John II was deposed in 1501, and Sten Sture the Elder again confirmed as leader.[5] However, the problem between the different parties and interests in the Swedish kingdom remained, and led once again to the establishment of the Union of Kalmar king, Christian II, as the king of Sweden in 1520. Christian II had to conquer most of Sweden before he was accepted and crowned, and his coronation celebration included the execution of more than eighty Swedish nobles, clerics, burghers, and peasants in Stockholm alone (and there were more such deaths all over Sweden which added to these numbers). These actions finally forced the Swedes to unite, and to agree once and for all that Danish rule, even as part of a Scandinavian union, was not the best strategy for the Swedish people.[6] Although the idea of such a Scandinavian union remained influential as a political alternative, it never again was considered in earnest.[7] The political conflict against Christian II between 1520 and 1523, and his deposition by means of his subjects renouncing their allegiance in all regions of Sweden, banishing his Danish officials, and subsequently raising the Swedish nobleman Gustav Vasa to the throne, enforced the idea that being part of the Swedish kingdom meant being ruled by a Swede, and not by a Dane. The later Northern Wars between (mostly) Sweden and Denmark-Norway from 1563 until 1721 enforced this view. After 1523, with the re-establishment of the independent Kingdom of Sweden, the country defined itself anew as a European monarchy which naturally came with some conflicts about religion, the role of different groups in the new kingdom, new institutions, a new military, laws, the royal dynasty, and finally the everlasting conflict about taxes.

Gustav I Vasa, who ruled from 1523 until 1560, managed not only to raise these important questions, but also to start finding some answers. Sweden began to develop a new political culture in the aftermath of 1523, which was partly based on older traditions as well as on making assumptions about such traditions.[8] One of the defining elements was the self-identification as a Protestant kingdom; whether it was a more Lutheran or a more Calvinist country, however, remained unsolved under Gustav I and his next two successors.[9] Another open question was the role different influential groups would play in this new monarchy. Different concepts of authority—*dominium regale* or *dominium politicum et regale*—were discussed long into the seventeenth century. These concepts were different answers to the question of how power should be distributed: should the monarch hold absolute power (*dominium regale*), or should the power be shared by aristocracy, the parliament, and crown (*dominium politicum et regale*, in England usually called "mixed monarchy").[10] However, what was already decided in the sixteenth century and in many ways confirmed by the events of 1599 was the increasing political relevance of peasants and townspeople.

In 1569, the oldest son of Gustav I, Erik XIV, was deposed by his two half-brothers, John (III) and Charles (IX). Officially, this was due to Erik suffering from bouts of madness, which supposedly led to tyrannical behaviour.[11] Yet, there was also another reason for this deposition. While Gustav I had benefited from the opportunity to re-build the Swedish kingdom mostly without any interferences from old, established noble families, most of whose numbers had been severely reduced in the bloody conflicts of the 1520s, Erik had to deal with a new generation of noble rivals. Moreover, in contrast to his half-brothers, who were born from Gustav's second marriage to a woman from the Swedish high aristocracy, Erik was not as closely related to this aristocracy. His mother was a German princess, and the Vasa dynasty had been a family of lesser nobles, previously supporters of the high noble family of Sture. In fact, most of the older Vasa dynasty (Gustav's siblings and parents) had perished in the 'Stockholm Bloodbath' or in Danish prisons after Gustav led the resistance against Christian II (see Table 4.2). Erik, therefore, was more or less isolated from the Swedish aristocracy, even though he was the legitimate king. His paranoia that he would suffer from a noble uprising led to increasingly radical reactions against the Swedish nobles, especially against

TABLE 4.2 Vasa kinship networks (simplified, includes adults only)

Generation 1	Erik Johansson Vasa († Stockholm Bloodbath, 1520) son of Johan Vasa and Birgitta Sture (daughter of a Sture and a Bielke) m. Cecila Månsdotter Eka (d. 1522): daughter of Måns Eka and Sigrid Báner (daughter of a Báner and a Gren)
Generation 2	1. Gustav I (1496–1560) m1 Katarina of Saxe-Lauenburg (1513–35): daughter of Magnus I, Duke of Saxe-Lauenburg, and Catherine of Brunswick-Lüneburg m2 Margareta Leijonhufvud (1516–51): daughter of Erik Abrahamsson Leijonhufvud († Stockholm Bloodbath, 1520) and Ebba Eriksdotter Vasa, second cousin of King Gustav m3 Katarina Stenbock (1535–1621): daughter of Gustaf Olofsson Stenbock and Brita Eriksdotter Leijonhufvud (the sister of Queen Margareta). [*no children*] 2. Margareta (1497–1536), married a Brahe then a Hoya 3. Magnus (1501–29) 4. Anna (1503–45), a nun 5. Märta (1507–22) 6. Emerentia (1507–22)
Generation 3	1. Erik XIV (1533–77) m. Karin Månsdotter *Half-siblings:* 2. John III (1537–92) m1. Katarina Jagiellonica; m2. Gunilla Bielke 3. Katarina (1539–1610) m. Edward II of East Friesland 4. Cecila (1540–1627) m. Christopher of Baden 5. Magnus (1542–95)—not married, no issue, early insanity 6. Anna (1545–1610) m. Georg Johan of Pfalz-Veldenz 7. Sophia (1547–1611) m. Magnus II of Saxe-Lauenburg 8. Elizabeth (1549–97) m. Christopher of Mecklenburg 9. Charles IX (1560–1611) m1. Maria of the Palatinate; m2. Kristina of Holstein-Gottorp

(continued)

TABLE 4.2 *(continued)*

Generation 4	Children of Erik XIV: 1. Gustav (1568–1607) 2. Sigrid (1566–1633) Children of John III, mg1: 1. Sigismund (1566–1632) 2. Anna (1568–1625) Children of John III, mg2: 3. John (1589–1618) Children of Charles IX, mg1: 1. Katarina (1584–1638) Children of Charles IX, mg2: 2. Gustav II Adolf (1594–1632) 3. Maria Elisabeth (1596–1618) 4. Karl Filip (1601–22)
Non-Swedish maternal kin of Eric XIV	Queen Katarina of Saxe-Lauenburg had siblings: Francis, Duke of Saxe-Lauenburg (1510–81); Dorothea, Queen of Denmark (1511–71); Klara, Duchess of Brunswick-Lüneburg-Giffhorn (1518–76); Sophia, Countess of Oldenburg-Delmenhorst (1521–71); and Ursula, Duchess of Mecklenburg-Schwerin (1523–77). Her father's siblings: the prince-bishops of Münster and Hildesheim; her mother's siblings: the Duke of Brunswick-Lüneburg and the prince-bishop of Minden.
Swedish maternal kin of John III and Charles IX	Queen Margareta Leijonhufvud had siblings: Abraham (1512–56); Birgitta (1514–72); Sten (1518–68); and Märta (1520–84). *Of these,* Märta Leijonhufvud married Svante Sture the Younger (1517–67), and had offspring: Sigrid (1538–1613) married a Bielke; Magdalena (1539–1610) married a Stenbock; Anna (1541–95) married another Bielke; Nils (1543–67); Sten (1544–65); Erik (1546–67); Margareta (1547–1617) married another Bielke; Mauritz (1552–92); Karl (1555–98); and Kristina (1559–1619) married a Banér. *From these marriages,* in the late 1560s, there were five Stenbock cousins, six Leijonhufvud cousins, and ten Sture cousins (several of whom perished in the Sturemurder of 1567).

Sources: Jan Samuelson, *Aristokrat eller förädlad bonde? Det svenska frälsets ekonomi, politik och sociala förbindelser under tiden 1523–1611* (Lund: Lund University Press, 1993), 160–61 (Table 24); 162–63 (Table 25); Michael Roberts, *The Early Vasas. A History of Sweden, 1523–1611* (Cambridge: Cambridge University Press, 1968), 470; Herman Hofberg, Frithiof Heurlin, et al., eds, *Svenskt biografiskt handlexikon: Alfabetiskt ordnande lefnadsteckningar af Sveriges namnkunniga män och kvinnor från Reformationen till nuvarande tid*, 2 vols (Stockholm: Albert Bonniers Förlag, 1906).

the Sture family, a growing reliance on counsellors from the commons, and an increased use of the parliament, which in Sweden included peasants, instead of the noble-dominated royal council. In regard to elements of an emerging national culture, the deposition of Erik therefore led to a resurgence of influence of the older aristocratic families (now more closely related to the new king, John III), but also to the wide acceptance of the parliament as the key political institution responsible for the legitimisation of a change of rulership.

Sigismund Vasa followed his father, John III, as king in 1592. His mother was the Polish-Lithuanian princess, Catherine Jagiellonica. Sigismund had been born in 1566, at a time when his parents were imprisoned at Gripsholm Castle in Sweden by Erik XIV. The conflict between Erik and his brother John was based on John's aspiration to establish a mostly autonomous realm in his dukedom of Finland, which was part of the Kingdom of Sweden but had several laws making it virtually independent from the main political body. This, combined with John's explicitly forbidden negotiations (for his marriage) with Poland-Lithuania at a time when Sweden and Poland-Lithuania were fighting for dominance in the Baltic region, made John a danger to a unified Swedish crown, and he was (with the support of the Council) imprisoned by Erik.[12] While Sigismund was still a child, John deposed Erik and became king of Sweden himself. John's kingship, though mostly dependent on aristocratic acceptance and more or less a *dominium politicum et regale*, was also shaped by his ambition to reach out across the Baltic Sea and establish a Swedish–Polish personal union under his rule. As the husband of a Polish princess—Catherine, the youngest sister of the last Jagiellonian monarch—he was a serious (but unsuccessful) candidate in the elections of 1572–73 and 1575.[13] After the death of the victor of the 1575 election, Stephen Báthory, in 1586, John promoted not his own candidacy but that of his twenty-year-old son, Sigismund. This time the Swedish candidate was successfully elected king of Poland-Lithuania, against Maximilian of Austria. It was considered in Sigismund's favour that he spoke Polish (his mother's tongue), was closely related to the Jagiellonians (his maternal aunt, the widow of Stephen Báthory, supported him after the death of his mother in 1583), and was a Catholic.[14] This last factor requires explanation: how could the heir to the Swedish throne, a kingdom officially Protestant since 1527, have grown up Catholic? This too was due to his Polish mother, who was obviously not only influential in choosing the name "Sigismund" for her son—the name of her father and her brother, both Polish kings—and a name without any tradition in Sweden, but who had also taught him her language and her religion. After John III became Swedish king in 1569 (when Sigismund was two-and-a-half years old), the Swedish council repeatedly tried to influence the young prince's education, especially his religious education, but were not successful.[15] Nor did they have much help from the King himself: due to his ambition to reach out across the Baltic Sea and become an ally—if not king—of Poland-Lithuania, John III also displayed leanings towards Catholicism, or at least to theological attempts to reunite Protestantism and Catholicism.[16]

By 1587, Prince Sigismund was ruling as Sigismund III in Poland-Lithuania, and his father, John III, in Sweden. Since a personal union between the Catholic Polish-Lithuanian elective monarchy and the Protestant Swedish hereditary monarchy was anticipated, John III and his council made sure to safeguard the Swedish Lutheran religion (among other things) in the Articles of Kalmar. These had been agreed already in 1587, before Sigismund was crowned in Poland.[17] However, the problems of a personal union between these two different realms proved too much to handle, especially since none of the political elites of these countries wanted to be under one rule. The rule of Sigismund in Poland-Lithuania could mostly be considered successful—at the very least, he died in 1632 with the crown on his head and his son was elected as his successor. He fit himself into Polish political culture even if there were some conflicts, not least because of his continued Swedish ambitions. Unfortunately for his Swedish crown, the Swedes did not care much for Sigismund's Polishness, just as they had not wanted a Danish king—they wanted a Swedish king. By this time, Swedish political culture had become even more precisely defined, aside from merely not being Danish, as a realm possessing a parliament with sufficient strength to have enacted so many royal depositions.

Foreignness, religion, and political representation as dynastic battlefields

When John III died in 1592, his son Sigismund became the new Swedish king—despite not having seen his country of birth for five years—due to a law of 1544 that formally established the monarchy as hereditary. He nevertheless continued his absences from Sweden due to requirements of his Polish throne: aside from the practical need to establish his rule in Poland, it was also a condition of his elected kingship in Poland that he not leave the country without the acceptance of the Polish Sejm, or parliament.[18] In his seven years of formal reign (1592–99), Sigismund spent only around fourteen months on Swedish territory. His Catholicism and perceived foreignness were thus the main reasons why his uncle Charles succeeded in representing him as an alien to Sweden, and thus unfit to wear the crown.

From the very start, Sigismund took nearly a year after his accession to the Swedish crown in November 1592 to come to Sweden, and when he did arrive, in September 1593, he spent less than a year and left for Poland again in August 1594. Nevertheless, in this time, all the necessary dynastic and royal rituals were performed: he attended the burial of his father, the former king, and had himself crowned and swore an oath to respect Swedish Protestantism. Compared to other personal unions of the time, his rule in Sweden should have come without problems since he was born a Swede, the oldest son of the former king, spoke the language, knew the country and the people, was related through his father to most of the Swedish aristocracy, and had spent the first twenty years of his life in the Kingdom.[19] However, two areas especially turned out to be political battlefields on which his father's brother, Duke Charles, could fight for more political influence in the Swedish realm: confession and representation.

Sweden had been Protestant since the reign of Gustav I, who enforced Protestantism as a means for his own political ends, mostly to enable him to repay foreign aid in his war against Christian II in the 1520s. This led to a confessional situation that endured until the end of the sixteenth century which Matthias Asche has called "basically open".[20] Large parts of the population, especially in peripheral regions outside of the Swedish centre around Lake Malar, still included strongly Catholic and pagan elements like pilgrimages, cults of saints, or magical practices in their religious life.[21] From the 1560s, under the reigns of Erik XIV and John III, the confessional question came under more intense scrutiny, and different ideas, from Lutheranism and Calvinism to Philippism and even Catholicism (supported by Jesuits at John's court, for example), were considered but not yet resolved.[22] This "openness" resulted from a combination of influences: a theological indifference by Gustav I, who was mostly interested in the economic and political effects of reformation; the Calvinist leanings of two of Gustav's sons (Erik and Charles); Catholic leanings from a third son (John); a predominantly Lutheran clergy in the bigger towns; and a slow implementation of the newer reformed ideas in the rest of Sweden, where it mixed with several older religious ideas and practices. This variety of theological influences made Sweden a multi-confessional kingdom in which, until the 1590s, nothing was definite and every outcome was still possible.

This openness came to an end with the "Uppsala Synod" (*Uppsala Kyrkomöte*) in March 1593. This meeting, however, can be viewed also as the first step by Duke Charles to alienate King Sigismund. Charles, who ironically was more of a Calvinist himself, had called for this meeting to safeguard the Lutheran religion against the new Catholic king. He was originally supported by several nobles and four of the seven Swedish bishops. More than 300 clerics came to Uppsala, and decided that Sweden should adhere to the Augsburg Confession of 1530. In the following months of 1593, the decisions of Uppsala were signed by all bishops, council members, more than 200 nobles, more than 1,500 clerics, and representatives from all Swedish provinces and counties.[23]

Before Sigismund could even think about whether he wanted to push for counter-reformation in Sweden or not, Charles had thus struck pre-emptively with this church meeting. While most of Sweden's population was not certain of the confessional differences, the clerics were more decided. The bishops were predominantly Lutheran, as were most of the lower clergy. And while the religious practice of the population more generally may not have been clear, there was certainly a consensus for anti-popery.[24] In this case, anti-popery should be understood as opposition to the imagined political influence of the pope in domestic affairs rather than opposition to Catholic beliefs. In this, Sweden was quite like seventeenth-century England, where people might not have known exactly what Catholicism was in its theological detail, but were convinced that the pope was the Antichrist.[25] This fear of popery and confirmation of the Protestant confession was made absolutely obvious in the declaration of the Swedish parliament when they deposed Sigismund in 1599: he was accused of following "popish doctrine" and trying to establish a "foreign rule [with] violence and tyranny".[26] Interestingly enough, it is not known if Sigismund would have actually tried for counter-reformation. There were some signs, but he did not get the chance to implement anything in Sweden.[27] On the surface, he accepted the resolutions of the Uppsala church meeting in 1593.[28] However, although forbidden to do so, he appointed Catholic nobles as his representatives in Stockholm and elsewhere. Since these were nobles from the most respectable families, this should not have been a problem. Even in England at its most hysterical there remained Catholic noble families in power throughout the early modern period. That it was different in Sweden is a signifier of another political battle taking place.

The resolution of the confessional question in Sweden at the church meeting of Uppsala is thus connected to another problem between Sigismund and Charles, which related directly to the developing Swedish political identity: the question of political influence and political representation. As with the closure brought to the "open" confessional situation, Charles used an old conflict between different political groups to establish a new consensus and to limit Sigismund's influence and political power. In this case, the problem had its roots in late-medieval political culture when Sweden could be described as an "aristocratic monarchy".[29] The *dominium politicum et regale* which was favoured by most of the political elite came, however, to a brutal end in the 'Stockholm Bloodbath' (and other such events) which dealt a nearly fatal blow to the Swedish political elite.[30] Important political leaders, including bishops, were killed (if they had not fallen already in the war against Christian II before), and their wives, sisters, mothers, and children were taken prisoner and brought to Denmark. This was also part of why Gustav I could establish the Swedish kingdom anew without much aristocratic opposition. Starting in the 1550s, however, a new generation had emerged which tried to re-establish their families' former political role, especially through the means of the royal council (*riksråd*).[31] In the meantime, the parliament (*riksdag*), with representatives from the aristocracy, the clergy, the towns, and miners, as well as peasants, had become a political institution which connected the crown to the people. Furthermore, Gustav I introduced in 1556–57 a new concept in Swedish territorial organisation: dukedoms. After Gustav's death, all of his sons were given a territory within Sweden to rule over, with the explicit condition that they would have to act in the interests of Sweden as a whole in regard to domestic and foreign policy.[32] This concept did not work, and was dropped again early in the seventeenth century, but in the second half of the sixteenth century it proved to be particularly troublesome for Erik XIV, John III, and finally, for Sigismund.

Charles, youngest son of Gustav I, was given the dukedom of Södermanland, and John the dukedom of Finland. The challenge of how such dukedoms should be ruled separately yet remain incorporated into the realm of Sweden was a central component of the relationship between Erik and John, and would continue to disturb the relationship between John and Charles after the deposition of Erik. This problem then continued under the reign of Sigismund. Additionally, since Sigismund had to spend much of his time in Poland-Lithuania, the situation was only made worse for the crown. In Södermanland, which is part of the heartland of Sweden, Duke Charles managed to establish his own court where he implemented his own politics, different from those of his brother John and, later, his nephew Sigismund. In particular, by means of religious tolerance he brought Calvinist (and other) refugees to his dukedom, which led to economic and technological gains in mining.[33] The conflict between these four groups (King Sigismund, the council, the parliament, and Duke Charles) intermingled with the confessional conflict as well as with other conflicts of this time, notably the war against Russia on Sweden's eastern border in Finland and the resulting Finnish "Cudgels War".[34]

To bring a bit of analytical order in the different groups and interests of the 1590s, the above-mentioned groups will be treated mostly as united parties, even though there were, of course, also differences within each group. Therefore, it could be said that in the conflict between crown (Sigismund) and duke (Charles), the parliament generally supported Charles, and the council (including much of the Swedish aristocracy) supported Sigismund, both as the legitimate king and also because Charles had managed to fall out with quite a lot of Swedish nobles.[35] Charles was able to gather around him much of the clergy, the peasants, the miners from Dalarna, and some of the towns—though not Stockholm—and to be chosen as new *Riksföreståndare*, a lieutenant-governor for the whole of Sweden, a position which had previously been used under Danish rule in the Union of Kalmar, but which was often more of an anti-king.[36] From this new position of power, Charles—now after the church meeting of Uppsala a Protestant champion as well as champion of the common man—called for several meetings of the parliament to further establish Protestantism on all levels, closing even the last Catholic convent of the Bridgettine Order in 1595.[37] In all this, Charles always emphasised that he had only the well-being of Sweden in mind. He did not strongly argue against Sigismund himself, but against Sigismund's governors and the nobles who supported him. Charles managed to establish himself as leader of political opinion for Swedes, especially clerics worried about counter-reformation, and for Swedes worried about an absentee monarch, and about too much noble influence. Charles legitimated a subsequent military conflict (1598–99) against Sigismund, who was supported by the Swedish nobles, with the argument that only he was truly supporting the King, whom the nobles were in fact working against by giving bad counsel: they were "unruly, untrue people [. . . and] disloyal counsellors".[38] In this way, he increased the gap between the aristocratic council and parliament, which was dominated by commons and clergy. Usually, the aristocracy was also represented in the parliament, and had quite a lot of influence; but since the parliaments of 1595 and 1597 were declared illegal by Sigismund, his chief supporters in Sweden stayed away and left the political field open to Charles and his supporters.[39] The parliaments of 1595 and 1597 became the arena in which Charles could present himself as a champion for Protestantism and for the common man, a task made even easier by the opposition, who stayed away according to the wishes of Sigismund. In this way, these parliaments became anti-aristocratic and Lutheran, characteristics which would soon define Swedish political culture more generally.

In 1598, Sweden was a country on the verge of civil war. In the summer of that year, Sigismund finally came to Sweden again, this time with an army to put Charles in his place. On his side were most of the nobility, some of the southern provinces and Finland, which nonetheless was too far away to really get involved. Sigismund had thus the more traditional support, whereas Charles had the clergy, parliament, most of the peasants and townspeople, and especially the ever-rebellious miners of Dalarna on his side.[40] In the battle of Stångebro on 25 September 1598, Charles' army won a decisive victory. This did not, however, mean that Sigismund lost his throne. Charles and his supporters wanted to enforce their vision of how the future Swedish kingdom should be. Besides being Swedish (instead of Polish-Lithuanian) and Lutheran, and with an influential parliament, Sweden should also remain a hereditary monarchy. And although it would be a monarchy limited and controlled by the parliament and laws, Sigismund was still the uncontested legitimate monarch. Thus, in the truce between Charles and Sigismund there was a condition that Sigismund should remain in Sweden for the time being until a new parliament could be called. Under the leadership of Sigismund and Charles, it would deal with all the problems raised by the allegedly disloyal noble counsellors. These counsellors would be brought to court and judged by neutral, foreign (that is, non-Swedish and non-Polish) nobles.[41]

At this critical moment, Sigismund made a mistake and in some ways proved that ruling over a composite state would be too difficult. The challenge Sigismund came up against was simply that of being in two kingdoms at once. He had already expressed this problem in February 1598 in a complaint against Charles, who should have supported his absent king, rather than exacerbating the problem.[42] This general challenge of composite monarchies was enhanced in the case of Poland-Lithuania and Sweden since one kingdom insisted on the presence of the king and the other kingdom developed (under the strong guidance of a member of the royal family) a strong political national identity. The mistake Sigismund made was that he left Sweden for Poland-Lithuania and even handed over his supporting counsellors to Charles. For whatever reason Sigismund left Sweden, it decided his fate as monarch to this kingdom. This action reinforced the belief that Sigismund was already too Polish, too Catholic, and not loyal enough to his Swedish subjects. Consequently, in July 1599, the Swedish parliament deposed Sigismund, but only after several times requesting that he come back to Sweden.[43] In this, the idea of a limited monarchy with a legitimate king remained stronger than anything Charles may or may not have wanted for the exercise of his own authority.

Political identity and the change of rulers of 1599

The civil war in Sweden had ended with the loss of the power of the aristocracy and that of the legitimate king. The new ruler, Charles IX, enforced a vision of Swedishness which was from then on used as self-identification and in many ways was embodied by Charles' son, Gustav II Adolph, the Protestant hero of the Thirty Years' War. Although he did not formally accept the crown until 1604, until Sigismund's younger half-brother John formally renounced his rights, after 1599 Charles had the Herculean task of bringing order and peace to a politically riven country, for which of course his own actions were mostly responsible. He started by literally removing all the remaining opposition, i.e. the nobles who had supported Sigismund. In the years leading up to 1605, there were several executions of aristocratic leaders who were handed over after Sigismund's return to Poland-Lithuania.[44] But Charles also tried to bring legitimacy to his rule by delaying his own acceptance of the crown until after the above-named John declined, leaving his uncle Charles legitimately as the next heir.[45] Reforms in law, politics, and administration helped to transform the new political identity of Sweden into concrete institutions and actions.[46]

Connecting the new Sweden with old Swedish traditions like performing the *Eriksgata*, a circuit through the core regions of Sweden, also helped to establish Charles IX as new ruler.[47] The complete replacement of the old council with a new one with less influence tightened the new political system with a strong crown, limited by several conditions such as adherence to the Lutheran faith and a dependence on popular support represented by the parliament, and a more controlled, weaker aristocracy.[48]

The events of the 1590s, and the deposition of Sigismund, showed that not only had Duke Charles succeeded in establishing a Swedish national identity and in linking himself with it, but also that Sigismund had failed completely at representing himself as Swedish. Sigismund, although born and raised in Sweden, appeared in the 1590s as too Polish and too Catholic. His actions confirmed his foreignness. And foreignness was, in countries with a developing national identity, perceived as a threat, even though composite states were still the norm in Europe. Charles' efforts were part of a long-term development, in which the change of rulership established a Swedish political culture which was then in turn used to legitimise the change.

Notes

1 See Heiko Droste, "Patrioten ausländischer Herkunft: Zum Patriotismus in Schweden im 17. Jahrhundert", in Robert von Friedeburg, ed., *'Patria' und 'Patrioten' vor dem Patriotismus: Pflichten, Rechte, Glauben und die Rekonfigurierung europäischer Gemeinwesen im 17. Jahrhundert*, Wolfenbütteler Arbeiten zur Barockforschung 41 (Wiesbaden: Harrassowitz, 2005), 314–17, for a discussion about Swedish national culture in the seventeenth century, and its roots in the sixteenth century. Heiko Droste emphasises language, geography, (invented) shared history, and religion as defining aspects of Swedish patriotism. In general, Michael Roberts, *The Early Vasas: A History of Sweden, 1523–1611* (Cambridge: Cambridge University Press, 1968) is still one of the best books on Sweden in the sixteenth and early seventeenth centuries.

2 For more on the Union of Kalmar, see Harald Gustafsson, "A State that Failed? On the Union of Kalmar, Especially its Dissolution", *Scandinavian Journal of History* 31, 3–4 (2006); Herman Schück, "The Political System", and Jens E. Olesen, "Inter-Scandinavian relations", both in Knut Helle, ed., *The Cambridge History of Scandinavia, Vol. 1* (Cambridge: Cambridge University Press, 2003).

3 For the economic relations between Dalarna, Stockholm, and the Hanseatic League, see Herman Schück, "Sweden's Early Parliamentary Institutions from the Thirteenth Century to 1611", in Michael F. Metcalf, ed., *The Riksdag: A History of the Swedish Parliament* (New York: St Martin's Press, 1987), 6 and 22. See also Gustafsson, "A State that Failed?", 208; and David Kirby, *Northern Europe in the Early Modern Period: The Baltic World 1492–1772* (London: Longman, 1990), 3–23.

4 See Werner Buchholz, "Schweden mit Finnland", in Matthias Asche and Anton Schindling, eds, *Dänemark, Norwegen und Schweden im Zeitalter der Reformation und Konfessionalisierung: Nordische Königreiche und Konfession, 1500 bis 1660*. Katholisches Leben und Kirchenreform im Zeitalter der Glaubensspaltung 62 (Münster: Aschendorf, 2003), 124–28.

5 On these military conflicts as background for the depositions around 1500, see J. L. I. Fennell, *Ivan the Great of Moscow* (London and New York: Macmillan, 1961), 172–78; and Kirby, *Northern Europe in the Early Modern Period*, 53–56.

6 See Droste, "Patrioten ausländischer Herkunft", 320, and for an extensive discussion of this point, Inken Schmidt-Voges, *De antiqua claritate et clara antiquitate Gothorum: Gotizismus als Identitätsmodell im frühneuzeitlichen Schweden*, Imaginatio borealis. Bilder des Nordens 4 (Frankfurt am Main: Peter Lang, 2004).

7 For more on this idea, see Michael Roberts, "On Aristocratic Constitutionalism in Swedish History, 1520–1720", in *Essays in Swedish History* (London: Weidenfeld & Nicolson, 1967).

8 See also Johan Holm, "King Gustav Adolf's Death: The Birth of Early Modern Nationalism in Sweden", in Linas Eriksonas and Leos Müller, eds, *Statehood Before and Beyond Ethnicity: Minor States in Northern and Eastern Europe, 1600–2000*, Multiple Europes 33 (Brussels and New York: P. I. E.-Peter Lang, 2005), 114–16. Holm argues here that Gustav I bound his subjects to himself, not to a national idea or a state, by emphasising a Swedishness which was separate from the Union of Kalmar. Rather than a Swedish nationalism, Holm notes the personal structure of power relations instead of statehood, which he identifies in the beginning of the seventeenth century. I argue that this bond between the Swedes and their king was easily transformed into a national identity where the ruling dynasty was just one part of it, instead of the focus point. While Holm states the existence of Swedish patriotism, at least among the political elite, in the 1630s, and traces its roots back to the beginning of Gustav II Adolf's reign (see 116–23), these roots can be seen already under Gustav's father, Charles IX.

9 A concise overview of the Reformation in Sweden is offered by Buchholz, "Schweden mit Finnland".

10 On these concepts of authority, see H. G. Koenigsberger, "*Dominium Regale* or *Dominium Politicum et Regale*: Monarchies and Parliaments in Early Modern Europe", in *idem*, ed., *Politicians and Virtuosi: Essays in Early Modern History* (London and Ronceverte: Hambledon Press, 1986): 1–25.

11 Emil Hildebrand, ed., *Svenska Riksdagsakter jämte andra handlingar som höra till statsförfattningens historia under tidehvarfvet 1521–1718: Andra Delen I. 1561–1568* (Stockholm: P. A. Norstedt & Söner, 1889), documents 367 and 381.

12 See Roberts, *The Early Vasas*, 207–09.

13 See Miia Ijäs, "The Rejected Candidate: John III Vasa, the Polish-Lithuanian Royal Elections (1573/1575) and Early-Modern Political Decision-Making", *Scandinavian Journal of History* 39, 4 (2014); and *idem*, *Res Publica Redefined? The Polish-Lithuanian Transition Period of the 1560s and 1570s in the Context of European State Formation Processes*, Eastern and Central European Studies 5 (Frankfurt am Main: Peter Lang, 2016).

14 See Roberts, *The Early Vasas*, 269–70.

15 See Anders Anton Stiernman, *Alla Riksdagars och Mötens Besluth: samt arfföreningar / Regements-Former, Försäkringar och Bewillningar / som / på allmenna Riksdagar och Möten / ifrån år 1521. intil år 1727. giorde / stadgade och bewiljade äro; med the för hwart och ett Stånd utfärdade allmenna Resolutioner* (Stockholm, 1728), 319–25.

16 John III was influenced by the works from George Cassander and Georg Witzel. See Buchholz, "Schweden mit Finnland", 193 and 198–99, for possible political reasons.

17 Olof S. Rydberg and Carl Hallendorf, eds, *Sverges Traktater med främmande magter jemte andra dit hörande handlingar: Femte Delens förra hälft, 1572–1632* (Stockholm: P. A. Norstedt & Söner, 1903), documents 9 and 9a.

18 See Buchholz, "Schweden mit Finnland", 200.

19 On personal unions and their challenges, see John H. Elliott, "A Europe of Composite Monarchies", *Past & Present* 137 (1992).

20 Matthias Asche, "Zentrum und Peripherie in der Geschichte Nordeuropas im Zeitalter der Reformation und Konfessionalisierung: Versuch eines Problemaufrisses", in Asche and Schindling, eds, *Dänemark, Norwegen und Schweden im Zeitalter der Reformation und Konfessionalisierung*, 17. For more on this, see Buchholz, "Schweden mit Finnland", 193–95. All translations, unless marked otherwise, are by the author.

21 The report from the Danish diplomat Peder Galt from the early 1620s described several magical practices, as well as superstition which was even spread from the pulpit in rural regions, here paraphrased by Nils Runeby, "Barbarei oder Zivilität? Zur Entwicklung einer organisierten Gesellschaft in Schweden im 17. Jahrhundert", in Göran Rystad, ed., *Europe and Scandinavia: Aspects of the Process of Integration in the 17th Century*, Lund Studies in International History (Lund: Scandinavian University Books, 1983), 206. Even as late as 1687, there were fears that inaction would lead the poorer population back to their pagan traditions and lose their faith in Christianity. See ibid., 209; and also Asche, "Zentrum und Peripherie in der Geschichte Nordeuropas im Zeitalter der Reformation und Konfessionalisierung", 19–20; and Buchholz, "Schweden mit Finnland", 125.

22 See Asche, "Zentrum und Peripherie in der Geschichte Nordeuropas im Zeitalter der Reformation und Konfessionalisierung", 20; and more extensively Buchholz, "Schweden mit Finnland", 193–201.

23 Roberts, *The Early Vasas*, 336.

24 Trygve R. Skarsten, "Reformation: Sweden", in Byron J. Nordstrom, ed., *Dictionary of Scandinavian History* (Westport: Greenwood Press, 1986), 509.

25 On English anti-Catholicism, see John Miller, *Popery and Politics in England, 1660–1688* (Cambridge: Cambridge University Press, 1973).

26 Stiernman, *Alla Riksdagars och Mötens Besluth*, 481 and 483.

27 See Buchholz, "Schweden mit Finnland", 206.

28 Stiernman, *Alla Riksdagars och Mötens Besluth*, 394–421.

29 See also Herman Schück, "Sweden as an Aristocratic Republic", *Scandinavian Journal of History* 9, 1 (1984).

30 See Roberts, "On Aristocratic Constitutionalism", 19.

31 Ibid., 20–23.

32 Roberts, *The Early Vasas*, 195–97.

33 Buchholz, "Schweden mit Finnland", 200–01.

34 Ibid., 200; Kirby, *Northern Europe in the Early Modern Period*, 127; and for more on the "Cudgels War", also known as the "War of Clubs", see John P. Maarbjerg, "The Economic Background to 'The War of Clubs'", *Scandinavian Journal of History* 17, 1 (1992); and Heikki Ylikangas, "The Historical Connections of European Peasant Revolts", *Scandinavian Journal of History* 16, 1–2 (1991).

35 See Mirkka Lappalainen, "Regional Elite Group and the Problem of Territorial Integration: The Finnish Nobility and the Formation of the Swedish 'Power State', *c.*1570–1620", *Scandinavian Journal of History* 26, 1 (2001), 18 (for reasons why nobles supported Sigismund); and Roberts, *The Early Vasas*, 300–01 (for noble opposition against Charles).

36 Gustafsson, "A State that Failed?", 208–09.

37 Stiernman, *Alla Riksdagars och Mötens Besluth*, 434–41.

38 Torvald Höjer and Lars Sjödin, eds, *Svenska Riksdagsakter jämte andra handlingar som höra till statsförfattningens historia: Första Serien. Tidevarvet 1521–1718. Avdelning I 1521–1611. Fjärde Delen 1597–1598* (Stockholm: P. A. Norstedt & Söner, 1909–1938), document 261, 751.

39 Roberts, *The Early Vasas*, 358–59. For more on this local level of conflict, see Piia Einonen, "The Politics of Talk: Rumour and Gossip in Stockholm During the Struggle for Succession (*c.*1592–1607)", *Scandia* 80, 2 (2014), 17.

40 Roberts, *The Early Vasas*, 379.

41 Rydberg and Hallendorf, eds, *Sverges Traktater med främmande magter jemte andra dit hörande handlingar*, documents Ia and Ib, 805–12.
42 Höjer and Sjödin, eds, *Svenska Riksdagsakter jämte andra handlingar som höra till statsförfattningens historia*, document 153, 410–11.
43 Roberts, *The Early Vasas*, 385.
44 Ibid., 388–91. See also Anu Lahtinen, "A Nobleman's Death: Power Struggle and Resistance in Accounts of a Political Execution in Early Modern Sweden", in Henrik Jensen, ed., *Rebellion and Resistance*, Power and Culture 4 (Pisa: PLUS-Pisa University Press, 2009), for such executions in Finland.
45 Buchholz, "Schweden mit Finnland", 215.
46 Tobias Bartke, "Zwischen Rechts- und Kulturtransfer: Die Funktion des Friedens in der versuchten Reform des schwedischen Rechts um 1600", in Inken Schmidt-Voges et al., eds, *Pax perpetua: Neuere Forschungen zum Frieden in der Frühen Neuzeit*, Bibliothek altes Reich 8 (Munich: Oldenbourg, 2010).
47 Fabian Persson, "'So that we Swedes are not more swine or goats than they are': Space for Ceremony at the Swedish Court within an International Context", in Birgitte Bøggild Johannsen, ed., *Beyond Scylla and Charybdis: European Courts and Court Residences outside Habsburg and Valois/Bourbon Territories, 1500–1700* (Odense: University Press of Southern Denmark, 2015), 128; or Schück, "Sweden's Early Parliamentary Institutions from the Thirteenth Century to 1611", 56.
48 See Roberts, *The Early Vasas*, 428–34.

Bibliography

Primary sources

Hildebrand, Emil, ed. *Svenska Riksdagsakter jämte andra handlingar som höra till statsförfattningens historia under tidehvarfvet 1521–1718: Andra Delen I. 1561–1568*. Stockholm: P. A. Norstedt & Söner, 1889.

Höjer, Torvald, and Lars Sjödin, eds. *Svenska Riksdagsakter jämte andra handlingar som höra till statsförfattningens historia: Första Serien. Tidevarvet 1521–1718. Avdelning I 1521–1611. Fjärde Delen 1597–1598*. Stockholm: P. A. Norstedt & Söner, 1909–38.

Rydberg, Olof S., and Carl Hallendorf, eds. *Sverges Traktater med främmande magter jemte andra dit hörande handlingar: Femte Delens förra hälft, 1572–1632*. Stockholm: P. A. Norstedt & Söner, 1903.

Stiernman, Anders A. *Alla Riksdagars och Mötens Besluth: samt arfföreningar / Regements-Former, Försäkringar och Bewillningar / som / på allmenna Riksdagar och Möten / ifrån år 1521. intil år 1727. giorde / stadgade och bewiljade äro; med the för hwart och ett Stånd utfärdade allmenna Resolutioner*. Stockholm, 1728.

Secondary sources

Asche, Matthias. "Zentrum und Peripherie in der Geschichte Nordeuropas im Zeitalter der Reformation und Konfessionalisierung: Versuch eines Problemaufrisses". In Matthias Asche and Anton Schindling, eds. *Dänemark, Norwegen und Schweden im Zeitalter der Reformation und Konfessionalisierung: Nordische Königreiche und Konfession, 1500 bis 1660*. Katholisches Leben und Kirchenreform im Zeitalter der Glaubensspaltung 62, 13–25. Münster: Aschendorf, 2003.

Asche, Matthias, and Anton Schindling, eds. *Dänemark, Norwegen und Schweden im Zeitalter der Reformation und Konfessionalisierung: Nordische Königreiche und Konfession, 1500 bis 1660*.

Katholisches Leben und Kirchenreform im Zeitalter der Glaubensspaltung 62. Münster: Aschendorf, 2003.

Bartke, Tobias. "Zwischen Rechts- und Kulturtransfer: Die Funktion des Friedens in der versuchten Reform des schwedischen Rechts um 1600". In Inken Schmidt-Voges et al., eds. *Pax perpetua: Neuere Forschungen zum Frieden in der Frühen Neuzeit*. Bibliothek altes Reich 8, 241–56. München: R. Oldenbourg, 2010.

Buchholz, Werner. "Schweden mit Finnland". In Matthias Asche and Anton Schindling, eds. *Dänemark, Norwegen und Schweden im Zeitalter der Reformation und Konfessionalisierung: Nordische Königreiche und Konfession, 1500 bis 1660*. Katholisches Leben und Kirchenreform im Zeitalter der Glaubensspaltung 62, 107–243. Münster: Aschendorf, 2003.

Droste, Heiko. "Patrioten ausländischer Herkunft: Zum Patriotismus in Schweden im 17. Jahrhundert". In Robert von Friedeburg, ed. *'Patria' und 'Patrioten' vor dem Patriotismus: Pflichten, Rechte, Glauben und die Rekonfigurierung europäischer Gemeinwesen im 17. Jahrhundert*. Wolfenbütteler Arbeiten zur Barockforschung 41, 309–34. Wiesbaden: Harrassowitz, 2005.

Einonen, Piia. "The Politics of Talk: Rumour and Gossip in Stockholm During the Struggle for Succession (*c.*1592–1607)". *Scandia* 80, 2 (2014): 9–35.

Elliott, John H. "A Europe of Composite Monarchies". *Past & Present* 137 (1992): 48–69.

Fennell, J. L. I. *Ivan the Great of Moscow*. London and New York: Macmillan, 1961.

Gustafsson, Harald. "A State that Failed? On the Union of Kalmar, Especially its Dissolution". *Scandinavian Journal of History* 31, 3–4 (2006): 205–20.

Helle, Knut, ed. *The Cambridge History of Scandinavia: Vol. 1, Prehistory to 1520*. Cambridge: Cambridge University Press, 2003.

Holm, Johan. "King Gustav Adolf's Death: The Birth of Early Modern Nationalism in Sweden". In Linas Eriksonas and Leos Müller, eds. *Statehood Before and Beyond Ethnicity: Minor States in Northern and Eastern Europe, 1600–2000*. Multiple Europes 33, 109–30. Brussels and New York: P. I. E.-Peter Lang, 2005.

Ijäs, Miia. "The Rejected Candidate: John III Vasa, the Polish-Lithuanian Royal Elections (1573/1575) and Early-Modern Political Decision-Making". *Scandinavian Journal of History* 39, 4 (2014): 403–24.

Ijäs, Miia. *Res Publica Redefined? The Polish-Lithuanian Transition Period of the 1560s and 1570s in the Context of European State Formation Processes*. Eastern and Central European Studies 5. Frankfurt am Main: Peter Lang, 2016.

Kirby, David. *Northern Europe in the Early Modern Period: The Baltic World 1492–1772*. London: Longman, 1990.

Koenigsberger, H. G. "Dominium Regale or Dominium Politicum et Regale: Monarchies and Parliaments in Early Modern Europe". In H. G. Koenigsberger, ed. *Politicians and Virtuosi: Essays in Early Modern History*, 1–25. London and Ronceverte: Hambledon Press, 1986.

Lahtinen, Anu. "A Nobleman's Death: Power Struggle and Resistance in Accounts of a Political Execution in Early Modern Sweden". In Henrik Jensen, ed. *Rebellion and Resistance*, 33–49. Power and Culture 4. Pisa: PLUS-Pisa University Press, 2009.

Lappalainen, Mirkka. "Regional Elite Group and the Problem of Territorial Integration: The Finnish Nobility and the Formation of the Swedish 'Power State', *c.*1570–1620". *Scandinavian Journal of History* 26, 1 (2001): 1–24.

Maarbjerg, John P. "The Economic Background to 'The War of Clubs'". *Scandinavian Journal of History* 17, 1 (1992): 1–24.

Miller, John. *Popery and Politics in England, 1660–1688*. Cambridge: Cambridge University Press, 1973.

Olesen, Jens E. "Inter-Scandinavian relations". In Knut Helle, ed. *The Cambridge History of Scandinavia: Vol. 1, Prehistory to 1520*, 710–70. Cambridge: Cambridge University Press, 2003.

Persson, Fabian. "'So that we Swedes are not more swine or goats than they are': Space for Ceremony at the Swedish Court within an International Context". In Birgitte Bøggild Johannsen, ed. *Beyond Scylla and Charybdis: European Courts and Court Residences Outside Habsburg and Valois/Bourbon Territories 1500–1700*, 121–33. Odense: University Press of Southern Denmark, 2015.

Roberts, Michael. "On Aristocratic Constitutionalism in Swedish History, 1520–1720". In *Essays in Swedish History*, 14–55. London: Weidenfeld & Nicolson, 1967.

Roberts, Michael. *The Early Vasas: A History of Sweden, 1523–1611*. Cambridge: Cambridge University Press, 1968.

Runeby, Nils. "Barbarei oder Zivilität? Zur Entwicklung einer organisierten Gesellschaft in Schweden im 17. Jahrhundert". In Göran Rystad, ed. *Europe and Scandinavia: Aspects of the Process of Integration in the 17th Century*. Lund Studies in International History, 203–18. Lund: Scandinavian University Books, 1983.

Schmidt-Voges, Inken. *De antiqua claritate et clara antiquitate Gothorum: Gotizismus als Identitätsmodell im frühneuzeitlichen Schweden*. Imaginatio borealis. Bilder des Nordens 4. Frankfurt am Main: P. Lang, 2004.

Schück, Herman. "Sweden as an Aristocratic Republic". *Scandinavian Journal of History* 9, 1 (1984): 65–72.

Schück, Herman. "Sweden's Early Parliamentary Institutions from the Thirteenth Century to 1611". In Michael F. Metcalf, ed. *The Riksdag: A History of the Swedish Parliament*, 5–60. New York: St Martin's Press, 1987.

Schück, Herman. "The Political System". In Knut Helle, ed. *The Cambridge History of Scandinavia: Vol. 1, Prehistory to 1520*, 679–709. Cambridge: Cambridge University Press, 2003.

Skarsten, Trygve R. "Reformation: Sweden". In Byron J. Nordstrom, ed. *Dictionary of Scandinavian History*, 507–09. Westport: Greenwood Press, 1986.

Ylikangas, Heikki. "The Historical Connections of European Peasant Revolts". *Scandinavian Journal of History* 16, 1–2 (1991): 85–104.

5

FREE ELECTION, DIVINE PROVIDENCE, AND CONSTITUTION

Legitimacy of royal power in the early modern Polish-Lithuanian Commonwealth

Jolanta Choińska-Mika and Katarzyna Kuras

When in January 1572, quite unexpectedly at this time of year, a ferocious storm hit the capital city of Cracow, a number of contemporaries saw it as a portent of difficulties and serious problems that would befall the Polish-Lithuanian Commonwealth in the coming year. The following months seemed to confirm those fears—a wave of famine struck as early as March, and later, in different parts of the country, an epidemic broke out. But even the natural phenomena and disasters did not frighten the citizens as much as the death of King Sigismund II Augustus in the first days of July. The chronicler of this time, Marcin Bielski, wrote: "his death frightened the Crown [i.e. the state], for he did not leave any offspring". The King died childless, and with his death the male line of the Jagiellonian dynasty expired, the family which (again quoting Marcin Bielski) "had happily reigned for two hundred years".[1]

The expiration of the dynasty, which had rooted itself so well in the national memory, caused great sadness and grave concern about the future of the country. During the life of Sigismund Augustus no contingency plans had been developed for the future of the Polish-Lithuanian throne in the event of a death of a childless monarch. With the death of Sigismund Augustus, the Commonwealth and its citizens were therefore faced with a myriad of threats. The appearance of a comet in the sky further heightened the mood of horror. The citizens were afraid of disintegration of the Commonwealth; just three years had passed since the Kingdom of Poland and the Grand Duchy of Lithuania had become unified into in a dual body, and separatist sentiments remained among part of the Lithuanian elite. They also feared an outbreak of religious conflict—the Commonwealth was at that time a multi-ethnic and multi-denominational country. Indeed, King Sigismund Augustus was regarded as the guarantor of the peaceful coexistence of different churches, religious peace, and state unity. He crafted a set of highly sophisticated policies, which, on the one hand, would comply with the Catholic

Church's position and, on the other, would ensure religious freedom for all citizens.[2] It was thanks to this dual commitment, coupled with careful diplomacy, that Poland and Lithuania experienced a time of relative security and stability in highly unstable and tension-ridden times, escaping the religious wars which plagued other European countries.

In addition to these problems, a number of extremely important issues regarding the future of the throne had to be resolved. Among them, an answer to the most important questions had to be found: How to set up a new ruler on the throne? Who, when, where, and following what procedures? How should the country function during the interregnum? How can public order and safety be maintained, as upon the death of the king all law courts stopped functioning? Finally, who should assume supreme authority during the interregnum or become an "interrex", the ruler between kings?

This chapter explores the ways in which the noble citizens responded to these questions, by establishing the so-called "free election"—a unique mode of electing the monarch that distinguished the Polish-Lithuanian Commonwealth from the rest of early modern Europe. We argue that this early model, based on a true commitment to republican ideals, ensured unprecedented levels of civic political engagement. In a paradoxical reversal, due to a complex web of internal and external socio-political developments of the eighteenth century, this highly participatory model later gave way to the establishment of a hereditary monarchy, accomplished in the 3 May 1791 Constitution. This development, paradoxical yet in tune with Enlightenment ideas shaping the European political sphere, was accompanied by a secularisation of notions of legitimacy and power, a transformation that reflected the wider ideological changes in the Polish-Lithuanian Commonwealth and its political nation.

The Polish-Lithuanian Commonwealth after the Union of Lublin (1569) and the origins of the free election

The Polish-Lithuanian Commonwealth was founded in 1569 by virtue of the Union of Lublin signed by two separate states: the Kingdom of Poland and the Grand Duchy of Lithuania. The two had been in a political relationship from the late fourteenth century, since the conclusion of the so-called Union of Krewo (1385) and the accession to the Polish throne of the Lithuanian Prince Jagiello. For most of the fifteenth and sixteenth centuries this relationship was merely a personal union.[3]

The Union of Lublin united two countries ruled by the same dynasty but with different political experiences. From the beginning of the fifteenth century, the Kingdom of Poland was an elective monarchy; however, the election was limited to the members of the Jagiellonian family. The Lithuanian throne, in contrast, was hereditary. The Kingdom of Poland had a quite long tradition, dating back to the fourteenth century, of participation in power by noblemen[4] (members of the political nation), and a well-functioning parliamentary system. It consisted of a bicameral Diet (or Sejm) and a network of regional, local assemblies or dietines. These institutions arose at the start of the fifteenth century, and in the ensuing decades gained a permanent place in the political system of the state. The crowning of this process was the decision of the Sejm of Radom in 1505 to adopt the so-called *Nihil novi* constitution. Under this system, any new law concerning public affairs (very broadly defined) had to be approved by the king, senators, and noble deputies. Thus the parliament became an inherent component of the decision-making processes and also the highest legislative authority in the Kingdom.

These processes were inspired by and embedded in a highly specific ideological context, one that combined classical history and culture, the works of St Thomas Aquinas and John of Salisbury, and the medieval constitutionalist movement. Those traditions gave birth to the early modern republican ideology and an extensive system of civic values. Among them, the key idea was the concept of *Res publica*—a community of citizens, united by rights, privileges, and common responsibilities. On the long list of ideological principles, a very important place was occupied by the belief in the sovereignty and supremacy of the common law.[5]

Lithuanian parliamentarism had a much shorter pedigree and was largely shaped by the earlier developments in Poland. It was not until the second half of the sixteenth century that, under the direction of King Sigismund Augustus, a network of local assemblies, with the right to send their delegates to the Diet, was established in Lithuania. Lithuanian noblemen were also much less independent and active than their Polish counterparts. Magnates—representatives of prominent aristocratic families—had a decisive role in the political life of Lithuania. These differences between the political traditions of the Kingdom of Poland and the Grand Duchy of Lithuania became even more pronounced during the interregnum period, shaping the course of events in that year. The interregnum of 1572–73 was the first joint political experience for Poland and Lithuania. The noble citizens of the Kingdom of Poland were the *spiritus movens* of the projects undertaken at that time, while Lithuanians for quite a long time merely observed the course of events with detachment.[6]

The death of the King in 1572 was an impulse which triggered a massive wave of civic activity. Noblemen, concerned with the fate of the state, began establishing an extraordinary form of local government: the so-called "confederacies". The first ones came into being as early as July 1572. Their mission was to maintain order and security in regional communities and the surrounding areas. For this purpose, special emergency courts (the so-called *kaptury*) were established. The confederations also made decisions concerning voluntary taxation of the local nobility for security purposes. By the end of 1572, the whole country was covered with a network of such local associations which should be regarded as a remarkable manifestation of the responsibility of citizens for their communities and the self-organising capacity of the nobility.

Simultaneously the matters concerning the future of the Polish-Lithuanian throne, especially those related to a prospective election, its legal and social framework, were discussed at regional and supra-regional meetings. Indeed, who should be entitled to participate in the election was on the top of the list of questions to be decided.

Previously, during the reign of the Jagiellonian dynasty, the outcome of royal elections had been decided by a narrow group of senators and high-ranking dignitaries. In 1538, the Diet allowed minor nobility to participate in the election, but the provisions of this act were vague.[7] The Union of Lublin decreed the joint election of the monarch of the Polish-Lithuanian Commonwealth,[8] but did not contain specifications about the nature of this election. It is no wonder that the Polish nobility feared that this time, just as had happened in the past, its role in the election process would be limited to a minimum—merely the acceptance of decisions taken by a smaller group. Yet they aspired to much more than that. Therefore, the right to participate in the election of the king became one of the more important questions to be decided during the interregnum.[9] The senators did not necessarily support the claims of the wider nobility, and some of them wanted to preserve the status quo. However, a remarkable wave of activity of the local noble communities quickly made the senators aware that the nobility was not going to give up its higher expectations: they wanted real, and not just nominal participation in the selection of the monarch, signalling that any decisions taken only by the elite would not be accepted.

Political debate during the interregnum took place not only during local or regional meetings. Equally important were the discussions in the "media" carried out with the help of contemporaneous tools: political writings and journalism. Mostly anonymous brochures and polemics were circulated throughout the country.[10] The authors discussed not only current affairs and disputes; they were also making numerous reform proposals, and voicing their opinions and thoughts on the political system of the Commonwealth. They evaluated possible candidates for the Polish throne and discussed the benefits and damages that could result from their respective election. The sheer number and the diversity of these texts and their subject matter bears further witness to the great interest of contemporary public opinion in the affairs of state and the desire for participation in decisions which could affect their lives.

This general context as well as direct pressures made by a nobility impatient with the protracted interregnum motivated the rival camps to action. The agreement was finally reached in the autumn of 1572 at the congress held in Kaski (October). According to the decisions of that meeting the role of Interrex passed to the Primate of Poland, the Archbishop of Gniezno, Jakub Uchański. The senators also accepted the idea of involving the wider masses of nobles in the electoral process. This resulted in the emergence of the concept of *electio viritim* ("one vote for each man"), promoted by senator Piotr Zborowski (the palatine, or governor, of Sandomierz province), as opposed to a representational vote, one for each of the local dietines.

The details concerning the implementation of the *electio viritim* were decided a few months later, in January 1573, at a meeting convened in Warsaw, called the "convocation" (*konwokacja*). It was attended by senators and delegates from all lands and provinces, nominated by their local assemblies. The decisions that were taken in Warsaw during the convocation paved the way for a new chapter in the history of the Polish-Lithuanian state. They confirmed the right of every nobleman to participate in the election of the monarch, setting Kamień, a village near Warsaw, as the place for the election, as well as the date (May) for the election. One major achievement (after long and heated disputes) was the signing by all participants of an obligation to respect religious differences and foster mutual tolerance between *dissidentes de religione*.[11] This act, unprecedented on a European scale, proved that, for the noblemen, the security of the Commonwealth was more important than religious differences.

On 5 April 1573 an elective congress began in the fields of suburban Warsaw. Crowds of nobility attended. There were approximately 30,000 people, which is a huge number, though several times smaller than some nineteenth-century historians claimed.[12] Before the actual election, however, the rules that would guarantee the security and order in the election field had to be laid down. A number of prohibitions were imposed (for example, a ban on carrying weapons and drinking alcohol) and severe penalties for breaking them were introduced. The election itself consisted of two stages. First, each palatinate (district) elected their representatives (a fixed number)—electors who would vote on their behalf. Second, the electors proceeded to vote while making sure that the interests of their districts were protected. Discussions seeking compromise played an extremely important part in the whole process.

In 1573, there were several candidates competing for the Polish crown. French diplomacy turned out to be most effective in their efforts and the French candidate—Henry, duc d'Anjou, brother of King Charles IX of France—gained the acceptance of those present in the election field.[13] The decision was announced on 11 May. The actual outcome of the election was the result of time-consuming negotiations. The counting of the votes was in a sense a mere formality.

The Henrician Articles: a quasi-constitution?

In parallel to the discussions about the candidates, the noblemen developed a list of terms that had to be accepted by the newly elected monarch. The noblemen referred to the traditional custom of "*confirmatio iuris*", confirming the rights of the Kingdom by the monarch assuming the throne. These efforts resulted in the Henrician Articles,[14] a collection of regulations setting legal boundaries for the future monarch. The Articles also confirmed the basic constitutional rights of the Commonwealth. In addition, they preserved extensive legislative prerogatives of the Diet, making it a requirement for the king to convene the Diet at least once every two years. The monarch was also required to consult the senators for his decisions. Finally, the Articles nominated a group of senators-residents who were to constantly remain at the king's side. These would offer advice and, at the same time, ensure that the monarch was acting in accordance with the law.

Moreover, the Articles stressed the inviolable principle of *electio viritim*. All future rulers were to be elected in this way. On the social level, the Articles reaffirmed the principle of tolerance between different faiths and denominations, committing the monarch to the maintenance of religious peace in the country. The last point of the document guaranteed citizens the right to renounce obedience to the king if he would break any of the sworn Articles. This provision therefore introduced the principle of political responsibility of the monarch, highlighting both the sovereignty and the primary role of law in the country.

However, this "constitution" prepared by the Polish nobility was difficult for Henry d'Anjou to accept. In particular, he did not agree to the point forcing him to ensure religious peace. Nevertheless, after dramatic negotiations between the Polish and French delegations in Paris, Henry promised to swear the Articles at the time of his coronation in Cracow. But matters took a different turn. Although Henry was crowned (25 February 1574), he skilfully managed to postpone swearing the Articles. Henry's rule lasted only a few months. At the news of the death of his brother, Charles IX (30 May 1574), the King secretly left Poland during the night of 18/19 June and returned to France. For the noble citizens, the disappearance of the recently elected monarch was a great surprise and threw everything into total confusion. Not much was known about whether the Polish-Lithuanian Commonwealth was in a state of regnum or interregnum.

After several months of fruitless waiting for the return of the King, and numerous attempts to persuade him to return, the nobles, impatient with Henry's attitude, took matters into their own hands. At the congress in Stężyca (May–June 1575) a second interregnum was officially announced.[15] It is worth emphasising that it was more turbulent than the previous one and ended in a walk-out on the election field and consequently a double election. Eventually it was Anna Jagiellon (the older sister of Sigismund Augustus) and Stephen Báthory, prince of Transylvania, who as a married couple were crowned and took power, swearing at the same time the Henrician Articles.[16] Those supporting Anna Jagiellon's candidacy strongly emphasised her "native" Jagiellonian origins and heritage, regarding them as the most important arguments in favour of her candidacy—her advantage and a firm guarantee of her ability to rule the country in a proper way.

This reference to "Jagiellonian blood" turned out to be a useful political tool, which revealed its persuasive power in public discourse during the third interregnum, after the death of Stephen Báthory. In 1587, Sigismund III Vasa was elected to the Polish-Lithuanian throne. The son of the king of Sweden, he was a nephew of Anna Jagiellon, and it is thanks to her intensive and effective campaigning that this eighteen-year-old son of Catherine Jagiellon gained the popular support that paved his way to the Polish-Lithuanian throne. During his reign, especially in visual propaganda, Sigismund willingly referred to his Jagiellonian heritage, further strengthening the already high regard of the public for the Jagiellons and Jagiellonian rule.[17] When Sigismund III Vasa died in 1632, the only candidate for the throne considered by the nobles was his oldest son, Ladislaus. The younger son, John Casimir, subsequently gained the royal title as a result of the next free election, in 1648. In the decades that followed, this noble attachment to dynastic continuity, while at the same time within the framework of *electio viritim*, continued alongside the nobility's commitment to play an active role in the decision-making process based on the will of free citizens, members of the political body of the Commonwealth.

The sacral character of royal power and the ceremony of coronation

The sacral character of the power of Polish elective monarchs was not very frequently invoked by the Polish nobility from the sixteenth to eighteenth centuries. Although monarchs used the phrase "by the grace of God", in fact their power did not come from God but resulted from a choice made by the nobles.[18] Competitors for the throne did not often invoke higher powers since the nobles that gathered for the sake of elections were more likely to be persuaded by the candidates' connections and dynastic traditions, which even required some of these to create imaginary and fictitious ancestry (for example, the father of Stanislaus Augustus Poniatowski claimed to be descended from the Torelli family, Italian aristocrats who settled in Poland in the middle of the seventeenth century, thus linking his family history to then-fashionable Italian culture and to the glories of ancient Rome).[19] Where invoking a family tradition was impossible, sometimes the argument of "a gift from Heaven" was used, and treated as a substitute for the official discourse whose objective was to convince the other nobles to cast their vote for a specific candidate.

In the history of all free elections in Poland the choice of the king was justified by a direct intervention of Divine Providence only once. This was in 1669, after the abdication of John II Casimir Vasa, since the elections turned out to be particularly turbulent and there was no agreement between the nobles and the senators as to the choice of the future Polish monarch. Consequently, making use of supernatural causes and miraculous events turned out to be necessary. Two days before the election, a white dove was seen to circulate over the election field. Another omen was even more evident. The Leczyca province observed a swarm of spring bees. They were said to have arrived from the east and hurt no one; they were extremely gentle. Another version says that these bees found Michael Korybut Wiśniowiecki, the future king, and settled beside him (some even claimed they formed a figure which bowed to the candidate).[20] The contemporary author Wespazjan Kochowski commented that it was indeed rare for bees to wander about in spring and that this should be read as a message from Heaven.[21] Bees—a sign of God's intervention—not only sanctified the election, but also predicted the new reign to be rich in honey. In actual fact, Michael Korybut Wiśniowiecki was a mediocre ruler and the way he governed hardly merited such a divine nimbus, which was nevertheless occasionally referred to in the official discourse during his reign.[22]

At the same time there is no doubt that the events of the late seventeenth and eighteenth centuries shifted the significance from elections to coronations in the process of the legitimisation of royal power. This was caused by immediate political circumstances and was not at all the result of intensive work of Polish theorists of state and law. Such was the case of the election Sejm of 1697, following the death of John III Sobieski. During the Sejm, Cardinal-Primate Michał Radziejowski, serving as the Interrex, pronounced the candidate of France, François-Louis de Bourbon-Conti, as the winner in the heated election contest. Conti was supported by the majority of Polish nobles. The chief runner-up in this election, Frederick Augustus I, Elector of Saxony, took advantage of Conti's delay in setting out for Poland from France, and challenged the outcome. When the Saxon arrived in Poland at the head of armed forces, his supporters broke into the treasury in the Wawel Castle in Cracow, secured the regalia, and succeeded in persuading Stanisław Dabski, Bishop-Senator of Brześć-Kujawski, to crown the challenger in the Royal Chapel in the Wawel, the traditional place for coronations.[23] Conti, who had travelled by sea from France (and with inadequate support of Louis XIV and his government), made only a brief landing at Oliwa on the Baltic coast near Gdańsk, and, hearing of the *fait accompli*, surrendered his claim and ingloriously returned to France.[24]

In 1697, it was not the number of votes but the coronation that decided the candidate's victory. Although as a result of such a procedure it was necessary to pacify the country and to make the nobles gradually accept Frederick Augustus (who took the name Augustus II), the fact that the ruler completed all the elements of the procedure of royal election was a strong argument in his favour. In particular, before the ceremony of coronation the Elector of Saxony had publicly announced his conversion, so that "the vanity of Catholic nobility was flattered by the idea that they had brought about the apostasy from the Lutheranism of the ruler of the country which had been the cradle of that 'heresy'".[25]

A similar situation occurred after the death of King Augustus II in 1733. The candidates for the Polish throne were: the son of the deceased monarch, Frederick Augustus II of Saxony; Stanislaus Leszczyński, the father-in-law of Louis XV of France (and a previous claimant of the throne); and a Portuguese prince, the Infante Emmanuel (younger brother of King John V). The latter was backed mainly by the Commonwealth's neighbours, who were against the Saxon and French candidates. The Poles themselves were not seriously considering the possibility of electing the Portuguese Infante; he was too exotic a candidate for noblemen's tastes. In 1733, the Interrex, Teodor Potocki, was able to persuade the Convocation Sejm of that year to exclude all foreigners from candidacy: in the pamphlets sent out on behalf of the Primate, it was argued that only "the Piast", which meant the Polish national candidate (a descendant of the ancient Piast dynasty in a metaphorical, if not literal, sense), would govern properly and smartly.[26] This did not prevent the candidate from the Saxon House from pressing his claim; his supporters distributed "Votum" signed allegedly by Pope Clement XIII through which electors would be released from the oath to choose "the Piast".[27] As a result, Stanislaus Leszczyński and Frederick Augustus of Saxony were elected simultaneously in separate elections held at Praga and Wola outside Warsaw. The Saxon candidate won around 4,000 votes, while Leszczyński received 13,000 ballots.[28] The difference was considerable, but in 1733 it was not the decisive factor.[29]

There is no doubt that the final victory of Frederick Augustus (who took the regnal name Augustus III) was secured by Russian help, which also made the quick coronation of the new king possible.[30] The coronation ceremony took place in January 1734 in the Wawel Castle in Cracow. On 15 January, funeral rites were held over the coffins of John III Sobieski and Augustus II, and two days later Augustus III was crowned king by Bishop Jan Lipski of Cracow. The surviving script of the ceremony indicates that it was an exceptionally modest event, but it met the requirements of such rites. The biggest problem was a lack of people for performing various functions during the ceremony: there were barely enough senators to carry the insignia of the King and Queen, and the decoration of the Wawel Cathedral was also modest.[31]

The Polish historian Jacek Staszewski wrote that Augustus III managed to capture the crown but not the throne.[32] The supporters of Stanislaus Leszczyński set up a General Confederacy at Dzików in the palatinate of Sandomierz. The confederate troops were routed by Russian and Saxon units, while Leszczyński escaped to France in dramatic circumstances. As a result of a few months' struggle, during which Russia provided military support, the Saxon candidate finally became king of Poland.[33] The final reconciliation between Augustus III and the *szlachta* took place over the next few years, during successive Sejm sessions in 1735 and 1736, which pacified the country and made the noble subjects accept the new king's rule. The process was long but effective;[34] after 1736 the legality of Augustus III's authority was not questioned, and in the Treaty of Vienna of 1738 Stanislaus Leszczyński renounced his claim to the Polish throne and recognised Augustus III.[35]

The last free election, 1764

The last free election, which took place in 1764, was equally problematic. Stanislaus Augustus Poniatowski was elected solely as a result of the favouritism of the Russian empress, Catherine II, who gave him her political and military backing.[36] During the competition for the crown, the candidate could not use any religious arguments or invoke clear dynastic links, except a distant genealogical connection with the Jagiellonian dynasty on the distaff side.[37] The voters tried to find arguments to accept the imposed candidature, although for some magnates even saying the King-elect's name was considered unpleasant. This was why during the service prior to the election, the Bishop of Smoleńsk, Gabriel Wodziński, did not mention divine intervention but spoke about the criteria which the candidate should meet: "the king's duty is to be better than others, therefore we need to elect a king better than others".[38]

During the coronation Sejm, the candidate's merits were recalled again in the speech of the Sejm Marshal, Jacek Małachowski, who mentioned the King-elect's parliamentary career and his political experience.[39] The King's power was therefore legitimised by his election (Poniatowski received over 5,000 votes on the election field) and the conviction that the candidate met the requirements necessary for a monarch.[40] The manner in which the election was explained reflected the changes

As a result of such a strategy and abandoning the tradition of emphasising the sacral nature of power, the King's position was strengthened, and debates no longer included topics which could lead to undermining the prestige of the King's majesty. Although it was therefore understood that according to Natural Law all power comes from God, at the same time the increasingly fashionable theory of the "social contract" was also accepted.

These tendencies were confirmed by the Four-Year Sejm, during which the process of de-sacralisation of the King's charisma—that is, a divinely conferred talent for rule—visibly accelerated. Between 1788 and 1792, Stanislaus Augustus continued to become more of a citizen and less the Anointed One (two of the top publicists of the period, Hugo Kołłątaj and Stanisław Staszic, contributed to the process[51]). Although during the Sejm proceedings Divine Providence was often invoked, religious beliefs were not linked to the monarch but to the problem of saving the Commonwealth and the nation. Ultimately, the Constitution adopted on 3 May 1791 proclaimed "Stanislaus Augustus, by the grace of God and the will of the people, King",[52] while in Article 5 the social contract was directly evoked in the words: "All authority in human society takes its origin in the will of the people."[53] It was then that a popular slogan was created: "the king with the nation, the nation with the king". This emphasised the new but essential alliance between the monarch and his subjects which made the adoption of the Constitution possible.

It is particularly important to note that the Constitution thus reformed the executive power, and addressed in depth the issue of succession to the Polish throne. For contemporaries this aspect was the most radical reform introduced by the Constitution.[54] The King's position was strengthened, and the Constitution abolished free elections. This is quite understandable considering what Poles experienced in the eighteenth century and the fact that in the Age of Enlightenment free elections were no longer a sufficient instrument of legitimising the king's power. Although the beginning of Article 7 of the Constitution contains the statement, "We desire and determine that the throne of Poland shall be forever elective by families",[55] this was merely a nod towards the traditionally inclined part of the Polish nobility. The following sentences, in contrast, directly attack free elections; they emphasise that interregnums were periods of considerable chaos in the country and opportunities for neighbouring countries to interfere in the Commonwealth's affairs. According to the provisions of the Constitution, the Polish throne would be passed on by right of succession; thus, accordingly, Stanislaus Augustus Poniatowski became the first hereditary monarch.[56] The Constitution created a unique situation: first, because the King did not have a legitimate son; and second, because in ascending the throne in 1764, he had sworn to uphold the Henrician Articles which forbade him to transform the elective throne into a hereditary one. At the time when the Constitution was adopted, the King was sixty years old; in order to avoid the necessity of electing a new ruling house—which would pose the risk of internal turmoil and external threat—the authors of the Constitution therefore decided to designate a new dynasty: after Stanislaus Augustus's death, the throne was to be taken over by the Elector of Saxony, Frederick Augustus III, King

Augustus III's grandson, as representative of the Saxon House. After Frederick Augustus, the Polish throne would then be passed on to his successors. The writers of the Constitution, to be thorough, even allowed for the succession, if necessary, of the Elector's daughter, Maria Augusta Nepomucena.[57]

The revolutionary provisions of the Constitution of 3 May 1791 were never enforced. However, the new Constitution reflected the changes in Polish political awareness, and in particular a new vision of the legitimisation of power. Interestingly, during the proceedings of the last Sejm of the Commonwealth, which was held in Grodno in 1793, deputies frequently invoked God's will, but no one tried to see Divine Majesty in Stanislaus Augustus any longer. This is quite understandable; as all supporters of the King and the reforms introduced by the Constitution of 3 May 1791 accepted the social contract theories of Jean-Jacques Rousseau. During the Sejm proceedings, the King as "first citizen" was shown utmost respect, as reflected in the ceremony of kissing his hand, performed as many as twenty-one times in Grodno in 1793 in order to calm down the various disputes.[58]

Conclusion

The legitimisation of royal power in the Polish-Lithuanian Commonwealth evolved through the sixteenth to eighteenth centuries. The idea of *electio viritim* was deeply rooted in republican tradition and values. It embodied noble desire to participate in every matter concerning their Commonwealth. Very soon, *electio viritim* was considered one of the most important rights of the nobility; this was reflected in its Latin description: *pupilla libertatis* ("pupil of freedom").

The need to address the challenges faced by the nation in 1572 and 1573 "liberated" all the positive qualities of the political culture of the nobility that had formed in the Jagiellonian era, notably the ability of reaching consensus and respect for the law. This commitment was best captured in a quote from the 1548 parliamentary speech delivered by the Speaker of the Chamber of Envoys, Jan Sierakowski: "the law is the soul of the Republic", without which "as the body without a soul, no Republic can exist".[59] With this belief came, among other things, the conviction of the supremacy of law in public life—even the king had to submit to the laws of the Kingdom. These assumptions were at the core of the Henrician Articles. Today, scholars consider the Articles a form of contract between the elected monarch and voters/electors, and even a manifestation of early modern constitutionalism, an expression of the desire to describe with law the relationship between the king and the citizens, the ruler and the ruled.[60] Although the stabilisation and "full" institutionalisation of elective procedures came only with the completion of subsequent elections, there is no doubt that it was the adoption of regulations after the death of Sigismund Augustus that was the crucial element for the development of the Polish-Lithuanian Commonwealth.

At the same time, in the official discourse, the charisma of each king of Poland was formally and traditionally linked to the power established on earth by God. These conceptions dominated in the seventeenth century, even though the power of Polish kings was successively weakening.[61] The eighteenth century brought changes. As a result of irregular elections of August II and August III and the birth of the new conceptualisation of the relationship between monarch and subjects in enlightened Europe, the process of transformation of the legitimisation of royal power began. The real changes occurred during the reign of Stanislaus Augustus Poniatowski (elected, like his predecessors, in the election field), when the ruler was transformed into the nation's servant, who, incidentally, perfectly fit the elective character of the king in the Commonwealth. On the other hand, the nation itself was promoted to the rank of sacredness and all pleas for the protection of "Divine Providence" involved only the nation. The divine charisma of the king was replaced by the nation's power.[62]

The eighteenth century was a period when previous methods of legitimising royal power underwent a crisis and a modern form of monarchy was born. As the ideas of the Age of Enlightenment developed, "God's Grace" was also replaced with the nation's sovereignty in the monarchy's titulature. In the Commonwealth, the problem was particularly important: each of the eighteenth-century free elections was free in name only; in reality the choice of the monarch was not determined by the number of noblemen's votes but by chance, a speedy coronation, or the help of a foreign army. Although each monarch was respected and "Divine Providence" was invoked in the official discourse, these efforts did not stop a gradual de-sacralisation of the monarchy, which culminated in the attempt to abduct King Stanislaus Augustus Poniatowski in 1771. As a result, the Commonwealth saw the birth of a new model of legitimisation of monarchy, codified in the Constitution of 3 May 1791, which was never enforced due to the collapse of the state in the years that followed.

List of Polish monarchs (XVI–XVIII centuries)

Sigismund I the Old (1506–48)

Sigismund II Augustus (1548–72) (sometimes known as Augustus I of Poland)

Henry of Valois (1573–74)

Stephen Báthory (1576–86)

Sigismund III Vasa (1587–1632)

Ladislaus IV Vasa (1632–48)

John II Casimir Vasa (1648–68)

Michael I Korybut Wiśniowiecki (1669–73)

John III Sobieski (1674–96)

Augustus II the Strong of Saxony (1697–1733)

Stanislaus Leszczyński (1704–09, 1733–36)

Augustus III of Saxony (1733–63)

Stanislaus Augustus Poniatowski (1764–95)

Notes

1 Marcin Bielski, *Kronika polska*, vol.VI (Warsaw: Gałęzowski, 1832), 7.
2 Regarding the complex context of Sigismund August's religious policy, see Anna Sucheni-Grabowska, *Zygmunt August król polski i wielki książę litewski 1520–1562* (Warsaw: Wydawnictwo Krupski i S-ka, 1996), 303–23.
3 Robert I. Frost, *The Oxford History of Poland-Lithuania. Volume 1: The Making of the Polish-Lithuanian Union, 1385–1569* (Oxford: Oxford University Press, 2015).
4 We use the terms "noblemen" or "nobility" when referring to the whole estate ("*szlachta*"), while the term "magnates" refers to the wealthy noble elite as opposed to ordinary or minor nobility.
5 On the subject of the system of political and civic values, see Anna Sucheni-Grabowska, *Wolność i prawo w staropolskiej koncepcji państwa* (Warsaw: Muzeum Historii Polski, 2009); and Anna Grześkowiak-Krwawicz, "Noble Republicanism in the Polish-Lithuanian Commonwealth (an Attempt at Description)", *Acta Poloniae Historica* 103 (2011): 31–65.
6 Stanisław Płaza, *Wielkie bezkrólewia* (Cracow: Krajowa Agencja Wydawnicza, 1988); Ewa Dubas-Urwanowicz, *Koronne zjazdy szlacheckie: w dwóch pierwszych bezkrólewiach po śmierci Zygmunta Augusta* (Białystok: Wydawnictwo Uniwersytetu, 1998).
7 Wacław Uruszczak, "Ustawy Zygmunta I z lat 1530 i 1538 w sprawie elekcji królewskiej", in *Prawo wczoraj i dziś: studia dedykowane profesor Katarzynie Sójce-Zielińskiej*, edited by Grażyna Bałtruszajtys (Warsaw: Liber, 2000).
8 Frost, *Making of the Polish-Lithuanian Union*, 492.
9 Jan Dzięgielewski, *Sejmy elekcyjne, elektorzy, elekcje 1573–1674* (Pułtusk: WSH im. Aleksandra Gieysztora; Oficyna Wydawnicza ASPRA-JR, 2003).
10 Jan Czubek, *Pisma polityczne z czasów pierwszego bezkrólewia* (Cracow: Akademia Umiejętności, 1906).
11 *Konfederacja warszawska 1573 roku, wielka karta polskiej tolerancji*, edited by Mirosław Korolko and Janusz Tazbir (Warsaw: Instytut Wydawniczy PAX, 1980).
12 On the subject of the controversies over the number of noblemen participating in the election, see Dzięgielewski, *Sejmy elekcyjne, elektorzy, elekcje*, 69–77.
13 Stanisław Grzybowski, *Henryk Walezy* (Wrocław: Zakład Narodowy im. Ossolińskich, 1985), 93–94.
14 Zdzisław Kaczmarczyk, *Artykuły henrykowskie* (Poznań: Księgarnia Akademicka, 1946).
15 Dubas-Urwanowicz, *Koronne zjazdy szlacheckie.*
16 It should be noted, however, that Anna quickly withdrew into the shadows, and actual rule was in the hands of Stephen Báthory.
17 Juliusz A. Chrościcki, *Sztuka i polityka. Funkcje propagandowe sztuki w epoce Wazów 1587–1668* (Warsaw: Państwowe Wydawnictwo Naukowe, 1983); and Stefania Ochmann-Staniszewska, *Dynastia Wazów w Polsce* (Warsaw: Wydawnictwo Naukowe PWN, 2006), 13–18.
18 About the "Dei gratia" formula, see Antoni Mączak, *Rządzący i rządzeni: władza i społeczeństwo w Europie wczesnonowożytnej* (Warsaw: PIW, 2002), 116.
19 Kasper Niesiecki, *Herbarz Polski*, vol. 7 (Lipsk: Breitkopf & Härtel, 1841), 376.
20 Jan Władysław Poczobut Odlanicki, *Pamiętnik: 1640–1684*, edited by Andrzej Rachuba (Warsaw: Czytelnik, 1987), 245.

21 Wespazjan Kochowski, *Roczniki Polski: klimakter czwarty (1669–1673)*, edited by Leszek Andrzej Wierzbicki (Warsaw: DiG, 2011), 61–62.

22 Hanna Widacka, *Piast na elekcyjnym tronie: Michał Korybut Wiśnowiecki w grafice XVII i XVIII wieku ze zbiorów polskich i francuskich* (Warsaw: Biblioteka Narodowa, 2009).

23 "Diariusz dostateczny wjazdu i aktu koronacjej Króla Jego Mości Augusta II szczęśliwie nam panującego" (1697). For full details of the varied manoeuvring leading up to the election and coronation, see Jutta Bäumel, *Auf dem Weg zum Thron: die Krönungsreise Augusts des Starken* (Dresden: Hellerau-Verlag, 1997).

24 Józef Andrzej Gierowski, *The Polish-Lithuanian Commonwealth in the XVIIIth Century: From Anarchy to Well-Organised State* (Cracow: Nakładem Polskiej Akademii Umiejętności, 1996), 64; Jerzy Lukowski, *Liberty's Folly: The Polish-Lithuanian Commonwealth in the Eighteenth Century, 1697–1795* (London; New York: Routledge, 1991), 121–22.

25 Gierowski, *The Polish-Lithuanian Commonwealth in the XVIIIth Century*, 63; Lukowski, *Liberty's Folly*, 121.

26 "Konstytucyje koronne i sentymenta o elekcyi królów polskich, vota et rationes obrania Piasta cum exclusione cudzoziemca podane ad deliberandum statibus Regni 1733" (1733), Biblioteka Książąt Czartoryskich, Cracow Ms 602, 56–84.

27 "Votum znacznych teologów", in *Gazety Polskie* 41 (1735): 366–69.

28 Jacek Staszewski, *August III Sas* (Wrocław: Zakład Narodowy im. Ossolińskich, 2010), 149.

29 Benjamin Franklin, reflecting on developments in Poland, wrote in *Poor Richard's Almanack* for September 1748: "On the first of this month, Anno 1733, Stanislaus, originally a private gentleman of Poland, was chosen the second time king of that nation. The power of Charles XII of Sweden, caused his first election, that of Louis XV of France, his second. But neither of them could keep him on the throne: for PROVIDENCE, often opposite to the wills of princes, reduced him to the condition of a private gentleman again." *Benjamin Franklin Papers*, vol. 3: http://franklinpapers.org/franklin/framedVolumes.jsp?vol=3&page=243a [accessed 28 February 2018].

30 As Jerzy Lukowski has written: "Leszczyński commanded much greater support than ever Conti had. Without active Russian military help, Augustus's position would have been untenable." Lukowski, *Liberty's Folly*, 159.

31 "Diariusz prawdziwy wjazdu do stołecznego Krakowa i koronacyi tamże, Fryderyka Augusta Elektora Saskiego wprzód pseudoelekta, a potem przez Sejm pacificationis roku odprawiony, po abdykacyi Stanisława, uznanego od zgromadzonych Stanów Rzeczypospolitej Polskiej, Augusta Króla Polskiego", in *Dwie koronacje Sasów, Augusta II i Augusta III, królów polskich*, edited by Władysław Syrokomla (Vilnius: 1854), 27–28; Michał Rożek, "Ostatnia koronacja w Krakowie i jej artystyczna oprawa", *Rocznik Krakowski* 44 (1973): 102.

32 Staszewski, *August III Sas*, 153.

33 Anna Grześkowiak-Krwawicz, *Queen Liberty: The Concept of Freedom in the Polish-Lithuanian Commonwealth* (Leiden and Boston: Brill, 2012), 21; Daniel Stone, *The Polish-Lithuanian State, 1386–1795* (Seattle: University of Washington Press, 2001), 261.

34 Lukowski, *Liberty's Folly*, 160. At the Pacification Sejm of 1736, Augustus III proclaimed a general amnesty, which facilitated the process of reconciliation.

35 As compensation, Stanislaus Leszczyński received the duchies of Lorraine and Bar, which were then to pass to France upon his death, which came about in 1766.

36 Gierowski, *The Polish-Lithuanian Commonwealth in the XVIIIth Century*, 183; Richard Butterwick, *Poland's Last King and English Culture: Stanisław August Poniatowski, 1732–1798* (Oxford: Clarendon, 1998), 158–59.

37 *Correspondance inédite du roi Stanislas-Auguste Poniatowski et de Madame Geoffrin (1764–1777)*, edited by Charles de Moüy (Paris: Plon, 1875), 101–02 (Stanislaus Augustus to Mme Geoffrin, Warsaw, 9 September 1764); Butterwick, *Poland's Last King*, 163; Richard Butterwick, "The Enlightened Monarchy of Stanisław August Poniatowski (1764–1795)", in *The Polish-Lithuanian Monarchy in European Context, c. 1500–1795*, edited by Richard Butterwick (London: Palgrave Macmillan, 2001), 198.

38 *Diariusz sejmu electionis między wsią Wolą i miastem Warszawą odprawionego* (Warsaw: Drukarnia Societatis Jesu, 1764), session of 27 August 1764.
39 *Diariusz sejmu coronationis* (Warsaw: Drukarnia Societatis Jesu, 1764), session of 3 December 1764.
40 Butterwick, *Poland's Last King*, 163. On the details, see Andrzej Stroynowski, "Stanisław August: król elekcyjny czy z łaski Bożej?", in *Staropolski ogląd świata. Kultura staropolska – poszukiwanie sacrum odnajdywanie profanum*, edited by Bogdan Rok and Filip Wolański (Toruń: Adam Marszałek, 2013), 515–30.
41 Adam Naruszewicz, *Poezye*, edited by Jan Nepomucen Bobrowicz (Lipsk: Breitkopf et Haertel, 1835), 181.
42 Stone, *The Polish-Lithuanian State*, 272.
43 Władysław Konopczyński, *Konfederacja barska*, vol. 2 (Warsaw: Volumen, 1991), 576–79; Piotr Ugniewski, "'Szkaradny występek królobójstwa' w międzynarodowej propagandzie Stanisława Augusta", *Przegląd Historyczny* XLV, 3 (2004): 327–47.
44 Butterwick, *Poland's Last King*, 166, 87–89.
45 "Przypadek, który się Najjaśniejszemu królowi . . .", in *Monitor* 95 (27 November 1771): 834.
46 Arkadiusz Michał Stasiak, *Patriotyzm w myśli konfederatów barskich* (Lublin: Tow. Nauk. Katolickiego Uniwersytetu Lubelskiego, 2005), 138–47; *idem*, *Teoria władzy monarszej czasów stanislawowskich: studium idei* (Lublin: Wydawnictwo KUL, 2013), 83–99.
47 Cited in Stroynowski, "Stanisław August: król elekcyjny czy z łaski Bożej?", 524.
48 Gierowski, *The Polish-Lithuanian Commonwealth in the XVIIIth Century*, 181; Grześkowiak-Krwawicz, *Queen Liberty*, 89–90.
49 Stanisław Konarski, *Wybór pism politycznych*, edited by Władysław Konopczyński (Cracow: Krakowska Spółka Wydawnicza, 1921), 326; Stasiak, *Teoria władzy monarszej czasów stanisławowskich*, 89–92.
50 *Diariusz sejmu wolnego ordynaryjnego warszawskiego . . . 1780* (Warsaw, 1781), 13, session of 3 October 1780.
51 Butterwick, *Poland's Last King*, 287; Lukowski, *Liberty's Folly*, 231–36. Staszic wrote: "Where law-making does not belong to the nation, there is no society, only a lord and his herd of cattle." Cited in Grześkowiak-Krwawicz, *Queen Liberty*, 52–53.
52 *Konstytucja 3 maja 1791. Statut Zgromadzenia Przyjaciół Konstytucji*, edited by Jerzy Kowecki (Warsaw: PWN, 1981), 81. See also: "Constitution of May 3, 1791 [English text]": www.polishconstitution.org/index1.html [accessed 1 October 2017].
53 *Konstytucja 3 maja 1791*, 86.
54 Jerzy Michalski, "The Meaning of the Constitution of 3 May", in *Constitution and Reform in Eighteenth-Century Poland: The Constitution of 3 May 1791*, edited by Samuel Fiszman (Bloomington and Indianapolis: Indiana University Press, 1997), 272.
55 *Konstytucja 3 maja 1791*, 91.
56 Ibid., 91–92. The republicans protested against the transformation of the elective throne into a hereditary one. See, for example: "Seweryna Rzewuskiego hetmana polnego koronnego o sukcesyi tronu w Polszcze rzecz krótka" (1789).
57 *Konstytucja 3 maja 1791*, 91–92; Butterwick, *Poland's Last King*, 295–97.
58 Stroynowski, "Stanisław August: król elekcyjny czy z łaski Bożej?", 530. For the ceremony of kissing the king's hand, see Joanna Kodzik, *Ceremoniał polskiego dworu królewskiego w XVII wieku z perspektywy niemieckich uczonych* (Warsaw: Muzeum Pałacu Króla Jana III w Wilanowie, 2015), 129.
59 Jan Sierakowski's parliamentary address to King Sigismund Augustus, 1 November 1548: *Dyaryusze sejmów koronnych 1548, 1553 i 1570 r.*, edited by Józef Szujski, Scriptores Rerum Polonicarum, vol. I (Cracow: Komisja Historyczna Towarzystwa Naukowego-Krakowskiego, 1872), 162.
60 Wacław Uruszczak, *Historia państwa i prawa polskiego*, vol. 1 (966–1795) (Warsaw: LEX a Wolters Kluwer business, 2015).
61 For details, see Urszula Augustyniak, *Wazowie i "królowie rodacy": studium władzy królewskiej w Rzeczypospolitej XVII wieku* (Warsaw: Semper, 1999).
62 Grześkowiak-Krwawicz, *Queen Liberty*, 75.

Bibliography

Primary sources

Bielski, Marcin. *Kronika Polska*, vol. VI. Warsaw: Gałęzowski, 1832.

"Constitution of May 3, 1791". www.polishconstitution.org/index1.html [accessed 1 October 2017].

Correspondance inédite du Roi Stanislas-Auguste Poniatowski et de Madame Geoffrin (1764–1777), edited by Charles de Moüy. Paris: Plon, 1875.

Czubek, Jan. *Pisma polityczne z czasów pierwszego bezkrólewia*. Cracow: Akademia Umiejętności, 1906.

"Diariusz dostateczny wjazdu i aktu koronacjej Króla Jego Mości Augusta II szczęśliwie nam panującego". 1697.

"Diariusz prawdziwy wjazdu do stołecznego Krakowa i koronacyi tamże, Fryderyka Augusta Elektora Saskiego wprzód pseudoelekta, a potem przez Sejm pacificationis roku odprawiony, po abdykacyi *Stanisława*, uznanego od zgromadzonych stanów *Rzeczypospolitej* Polskiej, Augusta Króla Polskiego". In *Dwie Koronacje Sasów, Augusta II i Augusta III, Królów Polskich*, edited by Władysław Syrokomla, 21–80. Vilnius, 1854.

Diariusz sejmu coronationis. Warsaw: Drukarnia Societatis Jesu, 1764.

Diariusz sejmu electionis między wsią Wolą i miastem Warszawą odprawionego. Warsaw: Drukarnia Societatis Jesu, 1764.

Diariusz sejmu wolnego ordynaryjnego warszawskiego . . . 1780. Warsaw: 1781.

Dyaryusze sejmów koronnych 1548, 1553 i 1570 r., edited by Józef Szujski. In *Scriptores Rerum Polonicarum*, vol. I. Cracow: Komisja Historyczna Towarzystwa Naukowego Krakowskiego, 1872.

Franklin, Benjamin. *Poor Richard's Almanack* (September 1748). *Benjamin Franklin Papers*, vol. 3: http://franklinpapers.org/franklin/framedVolumes.jsp?vol=3&page=243a [accessed 28 February 2018].

Kaczmarczyk, Zdzisław. *Artykuły henrykowskie*. Poznań: Księgarnia Akademicka, 1946.

Kochowski, Wespazjan. *Roczniki Polski: klimakter czwarty (1669–1673)*, edited by Leszek Andrzej Wierzbicki. Warsaw: DiG, 2011.

Konarski, Stanisław. *Wybór pism politycznych*, edited by Władysław Konopczyński. Cracow: Krakowska Spółka Wydawnicza, 1921.

Konfederacja warszawska 1573 roku, wielka karta polskiej tolerancji, edited by Mirosław Korolko and Janusz Tazbir. Warsaw: Instytut Wydawniczy PAX, 1980.

Konstytucja 3 maja 1791. Statut Zgromadzenia Przyjaciół Konstytucji, edited by Jerzy Kowecki. Warsaw: PWN, 1981.

"Konstytucyje koronne i sentymenta o elekcyi królów polskich, vota et rationes obrania Piasta cum exclusione cudzoziemca podane ad deliberandum statibus Regni 1733". (1733) Biblioteka Książąt Czartoryskich, Cracow. Ms. 602, 56–84.

Naruszewicz, Adam. *Poezye*, edited by Jan Nepomucen Bobrowicz. Lipsk: Breitkopf et Haertel, 1835.

Poczobut Odlanicki, Jan Władysław. *Pamiętnik: 1640–1684*, edited by Andrzej Rachuba. Warsaw: Czytelnik, 1987.

"Przypadek, który się Najjaśniejszemu królowi . . ." In *Monitor* 95 (27 November 1771), 830–36.

"Seweryna Rzewuskiego hetmana polnego koronnego o sukcesyi tronu w Polszcze rzecz krótka". Amsterdam: 1789.

"Votum znacznych teologów". In *Gazety Polskie* 41 (1735), 366–69.

Secondary sources

Augustyniak, Urszula. *Wazowie i "królowie rodacy": studium władzy królewskiej w Rzeczypospolitej XVII wieku*. Warsaw: Semper, 1999.

Bäumel, Jutta. *Auf dem Weg zum Thron: die Krönungsreise Augusts des Starken*. Dresden: Hellerau-Verlag, 1997.

Butterwick, Richard. *Poland's Last King and English Culture: Stanislaw August Poniatowski, 1732–1798*. Oxford: Clarendon, 1998.

Butterwick, Richard. "The Enlightened Monarchy of Stanisław August Poniatowski (1764–1795)". In *The Polish-Lithuanian Monarchy in European Context, C. 1500–1795*, edited by Richard Butterwick, 193–218. London: Palgrave Macmillan, 2001.

Chrościcki, Juliusz A. *Sztuka i polityka. Funkcje propagandowe sztuki w epoce Wazów 1587–1668*. Warsaw: Państwowe Wydawnictwo Naukowe, 1983.

Dubas-Urwanowicz, Ewa. *Koronne zjazdy szlacheckie w dwóch pierwszych bezkrólewiach po śmierci Zygmunta Augusta*. Białystok: Wydawnictwo Uniwersytetu, 1998.

Dzięgielewski, Jan. *Sejmy elekcyjne, elektorzy, elekcje 1573–1674*. Pułtusk: WSH im. Aleksandra Gieysztora; Oficyna Wydawnicza ASPRA-JR, 2003.

Frost, Robert I. *The Oxford History of Poland-Lithuania. Volume 1: The Making of the Polish-Lithuanian Union, 1385–1569*. Oxford: Oxford University Press, 2015.

Gierowski, Józef Andrzej. *The Polish-Lithuanian Commonwealth in the XVIIIth Century: From Anarchy to Well-Organised State*. Cracow: Nakładem Polskiej Akademii Umiejętności, 1996.

Grześkowiak-Krwawicz, Anna. "Noble Republicanism in the Polish-Lithuanian Commonwealth (an Attempt at Description)". *Acta Poloniae Historica* 103 (2011): 31–65.

Grześkowiak-Krwawicz, Anna. *Queen Liberty: The Concept of Freedom in the Polish-Lithuanian Commonwealth*. Leiden and Boston: Brill, 2012.

Grzybowski, Stanisław. *Henryk Walezy*. Wrocław: Zakład Narodowy im. Ossolińskich, 1985.

Jędruch, Jacek. *Constitutions, Elections and Legislatures of Poland, 1493–1993*. New York: EJJ Books, 1998. http://info-poland.buffalo.edu/JJ.html [accessed 19 May 2019].

Kodzik, Joanna. *Ceremoniał polskiego dworu królewskiego w XVII wieku z perspektywy niemieckich uczonych*. Warsaw: Muzeum Pałacu Króla Jana III w Wilanowie, 2015.

Konopczyński, Władysław. *Konfederacja barska*, vol. 2. Warsaw: Volumen, 1991.

Lukowski, Jerzy. *Liberty's Folly: The Polish-Lithuanian Commonwealth in the Eighteenth Century, 1697–1795*. London and New York: Routledge, 1991.

Mączak, Antoni. *Rządzący i rządzeni: władza i społeczeństwo w Europie wczesnonowożytnej*. Warsaw: PIW, 2002.

Michalski, Jerzy. "The Meaning of the Constitution of 3 May". In *Constitution and Reform in Eighteenth-Century Poland. The Constitution of 3 May 1791*, edited by Samuel Fiszman, 251–86. Bloomington and Indianapolis: Indiana University Press, 1997.

Niesiecki, Kasper. *Herbarz Polski*, vol. 7. Lipsk: Breitkopf & Härtel, 1841.

Ochmann-Staniszewska, Stefania. *Dynastia Wazów w Polsce*. Warsaw: Wydawnictwo Naukowe PWN, 2006.

Płaza, Stanisław. *Wielkie bezkrólewia*. Cracow: Krajowa Agencja Wydawnicza, 1988.

Rożek, Michał. "Ostatnia koronacja w Krakowie i jej artystyczna oprawa". *Rocznik Krakowski* 44 (1973).

Stasiak, Arkadiusz Michał. *Patriotyzm w myśli konfederatów barskich*. Lublin: Towarzystwo Naukowe KUL, 2005.

Stasiak, Arkadiusz Michał. *Teoria monarszej czasów stanislawowskich: studium idei*. Lublin: Wydawnictwo KUL, 2013.

Staszewski, Jacek. *August III Sas*. Wrocław: Zakład Narodowy im. Ossolińskich, 2010.

Stone, Daniel. *The Polish-Lithuanian State, 1386–1795*. Seattle, University of Washington Press, 2001.

Stroynowski, Andrzej. "Stanisław August: Bożej?" In *Staropolski ogląd swiata. Kultura staropolska – poszukiwanie sacrum odnajdywanie profanum*, edited by Bogdan Rok and Filip Wolański, 500–13. Toruń: Adam Marszałek, 2013.

Sucheni-Grabowska, Anna. *Zygmunt August król polski i wielki książę litewski 1520–1562*. Wydawnictwo Krupski i S-ka, 1996.

Sucheni-Grabowska, Anna. *Wolność i prawo w staropolskiej koncepcji państwa*. Warsaw: Muzeum Historii Polski, 2009.

Ugniewski, Piotr. "'Szkaradny występek królobójstwa' w międzynarodowej propagandzie Stanisława Augusta", *Przegląd Historyczny* XLV, no 3 (2004).

Uruszczak, Wacław. "Ustawy z lat 1530 i 1531 w sprawie elekcji królewskiej". In *Prawo wczoraj i dziś: studia dedykowane profesor Katarzynie Sójce-Zielińskiej*, edited by Grażyna Bałtruszajtys, 349–60. Warsaw: Liber, 2000.

Uruszczak, Wacław. *Historia państwa i prawa polskiego*, vol. 1 (966–1795). Warsaw: LEX a Wolters Kluwer business, 2015.

Widacka, Hanna. *Piast na elekcyjnym tronie: Michał Korybut Wiśnowiecki w grafice XVII i XVIII wieku ze zbiorów polskich i francuskich*. Warsaw: Biblioteka Narodowa, 2009.

6

LEGITIMACY THROUGH FAMILY TRADITIONS?

The Hanoverians represented as successors to the throne of Great Britain

Charlotte Backerra

In the early modern period, personal unions or composite monarchies were the dominant form of government. Kings and queens ruling over various people and territories bound together only by their personal rule were more common than sovereign, territorially united states with only one people.[1] At the same time, ideas of national identities and specific national cultures began to take root amongst the political elites in European kingdoms. These ideas were based on traditions, laws, history, religion, literature, and the language specific to a region.[2] Most importantly, these ideas could determine if a new monarch would be accepted on an old throne. If notions of divine right of kings and hereditary rights set the standards in times of dynastic change, it was the fulfilment of a kingdom's expectations of its rulers which decided the success (or not) of a change in dynasty. Therefore, new rulers who came from a different place or culture had to appeal to their new subjects by representing themselves as having adapted to the traditions, history, and values of the people, or—in more recent scholarly terminology—adapted to the national political culture. This chapter will re-examine the well-known but still remarkable—because at first glance unlikely—success of a German dynasty in eighteenth-century Britain. The basis of analysis will not be parliamentary discussions or court culture, as these have been examined thoroughly by other historians, such as Andrew Thompson[3] or Hannah Smith.[4] Rather, the focus will be on the adaptation of the Hanoverian dynasty to conform to the national culture—especially political culture—and expectations of the British Isles. In the following chapter, political culture will be seen as the fabric of values and attitudes regulating policy.[5] These values and attitudes, as well as the discussions and actions by members of the political system, can be determined through examining various media, not limited to written text, but including visual and material sources. As a case study, this chapter will focus on one of these, the medals produced in the context of the Hanoverian Succession, from the time of its first proclamation in 1701 until the second, non-contested accession of a Hanoverian king to the throne of Great Britain in 1727.

Great Britain and Hanover

The historical context for this chapter is well known: at the turn of the eighteenth century, the English parliament adopted the Act of Settlement in 1701 (and in Scotland, the Act of Security in 1704). The Act was meant to protect the law regarding the Protestant succession of the Bill of Rights, as it was determined after the "Glorious Revolution" of 1688. The Act of Settlement excluded the Catholic Stuarts, the family of King James II, and especially his son and heir James Francis Edward Stuart. Instead, Sophia, Electress of Hanover, granddaughter of King James I, was named heir apparent, and her heirs who were Protestant, if King William and Princess Anne (who became queen in 1702) would die without legitimate children. In 1714, the last Protestant Stuart, Anne, did indeed die without issue, leaving the throne to the House of Hanover. As Electress Sophia died before Anne, and her son therefore received the succession, he ruled in a personal union as King George I of Great Britain and Ireland and Elector Georg Ludwig of Hanover. In 1727, his son Georg August succeeded as King George II and ruled for thirty-three years until 1760. George II's wife Caroline aided the adaptation of the dynasty's image and behaviour until her death in 1736.

The House of Brunswick-Luneburg (Braunschweig-Lüneburg in German), also known as Guelph (after the name used by several of its earliest leaders, Welf) had ruled their territories in northern Germany since the early Middle Ages. In the late seventeenth century, one of the branches of the Guelph dynasty succeeded in gaining an electorate of the Holy Roman Empire (the ninth), which adopted the name Hanover after its capital city (and thus the dynasty also was called "Hanoverian"). The reigning duke of Brunswick-Luneburg was elevated to the rank of elector by the Emperor Leopold in 1692, in recognition of his military and political support.[6] The electoral status was, however, contested by other princes in the Empire for nearly twenty years, and also by the rest of the Guelph dynasty, whose senior branch, Brunswick-Wolfenbüttel, felt this honour was due to them instead. At the same time, the new electoral house competed with the House of Brandenburg and its new title "king in Prussia" (from 1701) to represent the leading Protestant power in the Empire.[7]

With the personal union, the first two Hanoverian kings had to manage two very different territories and the demands of completely different political cultures and systems. The electors could rule mostly unlimited within their German electorate, checked only by the estates and bound by the laws of the Holy Roman Empire.[8] In Great Britain, in contrast, there was a more rigorous system of checks and balances, including the permanent participation of both houses of Parliament (including a popularly elected House of Commons), an increasingly institutionalised government, and a growing public opinion eager to criticise and comment on royal politics.[9] This personal union of Great Britain and Hanover has been looked at by historians, recent studies covering various spheres, ranging from foreign policy and international relations involving religious and dynastic policies to scholarly exchanges. While much of this was initiated from the British side and with a focus on the "new"—at least for Great Britain—dynasty,[10] an effort has been made more recently in the former lands of the Guelph dynasty to cover the German side of the story, with research groups at the University of Göttingen and several exhibitions in Hanover in 2014.[11]

The publicly performed adaptation of the German Guelphs from Brunswick-Luneburg into a royal dynasty that would be acceptable in the British Isles as a process of legitimisation is the core of this analysis. Three areas in which the Hanoverians adapted to British political culture in the first half of the eighteenth century will be examined: dynasty, religion, and politics, with a special focus on the first. Even though Hannah Smith has adeptly drawn attention to the "Georgian Monarchy" and their acceptance in British politics and society once they were in Britain, this chapter will look at the problems they faced before they arrived and in their earliest days, as an ancient dynasty taking over an old but severely changed throne and country. As a whole, in Great Britain, the dynastic change was accepted, albeit with some exceptions: Jacobites would have preferred a continuous succession of the Stuarts (Catholic or not), while others feared the involvement in further European conflicts that had burdened the country under the rule of the Dutch King William, who led England against France and Louis XIV in two long and costly wars. This opposition, though limited, therefore meant that the continuation of the succession in the Hanoverian line was not a given, but had to be confirmed by the actions of the first rulers. This has previously been examined using written documents; in contrast, material culture has played only a minor role in historical research on the subject of political culture.

Medals as sources

Medals are some of the smallest historical sources, but can have profound meanings: they normally combine material—mostly gold, silver, and copper—with symbols or pictures and quite often a short phrase to emphasise the medal's meanings. Medals are not coins, but two-sided artistic representations commemorating a person or an event in durable material. In comparison to written texts, they carry subtexts through the material they are made of. Most images and symbols on medals work in different cultural and linguistic contexts without needing an actual translation. In this way, they are different from memoirs or pamphlets, the other commonly used media in interpreting early modern political culture. The design of a medal embodies the political and historical background of its production, symbolic meanings of images, and letters, as well as artistic arrangements and structures. The inscriptions, often in Latin, but sometimes, as in some of the medals presented in this chapter, also in vernacular languages, underline the meaning of the illustrations.

Invented in the Italian Renaissance period after the fashion of ancient Roman coins, commemorative medals became popular in court society and other parts of elite European societies. Until other types of souvenirs took their place in the late nineteenth and early twentieth centuries, medals were produced, distributed, and collected widely. They were sold in large quantities in different materials, pandering to the public's desire for souvenirs and collectables. Craftsmen all over Europe worked either independently or in official capacities—for example as masters of the mint—to produce medals.[12] Monarchs such as King Louis XIV of France[13] or Holy Roman Emperor Charles VI[14] used engraved metal objects to underline their dynasties' politics, supporting large workshops within their capital cities. Made with rare materials such as gold or silver, they were presented by princes to important visitors or supporters on special occasions. During public events such as coronations, weddings, or christenings, monarchs would distribute medals bearing their portrait, a symbolic picture, and the date, to guests and to the public by throwing them to the cheering crowd.

As material sources for dynastic history, medals show us the condensed, publicly available image of one monarch or dynasty. Normally, we are able to see the positive and heroicised representation of a monarchy, but sometimes also its caricatured depiction as distributed by its adversaries.[15] As with other sources, the context of a medal's origin needs to be taken into consideration. This might be a problem: there is often an artist's monogram and the year is to be found on the material; however, sources on the design process seldom survived. Yet even with knowing only the time of production, an interpretation is possible. The monarch or monarchs involved are easily detected, as the obverse or face of a medal normally shows his or her portrait together with the name and an abbreviated version of the title. To interpret the reverse or back, however, a sound grasp of symbols, metaphors, and allegories used at the time is required. Taken together with the historical context, these can be read just like written sources and demonstrate the values and attitudes conveyed by the medal.

Dynasty: Leibniz and the uses of Guelph history

To be placed in the line of succession to the English throne was a triumphal success for the Hanoverian dynasty. Two months after the Act had been passed in London, an English delegation under the leadership of the Earl of Macclesfield went to Germany to officially announce the result. But in Hanover, it was clear that a dynastic change in the British Isles had to be prepared carefully and in advance. Gifts were needed for the members of the delegation, material symbols that could be taken back to London. Soon after the announcement in 1701, the dynasty's official historian Leibniz therefore designed a medal pointing out the historical connections of the north German dynasty to England's ruling dynasties.

Polymath Gottfried Wilhelm Leibniz (1646–1716) had been appointed court historian to the Guelphs in the context of their ambitions of gaining an electorate.[16] The elevation in status would be based on military and financial support of the

Emperor in his campaigns against the Ottomans and the family's broad diplomatic relations—especially with the newly crowned King William III of England and Scotland. But it was the dynasty's history that was of vital importance to prove its claim of *ancienneté* and distinction amongst the German princely dynasties.[17] A legal fiction was generated as well, to justify an increase in status in the Holy Roman Empire: it was merely the recognition of long-existing dignities, and not a "new" creation at all. Leibniz was therefore charged with writing a general history of the Guelphs, from their origins in the Middle Ages to his time.[18] In this work, he demonstrated the dynasty's continuous succession from the tenth century, even visiting Italy to trace its genealogical connections there.[19] In general, Leibniz established a dynastic history that was based on records and reliable sources,[20] and was so well-founded that his employers were able to use the research as a basis to (re)claim rights and legal titles.[21] He published three volumes of sources containing documents, treaties, deeds, legal titles, and other proofs.[22] Although the dynasty's history was never finished, Leibniz' research was sufficient to aid in the consideration of just how to design a medal that could be used to connect the German Guelphs to England and the British Isles.

In the summer of 1701, Leibniz suggested a medal with parallel portraits of the Electress Sophia and Princess Matilda of England, an ancestress of the Guelph dynasty.[23] As he wrote to the Elector's vice-chancellor, a Latin inscription should be used to explain the relation between the two women.[24] Matilda (1156–89) was the daughter of King Henry II of England and Queen Eleanor of Aquitaine. In 1168, she married the Duke of Bavaria and Saxony, Henry the Lion, and gave birth to three sons, Emperor Otto IV, Henry the Elector Palatine, and William of Winchester, the founder of the Brunswick line of the Guelph dynasty. William's son Otto became the first duke of Brunswick-Luneburg in 1235. Sophia (1630–1714), the widowed Electress of Hanover, was born in the electoral dynasty of the Palatinate (a branch of the House of Wittelsbach, which also ruled Bavaria), the daughter of Elector Palatine Frederick V and Elizabeth Stuart, and therefore the granddaughter of James I and VI of England and Scotland. With her marriage to Duke Ernest August of Brunswick-Luneburg in 1658, she tied together the dynasties of Wittelsbach, Stuart, and Guelph. She also represented the connection to the future in her son, the Elector Georg Ludwig of Hanover, the future King George I of Great Britain. Leibniz also suggested including striding lions with the female portraits. Three lions would stand for England, two for Brunswick, and one for the Palatinate and Bavaria.[25] This concept was debated in the Hanoverian ministry, and the final medal was quite close to that proposed: with portraits on the obverse and reverse, the golden medal compared the successor to the crown, Electress Sophia, with Duchess Matilda, ancestress of the Brunswick family.[26] The craftsman was Samuel Lambelet, employed at the mint in Brunswick and a punch-cutter, engraver, and medallist commissioned by the Elector of Hanover.[27]

The medal (Figures 6.1 and 6.2) shows on the obverse the bust of Electress Sophia with a widow's veil, looking to the right. Below it is the signature "S. L." of Samuel Lambelet. Surrounding the portrait the text—in Latin abbreviations—reads in two lines: "Sophia of the Palatine lineage, granddaughter of James I, king of Great Britain, widow of Ernst August, elector of Brunswick and Luneburg—as successor to the English throne nominated in 1701."[28] The reverse shows Matilda, also as a widow looking to the right, with the signature "Lambelet" within the widow's veil. The Latin inscription reads: "Matilda, daughter of Henry II, king of England, wife of Henry the Lion, duke of Bavaria and Saxony, mother of Emperor Otto IV, once duke of Aquitaine, of Henry, count Palatine and William, ancestor of the house of Brunswick."[29]

As mentioned above, in August 1701, the Earl of Macclesfield came on official mission to Hanover. Three Whig lords, a royal herald, and a chaplain of the Church of England, as well as the Irish philosopher John Toland, accompanied the Earl. On 15 August, he formally presented the Act of Settlement to Electress Sophia. Elector George Louis, her son and now fourth in line to the English throne, received the regalia of the Order of the Garter.[30] Toland wrote in his *Account of the Courts of Prussia and Hanover* about the warm reception in Hanover, the Electress' kind words, and her active participation in an Anglican service.

FIGURE 6.1 Samuel Lambelet. *Medal on the Succession 1701*. Brunswick, 1701 (*obverse*).

FIGURE 6.2 Samuel Lambelet. *Medal on the Succession 1701*. Brunswick, 1701 (*reverse*).

Afterwards, all guests were given gifts according to their status, and the gold medal of Sophia and Matilda to honour the event.[31] This in itself was a substantial gift, as the medals were quite big and heavy, with a diameter of 64 millimetres and a weight of over 330 grams. Macclesfield and the others brought the medals to Great Britain, where they were shown to members of the political elite and apparently used as inheritance and family presents.[32] Some time later, probably in 1702, the medal was also struck in silver and copper, probably to be sold and further distributed.[33]

Sophia died in Herrenhausen on 8 June 1714, two months before Queen Anne. Therefore, her son George Louis was declared King George I of Great Britain on 1 August 1714.

Religion: defenders of the faith

The basis of the Hanoverians' rights to the succession was their Protestant faith. Consequently, Electress Sophia actively participated in the church service following the Anglican Book of Common Prayer with the official English delegation in Hanover in 1701.[34] But in fact, by tradition, the House of Brunswick-Luneburg was Lutheran, not Anglican, and they remained so when in Hanover. Only as sovereigns of Great Britain did they attend the Anglican church services at the Chapel Royal, had Anglican clergy at their court, and were active as heads of the Church of England.[35] This role was the basis for another medal, or rather *jeton* (a very small medal that would be thrown into the crowd), struck for the coronation of George I in 1714.[36]

The so-called *speaking side* of the medal shows an image of a church and the Latin inscriptions "the foundation of our repose" and "the Church of England".[37] Several dies were cut to be able to make enough of these small copper medals that were probably thrown to the crowds after the coronation and church service. The design originally came from Nuremberg in 1702, where medallist Lazarus Gottlieb Lauffer struck it with the bust of Queen Anne.[38] In 1714, only the obverse was changed to now show the portrait of King George I. The Church of England is here presented as the basis of the Kingdom's peace. Early in his reign, the new king declared the security of the Protestant faith as one of his main principles of rulership. He followed this policy by appointing largely moderate bishops and by supporting measures that tried to find a consensus between the Whigs and Tories in the Church of England.[39]

But Protestantism was not only necessary within Great Britain, but also in a wider European context. Contemporaries referred to the Hanoverian succession as the "Protestant Succession", and the newly installed dynasty was measured by its efforts to support their confession internally and externally.[40] The kings wanted to be seen as Protestant champions, as true defenders of the faith fighting against popery and arbitrary government. This tied in to the concept of *warrior-kings*—associated especially in the Empire with Protestant princes—which both George I and George II adhered to as a role model.[41] The personification of this was the (medieval) knight St George battling the beast, most often shown as a snake or dragon. Indeed, this image appeared on another coronation medal, this time designed by Georg Wilhelm Vestner, an artist from Nuremberg in Germany who sold his medals all over Europe, including in the British Isles.[42] This medal (Figure 6.3) shows the laureated bust of George I facing to the right with the inscription: "George Louis by the Grace of God King of Great Britain, France and Ireland, Duke of Brunswick and Luneburg, Elector of the Holy Roman Empire". The text continues on the reverse (Figure 6.4) with "Defender of the Faith and of Justice" and "crowned on the 31st October 1714".[43] The reverse shows St George stabbing the dragon while an angel is crowning him and guiding his spear. St George had been the patron saint of England since the thirteenth century,[44] and in the early eighteenth century the name shared by the saint and the King proved to be useful as an obvious link between them. The dragon, or any kind of monstrous beast, could at the time be understood as a negative

FIGURE 6.3 Georg Wilhelm Vestner. *Coronation Medal for King George I [Fidei Defensor]*, Nuremberg, 1714 (*obverse*).

FIGURE 6.4 Georg Wilhelm Vestner. *Coronation Medal for King George I [Fidei Defensor]*, Nuremberg, 1714 (*reverse*).

symbol for popery and arbitrary power—meaning France, and in this instance, also the French crown's support for the Catholic Stuarts.[45] The establishment of the House of Brunswick on the throne of England prevented a French intervention for a Catholic and Stuart restoration.[46] To the traditional religious title used by English kings since Henry VIII, "Defender of the Faith", is added "and of Justice", which is a reference to the king's role as highest judge in spiritual and temporal matters.

George II and his wife Caroline of Ansbach would continue to use this declaration in the next generation. Caroline, as Princess of Wales and as queen, actively supported the Protestant image of the dynasty. As a young woman, she had refused to convert to Catholicism to marry the Emperor's second son Charles (the future Emperor Charles VI, though at the time the Austrian claimant for the throne of Spain). Instead, she agreed to a marriage with the Hanoverian crown prince, from an equally Protestant dynasty as her own. Because of this, the Protestant elite of Europe saw her as a heroine for the faith—a role which she accepted. Caroline was interested in church politics and actively supported poor relief measures for Protestants in Europe. She was also seen as pious in public: with this image, she incorporated the German model of the Protestant mother of her country, the *Landesmutter*, the pillar of the dynasty's present and future, both in this world as support for her husband and mother of future rulers, and in the spiritual world as supplicant to God for heavenly aid for the dynasty and its people.[47] As crown princess she was compared to a "rose without thorns"—a common epithet of the Virgin Mary in reference to the Immaculate Conception—on a medal designed by John Croker.[48] But the rose also referred to the "English rose" and as such to a heraldic symbol for England. Her coronation medal (Figure 6.5) shows Caroline standing between Religion and Britannia, with the inscription "My Love – My Fatherland".[49] Thus, Caroline is the personified legitimisation of the Protestant Succession.

FIGURE 6.5 John Croker. *Official Coronation Medal for Queen Caroline in 1727.* London, 1727.

Politics: liberty and the people

With the beginning of the reign of King George I of Great Britain in 1714, further strategies to adapt to the political culture of their new home were used by George I, his son, the later George II, and Caroline. First of all, their coronations—in 1714 and 1727 for George II and Caroline respectively—followed old English ceremonial rules and protocols.[50] Court life continued on the foundations laid after the Restoration of 1660, and George II and Caroline especially showed a demonstrative use of the English language and favoured English courtiers and politicians. Caroline had only English maids of honour; the only German ladies were the little princesses' governesses.[51]

In regard to policy and politics, there existed values and traditions quite singular to Great Britain at the time. One was the value of the ancient liberties of the people, the belief in liberty, justice, and freedom for all free men.[52]

One of the coronation medals under examination here shows George I with the allegorical figures Liberty and the Christian Religion, walking towards Britannia, who is waiting to crown him. The inscription reads "The most excellent prince, guardian of Religion and Liberty", thus combining the Protestant faith with freedom as the central themes of British political culture. The medal was the official coronation medal, designed and struck by Ehrenreich Hannibal, another of the official Hanoverian medallists.[53] On the obverse is the usual bust of the King facing right with his titles as inscription, but this time wearing Roman-style armour, thus referring to his role as elector in the Holy Roman Empire. On the reverse, George is shown wearing the electoral cap and robes. To the left stands the allegory of Religion with the Christian standard, and to the right Liberty—as Athena with a Phrygian cap on a standard—holding a laurel wreath over the King's head. He moves towards the figure of Britannia who hands over the sceptre and the royal orb with a curtsey. Under her feet, a beast or dragon is lying dead, and behind her a lion holds the crowned royal shield. The text surrounding the display is "The most excellent prince, guardian of Religion and Liberty."[54] Below it, there is given the date of the public proclamation on 1/12 August 1714.

In this medal, everything comes together. George I as king and elector guards the Protestant religion and the ancient liberties of the people. Britain accepts him as ruler by handing him the royal insignia. The beast or dragon—again standing for popery and the Catholic Stuarts, arbitrary power, and France—is dead beneath Britannia's feet. The Protestant faith and with it the British way of life was thus defended by the establishment of the Hanoverian dynasty.

The symbolic figure of Britannia was also used for the official British coronation medal of George I, designed by the master of the Royal Mint, John Croker, which showed the enthroned King being crowned by Britannia. In 1727, for George II's coronation, the design was chosen again, but with a twist. As Prince of Wales he had clearly presented himself as accepting all things British, even more so than his father. So for his coronation medal, an inscription was added: *VOLENTES PER POPULOS*, or "willingly by the people".[55] This said it all: with the succession of

George II, the last doubts about the German princes ruling over Great Britain were cleared and replaced—at least officially—by the cooperation of king and people.

Conclusion

The change of dynasties from Stuart to Hanoverian in eighteenth-century Britain was successful because of the adaptation of the German dynasty to a British national political culture. Electress Sophia and George I, as well as George II and his wife Caroline, followed older English examples and even more the developing British traditions in their representation as defenders of the Protestant faith. They celebrated coronations and other ceremonies according to older examples, and bowed to national culture with their acceptance of political rules established in England and the ancient liberties of the people. The new kings' acceptance of British political and national culture played a major role in the successful change of dynasty in Great Britain against the forces of Jacobitism, isolationism, and rejection of a foreign ruling family. This process of adaptation can be seen—alongside various other ways—through medals produced by official British, Hanoverian, and other German medallists and artists, transforming political rhetoric into symbolic visual representations in metal.

Princess Matilda of England, daughter of King Henry II, and ancestress of the Brunswick-Luneburg line of the Guelphs, and Electress Sophia, granddaughter of King James VI and I, were compared on a medal to point out the dynastic logic and continuity of the Act of Settlement in 1701. For the occasion of the proclamation and coronation of the first Hanoverian king, George I, the images on the medals presented the continuity of religious and liberal politics. With his succession, George I, bearing the name of the patron saint of England, made secure the ascendancy of the Church of England as well as the rights and liberties of the English people. George I, George II, and their dynasty were the new "Defenders of the Faith", in Great Britain as well as in Germany and Europe. With George II and his wife Caroline, this development of a quest for legitimacy found an end point in the succession of George II that was undoubted and unperturbed by the people. Caroline stood as a queen in the middle of the people and their faith, representing the heavenly support for their reign.

The medals discussed in this chapter were produced by the dynasty to self-legitimise its position in Great Britain. By distributing them to the political elite even before the accession in 1714, and to the public on coronation days and ceremonial occasions, the Hanoverians demonstrated their adaptation to British political culture not through complex written texts, but through a source unbound by language, easily understood by contemporaries, and collected by broad strata of society.

Notes

1 See this author's chapter on the changes in dynastic rule from personal unions to composite monarchies in Ellie Woodacre, ed., *The History of Monarchy: A Handbook* (London: Routledge, 2019).

2 The classic study remains Linda Colley, *Britons: Forging the Nation 1707–1837* (New Haven: Yale University Press, 1992).

3 Andrew Thompson, *Britain, Hanover and the Protestant Interest, 1688–1756* (Woodbridge: Boydell Press, 2006).
4 Hannah Smith, *Georgian Monarchy: Politics and Culture, 1714–1760* (Cambridge: Cambridge University Press, 2006).
5 This follows the definition of political culture as it is used by the German historian Birgit Emich. See her *Territoriale Integration in der Frühen Neuzeit: Ferrara und der Kirchenstaat* (Cologne: Böhlau, 2005), 20–21.
6 Hans-Georg Aschoff, "Die welfischen Territorien und ihre Fürsten zwischen 1636 und 1714", in *Reif für die Insel: Das Haus Braunschweig-Lüneburg auf dem Weg nach London*, Catalogue for the Lower Saxon State Exhibition "Als die Royals aus Hannover kamen", Bormann-Museum Celle, Residence Museum in the Palace of Celle, 18 May to 5 October 2014, ed. Jochen Meiners (Dresden: Sandstein Verlag, 2014), 55–58.
7 Volker Press has shown that Prussia gained influence because of the Hanoverians' continuous absence from northern Germany due to the British succession. Volker Press, "Kurhannover im System des alten Reiches 1692–1803", in *England und Hannover / England and Hanover*, eds. Adolf M. Birke and Kurt Kluxen (Munich: K. G. Saur, 1986), 62. In my doctoral dissertation, I demonstrated the importance of the Hanoverian–Prussian conflict for British–Imperial relations in the early eighteenth century: Charlotte Backerra, "Wien und London, 1727–1735. Internationale Beziehungen im frühen 18. Jahrhundert" (Göttingen: Vandenhoeck & Ruprecht, 2018), esp. 382–87.
8 Press, "Kurhannover", 59–62.
9 See Hans-Christof Kraus, *Englische Verfassung und politisches Denken im Ancien Régime, 1689 bis 1789* (Munich: Oldenbourg, 2006), 61–66; or, more generally, Karl Tilman Winkler, *Wörterkrieg: Politische Debattenkultur in England 1689–1750* (Stuttgart: Franz Steiner, 1998).
10 Thompson, *Britain, Hanover and the Protestant Interest, 1688–1756*; Brendan Simms and Torsten Riotte, eds, *The Hanoverian Dimension in British History, 1714–1837* (Cambridge: Cambridge University Press, 2007).
11 Ronald G. Asch, ed., *Hannover, Großbritannien und Europa: Erfahrungsraum Personalunion 1714–1837* (Göttingen: Wallstein Verlag, 2014); Arnd Reitemeier, ed., *Kommunikation und Kulturtransfer im Zeitalter der Personalunion zwischen Großbritannien und Hannover: "to prove that Hanover and England are not entirely synonymous"* (Göttingen: Universitätsverlag Göttingen, 2014); Katja Lembke, ed., *Hannovers Herrscher auf Englands Thron 1714–1837*, Catalogue for the Lower Saxon State Exhibition "Als die Royals aus Hannover kamen", State Museum of Lower Saxony Hanover and Palace Museum Herrenhausen, 17 May to 5 October 2014 (Dresden: Sandstein Verlag, 2014). See also reviews by Tessa Murdoch ("The Art of the Hanoverians, 1714–2014") and Irène Diependaal ("Hanover: A German Dynasty and Its Symbols"), both in *The Court Historian*, 20, 2 (2015).
12 For commercial medallists see, for example, Marjan Scharloo, "Holtzhey and Son", *The Medal* 17 (1990): 23. Emperor Charles VI even established an academy for engravers: Heinrich Kábdebo, *Matthäus Donner und die Geschichte der Wiener Graveur-Akademie in der ersten Periode ihres Bestandes: Nach den Archivs-Acten der K. K. Hofkammer [. . .] dargestellt* (Vienna: Verlag der östereichisch-ungarischen Kunst-Chronik, 1880).
13 Robert Wellington, *Antiquarianism and the Visual Histories of Louis XIV: Artifacts for a Future Past* (Farnham and Burlington: Ashgate, 2015).
14 Maria Theresia Rath, "Kaiser Karl VI. in der Medaille (1685–1740)", (PhD diss., Katholieke Universiteit Leuven, 1980).
15 Philipp Attwood and Felicity Powell, eds, *Medals of Dishonour* (London: British Museum Press, 2009).
16 For Leibniz as historian of the Guelph dynasty, see the anthology Albert Heinekamp, ed., *Leibniz als Geschichtsforscher. Symposion des Istituto di Studi Filosofici Enrico Castelli und der Leibniz-Gesellschaft, Ferrara, 12. bis 15. Juni 1980*, Studia Leibnitiana, Sonderheft 10 (Wiesbaden: Steiner, 1982).

17 The most important publication on the role of history in the process of gaining the electorate is still Armin Reese, *Die Rolle der Historie beim Aufstieg des Welfenhauses 1680–1714* (Hildesheim: August Lax, 1967). A shorter version is provided in Nora Gädeke, "Die Rolle des Historikers. Gottfried Wilhelm Leibniz und der Aufstieg des Welfenhauses", in *Hannover und die englische Thronfolge*, ed. Heide Barmeyer (Bielefeld: Verlag für Regionalgeschichte, 2005), 157–78.

18 Reese, *Die Rolle der Historie*, 49.

19 See the recent chapter on Leibniz and the Italian connection by Matthias Schnettger, "Leibniz' Italienbild und die Bedeutung Italiens für die Geschichte und Politik des Welfenhauses", in *Umwelt und Weltgestaltung. Leibniz' politisches Denken in seiner Zeit*, eds Friedrich Beiderbeck et al. (Göttingen:Vandenhoeck & Ruprecht, 2015).

20 Nora Gädeke, "Leibniz als Gelehrter im höfischen Europa", in *Leibniz und Europa*, eds Albert Heinekamp and Isolde Hein (Hanover: Schlüter, 1994), 39–74, especially 53.

21 See, for example, Leibniz to Duke Ernst August (Hanover, Nov/Dec 1691), in Gottfried Wilhelm Leibniz, *Sämtliche Schriften und Briefe. Erste Reihe: Allgemeiner politischer und historischer Briefwechsel, Vol. 6*, ed. by the Leibniz Archive of the Gottfried Wilhelm Leibniz Library, Lower Saxon State Library Hanover (Berlin: Akademie Verlag, 2006), 58–61, www.gwlb.de/Leibniz/Leibnizarchiv/Veroeffentlichungen/I6A.pdf [accessed 15 June 2017].

22 Gottfried Wilhelm Leibniz, *Scriptores Rerum Brunsvicensium illustrationi inservientes, antiqui omnes et religionis reformatione priores* (Hanover: Förster, 1707–11).

23 Georg Schnath, *Geschichte Hannovers im Zeitalter der neunten Kur und der englischen Sukzession 1674–1714. Vol. IV: Georg Ludwigs Weg auf den englischen Thron. Die Vorgeschichte der Thronfolge 1698–1714* (Hildesheim:Verlag August Lax, 1982), 28. The medal was briefly discussed by Graham C. Gibbs, "Union Hanover/England. Accession to the Throne and Change of Rulers: Determining Factors in the Establishment and Continuation of the Personal Union", in *Die Personalunionen von Sachsen-Polen 1697–1763 und Hannover-England 1714–1837. Ein Vergleich*, ed. Rex Rexheuser, Deutsches Historisches Institut Warschau, Quellen und Studien 18 (Wiesbaden: Harrassowitz, 2005), 248–49.

24 Gottfried Wilhelm Leibniz to Ludolf Hugo, "Concept of a Medal on the Act of Settlement, Hanover, August 1701", in Gottfried Wilhelm Leibniz, *Sämtliche Schriften und Briefe. Erste Reihe: Allgemeiner politischer und historischer Briefwechsel*, vol. 20, ed. Leibniz Archive of the Gottfried Wilhelm Leibniz Library, Lower Saxon State Library Hanover (Berlin: Akademie Verlag, 2006), 24, no 18, www.gwlb.de/Leibniz/Leibnizarchiv/Veroeffentlichungen/I20A.pdf [accessed 16 June 2017].

25 Leibniz to Hugo, in Leibniz, *Sämtliche Schriften* 17, 24–25.

26 Samuel Lambelet, *Gold Medal on the Succession 1701* (Brunswick, 1701).

27 Wolfgang Leschhorn, "Lambelet, Samuel", in *Braunschweigisches Biographisches Lexikon, 8. bis 18. Jahrhundert*, eds Horst-Rüdiger Jarck, et al. (Brunswick: Appelhans Verlag, 2006), 423.

28 Inscription obverse: "SOPHIA · EX· STIRPE · EL: PAL: NEPT: IAC: I ·REG: M · BRIT :VIDVA ·ERN: AVG: EL: BRVNS : ET· L · / ANGLIAE · PRINCEPS ·AD· SVCCESS: NOMINATA· MDCCI ·".

29 Inscription reverse: "MATILDA · FILIA · H · II· R · ANGL:VX: H · LEON: D: BAV: ET· SAX: MATER· OTT: IV. IMP: PRIVS · DVCIS · AQVIT * / H · PAL: RHEN: D · S · WILH: SATORIS · DOMVS ·BRVNS:".

30 Adolphus William Ward, *The Electress Sophia and the Hanoverian Succession*, 2nd edn (London: Longman, Green and Co., 1909), 326; Schnath, *Geschichte Hannovers IV*, 42.

31 John Toland, *An Account of the Courts of Prussia and Hanover; Sent to a Minister of State in Holland* (London: John Darby, 1705), 62–63.

32 Gibbs, "Union Hanover/England", 248, footnote 27.

33 Sebastian Küster, "Medaillen hannoverscher Geschichte – Geschichte hannoverscher Medaillen", in *Ehrgeiz, Luxus & Fortune: Hannovers Weg zu Englands Krone*, ed. Sabine Meschkat-Peters (Hanover: Historisches Museum, 2001), 179–81; for the date, 180.

See the archived auction catalogue of Kuenker for the silver medal, www.kuenker.de/de/archiv/stueck/127269, as well as Kenom: Virtuelles Münzkabinett for the copper version, www.kenom.de/id/record_DE-MUS-163517_kenom_36319.

34 Toland, *An Account*, 62.

35 For a concise overview with the relevant literature see Michael Schaich, "Introduction", in *The Hanoverian Succession: Dynastic Politics and Monarchical Culture*, eds Andreas Gestrich and Michael Schaich (Farnham: Ashgate, 2015), 8–9.

36 Lazarus Gottlieb Lauffer, *King George I and the Church of England* (Nuremberg, 1714).

37 The Latin inscriptions are as follows: "FVNDAMENTVM QVIETIS NOSTRAE" – "ECCLES . ANGL."

38 Lazarus Gottlieb Lauffer, *Queen Anne and the Church of England* (Nuremberg, 1702).

39 William Gibson, *The Church of England 1688–1832: Unity and Accord* (London and New York: Routledge, 2001), 84–86.

40 See especially the works by Andrew Thompson, *Britain, Hanover and the Protestant Interest*; "Early Eighteenth-Century Britain as a Confessional State", in *Cultures of Power in Europe during the Long Eighteenth Century*, eds Hamish M. Scott and Brendan Simms (Cambridge: Cambridge University Press, 2007), 86–109; and "Hanover-Britain and the Protestant Cause, 1714–1760", in *The Hanoverian Succession*, eds Gestrich and Schaich, 89–106.

41 Hannah Smith, "The Idea of a Protestant Monarchy in Britain 1714–1760", *Past & Present* 185 (2004): 95–100.

42 Georg Wilhelm Vestner, *Coronation Medal of King George I* (Nuremberg, 1714).

43 Front: "GEORG LVD . D . G . M . BRIT . FR . ET HIB . REX DVX B & L . S . R . I . ELEC." Back: "FIDEI DEFENSOR ET AEQVI" and "CORONATVS 31 . OCT . MDCCXIIII". The coronation date is given in the new style, probably because the medal was by a German artist.

44 For the origins of the patronage of St George, see Jonathan Good, *The Cult of Saint George in Medieval England* (Woodbridge: Boydell Press, 2009).

45 See a contemporary example of Louis XIV as the Beast in Lionel Laborie, "Millenarian Portraits of Louis XIV", in *Louis XIV Outside In: Images of the Sun King Beyond France, 1661–1715*, eds Tony Claydon and Charles-Édouard Levillain (Farnham: Ashgate, 2015), 217–18.

46 For Jacobite attempts to regain the British throne with French support, see Daniel Szechi, *Britain's Lost Revolution? Jacobite Scotland and French Grand Strategy, 1701–8* (Manchester: Manchester University Press, 2015); John S. Gibson, *Playing the Scottish Card: The Franco-Jacobite Invasion of 1708* (Edinburgh: Edinburgh University Press, 1988); Frank McLynn, *France and the Jacobite Rising of 1745* (Edinburgh: Edinburgh University Press, 1981); and Doron Zimmermann, *The Jacobite Movement in Scotland and in Exile, 1749–1759* (Basingstoke: Palgrave Macmillan, 2003).

47 Smith, *Georgian Monarchy*, 32–37; Stephen Taylor, "Queen Caroline and the Church of England", in *Hanoverian Britain and Empire: Essays in Memory of Philip Lawson*, eds Stephen Taylor et al. (Woodbridge: Boydell Press, 1998).

48 John Croker, *Medal of Crown Princess Wilhelmina Charlotta [Caroline] as Rose* (London, 1718). Front: "WILHELMINA : CHARLOTTA : PRIN * WALLIÆ. Back: ROSA : SINE : SPINA."

49 John Croker, *Official Coronation Medal of Queen Caroline* (London 1727). Front: "CAROLINA D G MAG BR FR ET HIB REGINA". Back: "HIC . AMOR . HAEC . PATRIA . CORON . XI . OCTOB MDCCXXVII".

50 See Anonymous, *An Account of the Ceremonies Observed in the Coronations of the Kings and Queens of England; viz. King James II. and his Royal Consort; King William III. and Queen Mary; Queen Anne; King George I.; and King George II. and Queen Caroline* (London: G. Kearsley, 1760).

51 Andrew Thompson, *George II: King and Elector* (New Haven: Yale University Press, 2011), here, for example, 45–48; Andrew Hanham, "Caroline of Brandenburg-Ansbach and the 'Anglicisation' of the House of Hanover", in *Queenship in Europe, 1660–1815*, ed.

Clarissa Campbell Orr (Cambridge: Cambridge University Press, 2004), 286–87; and Christine Gerrard, "Queens-in-waiting: Caroline of Anspach and Augusta of Saxe-Gotha as Princesses of Wales", in *Queenship in Britain, 1660–1837: Royal Patronage, Court Culture and Dynastic Politics*, ed. Clarissa Campbell Orr (Manchester: Manchester University Press, 2002), 147–48. For Caroline's influence on the arts of the Georgian age, see Joanna Marschner, *Queen Caroline: Cultural Politics at the Eighteenth-Century Court* (New Haven: Yale University Press, 2014).

52 See the thought-provoking study by Harry Thomas Dickinson, *The Politics of the People in Eighteenth-Century Britain* (Basingstoke: Macmillan, 1994), here 165–66.

53 Ehrenreich Hannibal, *Medal on the Proclamation of George* (Brunswick, 1714). For Hannibal, see Rudolf Füssli, *Allgemeines Künstler-Lexicon, oder: Kurze Nachricht von dem Leben und den Werken der Mahler, Bildhauer, Baumeister, Kupferstecher, Kunstgiesser, Stahlschneider, ec.* (Zurich: Heidegger und Compagnie, 1763), 247.

54 "PRINC : OPT : RELIGIONIS ET LIBERTATIS CVSTODI."

55 John Croker, *Official Coronation Medal of King George II in 1727* (London, 1727).

Medals

Croker, John. *Medal of Crown Princess Wilhelmina Charlotta [Caroline] as Rose*. London, 1718. British Museum. M.8206, AN557148001. The Trustees of the British Museum. CC BY-NC-SA 4.0; www.britishmuseum.org/research/collection_online/collection_object_details/collection_image_gallery.aspx?partid=1&assetid=590535001&objectid=950605 [accessed 22 August 2017].

Croker, John. *Official Coronation Medal of King George II in 1727*. London, 1727. Niedersächsisches Landesmuseum Hannover, Kerstin Schmidt, Landesmuseum Hannover, 2014. CC BY-NC 4.0 DE; http://hdl.handle.net/428894.vzg/d5199fb3-4b9b-4e63-81dd-b1d5002fc4bc [accessed 16 July 2017].

Croker, John. *Official Coronation Medal of Queen Caroline in 1727*. London, 1727. Image 8: Bronze medal. Niedersächsisches Landesmuseum Hannover, Kerstin Schmidt, Landesmuseum Hannover, 2014. CC BY-NC 4.0 DE. [see also www.numisantica.com/, CC BY-SA 3.0 nl. Accessed 16 July 2017].

Hannibal, Ehrenreich. *Medal on the Proclamation of George I*. Brunswick, 1714. Niedersächsisches Landesmuseum Hannover, Ursula Bohnhorst, Landesmuseum Hannover, 2010. CC BY-NC 4.0 DE; http://hdl.handle.net/428894.vzg/3b6b438f-ff9e-435e-b821-8ebff-c7bbd12 [accessed 16 July 2017]

Lambelet, Samuel. *Medal on the Succession 1701*. Brunswick, 1701. Silver medal. Niedersächsisches Landesmuseum Hannover, Ursula Bohnhorst, Landesmuseum Hannover, 2013. CC BY-NC 4.0 DE; http://hdl.handle.net/428894.vzg/1d2be4a9-7428-4b1d-90fc-c2972aaa47ee [accessed 16 July 2017].

Lauffer, Lazarus Gottlieb. *King George I and the Church of England*. Nuremberg, 1714: M.8189, AN1612946846. The Trustees of the British Museum. CC BY-NC-SA 4.0; www.britishmuseum.org/research/collection_online/collection_object_details/collection_image_gallery.aspx?assetId=1612946846&objectId=950653&partId=1 [accessed 16 July 2017].

Lauffer, Lazarus Gottlieb: *Queen Anne and the Church of England*. Nuremberg, 1702; www.britishmuseum.org/research/collection_online/collection_object_details/collection_image_gallery.aspx?assetId=1612946802&objectId=950711&partId=1 [accessed 16 July 2017].

Vestner, Georg Wilhelm. *Coronation Medal for King George I [Fidei Defensor]*, Nuremberg, 1714: Niedersächsisches Landesmuseum Hannover, Ursula Bohnhorst, Landesmuseum Hannover, 2013. CC BY-NC 4.0 DE; http://hdl.handle.net/428894.vzg/2238e2f7-b32a-415f-bdfc-00e440df2133 [accessed 16 July 2017].

Bibliography

An Account of the Ceremonies Observed in the Coronations of the Kings and Queens of England; viz. King James II. and his Royal Consort; King William III. and Queen Mary; Queen Anne; King George I.; and King George II. and Queen Caroline. London: G. Kearsley, 1760.

Asch, Ronald G., ed. *Hannover, Großbritannien und Europa: Erfahrungsraum Personalunion 1714–1837.* Göttingen: Wallstein Verlag, 2014.

Aschoff, Hans-Georg. "Die welfischen Territorien und ihre Fürsten zwischen 1636 und 1714". In: *Reif für die Insel – Das Haus Braunschweig-Lüneburg auf dem Weg nach London.* Catalogue for the Lower Saxon State Exhibition "Als die Royals aus Hannover kamen," Bormann-Museum Celle, Residence Museum in the Palace of Celle, 18 May to 5 October 2014. Edited by Jochen Meiners, 49–58. Dresden: Sandstein Verlag, 2014.

Attwood, Philipp, and Felicity Powell, eds. *Medals of Dishonour.* London: British Museum Press, 2009.

Backerra, Charlotte. *Wien und London, 1727–1735. Internationale Beziehungen im frühen 18. Jahrhundert.* Göttingen: Vandenhoeck & Rupprecht, 2018.

Colley, Linda. *Britons: Forging the Nation 1707–1837.* New Haven: Yale University Press, 1992.

Dickinson, Harry Thomas. *The Politics of the People in Eighteenth-Century Britain.* Basingstoke: Macmillan, 1994.

Diependaal, Irène. "Hanover: A German Dynasty and Its Symbols". *Court Historian* 20, 2 (2015): 219–23.

Emich, Birgit. *Territoriale Integration in der Frühen Neuzeit: Ferrara und der Kirchenstaat.* Cologne: Böhlau, 2005.

Füssli, Rudolf: *Allgemeines Künstler-Lexicon, oder: Kurze Nachricht von dem Leben und den Werken der Mahler, Bildhauer, Baumeister, Kupferstecher, Kunstgiesser, Stahlschneider, ec.* Zurich: Heidegger und Compagnie, 1763.

Gädeke, Nora. "Leibniz als Gelehrter im höfischen Europa". In *Leibniz und Europa,* edited by Albert Heinekamp and Isolde Hein, 39–74. Hanover: Schlüter, 1994.

Gädeke, Nora. "Die Rolle des Historikers. Gottfried Wilhelm Leibniz und der Aufstieg des Welfenhauses". In *Hannover und die englische Thronfolge,* edited by Heide Barmeyer, 157–78. Bielefeld: Verlag für Regionalgeschichte, 2005.

Gerrard, Christine. "Queens-in-waiting: Caroline of Anspach and Augusta of Saxe-Gotha as Princesses of Wales". In *Queenship in Britain, 1660–1837: Royal Patronage, Court Culture and Dynastic Politics,* edited by Clarissa Campbell Orr, 143–61. Manchester: Manchester University Press, 2002.

Gibbs, Graham C. "Union Hanover/England. Accession to the Throne and Change of Rulers: Determining Factors in the Establishment and Continuation of the Personal Union". In *Die Personalunionen von Sachsen-Polen 1697–1763 und Hannover-England 1714–1837. Ein Vergleich,* edited by Rex Rexheuser, 248–49. Wiesbaden: Harrassowitz, 2005.

Gibson, John S. *Playing the Scottish Card: The Franco-Jacobite Invasion of 1708.* Edinburgh: Edinburgh University Press, 1988.

Gibson, William. *The Church of England 1688–1832: Unity and Accord.* London and New York: Routledge, 2001.

Good, Jonathan. *The Cult of Saint George in Medieval England.* Woodbridge: Boydell Press, 2009.

Hanham, Andrew. "Caroline of Brandenburg-Ansbach and the 'Anglicisation' of the House of Hanover". In *Queenship in Europe, 1660–1815,* edited by Clarissa Campbell Orr, 276–99. Cambridge: Cambridge University Press.

Heinekamp, Albert, ed. *Leibniz als Geschichtsforscher. Symposion des Istituto di Studi Filosofici Enrico Castelli und der Leibniz-Gesellschaft, Ferrara, 12. bis 15. Juni 1980,* Wiesbaden: Steiner, 1982.

Kábdebo, Heinrich. *Matthäus Donner und die Geschichte der Wiener Graveur-Akademie in der ersten Periode ihres Bestandes: Nach den Archivs-Acten der K. K. Hofkammer [. . .] dargestellt.* Vienna: Verlag der östereichisch-ungarischen Kunst-Chronik, 1880.

Kenom. "Virtuelles Münzkabinett. Medaille, Kupferabschlag, Sukzessionsmedaille, 1701 Kurfürstentum Hannover / Kurhannover Sophia". www.kenom.de/id/record_DE-MUS-163517_kenom_36319 [accessed 9 May 2019].

Kraus, Hans-Christof. *Englische Verfassung und politisches Denken im Ancien Régime, 1689 bis 1789.* Munich: Oldenbourg, 2006.

Kuenker. "Georg I. Ludwig, 1698-1714. Silbermedaille 1701, Brockmann 752". Auction catalogue. www.kuenker.de/de/archiv/stueck/127269 [accessed 9 May 2019].

Küster, Sebastian. "Medaillen hannoverscher Geschichte – Geschichte hannoverscher Medaillen". In *Ehrgeiz, Luxus & Fortune: Hannovers Weg zu Englands Krone*, edited by Sabine Meschkat-Peters, 179–81. Hanover: Historisches Museum, 2001.

Laborie, Lionel. "Millenarian Portraits of Louis XIV". In *Louis XIV Outside In: Images of the Sun King Beyond France, 1661–1715*, edited by Tony Claydon and Charles-Édouard Levillain, 209–28. Farnham: Ashgate, 2015.

Leibniz, Gottfried Wilhelm. *Scriptores Rerum Brunsvicensium illustrationi inservientes, antiqui omnes et religionis reformatione priores.* Hanover: Förster, 1707–1711.

Leibniz, Gottfried Wilhelm. *Sämtliche Schriften und Briefe. Erste Reihe: Allgemeiner politischer und historischer Briefwechsel, Vol. 6*, ed. by the Leibniz Archive of the Gottfried Wilhelm Leibniz Library, Lower Saxon State Library Hanover, 58–61. Berlin: Akademie Verlag, 2006; www.gwlb.de/Leibniz/Leibnizarchiv/Veroeffentlichungen/I6A.pdf [accessed 15 June 2017].

Lembke, Katja, ed. *Hannovers Herrscher auf Englands Thron 1714–1837.* Catalogue for the Lower Saxon State Exhibition "Als die Royals aus Hannover kamen," State Museum of Lower Saxony Hanover and Palace Museum Herrenhausen, 17 May to 5 October 2014. Dresden: Sandstein Verlag, 2014.

Leschhorn, Wolfgang. "Lambelet, Samuel". In *Braunschweigisches Biographisches Lexikon, 8. bis 18. Jahrhundert*, edited by Horst-Rüdiger Jarck et al., 423. Brunswick: Appelhans Verlag, 2006.

Marschner, Joanna. *Queen Caroline: Cultural Politics at the Eighteenth-Century Court.* New Haven: Yale University Press, 2014.

McLynn, Frank. *France and the Jacobite Rising of 1745.* Edinburgh: Edinburgh University Press, 1981.

Murdoch, Tessa. "The Art of the Hanoverians, 1714–2014". *Court Historian* 20, 2 (2015): 225–28.

Press, Volker. "Kurhannover im System des alten Reiches 1692–1803". In *England und Hannover / England and Hanover*, edited by Adolf M. Birke and Kurt Kluxen, 53–79. Munich: K. G. Saur, 1986.

Rath, Maria Theresia. "Kaiser Karl VI. in der Medaille (1685–1740)", PhD diss., Katholieke Universiteit Leuven, 1980.

Reese, Armin. *Die Rolle der Historie beim Aufstieg des Welfenhauses 1680–1714.* Hildesheim: August Lax, 1967.

Reitemeier, Arnd, ed. *Kommunikation und Kulturtransfer im Zeitalter der Personalunion zwischen Großbritannien und Hannover: "to prove that Hanover and England are not entirely synonymous".* Göttingen: Universitätsverlag Göttingen, 2014.

Schaich, Michael. "Introduction". In *The Hanoverian Succession: Dynastic Politics and Monarchical Culture*, edited by Andreas Gestrich and Michael Schaich, 1–22. Farnham: Ashgate, 2015.

Scharloo, Marjan. "Holtzhey and Son". *The Medal* 17 (1990): 16–27.

Schnettger, Matthias. "Leibniz' Italienbild und die Bedeutung Italiens für die Geschichte und Politik des Welfenhauses". In *Umwelt und Weltgestaltung. Leibniz' politisches Denken in seiner Zeit*, edited by Friedrich Beiderbeck, Irene Dingel, and Wenchao Li, 527–50. Göttingen: Vandenhoeck & Ruprecht, 2015.

Simms, Brendan, and Torsten Riotte, eds. *The Hanoverian Dimension in British History, 1714–1837*. Cambridge: Cambridge University Press, 2007.

Smith, Hannah. "The Idea of a Protestant Monarchy in Britain 1714–1760". *Past & Present* 185 (2004): 91–118.

Smith, Hannah. *Georgian Monarchy: Politics and Culture, 1714–1760*. Cambridge: Cambridge University Press, 2006.

Szechi, Daniel. *Britain's Lost Revolution? Jacobite Scotland and French Grand Strategy, 1701–8*. Manchester: Manchester University Press, 2015.

Taylor, Stephen. "Queen Caroline and the Church of England". In *Hanoverian Britain and Empire: Essays in Memory of Philip Lawson*, edited by Stephen Taylor, Richard Connors, and Clyve Jones, 82–101. Woodbridge: Boydell Press, 1998.

Thompson, Andrew. *Britain, Hanover and the Protestant Interest, 1688–1756*. Woodbridge: Boydell Press, 2006.

Thompson, Andrew. "Early Eighteenth-Century Britain as a Confessional State". In *Cultures of Power in Europe during the Long Eighteenth Century*, edited by Hamish M. Scott and Brendan Simms, 86–109. Cambridge: Cambridge University Press, 2007.

Thompson, Andrew. *George II: King and Elector*. New Haven: Yale University Press, 2011.

Thompson, Andrew. "Hanover-Britain and the Protestant Cause, 1714–1760". In *The Hanoverian Succession: Dynastic Politics and Monarchical Culture*, edited by Andreas Gestrich and Michael Schaich, 89–106. Farnham: Ashgate, 2015.

Toland, John. *An Account of the Courts of Prussia and Hanover; Sent to a Minister of State in Holland*. London: John Darby, 1705.

Ward, Adolphus William. *The Electress Sophia and the Hanoverian Succession*, 2nd edn. London: Longman, Green and Co., 1909.

Wellington, Robert. *Antiquarianism and the Visual Histories of Louis XIV: Artifacts for a Future Past*. Farnham and Burlington: Ashgate, 2015.

Woodacre, Ellie, ed. *The History of Monarchy: A Handbook*. London: Routledge, 2019.

Winkler, Karl Tilman. *Wörterkrieg: Politische Debattenkultur in England 1689–1750*. Stuttgart: Franz Steiner, 1998.

Zimmermann, Doron. *The Jacobite Movement in Scotland and in Exile, 1749–1759*. Basingstoke: Palgrave Macmillan, 2003.

7

THE REVERSAL OF DYNASTIES DURING THE BOURBON ERA IN THE KINGDOM OF NAPLES

Cinzia Recca

At the end of 1776, the fall of first minister Bernardo Tanucci from the government of the Kingdom of the Two Sicilies changed an entire era of civilian life in southern Italy and for the Neapolitan branch of the Bourbon dynasty. In terms of international alliances, the Kingdom broke free from its traditionally Spanish orbit, and entered, at least in appearance, into that of the Austrian Habsburg Monarchy. The immediate causes of the changes included the hostility of Queen Maria Carolina, who wanted to get rid of the strong power exercised by Tanucci; the ineptitude of the governing skills of King Ferdinand IV; and the pressures of Viennese diplomacy that sought to recover that part of Italy which Austria had lost earlier in the century.[1]

This virtual "reversal of dynasties" of 1776, as well as the one by which the Bourbons had re-asserted themselves in Italy in the 1730s—first in Parma, then in Naples—are usually overlooked in wider diplomatic studies of the eighteenth century which focus instead on the more well-known "reversal of alliances" of 1756. In that year the expansion of Prussian imperialism and the conquest of Silesia by Frederick II forced Austria to ally with France, to which the Spanish monarchy was already tied by the Bourbon family pact. With this reversal of alliances, the real ground on which the Treaty of Aranjuez (signed 14 June 1752) rested, dynasticism, ceased to exist. Under this treaty, Habsburg Austria and Bourbon Spain, along with the Kingdom of Sardinia, committed themselves to protect Italy against any foreign attack: as long as it did not conflict with the interests of France.[2] After 1756, the new close relations between Vienna and Paris produced momentous consequences borne by the south of Italy, where French interests in the Mediterranean greatly strengthened the claims of both allies, and at the same time weakened the effectiveness of Spanish protection, which were guaranteed only by Tanucci and his close personal relationship with his patron, the king of Naples and Sicily, Charles of Bourbon, who after 1759 reigned as King Charles III of Spain.[3] From his new position in Madrid, the interests of King Charles became the preservation of his southern Italian kingdom for his descendants, notably his second son, the Infant Ferdinand. As an inevitable consequence, the new arrangement of international alliances further weakened the much-needed defence of Neapolitan and Sicilian trade from the intrusiveness of the French government. Therefore, to avoid suffering under the new Vienna–Paris–Madrid axis, political players in Naples decided to make the best of the new situation, and create a direct connection, though still by means of a traditional dynastic method, between the future king of Naples (Ferdinand) and a daughter of the Empress Maria Theresa of Austria.[4] What they did not expect was the strength with which this Austrian princess, Maria Carolina, would achieve this goal through the force of her own individual personality, an echo of a similar push by another Bourbon consort, Elizabeth Farnese, in determining the fate of the Kingdom of Naples in a previous generation. This chapter intends to demonstrate how the balance of power and alliances changed within the Neapolitan branch of the House of Bourbon over the course of the eighteenth century, and in particular how the political and diplomatic role of two queens, Elizabeth Farnese and Maria Carolina of Austria, was effective in the acquisition, legitimisation, or maintenance of their Bourbon son's or husband's rule in the Kingdom of Naples.

Charles of Bourbon, Elizabeth Farnese, and a dynastic return to Italy

We usually consider Charles the first king of Naples of the Bourbon dynasty, and in fact he was definitely the great restorer of the Kingdom's independence, after two centuries of dominance by Spain.[5] But in reality, the first ruler of the new dynasty to reign in the south of Italy was Charles's father Philip V, who became king of Naples and Sicily when he ascended the thrones of Spain in 1700.[6] On his deathbed, Charles II, the last monarch of the previous dynasty—the Habsburgs—had settled the entire Spanish inheritance on Philip, duke of Anjou, second-eldest grandson of King Louis XIV of France. With Philip ruling in Spain, and the anticipation of his elder brother (Louis, duke of Burgundy) succeeding their grandfather eventually in France, the Bourbon dynasty would be able to secure great advantages, though some statesmen regarded a dominant House of Bourbon as a threat to European stability, jeopardising the balance of power. This fear was realised in the subsequent long and bloody War of the Spanish Succession (1701–14).[7] During the course of that war, Philip, though eventually the winner of the dynastic contest and the actual ruler of Spain, lost Spain's hold over Naples and Sicily in favour of the Austrian Habsburgs, whose aims of establishing a Mediterranean empire were thereby secured.

Nevertheless, the Italian territories would remain a major concern for the Bourbon dynasty. Philip V had struggled to keep them during the war, but by 1707 they were effectively lost, and the consequent peace treaty signed at Utrecht in April 1713 obliged him to relinquish his claims to his enemy, Charles of Austria.

Nevertheless, King Philip was not resigned to this loss, and the recovery of the Italian territories became one of his main political objectives. Furthermore, the King's new wife (since 1714), Elizabeth Farnese, played a key role in achieving this goal. Her position and actions are crucial for understanding the political history of the Spanish monarchy as a whole during the first part of the eighteenth century.[8] A clear portrait of her character emerges from the following quotation:

> Lady, of a mortal name,
> Lady who does not ignore anything;
> And although a Mother, and thus a Lady,
> She is a Manly Queen,
> I do not adulate, nor do I astonish you at seeing
> So foreign a Heroine
> And if passion does not deceive me in this scene there are only two,
> the Empress in Vienna, the Queen Mother in Spain.[9]

Elizabeth Farnese was the second wife of Philip V, and he could not have had a more faithful spouse.[10] The King was in fact a man who could not stay alone and lacked strength of character.[11] As queen, Elizabeth never left her husband's side, not only out of devotion but also because it was a way to get information to influence the monarch and to control the people that surrounded him. Giulio Alberoni described the Queen in a letter to the duke of Parma: "I know her Majesty to be tenacious in her affections and extremely wily and capable of profiting by a good opportunity and fooling her husband, of whom she is absolute mistress, without his entertaining the slightest suspicion."[12] In Spain the advent of the Bourbons had changed the system of Burgundian ceremonial historically employed by the House of Austria, which had decreed that the king and queen should live separately. Under the new regime of Philip V, the royal couple always stayed together, both in private life and in public life. Elizabeth Farnese went further and emerged as a more equal partner, fully sharing power with her husband the King.[13] She became a powerful queen and an adoring mother.[14] She gave Philip three sons, Charles, Philip, and Louis, and three daughters. Her political determination was marked by the strong will to place all of their children upon sovereign thrones. Of course, regarding the most important throne, that of Spain, there was continual tension because the King's eldest son and heir, Ferdinand, was his son by his first marriage. Therefore Elizabeth, who was only Ferdinand's step-mother, concentrated on the recovery of Naples and the duchies of Parma and Piacenza for her own sons. At the time of her marriage in 1714, it was already assumed that she would be the heir to these duchies upon the deaths of her childless Farnese uncles, Francesco and Antonio, which in the event came to pass when the latter died in 1731.[15] This position gave her a certain leverage as a potential sovereign in her own right. If as consort she had to be a loving and respectful spouse (and indications are that she was), as Queen she had to mediate between the King and his subjects, and bring him closer to them. An intelligent woman with very clear ideas, she personified the

As a mark of this continued family unity, shortly after the start of the War of Austrian Succession, in 1742 Charles sent troops north to Lombardy to the aid of his French and Spanish cousins. But when a British fleet appeared in the Bay of Naples and threatened to bomb the city, Charles decided to withdraw his forces, provoking the ire of Paris and Madrid. Nevertheless, in 1744, when he defeated an Austrian army completely in Velletri, thinking finally to end forever Habsburg claims over Naples, he also effectively freed himself from the tutelage of Madrid. With this victory, Charles began to be truly the king of independent realms in Naples and Sicily. This became even clearer in 1746, with the death of Philip V of Spain and the sidelining of his queen, Elizabeth Farnese, and her Italian ambitions. One aspect of these ambitions remained, however, in the pushing forward of another of her sons, Philip, to retake the Farnese inheritance in Parma and Piacenza, lost to the Habsburgs in the previous decade, as part of the treaty ending the War of Austrian Succession at Aix-la-Chapelle in 1748. In fact, on 29 July 1746, the Queen sent a letter to Louis XV in which she expressed her intention to follow the policy of her late husband in the Italian territories, demonstrating her willingness to make sacrifices for her two sons Charles and Philip: "what I care about is to ensure the kingdom of Naples and to place Philip in the duchies of Parma and Piacenza".[27] Thus Philip began yet another branch of the House of Bourbon in Italy: Bourbon-Parma (which persists to this day). Meanwhile, in Naples, Charles started to become a real Neapolitan monarch, fully in tune with his people and their needs. As the years passed, he eliminated the influence of his ministers, becoming a true sovereign and the real architect of his policy, concentrating power in his own hands.[28]

From viceroyalty to kingdom, the constitution of the monarchy of the Two Sicilies in the hands of Charles of Bourbon created the largest and most influential state of the entire Italian peninsula. On his arrival, the new sovereign was asked to come up with an effective policy for promoting the arts and building industries to make the new capital of the Kingdom of the Two Sicilies a renowned and respected court.[29] The crucial consequence in terms of space of this significant institutional change was evident. Naples became the largest royal capital of Italy and, consequently, developed a splendid court. This task of transformation was to be carried out by a young prince who, by experience, formation, and dynasty, had been exposed directly to four court cultures (the Spanish, the French, the Parmesan, and the Florentine) with different ways of perceiving and relating to the territory. Charles as duke of Parma and Piacenza and as heir of the grand duchy of Tuscany could appreciate the Parmesan and the Florentine cultures in particular, thanks to his mother Elisabeth, the heiress of the dynastic rights of the Farnese and the Medici, as he already had first-hand experience of them, between 1731 and 1734, during his first stay in Italy. Charles was to be an Italian Bourbon, a new breed of the ancient dynasty.

But on 10 August 1759, the king of Spain, Ferdinand VI, died without an heir, so according to the Treaty of Aix-la-Chapelle (1748) which established in a particular clause the system of succession, King Charles was called to Madrid to occupy the throne of Spain.[30] On 11 September 1759, Charles officially became king of Spain (as Charles III). On 3 October, the minister Tanucci, the Austrian ambassador, Count

Ludwig von Neipperg, and the duke of Parma signed a treaty that definitively sanctioned the irreversible process of the division of the Italian branch of the House of Bourbon into two sub-branches, Naples and Parma. Moreover it assured the succession to the throne of Naples and Sicily for Charles' third son, Ferdinand, in exchange for the assignment of the "Stato dei Presidi" (five garrison towns on the Tuscan coast) to Tuscany. In this way Charles assured the young sovereign in Naples the protection of another great power, Austria.[31] Finally, by virtue of another Bourbon family pact, the "Ordinance of Charles III of Spain regarding the cession of the of the Kingdom of Naples and Sicily to the third-born Ferdinando", it was determined that the two crowns—those of Spain and the Two Sicilies—would never be united.[32]

Nevertheless, all links were not entirely severed. At the time of the agreement, Ferdinand was only eight, so the regency in Naples was entrusted to eight ministers, among whom were Charles' now long-time faithful servant Tanucci, who served as Prime Minister and Foreign Minister, but always under the control of Charles from Madrid.[33] But as Ferdinand matured, this bond came to be seen more as shackles, and the last years of Charles III's life was characterised by a bitter discord with his son in Naples, and in particular with his son's wife, Queen Maria Carolina, daughter of Empress Maria Theresa of Austria, who was determined to break Spanish influence in Neapolitan affairs.[34] Indeed, the House of Austria's interests in southern Italy had not completely faded.

Maria Carolina and the re-Habsburgisation of southern Italy

For a long time the motto of the dynasty was *Bella gerant alii, tu felix Austria nube!* ("where others wage war, happy Austria, you marry!"), and we see in the career of Maria Carolina yet another example of the House of Austria's successful diplomatic marriage policy.[35] After her father's loss of Naples and Sicily in the 1730s, Empress Maria Theresa saw marriage as a typically Habsburg means to get back to a position of influence in southern Europe. During the minority of King Ferdinand, following years of bargaining between Madrid and Vienna, King Charles III agreed to let his son marry Maria Theresa's daughter, Johanna Gabriela, who promptly died of smallpox before the wedding could take place. The second choice was Maria Josepha, who was packed and ready to go when she, too, became ill and died. A third daughter, Maria Carolina, was swiftly designated to replace her. The marriage contract was very complicated, because the issue at stake was ultimately the control of the Italian territories over which the Habsburg and Bourbon dynasties had contended for much of the century.[36] Crucially, the contract implicitly sanctioned a return of Naples to Austrian influence via a clause which stipulated that Maria Carolina, after giving birth to her first male heir, would obtain the right to participate in the Council of State. This extraordinary clause implied that even if the future queen would not control the government—such a future is unlikely to have been envisioned—there would at least be a strong balancing force between the desires of the houses of Bourbon and Habsburg.[37]

The marriage took place by proxy in 1768 in Vienna. Although Maria Carolina was just sixteen when she was married to Ferdinand IV, at the Viennese court she had already learned the art of ruling that she would later exercise in Naples. There are several relevant sources regarding Maria Carolina's education, such as the correspondence with her mother,[38] and in particular the memorandum written by the Empress, *Informations secrètes de l'imperatrice Marie Thérèse pour Mme l'archiduchesse Caroline à l'occasion de son mariage avec Ferdinand roi de Naples.*[39] The guidance written by Wenzel Anton von Kaunitz-Rietberg is another significant piece of advice which forged the political formation of the young Queen. Kaunitz's reminder was intended to encourage her to deal with state affairs because, as he wrote, it was her duty as well as her right to deal with state matters along with affairs of economic and foreign policy.[40] Moreover, another important mentor for the art of ruling for Maria Carolina was no doubt her brother Grand Duke Leopold (known as Pietro Leopoldo in Italian) of Tuscany, as demonstrated by their numerous epistolary exchanges.[41] So Maria Carolina, charming, intelligent, and exuberant, was now sent to live with a king as young as she was but noticeably culturally inferior.

Ferdinand IV, in fact, did not speak German and barely knew Italian. He was known as the "Naughty King", a man who enjoyed the streets and who spoke with the masses in their Neapolitan dialect. Described by various sources as distracted, a bit naive, and lazy, Ferdinand had been instructed by the Prince of San Nicandro, Domenico Cattaneo, who had been in charge of the political and social preparation of the King, but preferred instead to instruct him to hunt and fish and encouraged rustic and vulgar behaviour.[42] The young king spent many hours each day hunting, socialising with fishermen and soldiers, neglecting his studies, and becoming, with the passing of time, increasingly rude and uncivilised and, most pointedly, disinterested in the government of the Kingdom. A recurring phrase in the letters of King Ferdinand to his father is: "I enjoy myself as best I can."[43]

Therefore, not having been appropriately prepared for the role he had to fulfil, Ferdinand IV rarely participated in any activities of his government, which remained instead in the hands of Minister Tanucci, and thus still under the influence of Charles III in Madrid. On 12 January 1767, when Ferdinand reached his majority, he gave his royal seal to Tanucci to spare himself the effort of signing executive orders, preferring other more enjoyable commitments. His innate disposition to have fun at the expense of anything serious became the typical image of his rule.[44] Nevertheless, despite his lack of learning, Ferdinand did have the sense to hold in high esteem people who knew how to distinguish themselves among others for their intelligence and their cultivation. After his marriage to Maria Carolina, he therefore delegated a share of the government to his wife. Maria Carolina was soon able to dominate the weak personality of her husband, and thereby gained significant influence in the politics of the Kingdom.[45]

Maria Carolina, aware of her strong influence on her husband, was convinced she had to bend him to her will and pleasure, so the only way to emancipate her Kingdom from Spanish influence was to eliminate Tanucci from the political scene. The Queen did not have much esteem for the minister; in fact, she considered him an intrusive and troublesome presence.[46] She described Tanucci as "loyal to his King and master Charles III, and servant of the court of Madrid, to whom he reported all the acts of the Neapolitan government".[47] On the other hand, Tanucci himself perceived that the court of Vienna relied on Maria Carolina to reorganise the Kingdom of Naples in Austria's favour: "there is so much Austricism which is going to spread out and to change the ancient rituals of the Court",[48] and "the Queen aims to interfere in the affairs of Government".[49] The Queen did indeed interfere, slowly changing several members of the court in her favour, such as her personal confessor, the gentlemen of the Chamber of the King, and her ladies-in-waiting, and ultimately influenced the fate of Tanucci himself.

Thanks to the clause that Maria Theresa—as we have seen—had included in the marriage contract, when Maria Carolina had her first son (in January 1775), she gained access to the State Council, thereby familiarising herself with power and opening the way for her reign as virtual regent, despite the fact that her husband, the sovereign, was alive and well. At this point Tanucci could not prevent the rising power of Queen Maria Carolina, and from that moment his fate was sealed: after forty-two years of service to the Crown and the Bourbon dynasty, Naples' most senior minister was sacked.[50]

But Ferdinand was not completely passive in this affair. Since 1775, his relationship with his spouse had been difficult, and Ferdinand confided this to his father, asking what he should do. There are some rather pathetic letters that divulge these confidences, and others where Charles III himself complains that his son listens too often to his wife's advice rather than to his father's. In a letter dated 28 May 1776 Ferdinand wrote to his father about Minister Tanucci:

> I would have placed the man on the list of those worth nominating, but my wife did not want him at all, and to live in peace and to not hear negative words I had to agree, but for God's sake do not mention anything in response to what I write because I will have even greater displeasure.[51]

So King Ferdinand had made the decision to avoid the pressures from his wife rather than reacting, concerned primarily about the tranquillity of his family and his leisure activities. He informed his father of his decision (persuaded, no less, by his wife) to dismiss Tanucci, and afterwards pretended that he had received consent which was never in fact given by Charles III.[52]

In removing Tanucci from the government of Naples, the Queen could rely on rising discontent in the Kingdom—Tanucci's reforms had caused displeasure, particularly among the conservative, feudal nobility—as well as the support of Freemasonry, for whom, unlike her husband, Maria Carolina showed open sympathy. Indeed, Maria Carolina had leaned immediately towards Freemasonry, forming a strong party opposed to Tanucci.[53] Enmities that Tanucci had accumulated during his long period of domination fuelled a strong opposition group which did not accept the government's close ties with Madrid. Maria Carolina's interest in the Freemasons was also linked to her desire to replace the influence of Charles III and Spain with the Austrian influence of her brothers, the Emperor Joseph II and Grand Duke Leopold of Tuscany (the future Leopold II), both themselves supporters of the Masonic movement.[54] From the exchange of letters between Maria Carolina and her brothers we see that they continued to help maintain caring familial relationships and that they sought both confirmation of her belonging to the House of Habsburg as well as alliances to continue the policy of marriage strategies undertaken by their mother, whose ultimate goal was to "allocate" the Habsburgs in all the major European courts and protect the interests of the House of Austria on the European scene.[55]

After Tanucci's removal, the long personal government of Maria Carolina began. The Queen's Masonic project took wing on a national basis that would become the source of the reform movements of the 1780s.[56] But Maria Carolina also had the idea of making Naples a springboard to facilitate the Habsburg Monarchy's domination of the Mediterranean. The advent of a Habsburg queen, for the Neapolitans, was almost a change of dynasty. It would be a Habsburg regime in Bourbon clothing. Maria Carolina, despite being so deeply Austrian, nevertheless tried to become a very credible Neapolitan patriot, publicly espousing the need to focus on national independence and the desire to escape from heavy foreign economic influences. In reality, the Kingdom of Naples continued to be contended between the Bourbons and the Habsburgs for the rest of the century.

In comparison, both queens—Elizabeth Farnese and Maria Carolina of Austria— in spite of their controversial and debated characters and actions, were female rulers who embodied powerful models of queenship. Even if they grew up in and belonged to two different dynasties, they had in common their strong capacity for achieving the goals of the most successful consorts, in maintaining and securing their kingdoms for their descendants. With the advent of the Habsburg queen-consort at the head of the government of Naples from 1775, we see a clear attempt to return to the previous status quo, with a Habsburg seated on the Neapolitan throne as one had been since 1516.

Notes

1 Roberto Tufano, "'Le renversement des alliances' europee e l'espulsione di Bernardo Tanucci dal governo delle Sicilie", *Frontiera d'Europa* no 2 (2003): 87–178; *idem*, *La Francia e le Sicilie. Stato e disgregazione sociale nel Mezzogiorno d'Italia da Luigi XIV alla Rivoluzione* (Naples: Arte tipografica, 2009), 40–46.

2 Rohan Butler, "The Secret Compact of 1753 between the Kings of France and Naples", in *Royal and Republican Sovereignty in Early Modern Europe*, eds Robert Oresko, G. C. Gibbs, and H. M. Scott (Cambridge: Cambridge University Press, 1997), 551–54.

3 Leopold Auer considers this international conjunction as essential for understanding the marriage strategies of the Bourbons of Spain and Naples: "Tanucci e le relazioni diplomatiche tra Austria e il Regno di Napoli", in *Bernardo Tanucci. Statista, letterato, giurista*, eds Raffaele Ajello and Mario D'Addio, Vol. I (Naples: Jovene, 1986), 241–58. See also Bernardo Tanucci, *Epistolario*, ed. Lamberto Del Bianco, Vol. IV (Rome: Edizioni di Storia e Letteratura, 1984), LXXVI–LXXVII.

4 Auer, "Tanucci e le relazioni diplomatiche", 243.

5 For details regarding the regnal number of King Charles (Charles VII of Naples and Charles V of Sicily), see Giuseppe Senatore, *Giornale storico di quanto avvenne ne' due reami di Napoli e di Sicilia l'anno 1734 e 1735* (Naples: Stamperia Blasiana, 1742).

6 In this regard, see the study of Pablo Vázquez Gestal, *Una nueva Majestad: Felipe V, Isabel de Farnesio y la identidad de la monarquía (1700–1729)* (Madrid: Marcial Pons, 2013), 97–166.
7 Marquis de Saint-Philippe [Vicente Bacallar y Sanna, marques de San Felipe], *Mémoires pour servir à l'histoire d'Espagne sous le règne de Philippe V,* trans. Maudave (Paris, 1756).
8 Charles C. Noel, "'Bárbara succeeds Elizabeth . . .': The Feminisation and Domestication of Politics in the Spanish Monarchy, 1701–1759", in *Queenship in Europe 1660–1815: The Role of the Consort*, ed. Clarissa Campbell Orr (Cambridge: Cambridge University Press, 2004), 161–65; Giulio Sodano and Giulio Brevetti, *Io la regina. Maria Carolina d'Asburgo-Lorena tra politica, fede, arte e cultura* (Palermo: Quaderni di Mediterranea, 2016), 21–22.
9 "Señora, de un mortal Nombre, señora que nada ignora; Y aunque Madre, y tan señora, es una Reyna muy Hombre; no adulo, no:ni hos asombre Heroyna ver tan extraña: y si la pasìon no engaña, solo ay dos en esta Scena, la Emperatriz en Viena, la Reyna Madre en España", Francisco Bengasi, *Décima de Francisco Bengasi en alabanza de la Reynna Madre, D. Ysabel de Farnesio*, quoted in Vázquez Gestal, *Una Nueva Majestad*, 169.
10 Since the twentieth century and more specifically during the last decade, the biographies of Luciano de Taxonera, Mirella Mafrici, Teresa Lavalle Cobo and Maria Ángeles Pérez-Samper have demonstrated how initiatives promoted by Queen Elizabeth Farnese had a key role in developing the political, social, and cultural scene of Spain in the first half of the eighteenth century. See Luciano de Taxonera, *Isabel de Farnesio* (Barcelona: Juventud, 1943); Mirella Mafrici, *Fascino e Potere di una Regina, Elisabetta Farnese sulla scena europea (1715–1759)* (Cava de'Tirreni: Avagliano, 1999); Teresa Lavalle Cobo, *Isabel de Farnesio. La reina coleccionista* (Madrid: Fundación Caja-Madrid, 2002); Maria Ángeles Pérez-Samper, *Isabel de Farnesio* (Barcelona: Plaza Janés, 2003). More recently, a new biographical study on her was edited by Gigliola Fragnito: *Elisabetta Farnese: principessa di Parma e regina di Napoli* (Rome: Viella, 2011).
11 On the kingship of Philip V, see Pedro Molas Ribalta, Rafael Cerro Nargánez, and Maria Adela Fargas Peñarrocha, *Bibliografia de Felipe V* (Madrid: Sociedad Estatal de Conmemoraciones Culturales, 2004). After the death of his son, King Philip was affected by depression, and Spain entered a period of rule characterised by his lack of government. See Henry Kamen, *Philip V of Spain: The King Who Ruled Twice* (New Haven/London: Yale University Press, 2001); Ricardo García Cárcel, *Felipe y los Españoles* (Barcelona: Debolsillo, 2003), 161–62; and Vázquez Gestal, *Una Nueva Majestad*, 105–11; and more recently, Christopher Storrs, *The Spanish Resurgence, 1713–1748* (New Haven: Yale University Press, 2016), 182–209.
12 Regarding the details of Elisabeth's marriage and her five-year virtual reign, the correspondence of Giulio Alberoni with the duke of Parma remains a source of extreme importance. This quote is from the Archivio di Stato di Napoli, *Carteggio Farnesiano*, 58, 24 March 1715, cited in Edward Armstrong, *Elisabeth Farnese: The Termagant of Spain* (London and New York: Longman and Green, 1892), 44.
13 Evidence for the deep levels of collaboration of the royal couple can be found in Louis de Rouvroy, duc de Saint-Simon, *Papiers inédits. Lettres et dépêches sur l'Ambassade d'Espagne. Tableau de la cour d'Espagne en 1721* (Paris: A. Quantin, 1880), 363–73.
14 Pérez-Samper, *Isabel de Farnesio*, 97–156; Vázquez Gestal, *Una nueva Majestad,* 170.
15 María Victoria López-Cordón Cortezo, "Elisabetta Farnese e il governo della Spagna", in *Elisabetta Farnese*, ed. Fragnito, 138–62.
16 See in this regard, George Moore, *Lives of Cardinal Alberoni, the Duke of Ripperda and Marquis of Pombal* (London: R. Faulder, 1806); Alfonso Professioni, *Il Ministerio in Spagna e il Proseco del cardinale Giulio Alberoni* (Turin: Giulio Gaspari, 1897); Pietro Castagnoli, *Il Cardenale Giulio Alberoni*, 3 vols (Piacenza: Collegio Alberoni, 1929–1932); Simon Harcourt-Smith, *Alberoni or the Spanish Conspiracy* (London: Faber and Faber, 1943); *idem, Cardinal of Spain: The Life and Strange Career of Giulio Alberoni* (New York: Knopf, 1955); Pablo Vázquez Gestal, "Giulio Alberoni", in *Diccionario Biográfico Español*, eds Aguirre de Viani and Allendesalazar y Muñoz de Salazar (Madrid: Real Academia de la Historia, 2009), 267–72.
17 Archivio di Stato di Napoli, *Carteggio Farnesiano*, 58, 23 June 1715, quoted in Armstrong, *Elisabeth Farnese*, 44.

18 William Coxe, *L'Espagne sous les rois de la maison de Bourbon: ou Mémoires relatifs à l'histoire de cette Nation*, Vol. 2 (Paris: Libraires du Roi, 1827), 252. "Je voyais l'abbé, qui est un personnage très puissant, parce qu'il exerce une influence illimitée sur la Reine et donc sur le Roi, qui n'aime pas les affaires et se laisse mener par sa femme: Je dois ajouter que je ne vois ici aucun parti qui puisse lui resister." (my translation).

19 See Adrian J. Pearce, *The Origin of Bourbon Reform in South America, 1700–1763* (New York: Palgrave Macmillan, 2014), 43–62; Storrs, *The Spanish Resurgence*, 209–15.

20 Noel, "'Bárbara succeeds Elizabeth . . .,' in Campbell Orr, *Queenship in Europe*, 162–64.

21 Pérez-Samper, *Isabel de Farnesio*, 111.

22 On these events, see Emilio Casa, "Memorie storiche di Parma dalla morte del duca Antonio Farnese alla dominazione dei Borbone di Francia (1731–1749)", *Archivio storico per le provincie parmensi* (1893): 1–145; George Hilton Jones, "La Gran Bretagna, la Toscana e la fine della questione della successione al trono granducale (1732–1737)", *Archivio storico toscano* 140 (1982): 443–87; *idem*, *Great Britain and the Tuscan Succession Question, 1710–1737* (New York: Vantage, 1998); Michelangelo Schipa, *Il Regno di Napoli al tempo di Carlo di Borbone* (Milan, Rome, and Naples: Dante Alighieri, 1923); Giuseppe Coniglio, *I Borboni di Napoli* (Milan: Corbaccio, 1995).

23 On King Charles and his Neapolitan kingship, see Schipa, *Il Regno di Naples al tempo di Carlo di Borbone*; Raffaele Ajello, "La vita politica napoletana sotto Carlo di Borbone. «La fondazione ed il tempo eroico» della dinastia", in *Storia di Napoli*, ed. Luigi La Bruna, Vol. VII (Naples: Edizioni Scientifiche Italiane, 1972), 461–717; *idem.*, "Carlo di Borbone", *Dizionario Biografico degli italiani*, Vol. 20 (1977): 961–84; Mirella Mafrici, *Il Re delle speranze: Carlo di Borbone da Madrid a Napoli* (Naples: Edizioni Scientifiche Italiane, 1998); Giuseppe Caridi, *Essere re e non essere re. Carlo di Borbone a Napoli e le attese deluse (1734–1738)* (Soveria Mannelli: Rubettino, 2006); Giuseppe Galasso, *Il regno di Napoli. Il Mezzogiorno Borbonico e Napoleonico* (Turin: Utet, 2007), 3–258.

24 See Pablo Vázquez Gestal, "'The System of this Court': Elizabeth Farnese, the Count of Santiesteban and the Monarchy of the Two Sicilies, 1734–1738", *Court Historian*, 14, 1 (2009), 38–42.

25 On the official entry into Palermo of King Charles and his coronation, see Pietro La Placa, *La reggia in trionfo per l'acclamazione e coronazione della Sacra Real maestà di Carlo, infante di Spagna* (Palermo: Antonio Epiro, 1736), 202–34; Senatore, *Giornale storico*; and Francesco Ceva Grimaldi, *Della città di Napoli dal tempo della sua fondazione fino al presente* (Naples: Stamperia e calcografia Vico Freddo Pignasecca 15, 1857), 721. "Two Sicilies" referred to the fact that in the Middle Ages, the rulers of mainland kingdom (Naples) refused to renounce the title "king of Sicily" after they had been driven off the island. See Tommaso Astarita, *Between Salt Water and Holy Water: A History of Southern Italy* (New York and London: W.W. Norton, 2005), 60, 264–65.

26 Galasso, *Il regno di Napoli. Il Mezzogiorno Borbonico e Napoleonico*, 71–79.

27 Pérez-Samper, *Isabel de Farnesio*, 414.

28 Ibid., 89–126.

29 Pablo Vázquez Gestal, "Los espacios de una nueva majestad. Carlos de Borbón y los Sitios Reales de la monarquía de las Dos Sicilias (1734–1759)", in *Una corte para el rey. Carlos III y los Sitios Reale*, eds José Luis Sancho Gaspar and Javier Ortega Vidal (Madrid: Comunidad de Madrid, 2016), 52–63.

30 See on this issue, Article 7 of the peace treaty signed 30 April 1748 concerning the succession rights of Philip of Parma to the dominions of his brother Charles. This was followed by the crucial Treaty of Versailles, 1 May 1757, between Austria and France in which was established the renunciation of Philip of Parma of any claims on the succession to Naples and, in Article 25, a specific confirmation of the succession of Charles's posterity as long as he renounced in turn any claim on the Medici and Farnese personal properties. In addition, on 30 December 1758, with the last Treaty of Versailles, it was also established that Maria Theresa renounced in favour of Philip of Bourbon the right of reversion of the duchy of Parma and confirmed the succession rights of Charles. Anna Maria Rao, *Il regno di Napoli nel Settecento* (Naples: Guida, 1983), 91–93; Galasso, *Il regno di Napoli. Il Mezzogiorno Borbonico e Napoleonico*, 225–58.

31 Michelangelo Schipa, *Nel Regno di Ferdinando IV di Borbone* (Florence: Vallecchi, 1938), 99–101.
32 The renunciation and cession by Charles of the Kingdom of the Two Sicilies and all further rights and titles to the estates and Italian properties in favour of his third-born son, Ferdinand, was established through an ordinance by King Charles, Ferdinand, and a regency council composed of Domenico Cattanico, Michele Reggio, Giuseppe Pappacoda, Pietro Bologna, Domenico Di Sangro, and Bernardo Tanucci. The ordinance was issued on 6 October 1759, which delineated specifically the line of succession in case of death, which was to follow the direct male line to infinity, but also stated that the order of succession could never bring about the union of the Spanish Crown with the Italian dominions. Österreichisches Staatsarchiv [henceforth ÖSt], Obersthofmeisteramt, Altere Zeremonialakten, Karton 80, 4, fols 49r–51v, "Ordinazione di Carlo III di Spagna riguardante la cessione del Regno di Napoli e Sicilia al terzogenito Ferdinando". The eldest son of Charles III, the Infante Felipe (1747–77), was excluded from the succession due to imbecility, so the crown of Spain was reserved for the second son, Infante Carlos, and Naples for the third.
33 On Bernardo Tanucci's ministry, see Enrica Viviani della Robbia, *Bernardo Tanucci ed il suo più importante carteggio* (Florence: Bibliografia, 1942); Raffaele Ajello and Mario D'Addio, "Bernardo Tanucci. Statista, letterato, giurista" (paper presented at "Convegno internazionale di studi per il secondo centenario, 1783–1983", Naples, 28–30 April 1986); Tufano, *La Francia e le Sicilie*, 165–60; *idem*, *Verso la giustizia produttiva. Un'esperienza di riforme nelle due Sicilie (1738–1746)* (Naples: Istituto Italiano per gli Studi Filosofici, 2015); Rosa Pia Onnis, "Bernardo Tanucci nel moto anticurialista del 700", *Nuova rivista storica* no 10 (1926): 328–65.
34 Tufano, *La Francia e le Sicilie*, 333–35; Cinzia Recca, *The Diary of Queen Maria Carolina of Naples 1781–1785: New Evidence of Queenship at Court* (New York: Palgrave Macmillan, 2016), 5–6.
35 Regarding the biographies and studies dedicated to Queen Maria Carolina, the following are particularly important: Alexander Freiherr von Helfert, *Königin Karolina von Neapel und Sizilien im Kample gegen die franzosische Weltherrschaft 1790–1814* (Vienna: Braumüller, 1878); *idem.*, *Maria Karolina von Österreich: Königin von Neapel und Sizilien* (Vienna: G. P. Faesy, 1884); André Bonnefons, *Une ennemie de la Révolution et de Napoléon. Marie Caroline reine des Deux-Siciles (1768–1814)* (Paris: Perrin, 1905); Mary Charlotte Bearne, *A Sister of Marie Antoinette: The Life-Story of Maria Carolina, Queen of Naples* (London: T. Fisher Unwin, 1907); Amalia Bordiga Amadei, *Maria Carolina d'Austria e il Regno delle Due Sicilie* (Naples: Cooperativa Editrice Libraria, 1920); Egon Caesar Corti, *Ich, eine Maria Theresias Tochter: Ein Lebensbild der Königin Marie Karoline von Neapel* (Munich: Bruckmann, 1950); Raffaele Ajello, "I filosofi e la regina. Il governo delle Due Sicilie da Tanucci a Caracciolo (1776–1886)", *Rivista Storica italiana* CIII, 3 (1991): 398–425; Giuseppe Astuto, "Dalle riforme alle rivoluzioni. Maria Carolina d'Asburgo: una regina austriaca nel Regno di Napoli e di Sicilia", in *Quaderni del dipartimento di studi politici*, eds Salvatore Aleo and Giuseppe Barone, vol. 1 (Milan: Giuffrè, 2007), 27–51; Friederike Hausmann, *Herrscherin im Paradies der Teufel: Maria Carolina Königin von Neapel. Eine Biographie* (Munich: Beck, 2014). More recently the image of this queen has been brought up to date by new studies analysing unpublished sources. See Recca, *The Diary of Queen Maria Carolina of Naples*; and Sodano and Brevetti, *Io la regina. Maria Carolina d'Asburgo-Lorena tra politica, fede, arte e cultura.*
36 On the marriage negotiation, see Corti, *Ich, eine Maria Theresias Tochter*, 108–09.
37 In a letter of Maria Theresa to Ferdinand IV, dated 8 December 1768, the Empress emphasises the importance of a union of lineages. ÖSt, Ministerium des k. k. Hauses Hausarchiv, Vermahlungen, Karton 14, 1r, fols 12r–12v.
38 This correspondence is in French and was published for the first time in 1881 by the Austrian historian and politician Alfred von Arneth: *Briefe der Kaiserin Maria Theresia an ihre Kinder und Freunde*, 4 vols (Vienna: Wilhelm Braumüller, 1881), vol. III, 27–64.
39 The memorandum has been partially published by Corti, *Ich, eine Maria Theresias Tochter*, 32; there is also a complete Italian version edited by Arsenio Frugoni, *Consigli matrimoniali alle figlie sovrane, di Maria Teresa d'Austria* (Florence: Passigli Editori, 2000), 37–78.

40 The memo is made up of twenty-six pages written in German by the diplomat Wenzel Anton von Kaunitz-Rietberg, who carefully describes the economic and political situation of the Kingdom of Naples and Sicily. ÖSt, Obersthofmeisteramt, Altere Zeremonialakten, Karton 80, 4, *Memoire des Hof- und Staatskanzler Kaunitz fur die Erzherzogin Maria Karoline betreffend das politische System des Erzhauses* (anlässlich ihrer Vermählung mit Ferdinand IV, König beider Sizilien), 17 March 1768, fols 1r–25v.

41 ÖSt, Sammelbände des Hausarchivs, Karton 10, 5/1, 5/2, 5/3.

42 After his first visit to Naples, Grand Duke Leopold wrote to his mother: "those who have had the King's education in their hands will have much to answer for in the presence of God for having neglected the talents of a prince who could have become perfect, if he had been cultivated." Adam Wandruszka, "Il Principe filosofo e il Re Lazzarone. Le lettere del granduca Pietro Leopoldo sul suo soggiorno a Napoli", *Rivista storica italiana* LXXII (1960): 508.

43 On the educational path of Ferdinand IV, see Galasso, *Il regno di Napoli. Il Mezzogiorno Borbonico e Napoleonico*, 387–90.

44 Concerning the weak personality of the King and his inability to govern, see the personal diary of King Ferdinand IV edited by Umberto Caldora, *Diario di Ferdinando IV di Borbone* (Naples: Edizioni Scientifiche Italiane, 1965).

45 Friederike Hausmann, *Maria Carolina Königin von Neapel. Eine Biographie*, 16–19; Recca, *The Diary of Queen Maria Carolina of Naples*, 3–4.

46 The Queen labelled Tanucci "pedantic and ambitious", accusing him of being an enemy of her house as well as herself. See: Ajello, *I filosofi e la regina*, 419–20; Recca, *The Diary of Queen Maria Carolina of Naples*, 4–5.

47 ÖSt, Sammelbände des Hausarchivs, karton 10, from a letter of Queen Maria Carolina to Grand Duke Leopold, 30 October 1779, fols 73r–74v.

48 There are several letters written by Minister Tanucci to King Charles that testify the perception of Queen Maria Carolina's ambitious intent. Excerpt of a letter written by Tanucci to Losada, 23 April 1776, lettera no 179, Archivo General de Simancas, *Estado*, lib. 306, fols 161–62.

49 See Rosa Mincuzzi, *Bernardo Tanucci ministro di Ferdinando di Borbone 1759–1776* (Bari: Dedalo libri, 1967), 500.

50 On 27 August 1776, Tanucci was dismissed but in the official dismissal message sent by Ferdinand IV to the Minister it was stated that a seat at the Council of State was still guaranteed. He spent the last years of his life in his country retreat at San Jorio, far from the affairs of the government. See in particular Luigi Barreca, *Il tramonto di Bernardo Tanucci nella corrispondenza con Carlo III di Spagna* (Palermo: Manfredi, 1976); Tufano, *La Francia e le Sicilie*, 315–23; Enrica Viviani della Robbia, *Bernardo Tanucci ed il suo più importante carteggio*, 409.

51 From a letter of King Ferdinand IV to his father, King Charles III, 28 May 1776, in Archivo General de Simancas, Estado, lib. 6081, fol. 365.

52 Corti, *Ich, eine Maria Theresias Tochter*, 108.

53 In 1775 Tanucci, concerned by the increase of many influential people belonging to the Masonic order, tried to convince Ferdinand IV to issue a new edict against Masonic meetings (in 1751 Charles had already issued an edict against Freemasonry without much success) but he found the young sovereign to be an obstacle. Giuseppe Giarrizzo, *Massoneria e illuminismo nell'Europa del Settecento* (Venice: Marsilio, 1994), 311.

54 Alessandro Mola, *Storia della Massoneria italiana dalle origini ai nostri giorni* (Milan: Bompiani, 1992); Antonio Trampus, *La massoneria nell'età moderna* (Rome and Bari: Laterza 2001); Anna Maria Rao, "La massoneria nel Regno di Napoli", in *Storia d'Italia, Annali*, 21, *La massoneria*, ed. Gian Mario Cazzaniga (Turin: Einaudi, 2006), 513–54.

55 There is a rich correspondence that testifies on the one hand to the confidence of Leopold in his younger sister's intelligence and her ability to educate her children, and on the other hand the certain presence of a far-sighted and older brother to whom she refers in moments of indecision and crisis, both familial and political. ÖSt, Sammelbände des Hausarchivs, Karton 10.

56 Recca, *The Diary of Queen Maria Carolina of Naples*, 5–6.

Bibliography

Primary sources

Archivo General de Simancas, *Estado*, lib. 306.
Österreichisches Staatsarchiv, Hausarchiv, Obersthofmeisteramt, Altere Zeremonialakten, Karton 80, 4.
Österreichisches Staatsarchiv, Hausarchiv, Ministerium des k. k. Hauses, Vermahlungen, Karton 14, 1.
Österreichisches Staatsarchiv, Sammelbände des Hausarchivs, Karton 10.

Secondary sources

Ajello, Raffaele. *Il problema della riforma giudiziaria e legislativa nel regno di Napoli durante la prima metà del secolo XVIII.* Naples: Jovene, 1961.
Ajello, Raffaele. "La vita politica napoletana sotto Carlo di Borbone. «La fondazione ed il tempo eroico» della dinastia". In *Storia di Napoli*, edited by Luigi La Bruna, Vol. VII, 461–17. Naples: ESI, 1972.
Ajello, Raffaele. "Carlo di Borbone". *Dizionario Biografico degli Italiani* Vol. 20 (1977): 961–84.
Ajello, Raffaele. "I filosofi e la regina. Il governo delle Due Sicilie da Tanucci a Caracciolo (1776–1886)". *Rivista Storica italiana* CIII, 3 (1991): 398–425.
Ajello, Raffaele, and D'Addio Mario. "Bernardo Tanucci. Statista, letterato, giurista" (paper presented at Convegno internazionale di studi per il secondo centenario, 1783–1983, Naples, 28–30 April 1986).
Armstrong, Edward. *Elisabeth Farnese. The Termagant of Spain.* London and New York: Longman and Green & Co., 1892.
Arneth, Alfred von. *Briefe der Kaiserin Maria Theresia an ihre Kinder und Freunde.* Vienna: W. Braumüller, 1881.
Astarita, Tommaso. *Between Salt Water and Holy Water: A History of Southern Italy.* New York and London: W. W. Norton, 2005.
Astuto, Giuseppe. "Dalle riforme alle rivoluzioni. Maria Carolina d'Asburgo: una regina austriaca nel Regno di Napoli e di Sicilia". In *Quaderni del dipartimento di studi politici*, edited by Salvatore Aleo and Giuseppe Barone, 27–51. Milan: Giuffrè, 2007.
Auer, Leopold. "Tanucci e le relazioni diplomatiche tra Austria e il Regno di Napoli". In *Bernardo Tanucci. Statista, letterato, giurista*, edited by Raffaele Ajello and Mario D'Addio, Vol. 1, 239–58. Naples: Jovene, 1986.
Barreca, Luigi. *Il tramonto di Bernardo Tanucci nella corrispondenza con Carlo III di Spagna.* Palermo: Manfredi, 1976.
Bearne, Mary Charlotte. *A Sister of Marie Antoinette: The Life-Story of Maria Carolina, Queen of Naples.* London: T. Fisher Unwin, 1907.
Bengasi, Francisco. "Décima de Francisco Bengasi en alabanza de la Reynna Madre, D. Ysabel de Farnesio". Quoted in *Una nueva Majestad. Felipe V, Isabel de Farnesio y la identidad de la monarquía (1700–1729)*, edited by Pablo Vâzquez Gestal (Madrid: Marcial Pons, 2013).
Bonnefons, André. *Une ennemie de la Révolution et de Napoléon. Marie Caroline reine des Deux-Siciles (1768–1814).* Paris: Perrin, 1905.
Bordiga Amadei, Amalia. *Maria Carolina d'Austria e il Regno delle Due Sicilie.* Naples: Cooperativa Editrice Libraia, 1920.
Butler, Rohan. "The Secret Compact of 1753 between the Kings of France and Naples". In *Royal and Republican Sovereignty in Early Modern Europe*, edited by Robert Oresko, G. C. Gibbs, and H. M. Scott, 551–79. Cambridge: Cambridge University Press, 1997.

Caldora, Umberto. *Diario di Ferdinando IV di Borbone*. Naples: Edizioni Scientifiche Italiane, 1965.
Campbell Orr, Clarissa, ed. *Queenship in Europe 1660–1815: The Role of the Consort*. Cambridge: Cambridge University Press, 2004.
Campolieti, Giuseppe. *Il re Lazzarone*. Milan: Mondadori, 1998.
Cantù, Cesare. *Storia degli Italiani*, Vol. 6. Naples: L'Unione Tipografica Editrice, 2005.
Caridi, Giuseppe. *Essere re e non essere re. Carlo di Borbone a Napoli e le attese deluse (1734–1738)*. Soveria Mannelli: Rubettino, 2006.
Casa, Emilio. "Memorie storiche di Parma dalla morte del duca Antonio Farnese alla dominazione dei Borbone di Francia (1731–1749)". *Archivio storico per le provincie parmensi* (1893): 1–145.
Castagnoli, Pietro. *Il Cardenale Giulio Alberoni*. 3 vols. Piacenza: Collegio Alberoni, 1929–1932.
Ceva Grimaldi, Francesco. *Della città di Napoli dal tempo della sua fondazione fino al presente*. Naples: Stamperia e calcografia Vico Freddo Pignasecca 15, 1857.
Coniglio, Giuseppe, *I Borboni di Napoli*. Milan: Corbaccio, 1995.
Corti, Egon Caesar. *Ich, eine Maria Theresias Tochter: Ein Lebensbild der Königin Marie Karoline von Neapel*. München: Bruckmann, 1950.
Coxe, William. *L'Espagne sous le rois de la maison de Bourbon: ou Mémoirs relatif a l'histoire de cette Nation*. Vol. 2. Paris: Libraires du Roi, 1827.
Croce, Benedetto. *Storia del Regno di Napoli*. Bari: Laterza, 1925.
D'Addio, Mario. "Carlo di Borbone e Tanucci nell'Epistolario (1726–1752)". In *Acta Napolitana, I Borbone di Napoli e di Spagna, Un bilancio Storiografico*, edited by Mario Di Pinto, 322–26. Naples: Guida Editori, 1985.
Fragnito, Gigliola, ed. *Elisabetta Farnese: principessa di Parma e regina di Napoli*. Rome: Viella, 2011.
Frugoni, Arsenio. *Consigli matrimoniali alle figlie sovrane, di Maria Teresa d'Austria*. Florence: Passigli Editori, 2000.
Gagnière, Albert. *La reine Marie Caroline de Naples, d'après des documents nouveaux*. Paris: Ollendorf, 1889.
Galasso, Giuseppe. *Il regno di Napoli. Il Mezzogiorno Borbonico e Napoleonico. Storia d'Italia*, Vol. 15, edited by Galasso Giuseppe. Torino: Utet, 2007.
García Cárcel, Ricardo. *Felipe y los Españoles*. Barcelona: Debolsillo, 2003.
Giarrizzo, Giuseppe. *Massoneria e illuminismo nell'Europa del Settecento*. Venezia: Marsilio, 1994.
Guimera, Augustin, and Petralta, Victor. *El Equilibrio de los Imperios: de Utrecht a Trafalgar*. Madrid: Fundación Española de Historia Moderna, 2004.
Harcourt-Smith, Simon. *Alberoni or the Spanish Conspiracy*. London: Faber and Faber, 1943.
Harcourt-Smith, Simon. *Cardinal of Spain: the Life and Strange Career of Giulio Alberoni*. New York: Knopf, 1955.
Hausmann, Friederike. *Herrscherin im Paradies der Teufel: Maria Carolina Königin von Neapel. Eine Biographie*. Munich, 2014.
Helfert, Alexander Freiherr von. *Königin Karolina von Neapel und Sizilien im Kample gegen die franzosische Weltherrschaft 1790–1814*. Vienna: Braumüller, 1878.
Helfert, Alexander Freiherr von. *Maria Karolina von Österreich: Königin von Neapel und Sizilien*. Vienna: G. P. Faesy, 1884.
Hilton Jones, George. "La Gran Bretagna, la Toscana e la fine della questione della successione al trono granducale (1732–1737)". *Archivio storico toscano*, 140 (1982): 443–87.
Hilton Jones, George. *Great Britain and the Tuscan Succession Question, 1710–1737*. New York: Vantage, 1998.
Kamen, Henry. *Philip V of Spain: The King Who Ruled Twice*. Madrid: Editorial tema de hoy, 1999.

La Cecilia, Giovanni. *Storie segrete delle famiglie Reali o Mister della vita intima de Borboni di Francia, di Spagna, di Parma, di Napoli, e della famiglia Lorena-Asburgo d'Austria e di Toscana.* Genova: Cecchi e Armanino Editori, 1861.
La Placa, Pietro. *La reggia in trionfo per l'acclamazione e coronazione della Sacra Real maestà di Carlo, infante di Spagna.* Palermo: Antonio Epiro, 1736.
Lavalle Cobo, Teresa. *Isabel de Farnesio. La reina coleccionista.* Madrid: Fundación Caja-Madrid, 2002.
López-Cordón, María Victoria, Maria Ángeles Pérez-Samper, and Maria Teresa Martìnez de Sas. *La Casa de Borbón. Familia, Corte y politica (1700–1808)*, Vol. 1. Madrid: Alianza Editorial, 2000.
López-Cordón Cortezo, María Victoria. "Elisabetta Farnese e il governo della Spagna". In *Elisabetta Farnese: principessa di Parma e regina di Napoli*, edited by Gigliola Fragnito, 139–62. Rome: Viella, 2011.
Mafrici, Mirella. *Il Re delle speranze: Carlo di Borbone da Madrid a Napoli.* Naples: Edizioni Scientifiche Italiane, 1998.
Mafrici, Mirella. *Fascino e Potere di una Regina, Elisabetta Farnese sulla scena europea (1715–1759).* Cava de' Tirreni: Avagliano, 1999.
Maiorini, Maria Grazia. *Tanucci L'Epistolario, Vol. IX 1760–1761.* Rome: Istituto Poligrafico e Zecca dello Stato, 1988.
Mincuzzi, Rosa. *Bernardo Tanucci ministro di Ferdinando di Borbone 1759–1776.* Bari: Dedalo libri, 1967.
Mola, Alessandro. *Storia della Massoneria italiana dalle origini ai nostri giorni.* Milan: Bompiani, 1992.
Moore, George. *Lives of Cardinal Alberoni, The Duke of Ripperda and Marquis Pombal.* London: R. Faulder, 1806.
Noel, Charles C. "'Bárbara succeeds Elizabeth . . .': The Feminisation and Domestication of Politics in the Spanish Monarchy, 1701–1759". In *Queenship in Europe 1660–1815: The Role of the Consort*, edited by Clarissa Campbell Orr, 155–85. Cambridge: Cambridge University Press, 2004.
Onnis, Rosa Pia. "Bernardo Tanucci nel moto anticurialista del '700". *Nuova rivista storica* N. X (1926): 328–65.
Pearce, Adrian J. *The Origin of Bourbon Reform in South America, 1700–1763.* New York: Palgrave Macmillan, 2014.
Pérez-Samper, Maria Ángeles. *Isabel de Farnesio.* Barcelona: Plaza Janés, 2003.
Professioni, Alfonso. *Il Ministerio in Spagna e il Proseco del cardinale Giulio Alberoni.* Torino: Giulio Gaspari, 1897.
Rao, Anna Maria. *Il Regno di Napoli nel Settecento.* Naples: Giuda, 1983.
Rao, Anna Maria. "La Repubblica Napoletana del 1799". In *Storia del Mezzogiorno*, edited by Giuseppe Galasso and Rosario Romeo, 469–539. Rome: Ed. del Sole, 1986.
Rao, Anna Maria. "La massoneria nel Regno di Napoli". In *Storia d'Italia, Annali*, 21, *La massoneria*, edited by Gian Mario Cazzaniga, 513–54. Turin: Einaudi, 2006.
Recca, Cinzia. *Sentimenti e politica. Il diario inedito della regina Maria Carolina di Napoli (1781–1785).* Milan: FrancoAngeli, 2014.
Recca, Cinzia. *The Diary of Queen Maria Carolina of Naples 1781–1785: New Evidence of Queenship at Court.* New York: Palgrave Macmillan, 2017.
Ribalta, Pedro Molas, Rafael Cerro Nargánez, and Maria Adela Fargas Peñarrocha. *Bibliografia de Felipe V.* Madrid: Sociedad Estatal de Conmemoraciones Culturales, 2004.
Rubio, María José. *Reinas de España. Siglos XVIII al XXI. De María Luisa Gabriela de Saboya a Letizia Ortiz.* Madrid: La Esfera de los Libros, 2009.
Saint-Philippe, marquis de [Vicente Bacallar y Sanna, marques de San Felipe]. *Mémoires pour servir à l'histoire d'Espagne sous le règne de Philippe V.* Translated by Maudave. Paris, 1756.

Saint-Simon, Louis de Rouvroy, duc de. *Papier inédits. Lettres et depéchês sur l'Ambassade de Espagne. Tableau de la cour 1721*. Paris: A. Quantin Imprimeur-Éditeur, 1880.
Schipa, Michelangelo. *Il Regno di Napoli al tempo di Carlo di Borbone*. Milan, Rome, and Naples: Dante Alighieri, 1923.
Schipa, Michelangelo. *Nel Regno di Ferdinando IV di Borbone*. Florence: Vallecchi, 1938.
Senatore, Giuseppe. *Giornale storico di quanto avvenne ne' due reami di Napoli e di Sicilia l'anno 1734 e 1735*. Naples: Stamperia Blasiana, 1742.
Sodano, Giulio, and Giulio Brevetti. *Io la regina. Maria Carolina d'Asburgo-Lorena tra politica, fede, arte e cultura*. Palermo: Quaderni di Mediterranea, 2016.
Storrs, Christopher. *The Spanish Resurgence, 1713–1748*. New Haven and London: Yale University Press, 2016.
Tanucci, Bernardo. *Epistolario*. Edited by Lamberto Del Bianco. Vol. IV. Rome: Edizioni di Storia e Letteratura, 1984.
Taxonera, Luciano de. *Isabel de Farnesio, retrato de una reina y perfil de una mujer, (1692–1766)*. Barcelona: Juventud, 1943.
Trampus, Antonio. *La massoneria nell'età moderna*. Rome and Bari: Laterza, 2001.
Tufano, Roberto. "'Le renversement des alliances europee' e l'espulsione di Bernardo Tanucci dal governo delle Sicilie". In *Frontiera d'Europa* (2003): 87–178.
Tufano, Roberto. *La Francia e le Sicilie. Stato e disgregazione sociale nel Mezzogiorno d'Italia da Luigi XIV alla Rivoluzione*. Naples: Arte tipografica, 2009.
Tufano, Roberto. *Verso la giustizia produttiva. Un'esperienza di riforme nelle due Sicilie (1738–1746)*. Naples: Istituto Italiano per gli Studi Filosofici, 2015.
Vázquez Gestal, Pablo. "Giulio Alberoni". In *Diccionario Biográfico Español*, edited by Aguirre de Viani and Allendesalazar y Muñoz de Salazar, 267–72. Madrid: Real Academia de la Historia, 2009.
Vázquez Gestal, Pablo. "'The System of this Court': Elizabeth Farnese, the Count of Santiesteban and the Monarchy of the Two Sicilies, 1734–1738", *Court Historian*, 14, 1 (2009), 38–42.
Vázquez Gestal, Pablo. *Una nueva Majestad. Felipe V, Isabel de Farnesio y la identidad de la monarquía (1700–1729)*. Madrid: Marcial Pons, 2013.
Vázquez Gestal, Pablo. "Los espacios de una nueva majestad. Carlos de Borbón y los Sitios Reales de la monarquía de las Dos Sicilias (1734–1759)". In *Una corte para el rey. Carlos III y los Sitios Reales*, edited by José Luis Sancho Gaspar & Javier Ortega Vidal, 52–63. Madrid: Comunidad de Madrid, 2016.
Viviani della Robbia, Enrica. *Bernardo Tanucci ed il suo più importante carteggio*. Florence: Bibliografia, 1942.
Wandruska, Adam. "Il Principe filosofo e il Re Lazzarone. Le lettere del granduca Pietro Leopoldo sul suo soggiorno a Napoli". *Rivista storica italiana* LXXII (1960).

PART II
Legitimising royal authority

8

PURPLE DREAMS OF THE MACEDONIAN DYNASTY OF BYZANTIUM IN MANUSCRIPT ILLUMINATIONS

Legitimising the usurping emperor, Basil I (867–86)

Alexandra Karagianni

Many monographs and studies have been devoted to the analysis of the historical, political, and ideological problems of the reign of Emperor Basil I, the founder of the Macedonian dynasty.[1] The rise of Basil I to the throne marked for the Byzantine Empire the beginning of a great political and cultural prosperity, which lasted about 200 years (867–1056). However, the dark past of the founder as well as the crimes he committed and the questionable methods he used to rise to power were undoubtedly an unsuitably negative legacy for his descendants and followers. For this reason, it was important for his unorthodox ascension to power to be interpreted through a series of royal dreams—visions seen by various people associated with Basil and his rise—that explained and justified his reign.

The historical sources about the origins of the Macedonian dynasty date back to the second half of the tenth century, during the reign of Basil's grandson, Emperor Constantine VII Porphyrogenitus. These historical sources are controversial, however, because they are not objective. In fact, we have no contemporary historical evidence at all for the rise to the throne of Basil I. As a result, the life and reign of Basil as recorded by contemporaries was mostly based on legends and rumours spread by royal propaganda and later became the source on which historians based the official historiography.[2]

This chapter examines five "purple" dreams of the Byzantine court as narrated in the second book of *Theophanes Continuatus* entitled *Vita Basilii*, attributed to Constantine Porphyrogenitus, and further illustrated in the manuscript of Ioannes Skylitzes, *Synopsis Historiarum*, both from the tenth to eleventh centuries.[3] These dreams justify the illegitimate rise of Emperor Basil I the Macedonian (867–86) to the Byzantine throne and the violent change his accession brought in through assassinations of the legitimate ruling dynasty. This chapter investigates how a prophetic or symbolic dream (or *chrimatismos*) could be used to legitimise the illegal actions of the simple peasant Basil and provide him with the opportunity to usurp the imperial throne from the reigning emperor Michael III (842–67).

Three of these symbolic dreams were attributed to Basil's mother: one of a golden tree growing out of her house, another of a visit of the Prophet Elijah, and the third of a golden cypress tree standing in the garden of her house. These dreams urged her to encourage her son to go to Constantinople to seek his fortune. Another dream, of the abbot of the Monastery of St Diomedes in Constantinople, features an appearance of St Diomedes himself, who persuades the Abbot to shelter Basil in the monastery and later to introduce him to a relative of the Emperor, Theophilitzes, who takes him into his service. Finally, the dream seen by Caesar Bardas, uncle of Emperor Michael III, showed Bardas himself entering along with his nephew into the church of St Sophia in Constantinople, then being slain by a guard on the orders of St Peter. This vision presages and latterly justifies Bardas' and Michael's violent assassinations by Basil in 866 and 867. As they became part of the official history, these dreams, the dreamers, and the dream interpreters served the political interests of the Emperor and strengthened the ties of religious authority to political power.

Even though the writings on dreams and dream interpretation from the ancient Greek and Byzantine eras are rare, theoretical references to dreams are quite common in the relevant historiography. Indeed, the origin and diagnostic value of dreams constitute elements that have awakened the interests of writers of various ages, resulting in the formation of a multiform dream tradition. The oldest text on dream interpretation that has survived intact from late antiquity, and was later used by the Byzantines, was the "Oneirocriticon of Artemidoros".[4] During the Byzantine period, the technique of dream interpretation, moving between magic and Christian belief, was highly appreciated and widespread in Byzantine society, as demonstrated by the existence of the so-called "Oneirocriticon of Achmet", a dream textbook dating from the tenth century.[5]

Byzantine scholars worldwide have debated the problem of Basil I's origins for many years without reaching a certain conclusion.[6] It is believed that Basil was born to peasant parents of Armenian origin in 811, or even in 830, in Charioupolis, a city in Byzantine Macedonia, which at that time was inhabited by Greeks, Armenians, Slavs, and Arabs. Information on the life and reign of Basil derives from the aforementioned *Vita Basilii*, as well as works by Hungarian Byzantinologist Gyula Moravcsik.[7] According to these sources, Basil traced his ancestry back to the Arsacid Empire,[8] on his father's side, while from his mother, who bore the Greek name Pangalo, he claimed descent from Constantine the Great and Alexander the Great.[9]

Basil's biographers embellished his life with various biblical and mythological motifs as well as various divine attributes, such as dreams, prophecies, and oracles. Thus, myth and truth are often confused while historical reality is shrugged off in favour of imperial propaganda. The attributes which prefigure the glorious future of this humble peasant were said to accompany him already in childhood:

for example, as his hair first began to grow, a purple nimbus appeared around his head as well as a purple border around his swaddling clothes. These symbols refer to the Purple or Porphyry Chamber of the Imperial Palace in Constantinople, where emperors were born.[10] The description of these purple symbols is attributed to Constantine Porphyrogenitus, who aimed to denote the imperial origins of his grandfather and at the same time to show that Basil's ascension to the imperial throne was God's will.

Another sign that prefigured Basil's future was the triple appearance of an eagle which flew above him in order to protect him from the burning sun.[11] The incident took place at a time when Basil was an unprotected child, while his parents were working in the fields inspecting and encouraging the harvesters.[12] The harvesters who saw the incident tried to chase away the eagle for fear that it would kill the child. But the eagle continued to provide shadow to Basil and reappeared two more times. In the meantime, his mother Pangalo, who witnessed the incident, was calm and considered the appearance of the eagle as a divine sign. Indeed, according to the Greco-Roman and Byzantine tradition, the eagle was considered a symbol of protection, victory, power, and ability to rule a kingdom.[13]

The first three Macedonian emperors—Basil I, his son Leo VI, and his grandson Constantine Porphyrogenitus—were very interested in dream narratives and dream interpretation, and used dreams to justify illegal actions, murders, and political wars for claiming, consolidating, and maintaining royal power.[14] This series of symbols and dreams thus have "propagandistic" function and justify Basil's rise.

The first dream predictions for Basil I come from the lower social classes; as is often seen, fate predestines them for the highest ranks.[15] Consequently, the first dream prediction comes from his mother Pangalo, who saw in three different phases symbolic and prophetic dreams concerning the brilliant future of her son. In her first dream, she saw a huge golden tree, full of flowers and fruits, which exceeded the height of her house. Its trunk was golden, as were its branches and leaves. Pangalo narrated her dream to a dream interpreter, who explained it, predicting the great destiny that awaited her son.[16] Her dream and its interpretation therefore comforted her worries about the future of her son. In addition, according to the narrator Constantine Porphyrogenitus, Mandani, the mother of Persian King Cyrus, had a similar dream of huge vine tendrils growing out of her house, a dream that predicted the rise of Cyrus to the Persian throne.[17] The similarity of Pangalo's dream with the dream of Mandani reveals the intention of Byzantine writers to imitate accepted royal narratives and to give Basil an imperial lineage.

Shortly afterwards, Basil's mother saw a second dream, which was not symbolic and did not need an interpretation. This dream was more straightforwardly prophetic, as a seer appeared to her and revealed the future. Pangalo dreamed of an old man, whose mouth emitted fire, telling her that she should urge her beloved son Basil to go to Constantinople, as God was going to hand over to him the sceptre of the Byzantine Empire. As the man who gave the divine message was not recognisable, the mother asked: "Who art thou, my lord, who brought such cheery tidings to me?" The man answered: "I am Elijah the Tishbite."[18] Constantine

Porphyrogenitus calls this second dream a divine revelation and a divinely validated explanation for the first symbolic dream.[19] The appearance of saints and prophets in the dreams of faithful Christians constitutes a quite common pattern in hagiographic literature.[20] Similarly, the official historiographers of the Macedonian dynasty connected the biblical personality of the Prophet Elijah to Basil I.[21]

After these early dreams, Basil, on the encouragement of his mother, set out for Constantinople, and after a long journey entered the city through the Golden Gate and rested beside the monastery of St Diomedes. Around midnight, St Diomedes appeared to the abbot of the monastery in a dream and ordered him to go out to the gate and call out the name "Basil". Whoever would answer the call should then be brought into the monastery, sheltered, and taken care of, as God had anointed him to be emperor and he would contribute to the restoration of the monastery. The abbot, believing that the dream was a vain illusion, paid no attention to it and turned over to sleep again. He saw the same dream for a second time and, as he continued to pay no attention to it, the saint appeared for a third time, and threatened angrily to punish him if he did not obey. So he awoke, cried "Basil", and discovered the peasant who was sleeping outside and led him inside the monastery.[22] The appearance of St Diomedes in the dream of the abbot is illustrated in the folio 83v° of the manuscript of Ioannes Skylitzes which is kept in Madrid.[23] It is a *chrimatismos* in three phases, namely a type of dream that consists of three identical repeated dreams that appear to one person during the same night.[24]

The abbot revealed the prediction of St Diomedes to Basil and asked him to remember him when the prophecy was fulfilled. He also introduced him to the courtier Theophilitzes, a frequent visitor to the monastery, who was also a relative of Emperor Michael III. By means of these dreams, therefore, the first contact of the peasant Basil with the royal court is achieved. Basil soon won the favour of Theophilitzes as he excelled in matters of physical strength and bravery and was prompt to carry out whatever orders were given to him. Theophilitzes took him into his service in the imperial palace and later promoted him to the position of *Protostrator*, the groom of the royal stable.[25]

In the meantime, Pangalo, worried that she was ignoring her son's fate, had another dream. She saw a large tree resembling a cypress standing in the courtyard of her house. The tree was covered with gilt foliage and had a golden trunk and branches. Basil was sitting on top of the tree.[26] This time Pangalo did not visit a dream interpreter but a pious woman named Anna who, according to Constantine Porphyrogenitus, had dedicated herself to prayers and fasting. The woman interpreted Pangalo's dream and encouraged her to be cheerful, as her son was destined to have the greatest fate and to become emperor of Byzantium.[27]

The narration and interpretation of Pangalo's three dreams is given by Constantine Porphyrogenitus in a scaled form. The narration starts with her first symbolic dream and its interpretation, continues with the prophecy of the Prophet Elijah, and concludes with her third dream and the consequent reassurance of a pious woman. This scalar presentation of dreams and interpretation aims to present the rise of Basil I to the imperial throne as God-chosen, and to justify both the pagan and the Christian methods and practices used by Basil's narrators in order to achieve this goal.

In the meantime, Basil, while serving Theophilitzes, decided to accompany him on an imperial mission to the city of Patras in Greece in 856. There he met the millionairess and widow Danielis, who was twenty years his senior, and started a romantic relationship with her. Danielis was very fond of Basil and bestowed on him lavish gifts of gold, rich clothes, and land. She later travelled to Constantinople with a large retinue in order to visit him after he had become emperor and there she was rewarded with the title of "King Mother".[28]

With newfound wealth, Basil returned to his homeland in Macedonia and purchased property for himself and his family. He even donated to the monastery of St Diomedes, where he had been sheltered during his first days in Constantinople, thus fulfilling the abbot's prophetic dream. But soon he returned to Constantinople and the imperial palace. At a banquet given by Theophilitzes and Antigonus, Caesar Bardas' son, Basil gained the attention of the emperor Michael III.[29] In the wrestling match that followed the banquet, Basil defeated a well-known Bulgarian wrestler who had claimed to be unbeatable. As a result of this, Basil was honoured with court offices and soon became the Emperor's confidant and bodyguard (*parakoimomenos*).[30] On Emperor Michael's orders, he even divorced his wife Maria and married Eudokia Ingerina, Michael's favourite mistress. However, Michael continued his relationship with Eudokia as well.[31]

As Imperial Parakoimomenos, Basil gained access to the intimate affairs of the palace and accompanied Emperor Michael on military expeditions of the Byzantine army in Asia Minor. In one of these expeditions against the Arabs, Basil convinced Michael that his uncle Caesar Bardas coveted the Byzantine throne and was organising a conspiracy against him. Together they organised a plot against Bardas which resulted in his assassination, on 21 April 866, inside the imperial tent during a campaign outside the city of Miletus.[32]

Caesar Bardas, just three months before his assassination, foresaw in a dream his own violent death as well as that of Michael. The dream is narrated by the Byzantine hagiographer Nicetas Paphlagon in his *Life of Patriarch Ignatius*.[33] According to this source, Bardas ran straight to his friend the courtier Philotheos Logothetes in order to narrate his nightmare:

> I have dreamt something that has broken all my bones and loosed my joints . . . one night I enter the Great Church in the company of the Emperor, as though in a procession . . . and I see images of archangels from all the windows. When I approach the ambo, I see two *cubicularii* (officials), harsh and severe. One of them seizes the Emperor, drags him to the right and attacks him violently as if to kill him; in the same manner, the other one takes me to the left. Suddenly I look up and see, sitting on the throne in the sanctuary, an aged man who resembles the image of Saint Peter and at his feet I see Patriarch Ignatius making a supplication. Then Ignatius turns round and points at me, saying: 'He is the one who caused me more grief than all the

> others'. Hearing this, the aged man with the image of Saint Peter, shouts: 'Seize Bardas who has brought the wrath of God and cut him in pieces in front of the narthex'. Immediately I am dragged off and attacked by the *cubicularii* as if to my death; and as I am trying to defend myself, I see the aged man shaking his finger at the Emperor, saying: 'Just wait, impious child'. Then, as if awake, I see myself being torn in pieces.[34]

In fact, Emperor Michael had deposed Patriarch Ignatius in 858 as he had disapproved of his religious policies. Ignatius, who was briefly replaced by Photios, was later restored on the patriarchal throne by Basil.

Shortly after the assassination of Bardas, Basil was invested with the dignity of Caesar (the title held by Bardas) and later was crowned co-emperor beside Michael in the Church of St Sophia on 26 May 866. The joint reign of Michael and Basil lasted for more than a year but the relations of the two men became strained when Michael started to favour the royal courtier Basiliskus with an eye to investing him with the imperial title. The favouritism that Michael clearly showed for Basiliskus infuriated Basil and motivated him to organise Michael's assassination. On the night of 24 September 867, when Michael, after a banquet, returned drunk to his chamber in the Palace of St Mamas, Basil and eight of his supporters, including his brothers Marinos and Symbatios, gained entry to the imperial chambers, attacked Michael, and killed him. In this heinous way Basil ascended the Byzantine throne.[35]

The five dreams concerning the life of Emperor Basil I legitimised his actions in usurping the imperial throne. They served Basil's political interests and strengthened ties between religious authority and political power. The illustration of the dreams in the manuscripts varies according to their content. In symbolic dreams which need to be interpreted, the dreamer and the dream coexist in the same scene. In some cases, the dreamer, although he has his eyes closed, actively participates in the dream. The dreamer and the dream interpreter, who is depicted explaining the content of the dream, are illustrated in the nearby scene. In the *chrimatismoi* a supernatural being appears to the dreamer and announces a prophecy or issues a command. The fulfilment of the prophecy or the command is depicted as an autonomous representation; it is, however, an extension and interpretation of the previous scene.[36]

It is remarkable that Basil, despite being a person with no education or military or administrative experience, became an effective and respected monarch, ruling for nineteen years. He overthrew the ruling Amorian dynasty, whose last descendant was Michael III, and established the Macedonian dynasty. As an emperor, he inaugurated the most glorious and prosperous era of the Byzantine Empire. He received little political criticism regarding the murder of Michael III due to Michael's unpopularity with the Byzantine populace. In fact, according to Constantine Porphyrogenitus, Michael appeared to be a monarch who had degraded the dignity of the imperial office. Byzantine sources describe Michael's habitual drunkenness (he was given the nickname "the Drunkard"), his obsession with chariot racing, and his passion for organising public displays in order to mock the processions and rituals of the Church.

In contrast, the prudent and skilful policy that Basil followed in the internal and external affairs of the Empire made Byzantium the strongest power in Europe and the eastern Mediterranean. Basil undertook an extensive building program in Constantinople, constructing many churches as well as hospitals and houses for the poor. He reorganised the judicial system and personally collected all the past laws into sixty books, the *Basilika*, and smaller legal manuals, the *Eisagoge*. Because of this great legislative work he is often called a "second Justinian". Further to this, he appointed educated, objective, and well-paid judges, multiplied the lower courts, and provided shelter and food to provincial citizens of the Empire who had to remain in Constantinople while their lawsuits were pending in the courts.[37]

In August 866, following a serious hunting injury and brief illness, Basil died after nineteen years of reign, leaving a peaceful and secure transition to his sons Leo and Alexander.[38] Yet, when historians compiled formal histories of this energetic and progressive emperor, they still felt the need to rely on divinely inspired dream narratives to validate Basil's reign and ensure that his memory was not tainted by the brutality and the illegitimate means by which he assumed power.

Notes

1 Norman Tobias, *Basil I, Founder of the Macedonian Dynasty: A Study of the Political and Military History of the Byzantine Empire in the Ninth Century* (New York: Edwin Mellen Press, 2007); Vasiliki Vlysidou, *Eksoteriki politiki kai esoterikes antidraseis tin epochi tou Vasileiou A. Ereunes gia ton entopismo ton antipoliteutikon taseon sta chronia 867–886* (Athens: Istorikes ekdoseis, S.Vasilopoulos, 1991).
2 Apostolos Karpozilos, *Vtzantinoi istorikoi kai chronografoi*, vol. C (Athens: Kanakis, 2009).
3 Ihor Ševčenko, ed., *Chronographiae quae Theophanis continuati nomine fertur liber quo Vita Basilii Imperatoris amplectitur*, Corpus fontium historiae Byzantinae, vol. XLII (Berlin and New York: De Gruyter, 2011); Hans Thurn, ed., *Ioannis Scylitzae Synopsis Historiarum*, Corpus fontium historiae Byzantinae, series 5 (Berlin: De Gruyter, 1973).
4 Maria Mavroudi, *Artemidorou Oneirokritica* (Athens: Istos, 2002), 32–33; Roger Ambrose Pack, ed., *Artemidori Daldiani Onirocriticon libri V* (Leipzig: Teubner, 1963).
5 Maria Mavroudi, *A Byzantine Book on Dream Interpretation. The Oneirocriticon of Achmet and its Arabic Sources* (Leiden: Brill, 2002).
6 Tobias, *Basil I, Founder of the Macedonian Dynasty*, 2–11.
7 Gyula Moravcsik, "Sagen und Legenden über Kaiser Basileios I", *Dumbarton Oaks Papers* 15 (1961): 59–126.
8 The Arsacid or Parthian Empire was in ancient Persia.
9 Ševčenko, *Theophanes Continuatus*, Book V, 215, verses 9–10.
10 According to the description of Anna Comnena, the walls and the floor of the Porphyry Chamber of the Imperial Palace were decorated with expensive porphyry marbles. Consequently the children of the emperors who were born there were named "Porphyrogenitus", or "born in the purple". Edgar Robert Ashton Sewter, trans., *Anna Comnena: The Alexiad* (London: Penguin, 2003), 190–97.
11 This image can be seen in Joannis Scylitzae, *Synopsis historiarum incipiens a Nicephori imperatoris a genicis obitu ad Isacii Comneni imperium* (Athens: Militos 2000), p. 174.
12 Ševčenko, *Theophanes Continuatus*, Book V, 218, verses 4–15.
13 Moravcsik, "Sagen und Legendenüber Kaiser Basileios I", 84–91.
14 George Calofonos, "Dream Interpretation: A Byzantinist Superstition?", *Byzantine and Modern Greek Studies* 9 (1984/85): 215–20.

15 Ilias Anagnostakis and Titos Papamastorakis, "Porphyres oneiraton opseis kai xriseis", *Arxaiologia & Texnes* 79 (2001): 26–33.
16 Ševčenko, *Theophanes Continuatus*, Book V, 215, verses 20–22.
17 Moravcsik, "Sagen und Legendenüber Kaiser Basileios I", 15, 89.
18 Ševčenko, *Theophanes Continuatus*, Book V, 222, verses 9–23.
19 Ševčenko, *Theophanes Continuatus*, Book V, 222, verse 23.
20 Germaine da Costa-Louillet, "Saints de Constantinople aux VIIIe, IXe et Xe siècles", *Byzantion* 24 (1954): 179–263.
21 Basil I showed a special interest in the veneration of Elijah and erected many churches and monasteries in his honour. See Paul Magdalino, "Basil I, Leo VI and the feast of the prophet Elijah", *Jahrbuch der Österreichischen Byzantinistik* 38 (1988): 193–96.
22 Ševčenko, *Theophanes Continuatus*, Book V, 223, verses 14–22.
23 Vassiliki Tsamakda, *The Illustrated Chronicle of Ioannes Skylitzes in Madrid* (Leiden: Alexandros Press, 2002), 130.
24 See image in Joannis Scylitzae, *Synopsis historiarum*, p. 176.
25 Ševčenko, *Theophanes Continuatus*, Book V, 229–33.
26 See image in Joannis Scylitzae, *Synopsis historiarum*, p. 177.
27 Ševčenko, *Theophanes Continuatus*, Book V, 215, verses 20–22.
28 Ševčenko, *Theophanes Continuatus*, Book V, 226, verses 10–11.
29 Michael III was the son of Emperor Theophilos and Empress Theodora. He was crowned co-emperor at his birth in 840, two years before the death of his father. From 856, power was exercised by Empress Theodora along with her powerful advisor, the eunuch Theoctistos. But Theoctistos was later murdered by Bardas, who became the actual ruler of the Empire.
30 The office of *parakoimomenos* was usually occupied by a eunuch. The *parakoimomenos* resided in or near the imperial rooms and was responsible for the emperor's safety during his resting. Basil I, however, was the first non-eunuch *parakoimomenos* in the imperial court.
31 Ševčenko, *Theophanes Continuatus*, Book V, 828, verses 3–8.
32 Tobias, *Basil I, Founder of the Macedonian Dynasty*, 65–70. Bardas was of Armenian origin and brother of Empress Theodora, Michael's III mother. "Caesar" was a title granted to the ruler second only to the emperor in authority. See image in Joannis Scylitzae, *Synopsis historiarum*, p. 169.
33 *Patrologiae Graecae cursus completus: seu bibliotheca universalis, integra, uniformis, commoda, oeconomica*, ed. Jacques-Paul Migne (Paris: Imprimerie Catholique, 1857–66), 105, coll. 533C–536D.
34 Quoted in Jeffrey-Michael Featherstone, "A Note on the Dream of Bardas Caesar in the *Life of Ignatius* and the Archangel in the Mosaic over the Imperial Doors of St Sophia", *Byzantinische Zeitschift* 74, 1 (1981): 42–43.
35 Tobias, *Basil I, Founder of the Macedonian Dynasty*, 73–77.
36 Anagnostakis and Papamastorakis, "Porphyres oneiraton opseis kai xriseis", 26–33.
37 Tobias, *Basil I, Founder of the Macedonian Dynasty*, 253–59.
38 Ševčenko, *Theophanes Continuatus*, Book V, 351, verse 22.

Bibliography

Primary sources

Migne, Jacques-Paul, ed. *Patrologiae Graecae cursus completus: seu bibliotheca universalis, integra, uniformis, commoda, oeconomica*. Paris: Imprimerie Catholique, 1857–66.

Oberhelman, Steven, ed. *The Oneirocriticon of Achmet. A Medieval Greek and Arabic Treatise on the Interpretation of Dreams*. Lubbock: Texas Tech University Press, 1991.

Oberhelman, Steven, ed. *Dreambooks in Byzantium: Six Oneirocritica in Translation with Commentary and Introduction*. Burlington: Ashgate, 2008.
Pack, Roger Ambrose, ed. *Artemidori Daldiani Onirocriticon libri V*. Leipzig: Teubner, 1963.
Ševčenko, Ihor. *Chronographiae quae Theophanis Continuati nomine fertur liber quo Vita Basilii Imperatoris amplectitur*. Berlin and New York: De Gruyter, 2011.
Sewter, Edgar Robert Ashton, trans. *Anna Comnena: The Alexiad*. London: Penguin, 2003.
Thurn, Hans, ed. *Ioannis Scylitzae Synopsis Historiarum*, Corpus fontium historiae Byzantinae, Book V. Berlin: De Gruyter, 1973.
Tsamakda, Vasiliki. *The Illustrated Chronicle of Ioannes Skylitzes in Madrid*. Leiden: Alexandros Press, 2002.
Tselikas, Agamemnon, ed. *Joannis Scylitzae, Synopsis Historiarum: incipiens a Nicephori imperatoris a genicis obitu ad Isacii Comneni imperium*. Athens: Militos, 2000.

Secondary sources

Anagnostakis Ilias, Titos Papamastorakis. "Porphyres oneiraton opseis kai xriseis", *Arxaiologia & Texnes* 79 (2001): 26–33.
Calofonos, George. "Dream Interpretation: A Byzantinist Superstition?" *Byzantine and Modern Greek Studies* 9 (1984/85): 215–20.
Da Costa-Louillet, Germaine. "Saints de Constantinople aux VIIIe, IXe et Xe siècles", *Byzantion* 24 (1954): 179–263.
Featherstone, Jeffrey-Michael. "A Note on the Dream of Bardas Caesar in the *Life of Ignatius* and the Archangel in the Mosaic over the Imperial Doors of St Sophia". *Byzantinische Zeitschrift* 74:1 (Jan 1981): 42–43.
Karpozilos Apostolos, *Vtzantinoi istorikoi kai chronografoi*, vol. C. Athens: Kanakis, 2009.
Magdalino, Paul. "Basil I, Leo VI and the Feast of the Prophet Elijah". *Jahrbuch der Österreichischen Byzantinistik* 38 (1988): 193–96.
Mavroudi, Maria. *A Byzantine Book on Dream Interpretation. The Oneirocriticon of Achmet and its Arabic Sources*. Leiden: Brill, 2002.
Moravcsik, Gyula. "Sagen und Legenden über Kaiser Basileios I". *Dumbarton Oaks Papers* vol. 15 (1961): 59–126.
Tobias, Norman. *Basil I, Founder of the Macedonian Dynasty: A Study of the Political and Military History of the Byzantine Empire in the Ninth Century*. New York: Edwin Mellen Press, 2007.
Vlysidou, Vasiliki. *Eksoteriki politiki kai esoterikes antidraseis tin epochi tou Vasileiou A. Ereunes gia ton entopismo ton antipoliteutikon taseon sta chronia 867–886*. Athens: Istorikes ekdoseis, S. Vasilopoulos, 1991.
Vogt, Albert. *Basile Ier empereur de Byzance et la civilization byzantine à la fin du IXe siècle*. Paris: Picard, 1908.

9

"KING BY FACT, NOT BY LAW"

Legitimacy and exequies in medieval England[1]

Anna M. Duch

When the tomb of Henry VI was opened at St George's Chapel, Windsor, in 1910, the sight that greeted investigators was disappointing. Within a lead coffin, the King's bones were lumped into a heap. Sir Alexander Macalister, a professor of anatomy, confessed he could not determine much beyond the fact the bones had once formed a forty-five- to fifty-five-year-old man who stood about 5'9"; the remains were in very poor condition. Macalister believed that the bones had been in an earthen grave,[2] suggesting that he saw evidence of insect activity, fungal involvement, animal disruption, or some other contaminating factor that would accelerate decomposition. In narrative and financial accounts of Henry's funeral, directed by Edward IV, in 1471, a lead coffin—a common preservative measure during the Middle Ages—was not mentioned. Thus, being interred only in a highly perishable wooden coffin, Henry partially returned to earth at Chertsey Abbey, in Surrey, permitting his remains to mix with those already present. This would explain not only the absence of Henry's right arm bones, but also the accidental inclusion of a pig's bone in the casket.[3] In 1484, when Richard III transferred Henry from Chertsey to Windsor, it is highly likely that the decayed body was disarticulated and placed inside the lead coffin that was then next seen in 1910.[4] The tomb was resealed with a simple slab with the King's name on it.

How could a consecrated king be buried in such a way? The same question was asked in 2012, when the remains of Richard III were rediscovered at Leicester Greyfriars. The grave had been dug too short, and Richard's bones had signs of peri-mortem abuse, that is, occurring around the time of death; although there were at least two fatal skull wounds, the ribs and pelvis were peppered with injuries that were likely inflicted after the body had been stripped of its armour at Bosworth in 1485.[5] Other kings had lost their crowns, such as Edward II in 1327 and Richard II in 1399, yet they had been accorded funerals and burials that remarked upon their station. This question of disparate circumstances was first considered by Joel

Burden in his chapter "How Do You Bury a Deposed King?"[6] Burden suggests that these "bad" exequies were performed on men like Henry VI and Richard III to deny the deceased their status as kings. This chapter will take up this argument and go further: in the eyes of those who buried them, Henry VI and Richard III were never legitimate kings, thus they were not subject to the rules of the medieval English royal funeral. In contrast, Edward II and Richard II, though they lacked kingly status at their death, were ultimately reconciled to the royal prescriptive texts of the English royal funeral, as well as contemporary political considerations, because they were undisputedly legitimate. Only the initial burials of these royal and formerly royal bodies will be addressed; discussion of the reburials of three of these kings would require a chapter all its own.[7]

Burying a king

Prescriptive texts pertaining to the royal funeral are found in a number of medieval manuscripts related to the ceremonial life of the monarchy. *De Exequiis Regalibus* is a short description of royal mortuary procedures found in the *Litlyngton Missal* (MS 37) and the *Liber Regalis* (MS 38) of Westminster Abbey, as well as Pamplona MS 197, and it has been copied into other, later manuscripts, including the *Liber Regie Capelle* and *Articles Ordained by King Henry VII for Regulation of His Household, 1494* (hereafter referred to as the *Household Articles*). The text, originally written sometime before the mid-fourteenth century,[8] briefly describes how the king's body should be preserved by bathing, evisceration, and embalming. Fashion and personal preferences changed with each monarch, but the text demanded that the body be prepared and dressed and arranged in his coffin honourably and fittingly (*honeste* and *decenter* in the text).[9]

The preservation of the medieval corpse was a vital element of the English royal funeral. The bodies of kings as early as Henry II were shown to high-ranking men of the kingdom prior to interment,[10] and it was common for medieval English kings to lay in their coffins above ground for months between death and funeral.[11] *De Exequiis Regalibus* addresses universal, preservative concerns of a dead body, but its practices predate any text. The grave goods that were enclosed with the body were important indicators of status; for an English king, the items explicitly identified were the rod and ball, the sceptre, and a crown. *De Exequiis Regalibus* is accompanied by an illumination in Pamplona MS 197, the *Litlyngton Missal*, and the *Liber Regalis*.[12] Each of these manuscripts has an illumination of a dead king lying on a *chare*, a specialised cart or wagon for carrying the deceased's coffin. The king depicted in the Pamplona MS holds a gold ball in his hands. The *Litlyngton Missal* king holds a gold rod and ball. *The Liber Regalis* king holds a rod and sceptre. These items corroborate the prescriptive text *De Exequiis Regalibus*, but they were also commonly associated symbols of monarchy by the late fourteenth century, particularly in England and France.[13]

In the mid-fifteenth-century *Liber Regie Capelle*, the guiding book for the Chapel Royal, the funerary section included *De Exequiis Regalibus* and then dictated not only the sequence of masses to be held for the dead but also that a certain amount of conspicuous consumption was required at a royal funeral. These demands were to be fulfilled for the funerals of both kings and queens; the consort was equal to her husband in this ceremonial matter.[14] Prior to the full funeral text, the *Liber Regie Capelle* has a small paragraph which dictates the expected dress of the attendees and the appearance of the chapel or church in cases of either a funeral or anniversary. The altars were to be covered in black, and the members of the Chapel were to be clothed in black cloth of gold, or black velvet. Those in attendance, including the new king and the dowager queen, were to wear black over their garments. If the body was present, then a *herse* was to be in the church as well.[15]

A *herse*, distinct from the modern hearse, was a large wooden structure in which the coffin was placed, and around the outside it supported numerous candles.[16] The greater the status of the deceased, the greater the *herse* and greater the number of candles. Likewise, the status of the dead dictated the numbers of cloths of gold to be offered, how many torches were to be held by mourners, the religious ceremonies at each stop, and other signs that indicated that this person had enough financial and political importance to be able to execute such features.[17] At every stop of the procession between the place of death and the site of burial, an Office of the Dead—Vespers, nine-lesson Matins, and Lauds—and three votive masses of the Trinity, Blessed Virgin, and Requiem were to be performed. These extensive religious offerings were signs of wealth; the minimum requirement for any Christian person's funeral was a Mass of Requiem, but additional offices and masses could be had for someone willing to pay for them in order to expedite the deceased king or queen's transit through Purgatory. Additionally, an archbishop officiated each of these events, further emphasising the status of the dead.[18]

Similarly, the *Household Articles*, which provided guidance for funerals of anyone of the nobility, indicate that the extent of the exequies should reflect the person's status at death. There were clear divisions between one rank and the next; those who were ranked as dukes or higher could expect a procession like that described above in the *Liber Regie Capelle* as well as formal welcome into each city, but those who were below this rank may not have such honours.[19] Additionally, for someone of such rank, "forty-eight torches is little enough",[20] and it is implied that those higher or lower than a duke would receive torches proportionate to his or her rank. In general, the *De Exequiis Regalibus* and *Liber Regie Capelle* funerary texts were designed to be used by those producing the exequies, while the *Household Articles* text was targeting those in attendance, informing the audience as to what was appropriate dress and conduct at a certain rank's exequies.

The funerals described in all these texts were far from plain. However, each text pivots on the status of the dead. The specific status of kings-who-were-not-kings when they died was therefore a very difficult problem to resolve for those planning their funerals. Considering that each king had been removed from power and stripped of his status as king in life, there was an understandable measure of uncertainty as to whether he should be awarded such honours in death. Certain changes had to be enacted to reflect his new station—whatever it was.

Fortunately, the royal prescriptive texts were flexible enough to accommodate a wide variety of events, including necessary departures from the standard order. The texts' principal function was to normalise and make ornate royal funerals manageable, not overcomplicate the proceedings. A successful funeral was one that adapted to complications external to the religious ceremonies, including a king who was not *the* king at his death. Although not all of the texts were written by the time of the funeral of Edward II in 1327 or that of Richard II in 1400, it is clear that certain features were already expected; practice often preceded commitment to parchment. However, differences must have been anticipated, due to the fact that both men had been removed from power. Edward had been replaced by his son Edward III after being deposed or forced to abdicate in January 1327,[21] and Richard was deposed or forced to abdicate in September 1399 and replaced by his cousin Henry IV.[22]

Both men were imprisoned after losing their crowns and lived for some time thereafter.[23] Edward of Caernarvon died on 21 September 1327 at Berkeley Castle, and Richard of Bordeaux was held at Pontefract Castle until his death on 14 February 1400. These places were deliberately far away from Westminster, so as not to distract from the new regimes. However, care for the formerly royal bodies was not ignored. In preparation for his funeral, Edward of Caernarvon was embalmed by a woman.[24] Little else is known about the preservation of Edward's body; there are no other comments about its appearance prior to the funeral, and Edward's tomb at Gloucester has never been opened. Richard of Bordeaux's body was treated very well; his bones were described as being in "near perfect" condition and dry by surgeon Charles Sangster, one companion of Arthur P. Stanley, Dean of Westminster, during the tomb's 1871 opening.[25] Thomas Tuttebury of the King's Wardrobe received £66 13s 4d on 17 February 1400 for the handling of Richard's corpse, which would have sufficiently embalmed and dressed the body.[26]

Unlike Edward of Caernarvon, Richard of Bordeaux had created a will that explicitly laid out what he wanted for his funeral, including how he was to be dressed, how the procession was to look, and other details.[27] Although the specificity of this will, right down to a white velvet (or satin) robe he was to wear, has been used as evidence of Richard's imperious demands, the minutiae dictated in Richard II's will were not addressed in the extant prescriptive text, *De Exequiis Regalibus*. Rather, Richard introduced his orders as instructions for how to do a funeral in *more regio*, in the royal way; he was reporting on what he viewed to *already* be the standard. This was not an improvisation, and indeed, certain features of Richard II's requests had been seen in prior kings' exequies. Many details provided in his will would finally appear as part of the royal prescriptive funerary texts in *Liber Regie Capelle* in 1449. Henry IV abided by some of these requests, though not all; Richard had asked for the funeral of a king—which he was not at his death.

There is limited information as to what Richard actually wore when he was buried. Eyewitnesses report that Richard's tightly wrapped body, face uncovered, was placed on a *chare* with black cloths, surrounded by torches and the banners of saints George and Edward the Confessor.[28] Possibly, Richard was dressed in whatever he had with him at Pontefract. In his will, he had specified the sceptre and jewellery to be included in his coffin. The survival of any of these items, if they existed, is unlikely; there had been holes in the shared tomb box of Richard and his queen, Anne of Bohemia, and items (including bones) are known to have been stolen from the tomb. This resulted in an oral tradition that there were copper crowns in the tomb, but upon opening in 1871, no such items were found.[29] The fragmented items in the tomb included what may have been parts of a sceptre,[30] but these may have been from Richard's reburial in 1413.

Evidence of the contents of Edward of Caernarvon's unopened coffin is more plentiful, due to information in accounts of the Great Wardrobe. Edward wore his undergarments (tunic, shirt, cap, gloves, and coronation coif) from his coronation, while his external garments appear to have been made for his exequies.[31] Uniquely, Edward of Caernarvon did have a funerary effigy, an image or mannequin of the deceased that was placed on top of the coffin during the exequies; this was the first of its kind, and until the sixteenth century it was a privilege reserved for the highest royal and ecclesiastic elites. However, despite wearing clothing fit for a king, Edward of Caernarvon was not issued a crown, rod, or sceptre by the Great Wardrobe.[32]

The crown, rod, and sceptre are explicitly mentioned requirements in *De Exequiis Regalibus*. David Carpenter, in discussing Henry III's exequies, determined that if an effigy was employed, the clothes it wore and the accessories it held were eventually returned to the Great Wardrobe, while those worn by the corpse never made it back for obvious reasons, which is explicitly noted in the jewel account.[33] Henry III, who did not have an effigy, thus took all his clothes and symbols of royalty to the grave. One set of Edward II's clothes (mantle, tunic, dalmatic, belt hose, shoes, cap, and spurs) made it back, and the undergarments did not. The external garments were more decorated and valuable, so they had been placed on the effigy to be retrieved later; the clothes made for Edward's corpse were probably not as ostentatious, though the value cannot be ascertained due to decay of the account. An interesting accessory was a gilt crown, valued at 7s 8d.[34] It is unlikely that Queen Isabella or Roger Mortimer, the de facto rulers, would have permitted the effigy to be crowned and visible to the public; Edward III, not Edward of Caernarvon, was king. Given that Edward of Caernarvon's coronation coif was not returned, the crown was probably paired with it, hidden from view, and went with the body to the grave. The crown was symbolic; it was just an artefact of Edward's previous status and power, much like the undergarments he wore. The reality was more reflected in what his hands held: nothing. His external garments in his coffin were likely pale copies of the valuable robes he wore the day he was crowned, memories of what had been.

Similarly, when looking at the illuminated *Chroniques* by Froissart held in the British Library (Harley MS 4380), the dead Richard II is seen in his procession, crowned but empty-handed.[35] Richard's hands had not been exposed during his procession, as only his face was visible.[36] Their appearance in the illumination should be seen as artistic license and political euphemism. The medieval audience was culturally aware about the problem of a deposed or usurped king's status; it was not by accident that these items were excluded from their funerals.

Neither Edward nor Richard were buried at Westminster, the centre of the English government. However, both bodies were viewed and sent on procession. Knights of Bristol and Gloucester were invited to view the body of Edward, probably at Berkeley, before its removal to Gloucester on 21 October 1327.[37] Edward's body was then taken on procession to Gloucester Abbey, which was less than twenty miles away from the site of Edward's death and far enough away from London to be out of sight and hopefully out of mind, as far as Queen Isabella and Mortimer were concerned.[38] The procession had at least some of the elements described in the *Liber Regie Capelle* and the *Household Articles*. Listed in an accounts roll at the Berkeley Castle Muniments are the expenses for dyeing a white canvas black for the funeral *chare*, the trappings for horses, decorations for the *chare*, oblations for the soul of the King, and the expenses for the Berkeley family to accompany the body to Gloucester Abbey.[39]

Richard of Bordeaux's body was taken from his place of death to London and then onward to King's Langley, thirty miles outside of London, for burial on 6 March 1400. The location of King's Langley for burial was a personally significant place for Richard; it was one of his favourite residences,[40] and he had interred his predeceased brother, Edward of Angoulême, there.[41] Along the processional route, there were mourners in black with torches, along with additional mourners with torches to greet the procession in London; Henry IV himself attended the services at St Paul's.[42] Froissart states that after St Paul's, Richard lay at Cheapside for two hours before being moved to King's Langley for his final exequies.[43] So far, Richard's funeral appears to have been appropriately carried out.

Henry IV paid out further sums for the body's transport and commemorative activity, including over 1,000 masses.[44] In the chronicles, very specific reports of the liturgical elements of Richard II's exequies are present, stating that the Office of the Dead took place, with Henry IV's approval and attendance.[45] Indeed, these items were required elements as set out by *Liber Regie Capelle*. As previously noted, all Christians needed a Mass of Requiem at their deaths, but a king was to receive the Office of the Dead and votive three masses (Trinity, Blessed Virgin, and Requiem) at each location where he was taken in procession. This reflected the king's status and his capacity for conspicuous consumption; only a man of a certain level of power and money could afford all of this. A king not having enough hours and masses was socially disturbing; his status was perceived to be undermined. Henry IV clearly provided enough to give Richard this courtesy.

Other courtesies were not afforded. The author of *Chronicque de la Traison et Mort de Richard Deux Roy Dengleterre* stated that Richard was buried *come un poure gentil home* or "like a poor gentleman".[46] Thomas Walsingham of St Albans complained that the abbot of St Albans was called upon late the night before the funeral and that the ceremonies the following morning were rushed. They were not well attended; Henry IV did not appear. Those that attended the final masses were not offered a meal afterwards.[47] The meal, or *convivium*, is a prescribed part of the funeral in the *Liber Regie Capelle.*[48] The Chapel Royal, the body governed by the *Liber Regie Capelle*, was a part of the King's Household; the implication is that the Household was to supply the *convivium* after the funeral and burial. It is ambiguous whether Henry IV was obliged to provide such a courtesy for his deposed predecessor, as Richard II was not king at his death and it was no longer his household. Walsingham's other complaints plausibly match up with that of the French narrative. The funeral of a "poor gentleman" did not meet social expectations due to the inability to spend money. Henry IV actively chose not to spend money on the secular features of Richard's exequies, thus denying him the status of king. Henry's tacit refusal to attend Richard's final funerary masses also undermined Richard's status.

The most glaring problem with Henry IV's funeral for Richard was the site of burial itself. As described above, King's Langley was not a terrible choice, but there was a complication: Richard had already completed his tomb—which was to be shared with his predeceased consort, Anne of Bohemia—by 1395, including the placement of recumbent statues of the (to-be) deceased.[49] This may well have tainted opinions regarding Henry IV and Richard II's exequies, regardless of how well they were executed.[50] Joel Burden rightly believes that Henry IV had tried to hedge between continuity with Richard and breaking away to establish his own ways. He attempted to grant Richard some elements of what would have been due to him, but also denied him others so as not to compromise Henry's own status.[51]

Edward II's funeral on 20 December 1327 was not as troublesome. There were at least two extensively decorated *herses*, standards, pennants, decorated coverings for harnesses, horses, and his coffin at Gloucester (all decorated with gold leaf), and appropriate clothing for the knights in attendance and other mourners.[52] These items can be placed in the contexts of the *Liber Regie Capelle* and the *Household Articles*. This was certainly a funeral for a man of status, even though there are no surviving narrative accounts from those in attendance. However, Edward could not be honoured as a king, as his son King Edward III had already been reigning since January 1327. This lack of status can be seen in the aforementioned appearance of the effigy and the clothing of the corpse, but was also manifest in the conspicuously absent torches and candles. So often described in both the wills of kings[53] and in the prescriptive texts,[54] the torches were to be dictated by rank: the higher the rank, the greater the number. What was Edward of Caernarvon's rank as a deposed king? Any rich man could have a lovely *herse*, but as mentioned above, the amount of candles and torches he had would identify his rank. Edward's exact position at his exequies was ambiguous, though there are no extant complaints about his exequies.

The funerals of Edward II and Richard II signified the importance of the deceased, yet also recognised that they were no longer kings. For Edward II, the goal of the funeral was never to delegitimise or negate Edward II as a king, because it was by virtue of his father's kingship that Edward III reigned.[55] For Richard II, some courtesies were afforded, such as a large number of masses and a procession, but others—including being buried where he wanted, and the demands of his will—could not. Although there were some unique features in Edward II's funeral, chroniclers never mentioned them. Close reading of the financial accounts and comparisons to other kings' exequies bring out these differences, not an eyewitness or contemporary complaining about them. The exequies were unremarkable and unobjectionable by contemporaries—they were a success. In contrast, chroniclers did complain about certain inconsistencies in Richard of Bordeaux's funeral, so this was less of a victory for the succeeding regime. Still, one must consider that the succession of Edward III was a much more direct and logical conclusion than Henry IV's own accession; Henry knew he was on precarious ground, so being too courteous to his rival may have endangered his own prospects.

In the *Household Articles* of 1494, a man was to be led into his funeral church with all his standards of rank, from least to greatest, and to have candles appropriate in number to his station.[56] Although this was newly committed to writing, it had been in practice for centuries. Even if a king was no longer king, the man still held some sort of station, unless he had been completely cast out. We therefore have the cases of Edward of Caernarvon and Richard of Bordeaux, no longer kings, but at least Edward was the Count of Ponthieu (through his mother), and Richard had held the titles of his father (Prince of Wales, Duke of Cornwall, Earl of Chester) for nearly a year prior to his accession. Their successors on the English throne viewed them as having been legitimate, though errant. Edward II and Richard II retained certain rights by their previous stations, and this was seen in how their funerals were conducted. They enjoyed funerals that were not kingly, but certainly noble, which is what they would have been if the crown had not passed to them. They were also subject to some process of deposition or forced abdication; they had been legitimate upon accession, so there had to be some action performed for them to release their power to their successor. This was the definitive difference between these two kings-that-were-not-kings in the fourteenth century and Henry VI and Richard III in the fifteenth century.

King by fact, not by law

In the Calendar of Charter Rolls, early on in Edward IV's reign, the phrase "king by fact, not by law" springs up repeatedly in reference to items issued by the Lancastrian kings from 1399 to 1461.[57] The Lancastrians, in the Yorkist mind, were never licit kings of England, though in fact laws and financial arrangements were ordered by them. These had to be honoured lest the kingdom descend into chaos,[58] but the power they had wielded was never rightfully theirs. Richard II had attainted Henry Bolingbroke,[59] and Edward IV may have considered that sentence to be in effect for his descendants. Edward IV ensured that Henry VI had this status by attainting him in the Parliament of November 1461, stripping him of the duchy of Lancaster.[60]

The phrase rang out again, though in a different choice of words, when Henry VII described Richard III's reign. Richard III was never considered to have been rightfully king from the moment he died, as he was succeeded by Henry VII, a man who felt that his rival's reign was completely illegitimate.[61] Although Richard III held the lands and titles of York by being his father's surviving, legitimate heir,[62] Henry VII made it a point to back-date his reign prior to Bosworth, deem Richard III a traitor, and attaint him post-mortem, stripping him of whatever titles he had. Henry VII did this at his first Parliament in November 1485. For both Henry VI and Richard III, the status of the deceased was completely nullified by attainder, and neither were afforded a formal process of deposition. As a result of their attainders, they were never kings. They were no longer princes of the blood royal. According to their attainders, these two men were not even nobles. There was no need to apply any prescriptive text with rigour. A rule not applied cannot be broken.

Refusing to adhere to the rules of the royal funeral had consequences, often immediately. The embalming stipulations in *De Exequiis Regalibus* were clearly disregarded by Edward IV when arranging for the exequies of Henry VI, oft referred to as Henry of Windsor. The 1910 tomb opening offers the physical evidence for this, but there is also narrative and financial evidence that corroborates the accusation of poor handling. The interval between Henry's death and burial in May 1471 was only three days, as he died at the Tower of London. Henry was paraded with an open visage, so that he could be identified.[63] According to *Warkworth's Chronicle*, Henry's body, while coffined, left blood on the ground, once at St Paul's and once at Blackfriars.[64] "Cruentation" was the medieval urban legend in which a victim always bled in the presence of his murderer. Henry theoretically bled in the presence of the pro-Yorkist courtiers and the royal house. Bleeding after death was also considered a sign of a martyr, and Henry quickly acquired a saintly following.[65] The report of blood might be dismissed as pro-Lancastrian propaganda, but given the condition of Henry's remains in 1910 and the stipulations of medieval preservation, the "bleeding" may have been the result of a poor embalming.

The costs of Henry's embalming were also low, as most of the money designated for his funeral was for the guarding of the corpse. Only £15 3s 6½d, given to Hugh Brice, was set aside for clergy, cloth, spices (the item that implied embalming), torches for the escort to St Paul's and to Chertsey, and other items, such as the unmentioned embalmer himself.[66] There was an additional payment of £9 10s 11d to Richard Martyn for twenty-eight yards of Holland linen and other items related to Henry's exit from the Tower, including the soldiers' salary for escort. Henry IV had spent far more than this amount caring for Richard's body in 1400 compared to what Edward IV spent in 1471 for Henry's body. In 1377, £21 had been spent solely upon the embalming of Edward III.[67] The poor condition of Henry's bones partially reflect the initial lack of a lead coffin—a measure recommended by the prescriptive texts the *Liber Regie Capelle*[68] and the *Household Articles*.[69] His exposure to the populace of London, the financial accounts, and the presence of tissue and hair clinging to the skull indicate that Henry was embalmed, though poorly.[70] The body did not withstand the centuries, or even the days before burial.

If we believe that Henry bled on the streets outside St Paul's and Blackfriars, then we may also believe he was denied divine services in those churches; it was forbidden to contaminate a church by shedding blood, whether by violence or due to an incontinent body.[71] If Henry's corpse was leaking, then he may have been denied entry. Alternatively, if he had not bled, this may have been part of Edward IV's disregard for him; it was a distinctly royal or elite feature to have the body in the church, rather than waiting outside. Although sources state that Henry had a procession with torches from the Tower to St Paul's with stops in between, these sources equally lack any mention of offices or masses for Henry in London. He was taken to churches to be seen, but there is no mention of anything happening at those churches. Hall reported that there were no Offices of the Dead, no masses, no tapers, no riders, and no mourners.[72] Others concurred, saying that there were only soldiers guarding the body, as if the dead Henry was being marched to execution.[73]

The Exchequer tells a slightly different story. The Carmelites, Augustinians, Dominicans, and Franciscans each received £1 and "other charities", while the Brothers of the Holy Cross received £2 for masses to be said for Henry in London. The Dominicans also received £2 12s 3d for masses and obsequies at Chertsey, for a total of £8 12s 3d.[74] There were certainly masses said for Henry in the City of London and at Chertsey on the day of his burial, but not necessarily during the procession in the days before. Unlike Richard of Bordeaux, there are no assurances by chroniclers that Henry of Windsor had masses offered for him while he was processed through London, nor any report of St Paul's receiving money for masses. The procession, funeral, and burial of Henry was a speedy affair. The corruption of Henry's corpse in public and the lack of any remedial action violated the spirit of *De Exequiis Regalibus* in its provisions for proper embalming and for giving a king a fitting funeral and burial. The exequies for Henry were thought to be pitiful.[75]

There is little evidence to suggest that Richard III, who had also lost his crown, received anything other than burial in holy ground. After his death on Bosworth Field on 22 August 1485, Richard was taken to the Church of the Annunciation in Leicester and lay in state for two days as evidence that he was dead.[76] He was transported to Greyfriars for burial, slung over a horse's back, tied up. Polydore Vergil indicates that Richard was buried naked, "without any pomp or solemn funeral".[77] David Baldwin postulated in 1986 that despite the disgraced state of the former king, he might have been interred in the choir of Greyfriars, a traditional place of honour.[78] He was not attainted and stripped of his titles until November.

Baldwin's theory was confirmed with the 2012 excavation of the Greyfriars' church in Leicester and the subsequent positive identification of Richard III's remains therein.[79] The ground near the skeleton's sacral area revealed the presence of roundworms,[80] indicating that Richard was buried with his intestines and not eviscerated. His two-day display in the Church of the Annunciation suggests that no preservative measures were taken. No evidence of a coffin or grave goods, such as cloth or jewellery, was found in the grave, which was too small.[81] If Richard had been shrouded by the friars, this would have decayed.[82]

Richard III's treatment resulted from the fact that he had never been considered king by Henry VII, and this status was made official by the post-mortem attainder.[83] His attainder meant that Henry VII was ultimately under little obligation to do anything more than to see that Richard was buried in holy ground. As Richard was never a true king, there was no reason to carry out the activities described in *De Exequiis Regalibus* and the *Liber Regie Capelle*. By loss of his titles, Richard would not have received the honours described in the *Household Articles* for princes of the blood royal either. Richard's reputation had already been marred by the manner in which he acquired the throne, the disappearance of his nephews, and rumours surrounding his marital ties. Despite this, chroniclers condemned those who did not treat his body well and expressed complicated feelings regarding Richard himself. As Polydore Vergil stated (later paraphrased by others), "And so the miserable man had suddenly such an end as wont is to happen to them that have right and law both of God and man in like estimation, as well [as] impiety and wickedness." In essence, Richard deserved his fate because he was a rotten person, but he was still king.[84] It must be considered that although Edward IV and Henry VII sought to undermine their predecessors' statuses, they could not control the perception of those who pitied Henry VI or those who were slightly perturbed by the treatment of Richard's body.

Although they had to be loyal to the new king, the Franciscan friars in Leicester still had an obligation to offer care for the souls of the poor, as they were (and are) charged in their vows; the prayers for burial were probably said, and Richard III's former status was recognised by being buried in the choir. If no offices and masses were said before Richard's interment, they may have been performed after Henry Tudor and his men departed from Leicester. An alternative order of burial presents itself in BL Arundel MS 26, the extant narrative of the exequies of Elizabeth Woodville, Edward IV's queen. In her will, the former consort had chosen not to have her full royal funeral as permitted by the *Liber Regie Capelle*, but rather a simpler, plainer one. Her only regal request was to be interred in the vault of Edward IV.[85] She was buried before any of her mourners arrived, in the dead of night, much to the horror of the manuscript's writer.[86] However, over the course of the following days, her hours and masses were said in the presence of her surviving children, save for Cecily and Queen Elizabeth.[87] There were general words of burial said for Elizabeth Woodville the night she was interred, but the Office of the Dead and three masses were executed days after; this was not liturgically unacceptable, or else those at Windsor would not have performed it. Socially, however, this event seems to have been an oddity; the writer of Arundel MS 26 aims his objections at the nature and order of events being below Elizabeth's station as a former queen and as mother of the current queen. His distressed tone is reminiscent of Henry VI's chroniclers in discussing his lack of liturgical hours and masses at every stop. Even though the prescriptive texts may have been applied appropriately and the private wishes of the deceased honoured, funerals for kings (and queens) that did not meet expectations were negatively commented upon. Chroniclers noticed when the traditional or the critical liturgical elements were missing. Failure to meet societal expectations pertaining to the deceased's status also provoked criticism, even if the funeral had met the necessary criteria of Christian burial and the prescriptive texts of the royal house. The writer of Arundel MS 26 was greatly displeased by the low-profile funeral and burial of Elizabeth Woodville, the queen dowager, even though it had been by her will and it was not liturgically inappropriate.[88]

Conclusion

Edward II and Richard II received exequies that were far more splendid than Henry VI and Richard III. More money was expended on the first pair, and their exequies had many royal features, although the handling of Richard II became awkward as Henry IV attempted to balance his claim with Richard's own indisputable one. Decoding the success of a royal medieval funeral partly depends on determining how contemporaries viewed it. No comment or complaint was rendered for the exequies of Edward II. The irregularities of Henry VI and Richard III's burials dominate chronicle accounts. Richard II lay somewhere in the middle. Save for Thomas Walsingham's chronicles and the *Chronicque de la Traison et Mort*, the written accounts of Richard II's funeral mention no overt problem or inappropriate arrangements. They are silent, not objecting to how the man was handled and buried. This implies that the majority thought the deposed king had received a funeral fitting to his station or they were too intimidated to suggest otherwise.

In contrast, Henry VI and Richard III had funerals and burials that were very different from the rituals described in the prescriptive texts; there were comments about the brief, piteous exequies for both men. Henry of Windsor's body decayed rapidly due a combination of certain prescriptive texts beings applied (procession, public view) and others not (embalming and preservation). Richard III was briskly interred, a loser of a great battle. The defining difference between these two sets of men was whether they were acknowledged as being of noble blood after they lost their crowns. For Edward II and Richard II, their status and inheritance granted them exequies as princes or at least noblemen. Henry VI and Richard III were attainted and stripped of any vestige of their former statuses, including the right to have a funeral fit for a king.

Notes

1 I have many people to thank for this publication, not least of which is Joel Burden, whose chapter "How Do You Bury a Deposed King?" was the spur. He also kindly exchanged ideas with me during my doctoral studies. I also must express gratitude toward W. M. Ormrod, who helped guide me through the larger work of my thesis, from which this piece is derived. I also must thank Jonathan Spangler, Ana Maria S. A. Rodrigues, and Manuela Santos Silva for their advice, editing, and support during this process.

2 W. H. St John Hope, "The Discovery of the Remains of King Henry VI in St. George's Chapel, Windsor Castle", *Archaeologia* 62, 2 (1911): 537.

3 Hope, "The Discovery of the Remains of King Henry VI", 537.

4 Ibid., 536.

5 R. Buckley, M. Morris, J. Appleby, T. King, D. O'Sullivan, and L. Foxhall, "'The King in the Car Park': New Light on the Death and Burial of Richard III in the Greyfriars Church, Leicester, in 1485", *Antiquity* 87 (2013): 536.

6 J. Burden, "How Do You Bury a Deposed King?" in *Henry IV: The Establishment of the Regime, 1399–1406*, eds Gwilym Dodd and Douglas Biggs (Woodbridge: York Medieval Press 2003), 50.

7 Because he was never crowned, Edward V will not be discussed here.
8 Bodleian MS Rawlinson C 425 is a "pontificale abbatiae Westmonasteriensis" with parts dating to the thirteenth century. J. W. Legg notes that the mortuary rite for kings is not in the original body of this manuscript; it is on the last folio and runs onto a page pasted into the back cover of the bound MS. It is also in a different, later hand; *Missale ad Usum Ecclesie Westmonasteriensis*, iii, ed. J. W. Legg, Henry Bradshaw Society 12 (Bury St Edmunds: Boydell, 1999), ix.
9 *Missale ad Usum Ecclesie Westmonasteriensis*, ii, ed. J.W. Legg, Henry Bradshaw Society 5 (Bury St Edmunds: Boydell, 1999), cols. 734–35.
10 R. Giesey, *The Royal Funeral Ceremony in Renaissance France* (Geneva: Droz, 1960), 22–23.
11 For example, Edward I died on 7 July 1307 on the Scottish border and was interred in Westminster Abbey on 27 October 1307, lying in state at various locations. Henry V died on 31 August 1422 in France and was not interred in Westminster Abbey until 7 November 1422. His body was displayed at churches along the route to the Abbey. This custom was not only for kings who died abroad. Edward III died at Sheen on 21 June 1377 and was interred on 5 July 1377 at Westminster, a gap of three weeks.
12 The illuminations are found in Pamplona MS 197, fol. 22v; *Litlyngton Missal*, fol. 224r; and *Liber Regalis*, fol. 33v.
13 This is particularly well illustrated by the sceptre of Charles V of France, crafted no later than 1380, which is topped by a figure of Charlemagne holding a long rod and a gold ball. It is currently on display at the Louvre as part of the French Crown jewels.
14 *Liber Regie Capelle*, ed. W. Ullmann, Henry Bradshaw Society 92 (Woodbridge: Boydell, 2010 [1959]), 115.
15 Ibid., 7.
16 As described in C. E. Woodruff and W. Danks, *Memorials of the Cathedral and Priory of Christ in Canterbury* (London: Chapman & Hall, 1912), 191.
17 *Liber Regie Capelle*, 112–14.
18 Ibid., 113–15.
19 *A Collection of Ordinances and Regulations for the Government of the Royal Household, made in divers reigns*, ed. J. Nichols (London: John Nichols for the Society of Antiquaries, 1790), 130.
20 Ibid., 131.
21 For a fuller discussion of the events of January 1327, see C. Valente, "The Deposition and Abdication of Edward II", *English Historical Review* 113, 453 (1998): 852–81.
22 N. Saul, *Richard II* (New Haven: Yale University Press, 1997), 418–25.
23 It is commonly accepted that both men met unnatural ends, though the exact nature of these events will likely remain subjects of debate.
24 S. A. Moore, "Documents Relating to the Death and Burial of King Edward II", *Archaeologia* 50 (1887): 218.
25 A. P. Stanley, "On an Examination of the Tombs of Richard II and Henry III in Westminster Abbey", *Archaeologia* 45, 2 (1880): 323.
26 *Issues of the Exchequer: being A Collection of Payments Made out of His Majesty's Revenue from King Henry III to King Henry VI Inclusive*, ed. Frederick Devon (London: John Murray, 1837), 275.
27 *A Collection of All the Wills, now known to be extant, of the Kings and Queens of England*, ed. John Nichols (London: John Nichols, 1780), 192–99.
28 *The Brut*, ii, ed. F. W. D. Brie (London: Kegan Paul, 1908), 591; *Chronicque de la Traison et Mort de Richart Deux Roy Dengleterre*, ed. and trans. by Benjamin Williams (Vaduz: Kraus Reprint, 1964), 103 and 261.
29 Stanley, "On an Examination", 314.
30 Ibid., 326–27.
31 Moore, "Documents Relating to the Death and Burial of King Edward II", 222.
32 D. A. Carpenter, *The Reign of Henry III* (London: Hambledon Press, 1996), 435, observes this in comparison to Henry III's Wardrobe; Moore, "Documents Relating to the Death and Burial of King Edward II", 221–22.

33 Carpenter, *The Reign of Henry III*, 429–32, citing The National Archives [henceforth TNA], E 372/116, m. 1v. My thanks to Paul Dryburgh for informing me of the jewel account's publication in *The Wardrobe Accounts of Henry III*, ed. B. Wild, Pipe Roll Society, 58 (96) (London: 2012), 155.
34 Moore, "Documents Relating to the Death and Burial of King Edward II", 221–22.
35 British Library [henceforth BL], Harley MS 4380 (Froissart's *Chroniques*), fol. 197b.
36 Thomas Walsingham, *The St Albans Chronicle*, ii, eds J. Taylor, W. Childs, and L. Watkiss (Oxford: Oxford University Press, 2011), 300; Jean Froissart, *Oeuvres: Chroniques*, xvi, ed. K. de Lettenhove (Osnabrück: Biblio Verlag, 1967), 235–36; *The Brut*, ii, 360; *Eulogium (Historiarum sive Temporis): etc.*, iii, ed. F. S. Haydon, RS, 9 (London: 1858), 387.
37 Moore, "Documents Relating to the Death and Burial of King Edward II", 220.
38 D. M. Palliser, "Royal Mausolea", in *Fourteenth Century England VI*, ed. W. M. Ormrod (Woodbridge: Boydell, 2010), 9; S. Phillips, *Edward II* (New Haven: Yale University Press, 2010), 550–52.
39 J. Smythe, *The Lives of the Berkeleys, Lords of the Honour, Castle, and Manor of Berkeley in the County of Gloucester from 1066–1618*, i, ed. Sir J. MacLean (Gloucester: John Bellows, 1883), 292–94.
40 J. H. Wylie, *History of England Under Henry the Fourth*, i (London: Longmans, Green, and Co, 1884), 117.
41 *Issues of the Exchequer*, 244.
42 *The Brut*, ii, 591; *Chronicque de la Traison et Mort*, 103 and 261.
43 Froissart, *Oeuvres*, xvi, 236.
44 *Issues of the Exchequer*, 275.
45 *The Brut*, ii, 360; Walsingham, *The St. Albans Chronicle*, ii, 300.
46 *Chronicque de la Traison*, 96 and 251.
47 Walsingham, *The St. Albans Chronicle*, ii, 301.
48 *Liber Regie Capelle*, 114.
49 TNA, E 101/473/7.
50 Paul Strohm, *England's Empty Throne: Usurpation and the Language of Legitimation, 1399–1422* (London: Yale University Press, 1998), 104.
51 Burden, "How Do You Bury A Deposed King?" 50.
52 Moore, "Documents Relating to the Death and Burial of King Edward II", 221–22.
53 For example, his son Edward III specifically asked that his tomb be well lit, possibly in reference to how his father could not be honoured; *A Collection of Wills*, 60.
54 *A Collection of Ordinances*, 130.
55 W. M. Ormrod, *Edward III* (New Haven: Yale University Press, 2010), 69.
56 *A Collection of Ordinances*, 130.
57 *Calendar of the Charter Rolls, [..] 1427–1516.* (London: His Majesty's Stationery Office, 1927), 139–67.
58 M. Hicks, *The Wars of the Roses* (London: Yale University Press, 2010), 170.
59 C. Given-Wilson, "Richard II, Edward II, and the Lancastrian Inheritance", *English Historical Review* 109, 432 (1994): 566–67.
60 *Parliament Rolls of Medieval England* [henceforth *PROME*], general ed. C. Given-Wilson (Scholarly Digital Editions and TNA: Leicester, 2005), Parliament of November 1461, items 17–28, with the loss of the duchy of Lancaster due to the attainder of Henry VI in item 26.
61 *PROME*, Parliament of November 1485, item 8.
62 T. B. Pugh, "Henry VII and the English Nobility", in *The Tudor Nobility*, ed. G. W. Bernard (Manchester: Manchester University Press, 1992), 85. By denying that the boys were legitimate heirs, Richard III asserted that the titles and holdings of York should have passed to him upon Edward IV's death. Thereafter, on Richard's death, if Henry VII had declared the now-legitimate boys dead, then the holdings and titles of York should have been divided among the surviving sisters. It was more beneficial for Henry for the boys to be simply absent and not legally dead, as the Crown would retain the lands and titles in their absence. Henry VIII ultimately had to make a settlement with his surviving aunts in 1511 to keep the York–Mortimer inheritance for himself.

63 *The Great Chronicle of London*, eds A. H. Thomas and I. D. Thornley (London: George W. Jones at the Sign of the Dolphin, 1938), 220.
64 T. Warkworth, "Warkworth's Chronicle: A Chronicle of the First Thirteen Years of the Reign of King Edward the Fourth", ed. J. O. Halliwell, in *Three Chronicles of the Reign of Edward IV* (Gloucester: Alan Sutton Publishing, 1988), 43.
65 E. Duffy, *Stripping the Altars: Traditional Religion of England, 1400–1580* (New Haven: Yale University Press, 1992), 161.
66 *Issues of the Exchequer*, 495–96.
67 C. Given-Wilson, "The Exequies of Edward III and the Royal Funeral Ceremony in Late Medieval England", *English Historical Review* 124, 507 (2009): 264.
68 *Liber Regie Capelle*, 113–14.
69 *A Collection of Ordinances*, 130.
70 Hope, "The Discovery of the Remains of King Henry VI", 537.
71 R. Horrox, "Purgatory, Prayer, and Plague: 1150–1380", in *Death in England: An Illustrated History*, eds P. C. Jupp and C. Gittings (Manchester: Manchester University Press, 1999), 103.
72 E. Hall, *Hall's Chronicle containing the History of England during the Reign of Henry the Fourth and the Succeeding Monarchs to the End of the Reign of Henry the Eighth* (London: J. Johnson, et al., 1809), 303.
73 *The Great Chronicle of London*, 220.
74 *Issues of the Exchequer*, 496
75 *The Great Chronicle of London*, 220; *Hall's Chronicle*, 330.
76 Charles Ross, *Richard III* (London: Eyre Methuen, 1981), 225; David Baldwin, "King Richard's Grave in Leicester", *Transactions of the Leicester Archaeological and History Society* 60 (1986): 21.
77 Polydore Vergil, *Three Books of Polydore Vergil's English History, Comprising the Reigns of Henry VI, Edward IV, and Richard III*, ed. Sir H. Ellis, Camden Society OS, 24 (London: 1844), 226.
78 Baldwin, "King Richard's Grave in Leicester", 24.
79 University of Leicester, "Richard III: Osteology", *The Discovery of Richard III*, accessed 12 May 2018, www.le.ac.uk/richardiii/science/osteology.html.
80 P. Mitchell, H. Yeh, J. Appleby, and R. Buckley, "The Intestinal Parasites of King Richard III", *The Lancet* 382 (4 September 2013), 888.
81 University of Leicester, "Archaeological Dig: Skeleton Found, Wednesday, 5 September Continued", *The Discovery of Richard III*, accessed 12 May 2018, www.le.ac.uk/richardiii/archaeology/5septembercont.html.
82 University of Leicester, "Richard III: Osteology".
83 *PROME*, Parliament of November 1485, item 8.
84 *Hall's Chronicle*, 421; Vergil, *Three Books*, 226; *The Great Chronicle of London*, 238.
85 *A Collection of Wills*, 350; BL, Arundel MS 26, fol. 29v.
86 BL, Arundel MS 26, fol. 29v.
87 BL, Arundel MS 26, fols 29v–30r.
88 Euan C. Roger has discovered some historical documentation that suggests Elizabeth Woodville may have died of plague, which would, in part, explain the rushed funeral: "'To Be Shut Up': New Evidence for Development of Quarantine Regulations in Early-Tudor England", *Social History of Medicine*, 11 April 2019.

Bibliography

Primary sources

Bodleian Library, Oxford, UK, MS Rawlinson C 425.
British Library (BL), London, UK, Arundel MS 26.

British Library (BL), London, UK, Harley MS 4380.
Museo de Navarra, Pamplona, Spain, MS 197.
The National Archives (TNA), Kew, UK, E 101/473/7.
Westminster Abbey, Westminster, UK, MS 37 (*Litlyngton Missal*).
Westminster Abbey, Westminster, UK, MS 38 (*Liber Regalis*).

Secondary sources

Baldwin, David. "King Richard's Grave in Leicester". *Transactions of the Leicester Archaeological and History Society* 60 (1986): 21–24.

The Brut. Ed. F. W. D. Brie. 2 vols. London: Kegan Paul, 1906–08.

Buckley, R., M. Morris, J. Appleby, T. King, D. O'Sullivan, and L. Foxhall. "'The King in the Car Park': New Light on the Death and Burial of Richard III in the Greyfriars Church, Leicester, in 1485". *Antiquity* 87 (2013): 519–38.

Burden, J. "How Do You Bury a Deposed King?" In *Henry IV: The Establishment of the Regime, 1399–1406*. Eds Gwilym Dodd and Douglas Biggs, 35–54. Woodbridge: York Medieval Press, 2003.

Calendar of the Charter Rolls, [. . .] 1427–1516. London: His Majesty's Stationery Office, 1927.

Carpenter, David A. *The Reign of Henry III*. London: Hambledon Press, 1996.

Chronicque de la Traison et Mort de Richart Deux Roy Dengleterre. Ed. and trans. Benjamin Williams. Vaduz: Kraus Reprint, 1964.

A Collection of All the Wills, now known to be extant, of the Kings and Queens of England, etc. Ed. J. Nichols. London: John Nichols for the Society of Antiquaries, 1780.

A Collection of Ordinances and Regulations for the Government of the Royal Household, made in divers reigns. Ed. J. Nichols. London: John Nichols for the Society of Antiquaries, 1790.

Duffy, E. *Stripping the Altars: Traditional Religion of England, 1400–1580*. New York: Yale University Press, 1992.

Eulogium (Historiarum sive Temporis): etc. Ed. F. S. Haydon. 3 vols. RS, 9. London: 1858.

Froissart, J. *Oeuvres: Chroniques*. Ed. K. de Lettenhove. 18 vols. Osnabrück: Biblio Verlag, 1967.

Giesey, R. *The Royal Funeral Ceremony in Renaissance France*. Geneva: Libraire E. Droz, 1960.

Given-Wilson, C. "Richard II, Edward II, and the Lancastrian Inheritance". *English Historical Review* 109, 432 (1994): 553–71.

Given-Wilson, C. "The Exequies of Edward III and the Royal Funeral Ceremony in Late Medieval England". *English Historical Review* 124, 507 (2009): 257–82.

The Great Chronicle of London. Eds A. H. Thomas and I. D. Thornley. London: George W. Jones at the Sign of the Dolphin, 1938.

Hall, E. *Hall's Chronicle containing the History of England during the Reign of Henry the Fourth and the Succeeding Monarchs to the End of the Reign of Henry the Eighth*. London: Printed for J. Johnson, et al., 1809.

Hicks, M. *The Wars of the Roses*. London: Yale University Press, 2010.

Hope, W. H. St John. "The Discovery of the Remains of King Henry VI in St. George's Chapel, Windsor Castle". *Archaeologia* 62, 2 (1911): 533–42.

Horrox, R. "Purgatory, Prayer, and Plague: 1150–1380". In *Death in England: An Illustrated History*. Eds P. C. Jupp and C. Gittings. Manchester: Manchester University Press, 1999.

Issues of the Exchequer: being A Collection of Payments Made out of His Majesty's Revenue from King Henry III to King Henry VI Inclusive. Ed. F. Devon. London: John Murray, 1837.

Liber Regie Capelle. Ed. W. Ullmann. Henry Bradshaw Society 92. Woodbridge: Boydell, 2010.

Missale ad Usum Ecclesie Westmonasteriensis. Ed. J. W. Legg. 3 vols. Henry Bradshaw Society 1, 5, 12. Bury St Edmunds: Boydell, 1999.

Mitchell, P., H. Yeh, J. Appleby, and R. Buckley. "The Intestinal Parasites of King Richard III". *The Lancet*, 382 (4 September 2013): 888.

Moore, S. A. "Documents Relating to the Death and Burial of King Edward II". *Archaeologia* 50 (1887): 215–26.

Ormrod, W. M. *Edward III*. New Haven: Yale University Press, 2010.

Palliser, D. M. "Royal Mausolea in the Long Fourteenth Century". In *Fourteenth Century England VI*. Ed. W. M. Ormrod, 1–19. Woodbridge: Boydell, 2010.

Parliament Rolls of Medieval England. General Ed. C. Given-Wilson. Scholarly Digital Editions and The National Archives: Leicester, 2005.

Phillips, S. *Edward II*. New Haven: Yale University Press, 2010.

Pugh, T. B. "Henry VII and the English Nobility". In *The Tudor Nobility*. Ed. G. W. Bernard, 49–110. Manchester: Manchester University Press, 1992.

Roger, Euan C. "'To Be Shut Up': New Evidence for Development of Quarantine Regulations in Early-Tudor England". *Social History of Medicine*, 11 April 2019. https://doi.org/10.1093/shm/hkz031.

Ross, Charles. *Richard III*. London: Eyre Methuen, 1981.

Saul, N. *Richard II*. New Haven: Yale University Press, 1997.

Smythe, J. *The Lives of the Berkeleys, Lords of the Honour, Castle, and Manor of Berkeley in the County of Gloucester from 1066–1618*. Ed. Sir J. MacLean. 3 vols. Gloucester: John Bellows, 1883.

Stanley, A. P. "On an Examination of the Tombs of Richard II and Henry III in Westminster Abbey". *Archaeologia* 45, 2 (1880): 309–27.

Strohm, Paul. *England's Empty Throne Usurpation and the Language of Legitimation, 1399–1422*. London: Yale University Press, 1998.

Valente, C. "The Deposition and Abdication of Edward II". *English Historical Review* 113, 453 (1998): 852–81.

Vergil, Polydore. *Three Books of Polydore Vergil's English History, Comprising the Reigns of Henry VI, Edward IV, and Richard III*. Ed. Sir H. Ellis. Camden Society OS, 24. London: 1844.

Walsingham, Thomas. *The St Albans Chronicle: The* Chronica Majora *of Thomas Walsingham*. Eds J. Taylor, W. Childs, and L. Watkiss. 2 vols. Oxford: Oxford University Press, 2003–11.

The Wardrobe Accounts of Henry III. Ed. B. Wild. Pipe Roll Society, 58 (96). London: 2012.

Warkworth, T. "Warkworth's Chronicle: A Chronicle of the First Thirteen Years of the Reign of King Edward the Fourth". Ed. James Orchard Halliwell. In *Three Chronicles of the Reign of Edward IV*. Gloucester: Alan Sutton Publishing, 1988.

Woodruff, C. E., and W. Danks, *Memorials of the Cathedral and Priory of Christ in Canterbury*. London: Chapman & Hall, 1912.

Wylie, J. H. *History of England Under Henry the Fourth*. 3 vols. London: Longmans, Green, and Co, 1884.

University of Leicester. *The Discovery of Richard III*. Excavation website. www.le.ac.uk/richardiii/.

10

THE EXALTATION OF THE "HOLINESS" OF THE BRAGANÇA DYNASTY AS A LEGITIMATING STRATEGY IN THE SEVENTEENTH CENTURY

Paula Almeida Mendes

Following the Portuguese Restoration of 1640, the European and international political framework of the second half of the seventeenth century meant that the newly inaugurated Bragança dynasty faced difficulties in having its legitimacy recognised. This study draws attention to the exaltation of the "holiness" of some of its members (Prince Teodósio, Princess Joana) or at least of their "virtue" (Queen Luísa de Guzman; Princess Catherine, queen of England; Princess Isabel Luísa Josefa), which became a strategy to support the legitimacy of this "illustrious" royal family that was able to "generate saints".

The disappearance of King Sebastian of Portugal, single and without children, in the Battle of Alcácer-Quibir in 1578, triggered a succession crisis regarding the Portuguese throne.[1] The Portuguese crown was at first delivered to Cardinal Henry, son of King Manuel I and Sebastian's great-uncle, who, sick and childless, died in 1580.[2] Thus the death of the old Cardinal-King opened a new succession crisis between three pretenders to the throne, all of them grandsons of King Manuel I: Philip II of Spain; Catherine, duchess of Bragança; and Anthony, the prior of Crato. The invasion of Portugal by Spanish troops commanded by the Duke of Alba, and the defeat of the prior of Crato in Alcântara, contributed to the imposition of Philip II of Spain as the best-placed candidate to ascend the Portuguese throne. Philip II also obtained the important support of the Portuguese nobility and of some sectors of the Portuguese bourgeoisie. This situation would culminate with the acclamation of Philip II as king of Portugal, at the Cortes of Tomar in 1581. Thus Portugal became part of a dual monarchy for sixty years.

An ambience of mourning after the disaster of Alcácer-Quibir and the subsequent loss of independence had gradually generated a malaise in Portuguese society.[3] This sentiment peaked in the 1630s and led to a revolt against rule by the Spanish Habsburgs. As Joaquim Romero Magalhães stresses, "the Union of Arms of 1639–1640, which would have been the pretext-agent for the restorationist rupture of 1640, culminates after these long years of connection [with the Habsburg monarchy]".[4] Thus on 1 December 1640, John, duke of Bragança, was acclaimed king of Portugal, as John IV. As underlined by Fernando Dores Costa, the Portuguese separation from the Spanish crown can be understood as an integral episode of the Thirty Years' War.[5] Spain was heavily involved with its military forces and also tied down by a rebellion in Catalonia, and was therefore unable to attend fully to the situation in Portugal.

The newly inaugurated Bragança dynasty faced several and various difficulties, however, in the political and international context of the second half of the seventeenth century, notably in its efforts to have its legitimacy recognised abroad. This concern for recognition drove it to send several embassies, not only to the major European courts, but also to the Holy See, where negotiations had been particularly difficult. King John IV sent several ambassadors, including the preacher and counsellor Father António Vieira, to various European kingdoms, while also attempting to negotiate the marriage of some of his children to other European princes. This strategy sought to reaffirm Portugal's prestige in the concert of European kingdoms. In this context, Portugal tightened its traditional alliance with England, dating back to the Treaty of Windsor in 1386; and obligingly, King Charles II of England gave military support to the Portuguese in their ongoing war of restoration with Spain which only ended in 1668.[6] Meanwhile, Portugal had also managed to expel the Dutch, arch-opponents of the Habsburgs, from Brazil and Angola, restoring Portuguese power in these Atlantic colonial spaces.

The construction of this political reality was carried out in part by this diplomatic activity, and also by the production of literature, from sermons[7] through to military or political texts,[8] produced over the period of the Restoration.[9] These factors were responsible, each in its own way, for defending the legitimacy of the rights of King John IV to the crown of Portugal. He was identified in some restorationist texts as *O Encoberto* ("the Hidden One") who would rise as a saviour to set free the fatherland from the Spanish and foreign oppression,[10] a figure already referred to by Gonçalo Anes Bandarra in his famous *Trovas* ("Verses"), written in the first half of the sixteenth century. Bandarra was a cobbler from Trancoso who wrote these based on his knowledge of the prophecies attributed to St Isidore and the writings of Pedro de Frias. These *Trovas* argued that a king, designated as the "Hidden One" because his identity is not explicit in the text, "seed of King Ferdinand the Catholic", would disrupt the Ottoman Empire and establish a world monarchy.[11] These *Trovas* were, as we shall see later, subject to different interpretations. In 1603, D. João de Castro published his *Paráfrase*: in his interpretation of these verses he identifies the "Hidden One" as King Sebastian;[12] later, as we shall see, the "Hidden One" would be King John IV.

Recent historical scholarship has primarily addressed the political, diplomatic, and military aspects that frame the Restoration in Portugal in the second half of the seventeenth century. But it is worth highlighting that other aspects, notably spiritual, of the lives of many Portuguese figures, particularly those of the Royal House, gleaned from various texts, can also contribute to complete understanding of this period. It is possible to study these aspects in texts of various types or paratexts about some members of the Bragança dynasty, constructing their portrait anchored in the concept of nobility through a reflection on their qualities and attributes, which matched together both "illustrious blood" and "good inclination" or virtue. This double set of notable qualities was, moreover, a theme prevalent throughout the seventeenth century, as shown in several texts;[13] for example, the *Cour Sainte* by Nicolas Caussin, deeply influenced by François de Sales, which was widely successful and was translated into Portuguese, published by António Pires Galante in 1652.[14]

Given this framework, centred on the debate and trying to articulate (true) nobility and virtue throughout the seventeenth century, it should not seem strange that several authors of this era convert this binomial into a *topos* with hagiographic contours. Indeed, in most of the saints' and devout "lives" published in the period, the protagonists are of noble descent and almost always the heirs of the moral and spiritual superiority that characterised their lineage. Thus biographers remained faithful to a long tradition, according to which holiness and nobility of birth are closely linked. Indeed, this tradition, which has been designated by André Vauchez as *beata stirps*,[15] can be linked to the Classical belief that there is an immediate connection between nobility of character and nobility of birth, which developed mainly in the High Middle Ages and eventually became a *topos* of hagiography. From this frame the emergence of the model of the "holy king", as studied by Robert Folz.[16] Folz defined it as a creation of medieval hagiography, accompanying the Christianisation of royalty, especially since the sixth century. It would undergo a profound change leading to the determination of the notion of "sacred kingship" and the paradigm of the "holy queen",[17] which, from the fourth century, with the figure of St Helen,[18] began to assert itself as an alternative access route to Christian perfection and "holiness". This was opposed to the model of the virgins and/or the martyrs who, from early Christianity, were considered the model of feminine holiness par excellence. In fact, even when forced to opt for a secular life, the holy queen expressed her religiosity through the practice of works of mercy, becoming a member of a religious third order, or tertiary, when her direct connection to power was ended (as with St Elizabeth of Portugal, during her widowhood). This practice also included the foundation of churches, monasteries, or convents, and even peacekeeping actions. These two male and female royal models have been the subject of attention of medieval scholarship, which has accentuated the scale of dynastic holiness, insisting on the issue of transmission of a family's charisma by blood.[19]

King John IV

The figure of King John IV[20] was surrounded by a messianic aura. The best-known written testimonies for this are provided in the interpretations of the prophetic *Trovas* of Bandarra, updated in the edition of Nantes (1644), published under the patronage of D. Vasco Luís da Gama, count of Vidigueira and marquis of Nisa, who at the time was ambassador of King John IV in Paris. In this edition, the monarch is identified as "the Hidden One". This interpretation is conditioned by historical circumstances: as we know, King John IV needed to be externally recognised as the legitimate king of Portugal and, in this way, many authors therefore began to replace the figure of King Sebastian, who had been previously identified by D. João de Castro in his *Paráfrase e concordância de algumas Trovas do Bandarra* (Paris, 1603) as the "Hidden One".

These interpretations share the providentialist destiny prophesied by a vision of Jesus Christ to D. Afonso Henriques (that is, Alfonso I, the first king of Portugal) on the eve of the Battle of Ourique in 1139.[21] The prophetic reading of the Ourique episode influenced the construction of the idea of the utopia of the "Fifth Empire" of Portugal and its global interests, developed by Father António Vieira, a Jesuit who was famous not only as a missionary in Brazil but also as a counsellor of King John IV.[22] As João Francisco Marques underlines, in some of Vieira's works, such as *História do Futuro* and *Esperanças de Portugal, Quinto Império do Mundo*, he points not only to the advent of a redeemer of the fatherland, but also to an emperor of the world.[23] King John IV died in 1656, but Vieira foretold the resurrection of the King, continuing to predict that John IV would be the Christian emperor of the world.

However, it should be taken into account that other texts also identify King John IV as this saviour figure who would rescue Portugal from the foreign yoke; it is an image we find in the work *Espelho de Lusitanos em o Christal do Psalmo Quarenta e Tres*, by António Veloso de Lira, published for the first time in 1643. Veloso de Lira, narrating various cases which, in his opinion, prophesied the end of the dual monarchy, the restoration of Portuguese independence, and the accession to the throne of a native king, tells us that a prodigious episode happened on the Tagus beaches in Lisbon, where "some pebbles appeared with letters that clearly said Duke, Duke", referring to the duke of Bragança.[24]

Queen Luísa de Guzman

Regarding the figure of Queen Luísa de Guzman,[25] wife of King John IV, it is above all in the studies of political history, as well as on various aspects of the Portuguese court in the mid-seventeenth century, that her figure has received some attention.[26] Several themes have guided the construction of the image of this queen by scholars, notably her influence over King John IV, leading him to accept the Portuguese crown and support the restorationist cause, and her role as regent after her husband's death in 1656, when their son Alfonso VI could not rule on his own due to his age.[27] Jean Fremont d'Ablancourt, French ambassador to the Portuguese court between 1659 and 1664, claimed that Luísa was "a Princess with a great knowledge", and D. Fernando Correia de Lacerda stressed her "strong spirit" and her "natural wisdom to reign".[28] Closely related to the exercise of governmental power is the appreciation given by some authors of the moral character of this queen, especially her "virtue" of prudence.[29] If we centre our attention on the dedications of some written works, these paratexts always exalt her virtues, especially her modesty, which has always been considered one of the exemplary female virtues. But the various works that were dedicated to Queen Luísa, especially those that fall within the category of spiritual literature, allow us to (re)construct her spiritual facets, as they reveal her favoured saints (St Augustine, St John the Evangelist) and her spiritual practices, solidified by the reading of devotional books and the practice of virtues.[30]

For example, we stress that Queen Luísa de Guzman retained a significant proximity to the Italian religious Father Alberto Maria Ambiveri († 1651), who came to Portugal in 1650. According to António Caetano de Sousa,

> the Queen was so comforted with the venerable presence of Father Alberto, and so satisfied with the efficacy of his words, that with fervent devotion she called him in particular, and she conversed with him privately about spiritual things of the soul; recommending herself in her prayers, she became a devotee of Saint Gaetan.[31]

After asking Father Alberto Maria Ambiveri to bless Prince Alfonso, who at the time was six and ill, with a relic of St Gaetano of Thiene, and

> when she said goodbye, she asked him to see her many times; because she wanted to communicate to him matters of her conscience, and assigned him Tuesdays for this conversation, in which business would be of the greatest importance, since they would belong to the Kingdom of Heaven.[32]

In 1663, Queen Luísa was unhappy with the actions and conduct of her son King Alfonso VI, as documented in some sources and sustained by scholars. She was perhaps also eager for a more modest or pious and "perfect" life, so she entered the convent of Augustinian nuns that she had founded in Lisbon, close to Grilo. In any case, this resolution seems to allow us to see the example of the Queen compared to the cases of other great women—especially widows—whose choice of life was deeply marked by the monastic model of spiritual life. This life insisted particularly and significantly on what were considered specifically feminine virtues or qualities, such as chastity, obedience, humility, honesty, and contempt of vanities, as, indeed, contemporary moralistic and didactic literature was prescribing.[33] In fact, the choice of a religious life—which echoed the disciplinary re-affirmation, by the Council of Trent, of the superiority of religious celibacy—was supported by several examples, many of them disseminated through devotional *vitae* ("lives") or religious chronicles, that generally aroused admiration and fed a desire for imitation.[34] During the period in which she was retired in the convent of Augustinian nuns, Queen Luísa de Guzman took upon herself the most humble exercises and tasks. An example is given in this account by D. António Caetano de Sousa, in his *vita* of the Augustinian nun Mariana da Soledade, included in the fourth volume of the *Agiologio Lusitano dos Santos e Varoens illustres em virtude do reino de Portugal e suas conquistas*: "Queen Luísa called her [Mariana] her kitchen companion [. . .],when this Serene Matron renounced the pomp of her majesty on earth in favour of the King of Heaven, humbling herself in such humble exercise."[35]

Moreover, this appreciation of the behavioural patterns of Queen Luísa will perhaps only be complete if we remember the moment of her death, in *Ultimas Acçoens da Serenissima Rainha D. Luiza Francisca de Gvsmam Nossa Senhora* (1666), by Friar Manuel da Conceição, which, by the tone that the author gives, takes on the contours of a "holy death", which would be the corollary of her, if not "holy", at least virtuous life.

Prince Teodósio

The figure of Prince Teodósio (1634–53), King John IV and Queen Luísa's firstborn son and heir to the Portuguese throne until his untimely death, is well known at the literary level, as demonstrated by the following works: *Theodosius Lusitanus, sive Principis perfecti vera effigies* (1680), by the Jesuit priest, Manuel Luís; *Vida do Príncipe D. Theodosio* (1747), by João Bautista Domingues; and an extensive notice included in the third volume of the *Agiologio Lusitano*, by Jorge Cardoso. The panegyric portrait of this prince can be completed with information that we can glean in the dedications of works addressed to him: for example, *Summa Politica* (1649), by Sebastião César de Meneses; *Armonia Política* (1651), by António de Sousa de Macedo; *Exhortação militar, ou lança de Achilles . . .* (1650), by Father Timóteo de Seabra Pimentel; and *Principios del Reyno de Portugal: con la vida y hechos de Don Alfonso Henriquez su primero rey* (1641), by António Pais Viegas. Considering this set of texts, it is perhaps Luís' *Theodosius Lusitanus*, and the details included by Cardoso in the *Agiologio Lusitano*, that paint the best picture of Prince Teodósio as the "perfect Catholic prince", with a particular hagiographic emphasis.

Luís dedicates the "liber primus" to "civil" aspects of the life of the Bragança prince: he recounts his childhood, his education (and his love for mathematics), presenting him as a *puer senex*,[36] to such an extent that, according to Jorge Cardoso, the Prince displaying

> since his childhood, in words and works, the capacity and maturity of an old man already inclined to the virtue of charity, everything that his parents gave him he ordered to be spent on the poor, reserving nothing for himself,

and "preserving in the traffic of the Palace, and in the labyrinth of the Court, a purity of conscience, and an innocence of life, similar to the ones he had in himself when he received Baptismal grace".[37] This aspect—the *puer senex*—had become a hagiographic *topos*, prevalent from Late Antiquity until the Middle Ages. This should not seem strange if we consider that this topic was suitable to the imitation of the life of Christ, through an immediate parallel with the episode of the young

Jesus, at twelve years old, who astonished with his wisdom the Doctors of Law in the Temple, explaining the Holy Scriptures and challenging his surprised masters.

Biographers also enhance Teodósio's military successes at Elvas, in the context of the Restoration Wars, as well as his distaste for wars between Christian princes, "to pursue the glorious conquests of the Kings of Portugal, not only to extend their Monarchy, but to expand the Catholic Religion".[38] Therefore, he offered himself to God as a missionary, aiming to suffer martyrdom, choosing as his patron St Francis Xavier, Apostle of the East, showing how martyrdom had continued since the beginning of Christianity to appeal to Christians, as a model to imitate. In fact, the martyr would be for centuries the "model" of holiness par excellence in that he or she sacrifices life for the sake of his or her faith, imitating the Christological paradigm.[39] Teodósio's prudence is especially valued by contemporary authors; in fact, his father, King John IV, held his advice in high esteem and, in private circles, referred to his son as "my Solomon", according to the words of D. António Caetano de Sousa.[40]

Especially significant is the fact that Father Manuel Luís devotes the extensive "liber secundus" of the *Vita*, "De Principis Theodosii eximiis dotibus, & virtutis politicis", to his virtues: wisdom, prudence, justice, mercy, kindness, fortitude, magnanimity, liberality, and love for the Portuguese, giving thus a focus that was not very common in hagiographic texts, but which was characteristic of treatises about Christian princes of the post-Tridentine era.

The "liber tertius", dedicated to "De Principis Theodosii Christianis virtutibus", fits naturally into the hagiographic genre tradition, specifically in the exaltation of "heroic virtues".[41] Moreover, it is worth remembering that Father Manuel Luís edited a volume entitled *Cuydai-o Bem: ensina o meyo breve fácil e seguro para se salvar; acrescentado com a Filosofia do verdadeiro christão e com hum exercício quotidiano para o mesmo fim que praticava o Principe de Portugal D. Theodosio* (Évora, 1674), in which he emphasises the spiritual and devotional aspects of the Prince, presenting him as a model for imitation, especially aimed at other young people. The Prince heard Mass every day and received Communion "all eight days"; he spent long hours

> in the presence of the Divine Sacrament, to which he was particularly devoted, either in public, attending the Canonical Hours, or in secret, praying in the tribune of the Royal Chapel. He was a devotee of the sacred Mysteries—Birth, Life, and the Passion of Christ—often in meditation with his arms stretched out on the Cross, weeping many tears, until he was 'transported'. He exalted Our Lady through his devotion: at seven years old he recited her Office every day, and the Divine Office at twelve, with great perfection.[42]

Cardoso adds that the Prince imitated the "heroic examples" of saints, particularly St John the Evangelist, St Thomas Aquinas, St Francis Xavier, St Francis Borgia, and St Catherine of Alexandria, and had a great love for the Society of Jesus, wishing passionately to be a Jesuit.[43]

The description of the death of Prince Teodósio, in the *Agiologio Lusitano*, is the corollary of his "holy life". In the wake of an itinerary marked by the rigours of ascetic life, practising "heroic virtues", the episode of "holy death" marks the end of the earthly life of Prince Teodósio and fits clearly into the frame of the edifying purposes of hagiographic literature. It converts the Prince's ultimate moments within a framework of gestures, attitudes, and behaviours similar to those prescribed in the *artes bene moriendi*, providing an ideal paradigm of a "good death". Prince Teodósio was buried in the Hieronymite Monastery (the Jerónimos) at Belém, dressed in the Franciscan habit. According to Jorge Cardoso, an extraordinary phenomenon occurred during the burial: "at eleven o'clock in the evening, when the body entered the Church, a dove was seen that accompanied him to main chapel, where it disappeared",[44] which the author interprets as a sign of his "holiness", a long institutionalised trope in hagiographic literature.

Princess Joana; Princess Catherine, Queen of England; and Princess Isabel Luísa Josefa

Like the boys, the princesses of the Bragança dynasty were celebrated in some texts, which focused above all on the praise of their nobility and virtue. The two daughters and grand-daughter of John IV and Luísa de Guzman had very different fates, but all were, in their way, celebrated for their "holiness".

Lucas de Andrade, chaplain of the Royal Chapel, authored *Breve Relaçam do que socedeo despois da morte da serenissima Senhora Dona Joana Infante de Portugal* (1654). This short text narrates the funeral and burial ceremonies of this princess, the eldest daughter of King John IV and Queen Luísa, who was born in 1636 and died aged just 17, in 1653. Lucas de Andrade's text has, in some ways, a hagiographic nature, to the extent that, if a little "covertly", it compares the case of Joana to the model of the "holy virgins", which was, from early Christianity, known as the paradigm of feminine holiness. At her funeral, she was dressed in the habit of St Francis, crowning, in this way, a life ruled by chastity and disease, the symptoms of which were first noticed at the age of four. The death of this princess caused great sadness, because the Portuguese had hoped to see her as queen of France. But the fact that she remained a maiden throughout her life thus seems to authorise the author to value the virtue of chastity, which, in the context of the Counter-Reformation, was highly valued as a feminine behavioural pattern.[45]

On the other hand, right from childhood, the behaviour of Princess Catherine (1638–1705),[46] the second daughter of John IV, was controlled according to an austere regulation, dominated throughout by a religious and pious atmosphere. According to Virgínia Rau, citing the words of the consul Masquard, "she had not left the Palace for five years and maybe not even ten times in her life".[47] In fact, if Queen Luísa had not needed to negotiate her marriage with Charles II of England for the sake of state interests, Princess Catherine would perhaps have chosen a religious life, not in a cloister, but with monastic contours—as seen in the example of Princess Maria of Portugal, daughter of King Manuel I—or even formally joined a religious order, indulging in prayer, the practice of virtue, and ascetic exercises. Yet in 1662, she married Charles II of England.

The dedications of works of spirituality addressed to Catherine as queen of England and Scotland always insist on her role as "protector" of Catholicism in Britain, manifesting this on various levels. For instance, Fr. António de São Bernardino, in *Caminho do Ceo descuberto aos viadores da Terra* (1665) writes in the dedication that Queen Catherine is often occupied with the Catholic exercises of her oratory and chapel, in which she spends most of the festival days, emphasising that the English nation should choose and follow "the path of her queen, as it alone is the true one, and erroneous is the diabolic malice invented for the perdition of so many souls".[48] Catherine de Bragança was in fact extremely zealous in promoting the Catholic faith in Britain, which led Pedro de Azevedo Tojal to publish in 1716 a heroic poem titled *Carlos Reduzido, Inglaterra Illustrada*, in which the author praises the figure of the Queen.[49] Another of these dimensions is, for example, the writing and editing of "lives" of saints (particularly the more recent ones) that could hardly find their place in the English editorial panorama. It is exemplified by the translation of St Rosa de Santa Maria's "life", made by ambassador Antonio de Sousa de Macedo, whose *Epitome panegyrico de la vida admirable, y muerte gloriosa de S. Rosa de Santa Maria, virgen dominicana* (1670), dedicated to Queen Catherine, who nurtured a strong devotion to this saint and reflects how the "lives" of saints were one of the most-read textual typologies by the female audience. The "lives" of saints, along with other works that are part of the contemporary spiritual literature, were strongly recommended by theologians and moralists as the most appropriate texts for the feminine gender, becoming even a kind of alternative literature in contrast to prose fiction, in particular books of chivalry, which were considered dangerous for women and young people.

The third of the trio of Bragança princesses, Princess Isabel Luísa Josefa (1669–90), was the only daughter of King Peter II and his first wife, Maria Francisca Isabel of Savoy.[50] For her we have a "life" entitled *Memorias da Serenissima Senhora D. Isabel Luiza Jozefa, que foy jurada Princeza destes Reynos de Portugal* (1748), by Pedro Norberto d'Aucourt e Padilha. The author especially praises her education ("the Queen [Maria Francisca Isabel of Savoy] employed all her love and talent in the education of a daughter unique in every sense, and she saw that Heaven rewarded her for her commitment to Christian piety"),[51] and her virtues.[52]

It is clear that Princess Isabel Luísa Josefa de Bragança was a privileged addressee of hagiographic works. When she was six years old, Fr. Miguel Pacheco dedicated to her his *Vida de la serenissima infanta D. Maria, hija delrey D. Manuel, fundadora de la insigne capilla de Nuestra Señora de la Luz* (1675), hoping she would imitate Maria's virtues. He points out that although several contracts had been drawn up for the marriage of Princess Maria, none were in fact concluded, particularly because she intended "to preserve her chastity until her death",[53] an attitude that compared her to the model of the "holy virgins". Maria was presented as a behavioural paradigm for royal and noble ladies, even those who in many cases were married. In this sense, according to Pacheco, the daily and spiritual or devotional practices of Maria reveal the influence of the monastic model, thus reflecting the continuity of this paradigm as a model of excellence for women, as shown by this excerpt:

> At certain times the table was set with the greatness due to her royal person, but in eating she had the temperance of a religious observant; and among such an abundance of seasoned delicacies, our Princess often fasted, ceasing to touch many by abstinence as others do by necessity.[54]

Moreover, the vicissitudes of Princess Isabel Luísa Josefa's life, determined by the political context, would eventually bring her closer to the case of Princess Maria, to the extent that she also never married, earning her the epithet of "the always bride". As a result, Duarte Ribeiro de Macedo dedicated to Princess Isabel Luísa Josefa the *Vida da emperatriz Theodora* (1677), praising her heroic virtues. But this dedication of a "life" of an empress, who took over the role of ruler after the death of her husband, the Byzantine Emperor Theophilus, is certainly connected to the fact that Princess Isabel Luísa Josefa was the sworn successor to the crown of the Portuguese kingdom (until a male heir was born, in 1689); in this way, the author intended to offer the Princess a kind of "specular" text that would work as an ideal feminine behaviour model to be followed by her as someone who was expected to give a perfect performance in future governmental functions.

Conclusion

For all this, it seems possible to say that the various authors discussed here had, each in his own way, intended to construct a portrait of some members of the Bragança dynasty strongly conditioned by moral, spiritual, and devotional aspects, in order to exalt a particular kind of "dynastic holiness" as a means of legitimising the dynasty and its assumption of the royal throne in 1640. Since the High Middle Ages, this literary strategy had worked as an element of prestige generation that was both political and spiritual in several European kingdoms. Indeed, the sources we have examined (and many others) seem to have intended, for reasons of the ideological construction and legitimisation of the Bragança dynasty, to provide an image of an exemplary model of a united, devout family that was able to 'generate saints'. In a sense, this allowed it to rub shoulders with other European reigning houses; for example, we can see the case of the Elector Palatine Philip William, father of King Peter II's second wife, Maria Sofia of Neuburg, who died in an "odour of sanctity". We read this in his "life", entitled *Vida do Serenissimo Principe Eleitor D. Felippe Wilhelmo [. . .] pay da Rainha D. Maria Sofia Isabella* (1692), by the Jesuit priest, Johann Bodler, and translated into Portuguese by another Jesuit, Francisco de Matos. This would be what Éric Suire calls the model of the *saint d'État*, or "saint of the state".[55]

In the Portuguese case, it seems to have been the Avis dynasty that originated an attempt to construct an image of "dynastic holiness", and it is important to note that their foundational matrix, as it would be for the Bragança dynasty, was based on choice and not on the natural succession of a king. However, there were, as far as I am aware, no actions put forward at that time in Rome for the beatification or canonisation of any of the kings or princes of the Bragança dynasty, as had happened with some members of the Avis dynasty, including Prince Fernando, son of King John I and Queen Philippa of Lancaster, who died in captivity in Fez in an "odour of sanctity"; and Princess Joanna, daughter of Alfonso V, a Dominican nun in the monastery of Jesus of Aveiro, who also died in an "odour of holiness".[56] In any case, the examples presented in this chapter also appear to contribute to building up an image of the Bragança dynasty as composed of people who were, if not holy, at least "virtuous", and whose behaviour should be imitated by all.[57]

In the case of the Braganças, the examples of virtue and "holiness" embodied through some of its members naturally came from the importance and revaluation, throughout the seventeenth century, of the model of royal or noble holiness. As an example, it is worth noting the canonisation of King Ferdinand III of Leon and Castile in 1671, and the beatification of Duke Amadeus IX of Savoy in 1677. But this framework also reflects a growing affirmation of the laity in the domain of holiness, if not officially recognised through the process of formal canonisation, at least through well-known "lives", to use the term employed by Sofia Boesch Gajano.[58]

On the other hand, these examples also reflect the level that sanctity, as a point of political reference, was inscribed within the logic of prestige in the seventeenth century. This was part of a wider framework of the construction of a history of "territorial sanctity",[59] one that would allow the Kingdom of Portugal to rival other European Catholic spaces—dynastic or territorial—who boasted of possessing more saints. But the truth is that, until the end of the century, and if we exclude those saints of ancient cults, especially martyrs or virgins of ancient Lusitania or Roman Galicia, Portugal had only four saints canonised, namely St Theotonius, St Anthony (who, at the time, was known in Europe as being from Padua or from Italy, and not as a native of Lisbon), St Elizabeth of Portugal (queen-consort of King Dinis), and St John of God (of the Order of Hospitallers, canonised in 1690), though he worked mostly in Spain. In any case, the fixation into public memory of the "holiness" of certain members of the Bragança dynasty through the written record should be read within the context of the period, insofar as these publications mirror models for imitation and behavioural guidelines to follow. While this brief study may illuminate some of these pathways into public perception of royal legitimacy, the broader canvas of production, editing, and reading of texts with hagiographic or exemplary content remains still rather understudied and therefore opaque, and may perhaps become clearer as other documentation and other sources—such as the processes of beatification and canonisation—come under closer scrutiny.

Notes

1 Maria Augusta Lima Cruz, *D. Sebastião* (Lisbon: Círculo de Leitores, 2006).
2 Amélia Polónia, *D. Henrique* (Lisbon: Círculo de Leitores, 2005).
3 Ana Cristina Nogueira da Silva and António Manuel Hespanha, "A identidade portuguesa", in *História de Portugal*, ed. José Mattoso, vol. IV (Lisbon: Círculo de Leitores, 1993), 33.

4 Joaquim Romero Magalhães, "Prefácio", in Rafael Valladares, *A Independência de Portugal. Guerra e Restauração (1640–1680)* (Lisbon: A Esfera dos Livros, 2006), 15.
5 Fernando Dores Costa, *A Guerra da Restauração. 1641–1668* (Lisbon: Livros Horizonte, 2004), 13.
6 Costa, *A Guerra da Restauração. 1641–1668.*
7 João Francisco Marques, *A parenética portuguesa e a Restauração* (Porto: INIC, 1989), 2 vols.
8 Rui Bebiano, "Literatura Militar da Restauração", *Penélope. Fazer e desfazer a História* 9/10 (1993): 83–98.
9 Vanda Anastácio, "'Heróicas virtudes e escritos que as publiquem': D. Quixote nos papéis da Restauração", *Revue der iberischen Halbilseln* 28 (2008): 117–36; and *idem*, "Conflitos e contactos na Ibéria: as relações entre Portugal e a Catalunha em 1640 nos 'papéis' da Restauração", in *A Construção do Outro: Espanha e Portugal frente a frente*, eds Tobias Brandenberger, Elisabeth Hasse, and Lydia Schmuck (Tübingen: Calepinus Verlag, 2008), 59–85.
10 José van den Besselaar, *O Sebastianismo – História Sumária* (Lisbon: Instituto de Cultura e Língua Portuguesa, 1987), 116–37.
11 Gonçalo Anes Bandarra, *Profecias do Bandarra (sapateiro de Trancoso)*, ed. António Carlos Carvalho (Lisbon: Vega, 2008), 41.
12 D. João de Castro, *Paraphrase et concordância de algumas Prophecias de Bandarra Çapateiro de Trancoso* (reprodução facsimile) (Porto: Edições Lopes da Silva, n.d.); João Carlos Gonçalves Serafim, introduction to *A Aurora da Quinta Monarquia (1604–1605)* by D. João de Castro (Porto: CITCEM/Edições Afrontamento, 2011).
13 Among others: Fr. Miguel Soares, *Serões do Príncipe*, ed. Maria Teresa Trigo Neto e Cova (Lisbon: Instituto de Alta Cultura/Centro de Estudos Históricos anexo à Faculdade de Letras da Universidade de Lisboa, 1966); Manuel Fernandes de Vila Real, *Epítome Genealógico do Eminentíssimo Cardeal Duque de Richelieu e Discursos Políticos sobre algumas acções da sua vida* [1641], ed. António Borges Coelho (Lisbon: Caminho, 2005). See also Maria Teresa Trigo Neto e Cova, "Características da Nobreza no século XVII" (BA dissertation, Faculdade de Letras da Universidade de Lisboa, 1965); Claudio Donati, *L'idea di nobiltà in Italia (secoli XIV-XVIII)* (Rome: Editori Laterza, 1988).
14 Zulmira C. Santos, "Da *Corte Sancta* à corte santíssima em Portugal", *Revista da Faculdade de Letras – Línguas e Literaturas. Anexo V – Espiritualidade e Corte em Portugal (séculos XVI-XVIII)* (Porto, 1993): 205–15.
15 André Vauchez, "'Beata stirps': sainteté et lignage en Occident aux XIIIe et XIVe siècles", in *Famille et parenté dans l'Occident médieval. Actes du Colloque de Paris, 1974*, eds George Duby and Jacques Le Goff (Rome: École Française de Rome, 1977), 397–407.
16 Robert Folz, *Les saints rois du Moyen Âge en Occident (VIe-XIIIe siècles)* (Brussels: Société des Bollandistes, 1984).
17 Robert Folz, *Les saintes reines du Moyen Âge en Occident (VIe-XIIIe siècles)* (Brussels: Société des Bollandistes, 1992).
18 Jo Ann McNamara, "*Imitatio Helenae*: Sainthood as an Attribute of Queenship", in *Saints: Studies in Hagiography*, ed. Sandro Sticca (New York: Binghamton, 1996), 51–80.
19 Gábor Klaniczay, "Sainteté royale et sainteté dynastique au Moyen Âge. Traditions, métamorphoses et discontinuités", *Cahiers du Centre de Recherches Historiques* 3 (1989): 69–80. For the Portuguese case: Maria de Lurdes Rosa, "A santidade no Portugal medieval: narrativas e trajectos de vida", *Lusitania Sacra*, 2ª série, 13–14 (2001–2002): 369–450.
20 King John IV (1604–56) was the son of D. João and D. Catarina, duke and duchess of Bragança. Leonor Freire Costa and Mafalda Soares da Cunha, *D. João IV* (Lisbon: Círculo de Leitores, 2006).
21 Ana Isabel Buescu, "Um mito das origens da nacionalidade: o milagre de Ourique", in *A Memória da Nação*, eds Diogo Ramada Curto and Francisco Bettencourt (Lisbon: Sá da Costa, 1991), 49–69; Ana Isabel Buescu, "Afonso Henriques no século XVI: momentos & imagens, corpos & lugares", in *Na corte dos reis de Portugal. Saberes, ritos e memórias. Estudos sobre o século XVI* (Lisbon: Edições Colibri, 2010), 185–209.

22 Developed by Vieira in part to legitimate the Bragança dynasty's claims to the throne, the utopia of the "Fifth Empire", based on the Old Testament "Dream of Daniel", predicted that Portugal would become the head of a Christian universal empire. In this vision, the other four empires were the Assyrians, the Persians, the Greeks, and the Romans.

23 João Francisco Marques, ed., *A Utopia do Quinto Império e os Pregadores da Restauração* (Vila Nova de Famalicão: Quasi Edições, 2007). See also Miguel Real, *Padre António Vieira e a Cultura Portuguesa* (Matosinhos: Quidnovi, 2008); van den Besselaar, *O Sebastianismo – História Sumária*.

24 António Veloso de Lira, *Espelho de Lusitanos em o Christal do Psalmo Quarenta e Tres* (Lisbon: na Officina de Domingos Rodrigues, 1753), 151: "sahirão alguns seixos com letras que claramente dizião Duque, Duque. Devia querer o mar desempenharse, em ser o que com os peixes espadas nos vaticinou tantas calamidades, agora com as letras nos traz o nome, e alivio a tantos males: ou ja apregoando o mar a justiça que a terra dissimulava".

25 Queen Luísa de Guzman (1613–66)—spelled Gusmão in Portuguese—was the daughter of the Spanish nobleman, Juan Manuel Perez de Guzman, duke of Medina Sidonia, and Juana de Sandoval.

26 See Hipólito Raposo, *Dona Luísa de Gusmão* (Lisbon: Empresa Nacional de Publicidade, 1947); Ana Paula Avelar, *D. Luísa de Gusmão. A Rainha Mãe (1613–1666)* (Vila do Conde: QuidNovi, 2011); Monique Vallance, *A rainha restauradora. Luísa de Gusmão* (Lisbon: Círculo de Leitores, 2012).

27 D. Luís de Meneses, count of Ericeira, *História de Portugal Restaurado*, vol. I (Lisbon: na Officina de João Galrão, 1679), 92–93; Gastão de Melo de Matos, "'Antes morrer reinando que acabar servindo'. Notas sobre o papel de D. Luiza de Gusmão em 1640", *Brotéria. Revista Contemporânea de Cultura*, vol. XXXI, fasc. 6 (1940): 601–20.

28 Fernando Correia de Lacerda, *Catastrophe de Portugal, na deposição d'el Rei D. Affonso o Sexto, & subrogação do Principe D. Pedro o único, justificada nas calamidades públicas* (Lisbon: a custa de Miguel Manescal, 1669), 16–17.

29 Giulio Sodano, "Prudenza e santità nell'età moderna", in *Repubblica e virtù. Pensiero politico e Monarchia Cattolica fra XVI e XVII secolo*, eds Chiara Continisio and Cesare Mozzarelli (Rome: Bulzoni Editore, 1995), 151–76.

30 Paula Almeida Mendes, "'Pera que ninguem com rezaõ se possa escusar de ter hum roteiro certo pera sua alma na peregrinação em o deserto deste mundo'. Sobre algumas dedicatórias de obras devotas e de espiritualidade a D. Luísa de Gusmão (1613–1666)", in *La Lengua Portuguesa. Vol. I: Estudios sobre literatura y cultura de expresión portuguesa*, ed. Ángel Marcos de Dios (Salamanca: Ediciones Universidad de Salamanca/Aquilafuente, 2014), 793–810.

31 D. António Caetano de Sousa, *Agiologio Lusitano dos Santos, e Varões Ilustres em virtude do Reino de Portugal, e suas Conquistas*, vol. IV [Lisbon: na Regia Officina Sylviana, 1744], ed. Maria de Lurdes Correia Fernandes (Porto: Faculdade de Letras da Universidade do Porto, 2002), 448: "ficou a Rainha tão edificada da veneravel presença de D. Alberto, e tão satisfeita da efficacia das suas palavras, que movida de fervorosa devoção o chamou particularmente, e logo com elle tratou particulares da sua alma; recommendando-se nas suas orações, começou a ser devota de S. Caetano".

32 Ibid., 448: "ao despedirse lhe disse, que a visse muitas vezes; porque queria communicarlhe materias da sua consciencia, e lhe assinou as terças feiras para esta conferencia, em que os negocios erão da mayor importância, por serem as materias pertencentes ao Reyno do Ceo".

33 Maria de Lurdes Correia Fernandes, "Viúvas ideais, viúvas reais. Modelos comportamentais e solidão feminina (séculos XVI-XVII)", *Faces de Eva* 1–2 (1999): 51–86.

34 Marina Caffiero, "Tra modelli di disciplinamento e autonomia soggestiva", in *Modelli di santità e modelli di comportamento. Contrasti, intersezioni, complementarità*, eds Giulia Barone, Marina Caffiero, and Francesco Scorza Barcellona (Turin: Rosenberg & Sellier, 1994), 265–78.

35 De Sousa, *Agiologio Lusitano dos Santos*, vol. IV, 268: "A Rainha D. Luiza lhe chamava a sua Companheira de cosinha, devia de ser a que a ajudava, quando esta Serenissima Matrona

abatia a pompa da Magestade da terra, em obsequio do Rey do Ceo, humilhando-se a tão humilde exercicio".

36 E. R. Curtius, "Boy and Old Man", in *European Literature and the Latin Middle Ages* (Princeton: Princeton University Press, 1990), 98–101.

37 Cardoso, *Agiologio Lusitano dos Santos*, vol. III [Lisbon: na Officina de Antonio Craesbeeck de Mello, 1666], 266: "mostrando de minino, em palavras, & obras, capacidade, & madureza de velho, sendo jà tam inclinado à virtude da esmola, que tudo quanto seus pães lhe dauão, mandaua dispender com os pobres, não reservando para si cousa algũa"; "conservando entre o trafego de Palacio, & labyrintho da Corte, huua pureza de cõsciencia, & innocencia de vida, igual á que nelle se achaua, quando recebeo a graça Baptismal".

38 Cardoso, *Agiologio Lusitano dos Santos*, vol. III, 272: "para prosseguir as gloriosas conquistas dos Reis de Portugal, não só para estender sua Monarchia, mas para dilatar a Religião Catholica".

39 Francesco Scorza Barcellona, "Dal Modello ai modelli", in *Modelli di santità e modelli di comportamento*, 9–18.

40 António Caetano de Sousa, *História Genealógica da Casa Real Portuguesa* (Coimbra: Atântida, 1946–55), vol. VII.

41 Romeo De Maio, "L'ideale eroico nei processi di canonizzacione della controriforma", in *Riforme e miti nella chiesa del Cinquecento* (Naples: Guida Editori, 1992), 253–74.

42 Cardoso, *Agiologio Lusitano dos Santos*, vol. III, 270: "na presença do Diuinissimo Sacramento, de quem era por extremo deuoto, & feruente amante, ou em publico, assistindo às Horas Canonicas, ou em secreto, orando na tribuna da Capella Real. Dos Mysterios sagrados, Nascimento, Vida, & Paixão de Christo, era deuotissimo, nella meditaua muitas vezes cos braços estendidos em Cruz, chorando imensas lagrimas, até que ficaua transportado. Na deuoção de N. Senhora era exímio, aos sette annos recitaua já todos dias o seu Officio, & o Diuino aos doze, com grandíssima perfeição".

43 Ibid., vol. III, 272.

44 Ibid., vol. III, 274: "sendo onze da noite, quando o corpo entrou pela Igreja, foi vista hũa aluissima Pomba, acompanhálo atê Capella mòr, onde desappareceo".

45 Lucas de Andrade, *Breve Relaçam do que socedeo despois da morte da serenissima Senhora Dona Joana Infante de Portugal* (Lisbon: por António Álvares, 1654).

46 Joana Almeida Troni, *Catarina de Bragança (1638–1705)* (Lisbon: Edições Colibri, 2008).

47 Virgínia Rau, *Dona Catarina de Bragança, rainha de Inglaterra* (Coimbra: Coimbra Editora, 1941), 8.

48 António de São Bernardino, *Caminho do Ceo descuberto aos viadores da Terra, pella determinação dos tempos, exercício da continuação da vida e do artigo da morte* (London, 1665), "Dedication".

49 "Dedication" addressed to King John V: "Este Poema, que ha doze annos anda continuamente na laboriosa officina do Parnaso, deve o impulso ao Catholico zelo, & fervoroso espirito, com que a Serenissima Rainha da Gram-Bretanha, sempre suspirada Infante de Portugal, Tia de V. Magestade, promoveo a Fè Romana a seu por todos os títulos felicissimo Esposo Carlos Segundo de Inglaterra", Pedro de Azevedo Tojal, *Carlos Reduzido, Inglaterra Illustrada* (Lisboa: Na officina de Antonio Pedrozo Galram, 1716), 3.

50 De Sousa, *História Genealógica da Casa Real Portuguesa*, vol. VII, 415; vol. VIII, 223.

51 Pedro Norberto d'Aucourt Padilha, *Memorias da Serenissima Senhora D. Isabel Luiza Jozefa, que foy jurada Princeza destes Reynos de Portugal* (Lisbon: na Oficina de Francisco da Silva, 1748), 6: "Empregou a Rainha todo o seu amor, e talento na educação de huma filha em todo o sentido única, e vio que o Ceo lhe premiava o empenho com que influía a piedade Christaã com aquellas soberanas partes, e excellentes virtudes, com que se hia adornando a sua índole, e chegando já áquelles annos em que quasi de repente se illumina o conhecimento humano com todas as luzes da intelligencia, se lhe conheceo logo a actividade dos seus distinctos resplendores, pois se admirava a Corte de como em huma idade taõ honra sabia a Princeza unir a Magestade com o amor, e o respeito com o agrado, fazendo-se ao mesmo tempo amar, e temer".

52 Ibid., 7.
53 Miguel Pacheco, *Vida de la serenissima infanta D. Maria, hija delrey D. Manuel, fundadora de la insigne capilla de Nuestra Señora de la Luz* (Lisbon: por João da Costa, 1675), 56v: "perseverar hasta la muerte en el estado de doncella".
54 Pacheco, *Vida de la serenissima infanta D. Maria*, 98r: "a sus horas se ponía a la mesa, con la grandeza debida a su real persona, mas en el comer com la templança de religiosa observantissima; y entre tanta abundancia de manjares sazonados, muchas vezes ayunaba nuestra Princesa, dexando de tocar en muchos por abstinencia como otros por necessidad".
55 Éric Suire, "Du 'saint dynastique' au 'saint d'État'", in *Des Saints d'État? Politique et sainteté au temps du concile de Trente*, eds Florence Buttay and Axelle Guillausseau (Paris: Presses de l'université Paris-Sorbonne, 2012), 173–80.
56 Legends of the holiness of Avis the dynasty include reports that shortly before the death of Prince Fernando, he had a vision of the Virgin Mary, the Archangel Michael, and St John the Evangelist; and when his body was placed in the coffin, a blinding light was seen; and when one night he appeared to an outlaw, the Prince had the body of a dove and the face of a man: Fr. João Álvares, *Chronica dos feitos, vida e morte do Infante Santo D. Fernando* (corrected by Jerónimo Ramos) (Lisbon: António Ribeiro, 1577), fols 112r.–113v., 129v. In Princess Joana's case, when she died, leaves and tree blossoms fell and fruit dried up; she also appeared to some nuns after her death, and some post-mortem miracles were attributed to her intercession: Fr. Nicolau Dias, *Vida da serenissima princesa D. Joana, filha del-rei D. Afonso V de Portugal* (Lisbon: António Ribeiro, 1585), fols 82r.–83r., 85v.–87v. and 88r.–88v.
57 Santos, "Da *Corte Sancta* à corte santíssima em Portugal".
58 Sofia Boesch Gajano, "Dal martirio all'ascesi: percorsi della santità femminile tra tardoantico e alto medioevo", in *Giustina e le altre. Sante e culti femminili in Italia settentrionale dalla prima età cristiana al secolo XII*, eds Andrea Tilatti and Francesco G. B. Trolese (Rome: Viella, 2009), 38.
59 Henri Fros, "Culte des saints et sentiment national. Quelques aspects du problème", *Analecta Bollandiana* 100 – *Mélanges offerts à Baudoin de Gaiffier et François Halkin* (1982): 729–35; Maria de Lurdes Correia Fernandes, "História, santidade e identidade. O *Agiologio Lusitano* de Jorge Cardoso e o seu contexto", *Via Spiritus* 3 (1996): 25–68.

Bibliography

Álvares, Fr. João. *Chronica dos feitos, vida e morte do Infante Santo D. Fernando* (corrected by Jerónimo Ramos). Lisbon: por Antonio Ribeiro, 1577.

Anastácio, Vanda. "Conflitos e contactos na Ibéria: as relações entre Portugal e a Catalunha em 1640 nos 'papéis' da Restauração". In *A Construção do Outro: Espanha e Portugal frente a frente*, ed. Tobias Brandenberger, Elisabeth Hasse, and Lydia Schmuck, 59–85. Tübingen: Calepinus Verlag, 2008.

Anastácio, Vanda. "'Heróicas virtudes e escritos que as publiquem': D. Quixote nos papéis da Restauração". *Revue der iberischen Halbilseln* 28 (2008): 117–36.

Andrade, Lucas de. *Breve Relaçam do que socedeo despois da morte da serenissima Senhora Dona Joana Infante de Portugal*. Lisbon: por António Álvares, 1654.

Avelar, Ana Paula. *D. Luísa de Gusmão. A Rainha Mãe (1613–1666)*. Vila do Conde: QuidNovi, 2011.

Bandarra, Gonçalo Anes. *Profecias do Bandarra (sapateiro de Trancoso)*. Lisbon: Vega, 2008.

Barcellona, Francesco Scorza. "Dal Modello ai modelli". In *Modelli di santità e modelli di comportamento. Contrasti, intersezioni, complementarità*. Ed. by Giulia Barone, Marina Caffiero, and Francesco Scorza Barcellona, 9–18. Torino: Rosenberg & Sellier, 1994.

Bebiano, Rui. "Literatura Militar da Restauração". *Penélope. Fazer e desfazer a História* n° 9/10 (1993): 83–98.

Besselaar, José van den. *O Sebastianismo – História Sumária*. Lisbon: Instituto de Cultura e Língua Portuguesa, 1987.

Bodler, Johann (S. J.). *Vida do Serenissimo Principe Eleitor D. Felippe Wilhelmo [. . .] pay da Rainha D. Maria Sofia Isabella*. Trans. by Father Francisco de Matos. Lisbon: Miguel Deslandes, 1692.

Boesch Gajano, Sofia. "Dal martirio all'ascesi: percorsi della santità femminile tra tardoantico e alto medioevo". In *Giustina e le altre. Sante e culti femminili in Italia settentrionale dalla prima età cristiana al secolo XII*. Ed. by Andrea Tilatti and Francesco G. B. Trolese, 37–64. Rome: Viella, 2009.

Buescu, Ana Isabel. "Um mito das origens da nacionalidade: o milagre de Ourique". In *A Memória da Nação*. Ed. by Diogo Ramada Curto and Francisco Bettencourt, 49–69. Lisbon: Sá da Costa, 1991.

Buescu, Ana Isabel. "Afonso Henriques no século XVI: momentos & imagens, corpos & lugares". In *Na corte dos reis de Portugal. Saberes, ritos e memórias. Estudos sobre o século XVI*, 185–209. Lisbon: Edições Colibri, 2010.

Caffiero, Marina. "Tra modelli di disciplinamento e autonomia soggestiva". In *Modelli di santità e modelli di comportamento. Contrasti, intersezioni, complementarità*. Ed. by Giulia Barone, Marina Caffiero, and Francesco Scorza Barcellona, 265–78. Torino: Rosenberg & Sellier, 1994.

Cardoso, Jorge. *Agiologio Lusitano dos Santos, e Varões Ilustres em virtude do Reino de Portugal, e suas Conquistas*, vol. III [Lisbon: na Officina de Antonio Craesbeeck de Mello, 1666]. Ed. by Maria de Lurdes Correia Fernandes. Porto: Faculdade de Letras da Universidade do Porto, 2002.

Castro, João de. *Paraphrase et concordância de algumas Prophecias de Bandarra Çapateiro de Trancoso* (reprodução facsimile). Porto: Edições Lopes da Silva, n.d.

Conceição, Fr. Manuel da. *Ultimas Acçoens da Serenissima Rainha D. Luiza Francisca de Gvsmam Nossa Senhora*. Lisbon: Officina de Diogo Soares de Bulhoens, 1666.

Costa, Fernando Dores. *A Guerra da Restauração. 1641–1668*. Lisbon: Livros Horizonte, 2004.

Costa, Leonor Freire, and Mafalda Soares da Cunha. *D. João IV*. Lisbon: Círculo de Leitores, 2006.

Cova, Maria Teresa Trigo Neto e Cova. "Características da Nobreza no século XVII". BA dissertation, Faculdade de Letras da Universidade de Lisboa, 1965.

Cruz, Maria Augusta Lima. *D. Sebastião*. Lisbon: Círculo de Leitores, 2006.

Curtius, E. R. "Boy and Old Man". In *European Literature and the Latin Middle Ages*, 98–101. Princeton University Press, 1990.

D'Ablancourt, Jean Fremont. *Mémoires de Monsieur d'Ablancourt, Envoyé de Sa Majesté très-Chrétienne Louis XIV en Portugal, contenant l'Histoire de Portugal, depuis de Traité des Pyrenées de 1659 jusqu'à 1668*. Amsterdam: chez J. Louis de Lorme, 1701.

De Maio, Romeo. "L'ideale eroico nei processi di canonizzazione della controriforma". In *Riforme e miti nella chiesa del Cinquecento*, 253–74. Napoli: Guida Editori, 1992.

Dias, Fr. Nicolau. *Vida da serenissima princesa D. Joana, filha del-rei D. Afonso V de Portugal*. Lisbon: por António Ribeiro, 1585.

Domingues, João Bautista. *Vida do Príncipe D. Theodosio*. Lisbon: na Officina dos Herdeiros de Antonio Pedrozo Galram, 1747.

Donati, Claudio. *L'idea di nobiltà in Italia (secoli XIV-XVIII)*. Roma: Editori Laterza, 1988.

Fernandes, Maria de Lurdes Correia. "História, santidade e identidade. O *Agiologio Lusitano* de Jorge Cardoso e o seu contexto." *Via Spiritus* 3 (1996): 25–68.

Fernandes, Maria de Lurdes Correia. "Viúvas ideais, viúvas reais. Modelos comportamentais e solidão feminina (séculos XVI-XVII)". *Faces de Eva* 1 2 (1999): 51–86.

Folz, Robert. *Les saints rois du Moyen Âge en Occident (VIe-XIIIe siècles)*. Brussels: Société des Bollandistes, 1984.

Folz, Robert. *Les saintes reines du Moyen Âge en Occident (VIe-XIIIe siècles)*. Brussels: Société des Bollandistes, 1992.
Fros, Henri. "Culte des saints et sentiment national. Quelques aspects du problème". *Analecta Bollandiana* 100 – *Mélanges offerts à Baudoin de Gaiffier et François Halkin* (1982): 729–35.
Klaniczay, Gábor. "Sainteté royale et sainteté dynastique au Moyen Âge. Traditions, métamorphoses et discontinuités". *Cahiers du Centre de Recherches Historiques* 3 (1989): 69–80.
Lacerda, Fernando Correia de. *Catastrophe de Portugal, na deposição d'el Rei D. Affonso o Sexto, & subrogação do Principe D. Pedro o único, justificada nas calamidades públicas*. Lisbon: a custa de Miguel Manescal, 1669.
Lira, António Veloso de. *Espelho de Lusitanos em o Christal do Psalmo Quarenta e Tres*. Lisbon: na Officina de Domingos Rodrigues, 1753.
Luís, Father Manuel. *Cuydai-o Bem: ensina o meyo breve fácil e seguro para se salvar; acrescentado com a Filosofia do verdadeiro christão e com hum exercício quotidiano para o mesmo fim que praticava o Principe de Portugal D. Theodosio*. Évora: na Imprensa da Universidade, 1674.
Luís, Father Manuel. *Theodosius Lusitanus, sive Principis perfecti vera effigies*. Évora: ex Typ. Academiae, 1680.
Macedo, António de Sousa de. *Armonia Política*. Haga do Conde: Officina de Samuel Broun, 1651.
Macedo, António de Sousa de, trans. *Epitome panegyrico de la vida admirable, y muerte gloriosa de S. Rosa de Santa Maria, virgen dominicana*. Lisbon: Antonio Craesbeeck de Melo, 1670.
Macedo, Duarte Ribeiro de. *Vida da emperatriz Theodora*. Lisbon: na Officina de Ioam da Costa, 1677.
Magalhães, Joaquim Romero Magalhães. "Prefácio". In Rafael Valladares, *A Independência de Portugal. Guerra e Restauração (1640–1680)*, 15–18. Lisbon: A Esfera dos Livros, 2006.
Marques, João Francisco. *A parenética portuguesa e a Restauração*, 2 vols. Porto: INIC, 1989.
Marques, João Francisco Marques, ed., intr., and notes, *A Utopia do Quinto Império e os Pregadores da Restauração*. Vila Nova de Famalicão: Quasi Edições, 2007.
Matos, Gastão de Melo de. "'Antes morrer reinando que acabar servindo'. Notas sobre o papel de D. Luiza de Gusmão em 1640". *Brotéria. Revista Contemporânea de Cultura* XXXI, 6 (1940): 601–20.
McNamara, Jo Ann. "*Imitatio Helenae*: Sainthood as an Attribute of Queenship". In *Saints: Studies in Hagiography*. Ed. by Sandro Sticca, 51–80. New York: Binghamton, 1996.
Mendes, Paula Almeida. "'Pera que ninguem com rezaõ se possa escusar de ter hum roteiro certo pera sua alma na peregrinação em o deserto deste mundo'. Sobre algumas dedicatórias de obras devotas e de espiritualidade a D. Luísa de Gusmão (1613–1666)". In *La Lengua Portuguesa. Vol. I: Estudios sobre literatura y cultura de expresión portuguesa*. Ed. by Ángel Marcos de Dios, 793–810. Salamanca: Ediciones Universidad de Salamanca/Aquilafuente, 2014.
Meneses, D. Luís de (count of Ericeira). *História de Portugal Restaurado*. Vol. I. Lisbon: na Officina de João Galrão, 1679.
Meneses, Sebastião César de. *Summa Politica*. Lisbon: Antonio Alvarez, 1649.
Nogueira da Silva, Ana Cristina, and António Manuel Hespanha. "A identidade portuguesa". In *História de Portugal*, ed. by José Mattoso, vol. IV, 18–37. Lisbon: Círculo de Leitores, 1993.
Pacheco, Fr. Miguel. *Vida de la serenissima infanta D. Maria, hija delrey D. Manuel, fundadora de la insigne capilla de Nuestra Señora de la Luz*. Lisbon: por João da Costa, 1675.
Padilha, Pedro Norberto d'Aucourt. *Memorias da Serenissima Senhora D. Isabel Luiza Jozefa, que foy jurada Princeza destes Reynos de Portugal*. Lisbon: na Oficina de Francisco da Silva, 1748.
Piccolomini, Enea Silvio. *Tractado de la miseria de los cortesanos*. Coimbra: por João de Barreira, 1563.

Pimentel, Father Timóteo de Seabra. *Exhortação militar, ou lança de Achilles*. Lisbon: na Officina Craesbeeckiana, 1650.

Polónia, Amélia. *D. Henrique*. Lisbon: Círculo de Leitores, 2005.

Raposo, Hipólito. *Dona Luísa de Gusmão*. Lisbon: Empresa Nacional de Publicidade, 1947.

Rau, Virgínia. *Dona Catarina de Bragança, rainha de Inglaterra*. Coimbra: Coimbra Editora, 1941.

Real, Miguel. *Padre António Vieira e a Cultura Portuguesa*. Matosinhos: Quidnovi, 2008.

Rosa, Maria de Lurdes. "A santidade no Portugal medieval: narrativas e trajectos de vida". *Lusitania Sacra*, 2ª série, 13–14 (2001–2002): 369–450.

Santos, Zulmira C. "Da *Corte Sancta* à corte santíssima em Portugal". *Revista da Faculdade de Letras – Línguas e Literaturas. Anexo V – Espiritualidade e Corte em Portugal (séculos XVI-XVIII)* (Porto, 1993): 205–15.

São Bernardino, Fr. António de. *Caminho do Ceo descuberto aos viadores da Terra, pella determinação dos tempos, exercício da continuação da vida e do artigo da morte*. Londres, 1665.

Serafim, João Carlos Gonçalves. Introduction to *A Aurora da Quinta Monarquia (1604–1605)* by D. João de Castro. Porto: CITCEM/Edições Afrontamento, 2011.

Soares, Fr. Miguel. *Serões do Príncipe*. Ed. by Maria Teresa Trigo Neto e Cova. Lisbon: Instituto de Alta Cultura/Centro de Estudos Históricos anexo à Faculdade de Letras da Universidade de Lisboa, 1966.

Sodano, Giulio. "Prudenza e santità nell'età moderna". In *Repubblica e virtù. Pensiero politico e Monarchia Cattolica fra XVI e XVII secolo*. Ed by Chiara Continisio and Cesare Mozzarelli, 151–76. Roma: Bulzoni Editore, 1995.

Sousa, D. António Caetano de. *História Genealógica da Casa Real Portuguesa*. Vols. VII and VIII. Coimbra: Atlântida, 1946–55.

Sousa, D. António Caetano de. *Agiologio Lusitano dos Santos, e Varões Ilustres em virtude do Reino de Portugal, e suas Conquistas* [Lisbon: na Regia Officina Sylviana, 1744]. Vol. IV. Ed. by Maria de Lurdes Correia Fernandes. Porto: Faculdade de Letras da Universidade do Porto, 2002.

Suire, Éric. "Du 'saint dynastique' au 'saint d'État'". In *Des Saints d'État? Politique et sainteté au temps du concile de Trente*. Ed. by Florence Buttay and Axelle Guillausseau, 173–80. Paris: Presses de l'Université Paris-Sorbonne, 2012.

Troni, Joana Almeida. *Catarina de Bragança (1638–1705)*. Lisbon: Edições Colibri, 2008.

Valladares, Rafael. *A Independência de Portugal. Guerra e Restauração (1640–1680)*. Lisbon: A Esfera dos Livros, 2006.

Vallance, Monique. *A rainha restauradora. Luísa de Gusmão*. Lisbon: Círculo de Leitores, 2012.

Vauchez, André. "'Beata stirps': sainteté et lignage en Occident aux XIIIe et XIVe siècles". In *Famille et parenté dans l'Occident médieval. Actes du Colloque de Paris, 1974*. Ed. by George Duby and Jacques Le Goff, 397–407. Rome: École Française de Rome, 1977.

Viegas, António Pais. *Principios del Reyno de Portugal: con la vida y hechos de Don Alfonso Henriquez su primero rey*. Lisbon: Paulo Craesbeeck,1641.

Vila Real, Manuel Fernandes de. *Epítome Genealógico do Eminentíssimo Cardeal Duque de Richelieu e Discursos Políticos sobre algumas acções da sua vida* [1641]. Ed by António Borges Coelho. Lisbon: Caminho, 2005.

11

CONSOLIDATING AUTHORITY IN SEVENTEENTH-CENTURY MOROCCO

Sultan Moulay Ismail's strategies for legitimacy

Fatima Rhorchi

Since the late eighth century, Morocco has been ruled by a sultan, a monarch who monopolised the levers of power and represented the focal point of the *makhzan* system. The notion of *makhzan*, the traditional name of Moroccan central government, while still part of the Moroccan lexicon, has mostly been replaced by the word "*dawla*", or "state", as used by the media and associated with the era of modernity. Moroccan royal tradition was launched by sharifs, descendants of the Prophet Mohamed, and the modern Moroccan state traces its origins to the establishment of the Idrissid dynasty in the ninth century. They founded their state in the Islamic far west as a form of revenge for the Battle of Fakh (786) in which they were dispossessed of their power in the Arab heartland and forced to disperse.[1] Idris I and his successors (who ruled until 974) were able to secure substantial political legitimacy thanks to their descent from the Prophet Mohamed. Their being members of *ahl al-bayt*, the Prophet's household, conferred on them the special status of being sharifs. Since then, "Sharifism" as the religious element of the state has spread out from its primary genealogical denotation to become a legitimising ideology, and it was maintained as such in the ideologies of the various dynasties that followed in Morocco. Their dynasty did not stay in power for long, as the combination of their power and their ancestry made them a regular target of Abbasid persecution; indeed, even the founder Idris I was poisoned and killed by an Abbasid agent. Nevertheless, the mausoleum of his son Idris II, situated in the heart of Fez, became an everlasting "symbolic aspect of Moroccan stateness", which people requesting divine intercession continue to visit regularly.[2] According to historians, no other Arab-Muslim state venerates its founder in such a fashion, combining political and religious attributes in a daily rite of affirmation. Fez itself became a symbolic setting in which was situated the origins of legitimate power.

In the early modern period, the Saadi dynasty (1554–1659) also contributed to the process of embedding Sharifism as the main characteristic of the political arena.

to arbitration in economic issues. They maintained neutral relationships with central governing power and did not try to mobilise their members to challenge the rule of the sultanate. The second type had more political interests. They tended to challenge the central government, which is why they represented a real threat to the *makhzan* powers. Starting from the fifteenth century, a significant Sufi-Jihadi ideology represented by the Shadily-Jazuli *tariqa* (school or order) spread. This Sufi school relied heavily on the veneration and glorification of the Prophet and mobilised the population for the defence of Dar al-Islam, the Islamic community, as the rule of the Marinid and Wattassid dynasties weakened.[18] In fact the weakness of central control that characterised Moroccan politics through the Marinid, Wattassid and late Saadi dynasties created an environment where local saints and religious brotherhoods were able to flourish. At that time, the sultanate was unable to repulse the threat of the Portuguese and Spanish invasion on its own; it relied on the local *marabouts* to organise resistance. Before the advent of the Alawis, Morocco's rural populations lived in a tribal, anarchic system that historians call the "maraboutic crisis",[19] in which saints and trans-tribal religious brotherhoods played a crucial role in maintaining a level of political stability. As a result, the power of *zawiyas* that expanded their political role by collecting members and drawing together people from various tribes was in constant amplification.[20]

Unlike the Saadis, the Alawis were sharifs but were not supported by *marabouts* and *tariqas*. At the beginning, their power was challenged by ruthless contenders. It should be noted that throughout the reign of the Alawi sultanate, the fluid system of *bled al-makhzan* and *bled siba* ("land of order" and "land of lawlessness") still existed. In this system, the sultanate was not the absolute centre of power and legitimacy in the country. Instead, it was composed of several contending centres of power. *Bled al-makhzan* comprised the tribes that swore allegiance to the sultan, paid taxes, and provided troops for the army, whereas *bled siba* encompassed the tribes that rejected the administrative authority of the sultan.[21] The dynasty was on the verge of collapsing until Sultan Moulay Rachid, Moulay Ismail's predecessor, provided the necessary funds for the war against the *zawiyas* by opening the land route between Sijilmassa, a city deep in the interior, and the Mediterranean in order to get resources from reactivated trade.[22]

Therefore, although Baraka represented power, Sharifism stood for what best legitimised power in Moroccan society. Although these two notions seemed to be distinct, they overlapped. Sharifism bestowed Baraka, and the possession of Baraka warranted that a person claimed Sharifism. This accounts for the permanent antagonism between kings and saints; in other words, between the *makhzan*, as a central power, and the *zawiyas* as centres of local power. These tensions grew higher and higher between the ruling power and the powerful *zawiyas*, namely the Dilai *zawiya* and the Sharqawi *zawiya*, whose control went far beyond the region. The Dilai rulers claimed descent from the first caliph and companion of the Prophet, Abu Bakr, and the Sharqawi from the Caliph Omar.

Moulay Ismail, the second king of the Alawi dynasty, proclaimed himself king after the sudden death of his half-brother Moulay Rachid in a riding accident.

He inherited a country weakened by tribal warfare. He established his legitimacy amid the internal disorder of the "maraboutic crisis", and the external threats posed by Iberian incursions on both the Atlantic and Mediterranean coasts as well as the Ottoman threat from the east. Since his accession to power, the new sharifian monarch imposed a "redistribution" of the sacred. That is, the various sharifian groups had to adapt themselves to a new situation in which the ruling sultan claimed his legitimacy not only as a sharif endowed with Baraka but also as a warrior with the requisite military and political powers, and a saint with religious superiority. This changed the playing field of Morocco's political sphere for good.[23] His fifty-five-year rule was the longest in Moroccan history and is regarded as one of the greatest; though some qualify it as the most tyrannical, characterised by a ruthless centralisation of all decisions and the fear with which the Sultan reigned.[24]

In order to consolidate his authority and obtain the title of "commander of the faithful" and to declare that in his person the synthesis between Khilafa ("caliph", successor of the Prophet) and Imama (spiritual guide) was realised, Moulay Ismail used a plethora of measures. First, it was necessary for him to obtain a *bey'a* (oath of allegiance) from the *ahl al-hal wa al-'aqd* ("those who tie and untie"); that is, the representatives of the population, namely the *ulama* (scholars), the sharifs, the merchants, notables, and *al-achraf* (aristocratic families). In this respect, it is worth mentioning that the *bey'a* to the sultan as a ritual of allegiance and as a written text is reminiscent of the *bey'a al- ridwan* or the allegiance of benediction that was accorded by God to the Prophet Mohamed. These texts of allegiance were displayed on the walls of the shrine of Moulay Idris II so that people could obtain their Baraka.[25]

By integrating the religious and the saintly elements, the oath of allegiance served as a sort of endorsement and further recognition of the sultan as the foremost figure of religious authority in the country.[26] Henceforth, the sharifs and the saints became integral parts of the royal ceremonial. Whether the sultan was in his capital or on the move throughout the country, their presence was essential in order to bestow legitimacy on his actions.[27] As a strong centralising sultan, Moulay Ismail had to assert that spiritual power remained concentrated in his person as *amir al-muminin* ("prince of believers") and head of the sharif class. Therefore, he sought to induce intra-sharifian rivalries by promoting and granting privileges to some powerful and popular sharifian groups who thus became the *makhzan* allies, while at the same time curtailing the powers of other religious groups with less powerful sharifian lineages by putting them under close supervision through the successive campaigns of expurgation and the practice of creating formal lists.[28] This campaign of investigation was another strategy meant to confirm the sharifian sultan's supremacy as the ultimate guardian and protector of the holy lineages. As a consequence, the solidarity of the sharif class was undermined and these investigations triggered division and genealogical uncertainty. In fact, they resulted in the elaboration of two registers of the Idrissid sharifs of Morocco. Moulay Ismail's *kunnash* (register) was considered the basic reference for Alawi sultans. He classified sharifs into six *tabaqas* (categories), which encompassed *al-machahir*, the well-known sharifian families; those who possessed authenticated *zahirs* (formal documentation) of *attawqir wa al-ihtiram* ("veneration and respect"); those who possessed other documents attesting their sharifian status; those whose *zahirs* were contested; and finally, two other categories for those who were either claimants with no documents or those dismissed for being false claimants.[29] And yet, the *makhzan* representing Ismail's authority continued to be contested by both tribal and urban saints as well as by the *ulama*, or religious scholars.

The ability of a sharifian sultan to rule did not mean that the governing authorities went unchallenged. There were frequent revolts against Moulay Ismail's efforts to assert political control. In fact, he had to face many enemies from inside and outside. His authority was contested by members of his own family as well as by urban saints and *shurafa*, especially those belonging to prestigious families like the Idrissi in Fez who felt challenged by southern *shurafa* families coming from the fringes of the desert and taking power.[30] Moulay Ismail spent the first fifteen years of his reign uprooting opposition from his nephew, Ahmed Ibn Mahraz; his half-brother, Moulay Harran; and his own son, Moulay Mohamed Ibn Ismail, whose arm and leg he ordered to be amputated and left uncured until he died.[31] When the Sultan returned from Marrakech, where he had to fight Ahmed Ibn Mahraz, the people of Fez revolted against the Sultan and supported his nephew. They sent archers to face him and clung to their allegiance to Ahmed.

The relations between Moulay Ismail and the city of Fez were always strained. People in Fez were waiting for any opportunity to turn their back on the Sultan. The authoritarian and centralising policies of this sultan jostled the interests of the wardens of Fez as the traditional centre of sharifdom. The people of Fez revolted against the *makhzan*'s heavy taxation. They also criticised the Sultan for recruiting slaves in his slave army. The conflict with the *ulama* there included issues in which the religious and the political overlapped. In order to subjugate a city like Fez and to respond to all these threats, he had to face the hardest task in his reign. His use of absolute force to curb the rebellious spirit of the city was in vain. Continuing tensions are reflected in a letter addressed to the Sultan by Abu Ali al-Hasan al-Yusi concerning the illegal taxation the Sultan levied which exceeded the amount permitted under the *shari'a*, and in the negative attitude of scholars and other *ulama* towards the ownership of slaves, objecting mostly that the Sultan had enslaved free-born Muslims.[32]

One of these scholars, Abdessalam Gessous, suffered an infamous ordeal confronting the Sultan, reported by one of his disciples called Ali Mesbah as cited in the *Tarikh al-Du'ayf*, by Mohammed al-Du'ayf al-Ribati. The events presented range between reality and fiction and between justification and condemnation. One of the documents tells the story in detail. It recounts that in 1709 the Sultan ordered that Gessous should be thrown in jail and pay twenty quintals of copper coins as a fine for his letter of complaint. In addition to suffering a beating and humiliation, he was taken on a circuit around the city to call on the people to provide him with the money to pay his fine. Since the amount of money was gathered by the people of Fez quickly and exceeded the amount expected, the scholar was released, but the elite warned the Sultan that Gessous' popularity represented a real threat to the monarchy. As a result, he was jailed and strangled the next day. According to Mezzine, such a punishment characterised this period, and was the normal way to eliminate any opponent of the Ismaili *makhzan*, including the Sultan's children and relatives and his officials.[33]

The Sultan also needed to consolidate his Baraka through another legitimising ideology, military power. Therefore, Moulay Ismail set out to maintain the territorial integrity of his country, which was at the time being targeted by the expansionist endeavours of both European powers to the north and Ottomans to the east. For this purpose, he imported a slave army from south of the Sahara to supplement the existing Arab and Berber tribes' army called the Oudaya Jaysh. He ensured the loyalty of the latter through gifts of lands, grants, and tax exemptions. The Abid Alboukhari (slave army) swore allegiance and loyalty exclusively to the Sultan independently of any local loyalties. The Abid were used as a brutal instrument of his authoritarian regime to impose obedience and taxation. He also built a string of *kasbas*, fortresses along the eastern border of Morocco in Oujda and Taourirt and into the middle Atlas near Azrou and Sefrou. These important garrisons were formed as a network across the country.[34] Further to this, Moulay Ismail sought to consolidate his Baraka by virtue of military success through *harkat*.[35] These *harkat*, which referred to military expeditions organised for punitive or fiscal purposes, encompassed both urban and rural targets. Since his enthronement Ismail had ceaselessly campaigned against recalcitrant tribes and *zawiyas* in order to ensure the integrity of the country, to fight the rebel Berber chiefs in the south, the urban saints in the cities, and the Europeans entrenched along the Moroccan coasts.

In a similar manner, Ismail founded the Dar al-Makhzan ("house of government") as the centre from which his power emanated. It became a place of *al-Hayba wa al-Waqar* ("fear and reverence").[36] Hammoudi states that the Dar al-Mulk ("house of power") served to justify the use of terror by invoking the law. The disobedient ones or those who revolted or contested the monarch's authority would undergo punishment, death, or torture there because they had placed themselves outside the law and challenged the *ummah* ("nation"). The Sultan evoked the patriarch's right of life and death over his children. Hence the memorable cases of torture and the ritualised procedures of decapitation. In such a system of governance, unlike any other, terror met the sacred in the figure of the sultan as both saint and executor.[37] Moulay Ismail was described as "bloodthirsty" for his legendary cruelty. In order to intimidate rivals, he ordered that a rebel city's walls be adorned with 10,000 heads of slain enemies. The most remembered detail, based on Moroccan popular memory and Western accounts, is that Moulay Ismail used Christian captives, among others, to build the monuments in his imperial city, Meknes, and that if a worker slowed down or fell ill during construction, he was sealed into the wall on which he was working. Moreover, the huge underground prison that Ismail built in his imperial city attests to this day the harshness of his rule.[38] However, when he realised that the iron fist needed to be softened, he tried different strategies to gain support inside the city and appease tensions. He rebuilt the tomb of Moulay Idris as a powerful symbol of legitimacy. Then, he granted privileges as a political means to defeat some of his opponents and create alliances. Being aware that sharifian descent was one of his main sources of legitimacy, he made all *tariqas* or religious orders move their mother houses to Fez, the capital of Sharifism. According to Darif, the political significance of such a decision was to deprive the *zawiyas* of their strategic and military position of strength by uprooting them from the mountains in the heart of their tribal lands and confining them in the city of Fez. He describes this as an extreme level of "domestication".[39]

Furthermore, Moulay Ismail elevated the *zawiya* of Abd al-Rahman al-Fassi to the rank of sanctuary *hurm*, a religious sanctuary or refuge. According to El-Mansour, the *hurm* as a religious institution played an essential part in the overall politico-religious order. The acceptance of this institution by the Sultan symbolised a power distribution between temporal authorities and religious groups.[40] In addition to its being a privilege granted to a religious group, this elevation proved to be of great help to the *makhzan* itself. By offering shelter to the persecuted and defending the helpless, the sanctuary provided an outlet for suppressed frustrations and feelings of despair, giving at the same time an opportunity to the monarch to re-arrange negotiations and find a way out of a deadlock in resolving a political crisis. Therefore, Moulay Ismail relied on the special relationship he forged with one of the most eminent of the *ulama* of the time, Abd al-Qadir al-Fassi and his son Muhammad, whose grandfather had been a great mystic who founded a *zawiya* in the Qarawiyin sector. As a gesture of good will towards the al-Fassi family, Sultan Moulay Ismail ordered his governor in Fez to enlarge the *zawiya* and accord it much greater importance as a religious institution within Fez society.[41] When construction was completed, the *zawiya* was four times its original size as it was augmented with a number of houses surrounding it. This religious lodge was furthermore granted a number of *ahbbas*, or endowments, allowing it to stand out as an important place of worship and learning where the Sultan's messages were read out to the city and crucial issues were debated.[42]

Moulay Ismail also tried to confine the various sharifian lineages to the religious field, rather than political, by granting them a wide range of privileges in the form of donations, endowments, tax exemptions, and the right to sanctuary, or the right to provide shelter. In doing so, he enhanced his relations with the *shaykhs* of the Wazzani, Sharqawi and Nassiri *zawiyas* and *tariqas* who had been persecuted by his brother Moulay Rachid.[43] The special *Zahir al-tawqir wa al-Ihtiram* ("consideration and respect decree") he promulgated was meant to control and regulate these privileges. These decrees were simply routine documents granting the beneficiaries preferential treatment by the Ismaili *makhzan* officials.[44] It should be noted that the Wazzani *zawiya* based in northern Morocco, unlike the others located further to the south, enjoyed more considerable advantages by cooperating with the ruling sultan in the aim of boosting sharifian ideology. In addition to enjoying privileges on fiscal and administrative levels, they were authorised to found branches of their order both inside and outside the realm. In return, the Wazzani sharifs contributed to the consolidation of the Alawi state. According to Harrak, hagiographic works of the founding *shaykh* of the Wazzani *zawiya*, Moulay Abdallah al-sharif (d. 1705), express the widely accepted belief disseminated among his followers that the "spiritual caliphate" exercised by the House of Wazzan was higher than the "temporal caliphate" exercised by the Alawi sultan, since the former was a response to a mystical revelation, executed as a *bey'a*, which had been proclaimed in his name by the elements of the universe, "the soil, the rocks, the plants and the trees". He named his *zawiya* "Dar ad-damana", or "the house of guarantee", meaning that whoever entered it or served it would be safe. Although the Wazzani sharifs considered their caliphate to be superior to political power, they recognised nevertheless that the temporal caliphate was necessary for maintaining the righteousness of the community. Hence, they gave their blessing to the ruling sultan in public prayers, exhorted the population to obey him and incited the members of their brotherhood to participate in *jihad* under their warlords.[45]

For all these reasons, although the monarch possessed religious legitimacy in an Islamic state, Sufi orders, local *zawiyas*, and sharifian families all also shared in that legitimacy and claimed a number of consequent privileges.[46] The notion that these "saints" were endowed with special qualities of ethical and social efficacy underscores the fact that they were antagonistic community leaders who formed a counterweight to sultanic authority. Hammoudi explains that "Sultans and saints shared a similar kind of spiritual ascendance that made their relationship one of tension, rivalry, and mutual attraction. They both possessed Baraka, which placed them on equal footing in terms of a spiritual claim to rule."[47] Thus, it was difficult for the Sultan to attack the ideological basis for *maraboutism*, even though these saints and *zawiyas* could potentially command influence over political legitimacy, and could thus present a serious challenge to his authority simply by blaming the deterioration of the country upon him.[48] Epidemics, droughts, or famines were usually blamed upon the decadence of the ruler and the corruption of the society he misruled.[49]

In this context, several hagiographic writings recount instances in which Moulay Ismail's powers clashed with those of some saints. These texts are full of cultural significance, which most researchers consider good illustrations of the dynamics of the miraculous and genealogical Baraka and Sharifism. Abd al-Salam al-Qadiri (1698) reports the case of a runaway slave who took refuge in the *zawiya* of Ahmed Ibn Abd Allah Ma'an in Fez and received the saint's protection when the Sultan ordered the slave to be killed. Al-Qadiri says that the slave went on pilgrimage and roved as he pleased without being arrested, "thanks to the Baraka of Lord Ahmed, may God be pleased with him".[50] In another case, the same saint Ahmed Ibn Abd Allah Ma'an extended his protection to a deserter from the city militia of *rumat* (archers) of Fez. When the ex-soldier came to the sanctuary, the saint looked at him and said: "Just go. You have nothing to fear!" The deserter left the *zawiya* and found a job transporting limestone from one part of the city to another. People were impressed to hear that he finally was dropped from the roster of the militia without being bothered by any government official.[51] These examples show how saints intervened and provided shelter from abuses of power, especially against the

Idris in Fez included the shrine and the surrounding blocks of houses. Its limits were indicated in wooden bars that cut across the neighbouring streets, which can still be seen today. The same privilege was accorded to the Alami sharifian sanctuary by extending it over the lands of several tribes of Jbala. This decree issued by al-Mansour (1578) and renewed by succeeding sultans emphasised the immunity of the *hurm*, and any fugitive who took refuge in it was immune from pursuit. See Mohammed El-Mansour, "The Sanctuary (Hurm) in Pre-colonial Morocco", in *In the Shadow of the Sultan: Culture, Power, and Politics In Morocco*, eds Rahma Bourqia and Susan Gilson Miller (Cambridge: Harvard Centre for Middle Eastern Studies, 1998), 53.

3 B. A. Mojuetan, "Legitimacy in a Power State: Moroccan Politics in the Seventeenth Century during the Interregnum", *International Journal of Middle East Studies* 13 (Aug. 1981), 348. Although their sharifian descent was denied by some of their enemies (see Ibn Khaldoun: *al-Moqadima*), the Saadi dynasty succeeded the crumbling Wattassid sultanate in Fez. The latter was caught between the Portuguese, the Sufi movement and the *zawiyas*. The Saadis brought a new political legitimacy built on the alliance between *zawiyas*, Sharifism, and *jihad*, which was substituted for the tribally based state of the Marinids and Wattassids.

4 Rahma Bourqia and Susan Gilson Miller, Introduction to *In the Shadow of the Sultan*, 2. In the thirteenth century, Moulay Hassan al-Dakhil, a descendent of Ali, the fourth caliph of Islam, and Fatima, the Prophet's daughter, had arrived in Morocco. The Alawis settled in Sijilmassa as sharifs. In the 1430s, Moulay Ali al-Sharif joined the war against the Portuguese in the north, and in the seventeenth century they became political leaders. In 1640, his son Mohamed expelled the *zawiya* of Dilae's warlord, Abu al-Hassan al-Simlali, took control of Sijilmassa and proclaimed himself sultan. See Richard C. Pennell, *Morocco: From Empire to Independence* (Oxford: One World, 2003), 97–98. "Moulay", as a title or honorific, has been and is still used in various regions of the Muslim world. In the Maghrib and Andalusia, it was applied to saints or Sufis, as well as to various ruling houses that based their legitimacy upon descent from the prophet Mohamed. In the Alawi dynasty *Moulay* and *Sidi* were used equally as honorific titles. Today, both are used mostly as signs of respect or civility.

5 Abdallah Hammoudi, *Master and Disciple: The Cultural Foundations of Moroccan Authoritarianism* (Chicago: University of Chicago Press, 1997), chapter 2; *idem*, "Sainteté, pouvoir et société: Tamgrout aux XVIIe et XVIIIe siècles", *Annales, E. S. C.* 3–4 (1980), 615–41; *idem*, "The Path to Sainthood: Structure and Danger", *Princeton Papers* 3 (1994), 71–88.

6 Abdul Rahman bin Mohammed ibn Khaldoun, *Al-Moqadima* (Beirut: Dar al-Kitab al-Arabi, 2004), 311. Ibn Khaldoun describes how the Almohads relied on nomadic tribes for military service. The Marinids forged their reputation as warriors fighting the Christians. The Almoravids were nomads and warriors, and their men distinguished themselves by covering their faces with a veil *al-moulathamoun*. Only Islam could have brought unity to these desert tribes: the Sanhaja, Gudala, Masufa, and Lamtuna on one side, and the Maghrawa and Zenata on the other. Hence the vitality of the cities was dying out as power dispersed among leaders of mercenaries and the tribal chiefs; by the late fourteenth century this created a serious problem of political legitimacy. See Pennell, *Morocco: From Empire to Independence*, chapter 4.

7 Pennell, *Morocco: From Empire to Independence*, 98–99. Sharifism had carried an undercurrent resistance to the Marinids, although they attempted to contain it. The Marinids and the Wattassids placed the sharifs in such a privileged position that they appeared as the pillars of their political legitimacy. See Mohammed Kably, "Musahama fi Tarikh al-Achraf", in *Majallat kuliyat al-Adab*, nos 3–4 (Rabat, 1968), 7–19.

8 Mohammed Kably, "Legitimacy of State Power and Socio-Religious Variations in Medieval Morocco", in *In the Shadow of the Sultan*, eds Bourqia and Miller, 133. On this point, see also Kably, *Société, pouvoir et religion au Maroc à la fin du 'Moyen-Age' (XIVe-XVe siècle)* (Paris: Maisonneuve et Larose, 1986), 246–53; and *idem*, "Hawla ba'd mudmarat al-tashawwuf", in *Al-Tarikh wa adab al-manaqib* (Rabat: Editions Okad, 1989), 67–69.

9 Rahma Bourqia, "The Cultural Legacy of Power in Morocco", in *In the Shadow of the Sultan*, eds Bourqia and Miller, 243. According to Bourqia, "The Moroccan political system seems not to fit readily into existing frameworks of analysis developed in western political theory but requires instead its own distinctive paradigms in order to be fully understood." See also *idem*, "L'Etat et la gestion du symbolique au Maroc précolonial", in R. Bourqia and N. Hopkins, *Le Maghreb: approches des mécanismes d'articulation* (Casablanca: Al-Kalam, 1991), 137–51.

10 Harrak, "Sharifism and the Sharifs", 19. The act delivered by the sultan, "*zahir al-Tawqir wa al- Ihtiram*", constituted a sort of "patent of nobility". This *zahir* is reproduced in Al-Tahiri, *Tuhfat al-Ikhwan bi Ba'd Manaqib Shurafa' Wazzan* (Fez: Lithograph Press, 1906), 39.

11 Edmund Burke III, "The Moroccan Ulama, 1860–1912: An Introduction", in *Scholars, Saints, and Sufis: Muslim Religious Institutions since 1500*, ed. N. R. Keddie (Berkeley: University of California Press, 1972), 98. See also Beck, *L'image d'Idris II.*

12 Ibn Khaldoun, *al-Moqadima*, 254. Ibn Khaldoun served in the court of the Merinid Sultan Abou Inan.

13 El-Mansour, "The Sanctuary (Hurm) in Pre-Colonial Morocco", 60. The *naqib* was chosen by the sharifian group to which he belonged in order to protect the sharifian lineage, serve as the representative of his group before the *makhzan*, and arbitrate in intra-sharifian conflict. See Abu al-Rabii Sulayman ibn 'Abd Allah al-Shafshawni al-Hawwat, *Al-Sirr al-ẓāhir fī-man abraza bi-Fās al-sharaf al-bāhir min a'qāb al-shaykh 'Abd al-Qādir* (Fez: Litho, 1932), 8.

14 Bourqia. "The Cultural Legacy of Power in Morocco", 246. The difference between a saint in Christian theology and a *marabout* was that the latter was worshipped while he was alive, because of his possession of Baraka, which he could transfer to one of his successors, usually a close male relative, a son, a trusted friend or a disciple. See Dale F. Eikelman, *Moroccan Islam: Tradition and Society in a Pilgrimage Centre* (Austin: University of Texas Press, 1976), 25–26.

15 Clifford Geertz offers a detailed and insightful analysis of Baraka in his *Islam Observed: Religious Development in Morocco and Indonesia* (New Haven: Yale University Press, 1968), 33–35. See also his "Centers, Kings, and Charisma: Reflections on the Symbolics of Power", in Geertz, *Local Knowledge: Further Essays in Interpretive Anthropology* (New York, 1993), 121–23.

16 Driss Ksikes, "Les Chorfa mènent la danse", *Tel Quel* 165 (March 2005). On this point, see also Ernest Gellner's *Saints of the Atlas* (London: Weidenfeld and Nicolson, 1969), 88.

17 Edward Westermarck, *Ritual and Belief in Morocco*, 2 vols (London: Macmillan, 1926), 1–64. For more details on Baraka and sainthood, refer to Vincent J. Cornell, *Realm of the Saint: Power and Authority in Moroccan Sufism* (Austin: University of Texas Press, 1998). See also Alfed Bel, *La religion Musulmane en Berbérie*, vol. 1 (Paris: Paul Gerthner, 1938), 357–407.

18 Harrak, "Sharifism and the Sharifs", 19. Vincent J. Cornell, "The Logic of Analogy and the Role of the Sufi Shaykh in Post-Marinid Morocco", *International Journal of Middle East Studies* 15, 1 (Feb. 1983).

19 Abdelfatah Kilito, "Speaking to Princes: Al-Yusi and Mawlay Ismail", trans. Michael Cooperson, in *In the Shadow of the Sultan*, 40. Driss Ksikes' "Les Chorfa mènent la danse" sheds light on the intricate administrative process involved in obtaining a certification of sharif, especially of "Alawi Origin".

20 El-Mansour, "The Sanctuary (Hurm) in Pre-Colonial Morocco", 58. In his *Between Caravan and Sultan: The Bayruk of Southern Morocco – A Study in History and Identity* (Leiden: Brill, 1959), 6, Mohamed Hassan Mohamed refers to the totemic use of the term "*siba*" as a free unfettered camel, which became an allegory of "wayward" rebels and lawlessness.

21 Fatima Ghoulaichi, "Of Saints and Sharifian Kings in Morocco: Three Examples of the Politics of Reimagining History through Reinventing King/Saint Relationships" (PhD diss., University of Maryland, College Park, 2005). On the history of *makhzan* and *siba*,

see Robert Montagne, *The Berbers: Their Political and Social Life*, trans. David Seddon (London: Frank Cass, 1973).
22 Pennell, *Morocco: From Empire to Independence*, 98.
23 Harrak, "Sharifism and Sharifs", 26; Pennell, *Morocco: From Empire to Independence*, 98–99.
24 Ghoulaichi, "Of Saints and Sharifian Kings in Morocco", 18.
25 Bourqia, "The Cultural Legacy of Power in Morocco", 245. For more on *bay'a*, see Bettina Dennerlein, "Legitimate Bounds and Bound Legitimacy: The Act of Allegiance to the Ruler (Bai'a) in 19th Century Morocco", *Die Welt des Islams* 41, 3 (2001), 287– 310. See also Abd al-Rahman ibn Zaydan, *Al-Durar al-fakhira bi-maathir al-muluk al-Alawiyin bi Fas al-zahira* (Rabat: Al-Matba'a al- Iqti Sadiya, 1937), 247; and *idem, al-Izz wa al-salwa fi ma'lim nuzum al-dawla*, 2 vols (Rabat: Al-Matba'a al-Malakiya, 1962).
26 Ghoulaichi, "Of Saints and Sharifian Kings in Morocco", 17.
27 Mohamed El-Mansour, "The Religious and Social Practice of the Wazzani Zawiya", in *Tribe and State: Essays in Honour of David Montgomery Hart*, eds E. G. Joffé and C. R. Pennell (Wisbech, Cambridgeshire: Menas Press, 1991), 69–83.
28 Harrak, "Sharifism and Sharifs", 20.
29 Ibid., 30.
30 El-Mansour, "The Sanctuary (Hurm) in Pre-colonial Morocco", 70.
31 Muhammed al-Saghir, *Nozhat-Elhadi, Histoire de la dynastie saadienne au Maroc*, trans. O. Houdas (Paris, 1889), 179.
32 Larbi Mezzine, *Le Tafilalt: Contribution à l'histoire du Maroc aux XVIIe-XVIIIe siècles, Publications de la Faculté des Lettres et des Sciences Humaines*, vol. 13 (Rabat: 1987), 199. For the letters of al-Yusi, see *Rasa'il Abi 'Ali al Yusi*, ed. Fatima Khalil Qabli, 2 vols (Casablanca: Dar al-Thaqafah, 1981). See also Ghoulaichi, "Of Saints and Sharifian Kings in Morocco", chapter II: "Moulay Ismail and Lyusi. The Politics of Baraka and Sharifism", 18–28.
33 Mezzine, "Le Tafilalt", 221. For the ordeal of Gessous, see Mohammed al-Du'ayf al-Ribati, *Tarikh al-Du'ayf (Tarih al-Dawla al-Saida)*, ed. Ahmad al-Amari (Rabat: Dar al-Maturat, 1986).
34 Pennel, *Morocco: From Empire to Independence*, 99.
35 Ghoulaichi, "Of Saints and Sharifian Kings in Morocco", 12.
36 *Dar al-makhzan* refers to both the administration and the seat of government, but also the dominant official class. There is an extensive literature on this ancient word and related institutions. Both are mentioned in the Arabic sources: see for example, E. Lévi-Provençal, *Documents inédits d'histoire almohade* (Paris: Paris Librairie Orientaliste, 1928), text 71 and glossary; and Abu al-Qasim Ahmed al-Zayani, *Al-tujaman al-mu rib 'an duwal am-machriq wa-al-Maghrib*, ed. and trans. O. Houdas, *Le Maroc de 1631 à 1812* (Paris: E. Leroux, 1886). Kilito, "Speaking to Princes", 38.
37 Hammoudi, "The Reinvention of Dar al-mulk: The Moroccan Political System and Its Legitimation", in *In the Shadow of the Sultan*, 139.
38 Ghoulaichi, "Of Saints and Sharifian Kings in Morocco", 18.
39 Mohamed Darif, *Muassasat az-Zawaya bil-Maghreb, manchourat al-majala al-maghribiya li'ilm al-ijtima' al-siyasi* (Rabat: Matba'at al-Ma'arif al-Jadida, 1992), 238.
40 El-Mansour, "The Sanctuary (Hurm) in Pre-colonial Morocco", 59.
41 Muhammad Ibn al-Tayyib al-Qadiri, *Nashr al-mathani li-ahl a qarn al-hadi 'ashr wa al-thani*, eds A. Tawfiq and M. Hijji, 4 vols (Rabat: Dar al-Maghrib, 1977), 153.
42 Ibid., 117.
43 Pennell, *Morocco: From Empire to Independence*, 99. Although representatives of the other branches of the Prophet's House did exist in Morocco, for example the Naciris of Tamegrut who claimed descent from Jaafar ibn Abi Talib, only the descendants of Ali figured in the various registers of Moroccan Sharifs, and profited from the advantages offered to this cast (see Harrak, "Sharifism and the Sharifs", 19).
44 Bourqia, "The Cultural Legacy of Power in Morocco", 246.
45 Harrak, "Sharifism and the Sharifs", 25. Westermarck, *Ritual and Belief in Morocco*, 194, states that in Fez when the new Sultan mounted his horse during the allegiance

ceremony, the head of the Wazzani *sharifs* living in the place where he was proclaimed would hold the stirrup and help him mount his horse, thus bestowing on him the *Baraka* of Dar ad-Damana Wazzan. The same anthropologist alludes to "a saying that although no Wazzan sharif can rule as sultan, no sultan can rule without the support of the great sharif of Wazzan".

46 El-Mansour, "The Sanctuary (Hurm) in Pre-Colonial Morocco", 56.

47 Hammoudi, referenced by Miller and Bourqia's introduction to their *In the Shadow of the Sultan*, 10.

48 B. A. Morjeten, "Legitimacy in a Power State: Moroccan Politics in the Seventeenth Century during the Interregnum", 347.

49 Sahar Bazzaz, *Forgotten Saints: History, Power and Politics in the Making of Modern Morocco* (Cambridge: Harvard University Press, 2010), 64.

50 El-Mansour, "The Sanctuary (Hurm) in Pre-Colonial Morocco", 55.

51 Ibid., 56.

52 Kilito, "Speaking to Princes: Al-Yusi and Mawlay Ismail", 129. See also Geertz, *Islam Observed*, 33–35, for a reconstruction of this confrontation.

53 Pennell, *Morocco: From Empire to Independence*, 106.

54 Ghoulaichi, "Of Saints and Sharifian Kings in Morocco", 21.

55 Ghoulaichi, "Of Saints and Sharifian Kings in Morocco", 22.

56 Darif, *Muassasat az-Zawaya bil-Maghreb*, 128–33. For more details on Moulay Ismail's strategies against *zawiyas* and tribal groups, see Georges Drague, *Esquisse d'histoire religieuse du Maroc: Confréries et Zaouias* (Paris: Peyronnet, 1951).

Bibliography

Al-Du'ayf al-Ribati, Mohammed. *Tarikh al-Du'ayf (Tarih al-Dawla al-Saida)*. Edited by Ahmad al-Amari. Rabat: Dar al-Maturat, 1986.

Al-Hawwat, Abu al-Rabii Sulayman ibn 'Abd Allah al-Shafshawni. *Al-Sirr al-ẓāhir fī-man abraza bi-Fās al-sharaf al-bāhir min a'qāb al-shaykh 'Abd al-Qādir*. Fez: Litho, 1932.

Al-Qadiri, Muhammad Ibn al-Tayyib. *Nashr al-mathani li-ahl a qarn al-hadi 'ashr wa al-thani*. Edited by A. Tawfiq and M. Hijji. 4 vols. Rabat: Dar al-Maghrib, 1977.

Al-Tahiri, Ahmad ibn Hamdun. *Tuhfat al-Ikhwan bi Ba'd Manaqib Shurafa' Wazzan*. Fez: Lithograph Press, 1906.

Al-Zayani, Abu al-Qasim Ahmed. "Al-tujaman al-mu rib 'an duwal am-machriq wa-al-Maghrib". Edited and translated by O. Houdas. In *Le Maroc de 1631 à 1812*. Paris: E. Leroux, 1886.

Bazzaz, Sahar. *Forgotten Saints: History, Power and Politics in the Making of Modern Morocco*. Cambridge: Harvard University Press, 2010.

Beck, Herman. *L'image d'Idris II, ses descendants de Fas et la population sharifienne des Sultans Marinides (1258–1465)*. Leiden: Brill, 1989.

Bel, Alfred. *La religion Musulmane en Berbérie*, vol. 1. Paris: Paul Gerthner, 1938.

Bourqia, Rahma. "L'Etat et la gestion du symbolique au Maroc précolonial". In *Le Maghreb: approches des mécanismes d'articulation*, edited by R. Bourqia and N. Hopkins, 137–51. Casablanca: Al-Kalam, 1991.

Bourqia, Rahma. "The Cultural Legacy of Power in Morocco". In *In the Shadow of the Sultan: Culture, Power, and Politics in Morocco*, edited by R. Bourqia and S. G. Miller, 243–58. Cambridge: Harvard Centre for Middle Eastern Studies, 1998.

Burke, Edmund, III. "The Moroccan Ulama, 1860–1920: An Introduction". In *Scholars, Saints, and Sufis: Muslim Religious Institutions since 1500*, edited by N. R. Keddie, 93–125. Berkeley: University of California Press, 1972.

Cornell, Vincent J. "The Logic of Analogy and the Role of the Sufi Shaykh in Post-Marinid Morocco". *International Journal of Middle East Studies* 15, 1 (Feb. 1983), 67–93.

12

DOMINAE IMPERIALES

Ottonian women and dynastic stability, strength, and legitimacy in tenth-century Germany

Penelope Nash

At the beginning of the tenth century the rulers in Germany lacked clear succession criteria. The first ruler of what was to become the Ottonian dynasty, Henry I, accepted the title of king from the people in 909, purportedly with reluctance. Henry had to deal with the threat of usurpation and the lack of clear succession criteria, which destabilised his regime. The four successive Ottonian rulers received a higher title, that of emperor, at a coronation by the pope. By the early eleventh century, the fifth Ottonian and last emperor, Henry II, operated in a more stable ruling milieu. Primogeniture had been established in the Holy Roman Empire and, although Henry II had no children, the succession of the new Salian dynasty after his death in 1024 occurred with relatively little turmoil, in contrast to the bloody battles that had been waged in the first half of the previous century to establish precedence.

This chapter examines the issues arising from such difficulties and their effect on Ottonian politics. Illegitimate sons and second marriages, with the consequent downgrading of earlier offspring, caused dissension and military conflict. The chroniclers write uneasily of these conflicts, often to justify the legitimacy of the new rulers. How did the chroniclers treat those events? In hindsight we can see a pattern of greater stability developing over the century. But that pattern was not clear to those living through the events, and the fear of choosing the wrong side shows through in the contemporary reports and in the actions and reactions of their subjects of study.

The Ottonian dynasty began in 919 after Conrad I, the East Frankish king, surprised everyone at his death bed by nominating the Saxon Henry, who was not his kin, as the next ruler. He "admonished them in a paternal voice that in choosing his successor there should be no division in the kingdom".[1] The leading men accepted Conrad's choice and acclaimed the new King Henry I. Henry concluded a treaty with Charles the Simple of West Francia in 921. He followed some Carolingian precepts. For example, he was crowned and he ruled as an itinerant king, moving from palace to palace.[2] In other matters Henry rejected Carolingian customs.

TABLE 12.1 The Ottonian rulers and selected family

Ruler	*Birth* *(co-regent with father)* *Independent kingship (k.)* *[co-emperor with father]* *Independent imperial reign (e.)*	*Wife*	*Sister (S), brother (B), cousin (C)*	*Comment*
Henry I (Henry the Fowler)	b. 876 k. 919–36	Queen Mathilda		First Ottonian
Otto I	b. 912 k. 936–73 e. 962–73	Queen and Empress Adelheid	Gerberga (S); Duke Henry I of Bavaria (B)	
Otto II	b. 955 (961–73) k. 973–83 [968–73] e. 973–83	Queen and Empress Theophanu	Abbess Mathilda of Quedlinburg (S); Duke Henry II of Bavaria (aka Henry the Wrangler) (C)	
Empress Adelheid	*974–75*	*n/a*		*Regent for Otto II*
Otto III	b. 980 k. 994/95–1002 e. 996–1002	unmarried	Abbess Adelheid of Quedlinburg (999–1043) (S), Abbess Sophia of Gandersheim (1002–39) (S)	
Empress Theophanu, Empress Adelheid, *Abbess Mathilda of Quedlinburg*	*983–June 991*	*n/a*		*Regents for Otto III during this period*
Empress Adelheid, *Abbess Mathilda of Quedlinburg*	*June 991–94/95*	*n/a*		*Regents for Otto III during this period*
Henry II	b. 973 k. 1002–24 e. 1014–24	Queen and Empress Cunegunde		Last Ottonian

He refused anointing. He signalled that he would rule with his leading men, not over them. He sought alliances with the dukes of Swabia and Bavaria who were magnates outside his near family. At the end of his life he called a meeting with the rulers of West Francia and Burgundy at which he appeared as the senior man.[3]

In 1024, 100 years after Henry I's election as king, the fifth and last member of the Ottonian dynasty, Emperor Henry II, died without issue, and the succession passed to a new line, whose members came to be known as the Salians (see Table 12.1). With good reason, historians have seen the Ottonian dynasty as one that progressed from an uncertain beginning to one of relative stability.[4] This has been attributed primarily to the efforts of the male leaders. In contrast, while their wives, sisters, aunts, and daughters are known as powerful women, they are usually relegated to the background when dynastic competence is examined. In this chapter I propose a different reason for the continuance of the stability of the regime, and argue that the ruling women rather than their men maintained that stability after Otto I died in 973, up to and including the start of the reign of Henry II in 1002.

Background

The story of the Ottonian dynasty is typically told as follows. King Henry I consolidated his kingship by concluding a truce with the Magyars in 926. His son Otto I crushed the last major rebellion of his reign in 954, and destroyed the Magyar threat at the Battle of the Lech in 955. His son Otto II succeeded at Otto I's death in 973. In June 982 Otto II suffered a major defeat at Crotone in southern Italy. Sensing weakness in the Empire, the Slavs in the East rose up in rebellion. In late 983 Otto II died. After a short, albeit serious, dispute over who would undertake the regency for Otto III, Empress Adelheid, Empress Theophanu, and Abbess Mathilda of Quedlinburg (grandmother, mother, and aunt of Otto III) became joint regents. The imperial charters were issued in the name of Otto III, even though he was only three. The leading men of the realm defeated the Slavs and other rebels in the East. Otto III came of age between mid-994 and early 995, and ruled until his death in 1002.[5]

This story normally gives credit to Otto II and Otto III for maintaining the stability of the Kingdom in the latter third of the tenth century with help from the leading men, but without much contribution from the women in the family. I propose instead that not only were the women prominent, but that they were the backbone of the Empire from 983, after Otto II died, until at least mid-994, when Otto III reached maturity. Furthermore, the support of Otto III's two sisters, Abbesses Adelheid and Sophia, was the principle reason Henry II succeeded to the kingship in 1002.

The two empresses, Adelheid and Theophanu, did not come into their own only after their husbands died, when they became regents for their sons or grandsons.[6] Much earlier, Queen Adelheid had undertaken a decisive role with her first husband, King Lothar of Italy (r. 947–50). After his death in 950, she operated as queen in Italy and she exercised a wide range of powers there and in Germany during the reign of her second husband, Otto I (r. 936–73).[7] One mark of the power and influence that a person exercised in the Middle Ages was the number of interventions that are recorded for her or him in the court records, especially in the charters (or *diplomata*) of the ruler. Adelheid's overall intervention rate of approximately 37 per cent in all of Otto I's (extant) diplomata during their marriage indicates her high level of influence.[8]

Adelheid's interactions with or interventions on behalf of two doges of Venice—Vitale Candiano and Pietro IV Candiano—are salutary and provide examples of sustained effective involvement. She continued the alliances formed during Otto I's reign. In 963 the imperial court gifted property and other goods at Musestre, 10 kilometres from Torcello in the province of Treviso, to Vitale Candiano, an eminent Venetian and a future doge (r. 978–79).[9] On 2 December 967 an imperial charter (*diploma*) records in affectionate words that Otto I had acceded to the request brought to him by his wife Empress Adelheid ("... per Adeleidam dilectam coniugem nostrum") and two other intercessors on behalf of Doge Pietro IV Candiano (r. 959–76). Otto I renewed and revised the highly significant pact between the Empire and Venice originally negotiated by Charlemagne that included details of the protection within the imperial borders of certain Venetian possessions and confirmed the basis of mutual trade and intercourse.[10] Adelheid's ongoing influence in Venetian affairs can be seen once more four years later. On 8 January 972 at Ravenna Otto I gifted more property (this time Isola, situated in Istria) to Vitale Candiano as his free property and with immunity, at the intercession of Adelheid.[11]

Adelheid's direct intervention can be seen at Piacenza in later 976. Earlier in that year Doge Pietro IV Candiano and his young son from his second marriage with Waldrada, the daughter of Willa and Margrave Humbert of Tuscany, were murdered. Waldrada's maternal grandmother (another Waldrada) was the sister of Empress Adelheid's father, Rudolf II (king of Burgundy 912–37, king of Italy 924–26).[12] In addition, the younger Waldrada's paternal grandfather was King Hugh of Italy (r. 926–47). Hugh, through his marriage to Bertha of Swabia, became Adelheid's stepfather, and through Adelheid's marriage to his son King Lothar of Italy (her first marriage) also became her father-in-law.[13] Consequently Empress Adelheid was "aunt" by marriage to the younger Waldrada through two different genealogical paths.

That relationship was important when at her niece's entreaty Empress Adelheid presided personally over a court sitting in Piacenza on 25 October 976 in order to rule over a dispute about the legal rights of her now-widowed niece. The new political leadership in Venice wanted to retrieve the reverse dowry (that is, the gifts that the groom gave his bride on their marriage) from the widow, who wrote to the Empress to request the admission of her lawyer before the court.[14] Sean Gilsdorf notes the many "bonds of lordship, trust, and even affinity" that connected Adelheid with the Venetians.[15]

The second imperial woman of interest, Theophanu, came from the Byzantine court as a *puella*, exact age unknown, to the East Frankish court of Otto I to marry his son, Otto II, in 972. After Otto I's death in 973 Empress Adelheid acted as regent for a year for the newlyweds. Then the young couple took over the responsibility for the Empire. Adelheid spent much of her time in Italy and at the kingdom of her brother Conrad in Burgundy. Like Adelheid, Theophanu participated firmly and extensively in rulership. She too acted as intervener on behalf of petitioners seeking favours early in her marriage to Otto II. His charters show that she intervened in approximately 36 per cent of all the Emperor's diplomata (at least of those that are extant).[16] After Otto II's unexpected death in December 983 the two women met at Pavia and worked together to set the direction for the realm, which was now in the nominal charge of a three-year-old boy, Otto III, their grandson and son.

Otto II's death

Otto II left behind a troubled and rebellious empire. In the East the newly conquered Slavs and others were in revolt. In the West there was uncertainty over who would rule the West Franks. In the Ottonian house members of the family were contending with each other for rulership of the Empire. Otto II's unexpected death in December 983 triggered the crisis of succession. Otto had taken the precaution in May 983 of having his son, Otto III, crowned joint king at Verona and acclaimed by the leading men, which strengthened the young boy's chance of succeeding him as king. Hereditary succession was more firmly entrenched than when Otto I first became ruler after his father, Henry I, died in 936, but was still not absolutely assured. The vital question was who should become regent and rule for the three-year-old Otto III. The obvious choice was one of his uncles: Duke Henry the Wrangler, King Lothair of West Francia, or Duke Charles of Lower Lotharingia. Instead, the leading men chose three women as joint regents.[17]

A strong queen could in effect rule even if an underage ruler held the throne. The queen's success as regent "was predicated not simply on her traditional occupation of it, nor on some structural property of familial or royal succession"; she also had to put into practice the "personal, material, and symbolic resources at her disposal".[18] The three *dominae imperiales* (Empress Adelheid, Empress Theophanu, and Abbess Mathilda of Quedlinburg) ruled as regents at various times in the period before Otto III reached his majority.[19] Nevertheless, Adam of Bremen ignored the women's practical rule. In discussing Otto III's life he counted Otto's reign from the age of three:

> The third Otto, although still a boy, succeeded to the throne and for eighteen years distinguished the sceptre by a strong and just rule.[20]

Despite that tradition, robust evidence exists for the direct rule of Empress Theophanu, Empress Adelheid, and Abbess Mathilda, with the church hierarchy providing advice and chancery support. Let us take some examples of how the women ruled, favouring collaboration and negotiation over conflict.

Stability and strength of the realm, 983–95

There is good evidence that the stability of the dynasty in the last twenty years of the tenth century depended on the three *dominae imperiales*. From the early death of Otto II in 983 until Otto III reached his majority, probably in late 994, their actions in the Empire show how in the main their strategy was negotiation rather than confrontation to resolve disputes. In the West Frankish kingdom, King Lothair, his son King Louis V, Duke Charles of Lower Lotharingia, and Hugh Capet at different times competed for the throne. The situation was even more complex. The East Frankish and West Frankish families were connected by marriage. Emma, the daughter of Empress Adelheid and her first husband, King Lothar of Italy, had married King Lothair of West Francia. Emma was consequently the sister-in-law of the reigning Empress Theophanu.

Theophanu used a number of strategies to alleviate the tensions in the West Frankish kingdom. She persuaded Hugh Capet to relinquish Lotharingia. She decided not to support Hugh's Carolingian rival, Duke Charles of Lower Lotharingia, because he would have separated Lotharingia from the Empire. King Lothair died in 986 and King Louis V in 987. Theophanu did not attempt to intervene in the skirmishes for the throne in the West as had her father-in-law, Otto I, nor did she interfere after Hugh gained the upper hand in the government. From 982 the Capetians consequently took over in France completely independently, though with the agreement of the Germans under Theophanu's watch.[21]

In the East Theophanu was unable to recover the enormous losses caused by the great Slav revolt of 983. However, she was able to secure the North March and the March of Meissen, and to sign peace agreements with Mieszko of Poland and with Boleslav of Bohemia.[22] It is worth examining in more detail how Theophanu handled politics in the East. The Elbe Slavs remained incorporated ecclesiastically into the Magdeburg See. Here Theophanu followed the earlier aims of King Henry I and Emperor Otto I. She conducted herself differently against the people who were to be significant in the formation of Poland and Bohemia. She took sides in dynastic disputes, in favour of the Piasts in Poland and against the Přemyslids in Bohemia. She was even ready to give military help to the Polish duke Mieszko I. With those actions the Empress sanctioned the formation of a Piast state (the basis of a future larger Poland) ruled by Mieszko, whose tribute duty she kept, but she decided against a strong Bohemian (that is, Czech) duchy. She consequently set the critical direction for future development. Poland moved towards independence while the attachment of Bohemia to the Empire only increased (and would continue until the dissolution of the Empire in the early nineteenth century).[23]

In Italy, Theophanu, acting decisively for her young son, issued charters in her own name as *imperator augustus*.[24] Josef Fleckenstein acknowledges her important role from 984 until her death in 991: the

> greatest achievement of the regency [of Otto III] with the Empress Theophano at its head was to ward off the worst dangers facing the Empire and to preserve the minor king's patrimony of authority. With the support

of [the senior clergy] . . . Theophano displayed a sure hand both at home and abroad.[25]

During the early years of Otto III's regency, Theophanu ruled mainly in Germany, and Empress Adelheid continued her important ruling role in Italy. Adelheid acted as regent three times between 974 and 994: one year for her son Otto II and his new young bride Theophanu; eight years with Theophanu and Abbess Mathilda of Quedlinburg for the underage Otto III after Otto II's death; and then three years as sole regent for Otto III after Theophanu's death. Adelheid spent twelve years as regent or ruler in Italy out of the twenty-one years after the death of her husband Otto I.[26] When Theophanu died there was no debate about the ability and the right of Adelheid to continue the regency alone until her grandson Otto III reached his majority. During that period Adelheid confirmed large financial contributions to her favourite monastery at Selz.[27] In late 994 Otto III added further riches to Selz soon after he came of age and took control of the Kingdom.[28]

Whoever controlled the roads controlled the Kingdom. The mark of Adelheid's influence there is shown in a document dated to 995 in which she expects and obtains accommodation and victuals for the travelling court and the animals on an overnight stay. The safety of the German roads and Adelheid's demonstration of her control over them towards the end of her sole regency for Otto III is shown in her letter to "G", probably either a Würzburg clerk or Gozpert, the abbot of Tegernsee, in which she orders the abbey to prepare for the arrival of her royal party. They were to provide accommodation, funds, and food for her and her travelling household, and fodder for her animals.[29] Adelheid held not only control of the roads but also the royal right to the goods of the monastery.

The two imperial widows Theophanu and Adelheid limited themselves to conducting the regency for their son and grandson, Otto III, but never strove for a truly independent power of rule. Consequently, transition to the autonomous rule of Otto III proceeded seamlessly without friction. As soon as the young king had reached the prescribed age limit, his full authority to conduct business was recognised, and there was no longer any doubt about who exercised the de facto *potestas* over the realm.[30] In contrast to the measured decisions of the female regents, Otto III's immediate actions indicated his differing views. In 995 Otto III unsuccessfully attacked the Abodrites and the lands of the Wiltzi (Slavs along the Baltic coast, now north-eastern Germany).[31] In 996 he left Germany for Italy, leaving behind his aunt, Abbess Mathilda of Quedlinburg, as ruler. That visit and his return there in 997 provoked widespread disapproval because of various cruelties that he inflicted on those who opposed him. For example, he ordered that the eyes, nose, and tongue of the anti-pope Johannes Philagathos be cut off, and that the prefect of Rome, Crescentius, be beheaded and that his body be hung upside down on the Monte Mario.[32] In contrast, Otto III showed the ongoing importance he placed on the third member of the *dominae imperiales* in giving her control of the Kingdom.

His mother Theophanu kept Archchancellor Willigis of Mainz and Chancellor Hildibald of Worms (the senior clergy in the German lands) on side.

Her collaboration with men like St Adalbert of Prague and Bishop Unger of Memleben and Posen—important leaders of missions to the Slavs—would probably have been greater than the sparse sources show. The foreigner Theophanu could evaluate the situation with some independence because although her world view was fashioned in Byzantium it was tempered by her later experiences in the West.[33] An example of the successful outcome of negotiations in general can be seen in the presence of Margrave Hugh of Tuscany and Mieszko of Poland at Quedlinburg with Theophanu and Otto III for the Easter celebration in 991. Visitors and the imperial party gave gifts, and received gifts in return.[34]

Theophanu and Adelheid, with occasional support from Abbess Mathilda of Quedlinburg, ruled the Empire without doubt, but they did not appropriate the Empire for themselves. We must not forget that Henry the Wrangler had attempted to usurp the throne immediately after Otto II died and that he and his father, Duke Henry I of Bavaria, had acted in constant opposition to the elected Ottonian rulers. It is no mean feat that the women persuaded Henry the Wrangler to submit to them and to the young King Otto III. Henry's reconciliation lasted through the rest of the regency of the three women (983–91) and into Adelheid's sole regency (991–94). He died in 995.[35]

One further example of the contribution by Ottonian women, a generation after Theophanu, is relevant. After Otto III died in 1002 without a direct heir, more than one claimant to the throne stepped forward. The future Henry II (son of Henry the Wrangler) sought the kingship. Henry II had legitimate claim as grandson of Duke Henry I of Bavaria (brother of Otto I) but so did others. Theophanu's two daughters, sisters of the recently deceased Emperor Otto III, Abbess Adelheid of Quedlinburg and Abbess Sophia of Gandersheim, attended the gathering of all the great men of the realm at Werla in 1002. Karl Leyser's comment on the report by Bishop Thietmar of Merseburg is pertinent: a

> table had been set for Adelheid's and Sophia's dinner, and the food was already there when Margrave Ekkehard of Meissen and his supporters . . . seized it ahead of the two sisters and sat down to the meal. It was the most obvious, public and visible way to strike at and repudiate the old [Ottonian] dynasty.

Ekkehard's message was that he did not need to be of royal blood to become king.[36] Ekkehard's insult, directed to the sisters and not to the unnamed leading men, shows the pivotal role and consequently the legitimacy that he, the leading men and the chronicler of the event, Bishop Thietmar, gave to the sisters in the selection of the new king. Though Henry's ancestors had rebelled frequently against the elected kings, the sisters demonstrated their harmony with and support of their cousin by attending. As direct descendants of the imperial line their support was essential to Henry II's successful election to the kingship. Count Ekkehard and his men were repudiated, and Henry II was elected king and later crowned emperor.

Context and conclusion

The progression of the Ottonian dynasty's power into a third consecutive generation marked by Otto II's succession was very unusual in post-Carolingian Europe. Nevertheless, Otto II's achievements were circumscribed and he died leaving the Empire in crisis. As we have seen, it is clear that the decisive actions of three Ottonian women during the reigns of the last three Ottonian emperors were the main determinates of the stability of the Germanic kingdom and empire in this period. We can name their success as "agency" or "power". The concept of and term "agency" has been applied mostly to women as another option when political authority was not available.[37] Theresa Earenfight distinguishes between power, authority, influence, and agency. She also argues for a better understanding of the spectrum of power encompassing resistance, coercion, intercession, and tutelage. Hard power (such as "executing a traitor") is often associated with men; soft power (such as "pardoning a traitor through intercession") is often associated with women.[38] Empress Adelheid, Empress Theophanu, and Abbess Mathilda of Quedlinburg (the three *dominae imperiales*) were not only influential when acting as regents at various times for Otto I, Otto II, and Otto III, but also operated well beyond "agency" at all times to rule the Empire using the full spectrum of power.

I have two caveats about my discussion in this chapter. First, I do not want to imply that the views of the contemporary Bishop Thietmar of Merseburg in chronicling the events of the late tenth and early eleventh centuries were unaffected by the situation in which he found himself. He wrote when Henry II was well established as king, and was in the process of becoming emperor.[39] Bishop Thietmar naturally sought to preserve himself and his diocese and needed to keep favour with the incumbent ruler. He also needed to present the rulers before Henry II somewhat favourably, but not too favourably, since although Henry was closely related to them, his ancestors had rebelled fiercely and often.

Second, not all modern writers have ignored or underestimated the power of the Ottonian women, but few have positioned their contribution to the stability of the dynasty at the end of the tenth century so highly. My argument has been that the Ottonian women contributed far more to the stability of the latter third of the Ottonian dynasty by negotiation than the men did by war. The proofs for this proposition are often hidden and diffuse. I hope I have indicated where the evidence lies, and shown that the ruling women subtly shaped their neighbours' futures by choosing different tactics from those that their masculine near-kin more often selected.

Notes

1 ". . . ne in eligendo post se rege discidium regni fieret, paterna eos voce premonuit", Adalbert of Magdeburg, *Continuatio Reginonis*, ed. Albert Bauer and Reinhold Rau, *Ausgewählte Quellen zur deutschen Geschichte des Mittelalters* [hereafter *AQDG*] 8 (Darmstadt: Wissenschaftliche Buchgesellschaft, 2002), s.a. 919, 192, trans. Simon MacLean, *History and Politics in Late Carolingian and Ottonian Europe: The Chronicle of Regino of Prüm and Adalbert of Magdeburg* (Manchester: Manchester University Press, 2009), s.a. 919, 235.

See also Karl J. Leyser, *Rule and Conflict in an Early Medieval Society: Ottonian Saxony* (London: Edward Arnold, 1979), 27.

2 For the Carolingians as travellers rather than true itinerants, see John W. Bernhardt, "'On the Road Again': Kings, Roads, and Accommodation in High Medieval Germany", in *Every Inch a King: Comparative Studies on Kings and Kingship in the Ancient and Medieval Worlds*, ed. Lynette Mitchell and Charles Melville (Boston: Brill, 2012), 304.

3 For how far Carolingian ways were followed or not by the Ottonians and a summary of the polity of the Ottonians themselves, see Timothy Reuter, "The Ottonians and Carolingian Tradition", in *Medieval Polities and Modern Mentalities*, ed. Janet L. Nelson (Cambridge: Cambridge University Press, 2006), 268–83. See also Karl J. Leyser, "Henry I and the Beginnings of the Saxon Empire", *English Historical Review* 83, 326 (Jan. 1968): 1–32, esp. 1–5.

4 Eckhard Müller-Mertens, "The Ottonians as Kings and Emperors", in *New Cambridge Medieval History, Volume III, c.900–c.1024*, ed. Timothy Reuter (Cambridge: Cambridge University Press, 1999), 233–66; Timothy Reuter, *Germany in the Early Middle Ages c. 800–1056* (London: Longman, 1991), 183–214; Benjamin Arnold, *Medieval Germany, 500–1300: A Political Interpretation* (Basingstoke: Macmillan, 1997), esp. 133–48.

5 David Bachrach, "Exercise of Royal Power in Early Medieval Europe: The Case of Otto the Great 936–73", *Early Medieval Europe* 17, 4 (2009): 389–419; Gerd Althoff, *Otto III*, trans. Phyllis G. Jestice (University Park, PA: Pennsylvania State University Press, 2003).

6 The most important contemporary sources are: Odilo of Cluny, *Epitaphium domine Adalheide auguste or 'Das Epitaphium'*, ed. Herbert Paulhart, *Die Lebensbeschreibung der Kaiserin Adelheid von Abt Odilo von Cluny* (Graz and Cologne: Böhlau, 1962), 27–45; *Vita Mathildis reginae antiquior (Die Lebensbeschreibungen der Königin Mathilde)* and *Vita Mathildis reginae posterior (Die Lebensbeschreibungen der Königin Mathilde)*, ed. Bernd Schütte, *Monumenta Germaniae Historica* [hereafter *MGH*], *Scriptores rerum Germanicarum in usum scholarum separatim editi* 66 (Hanover: Hahn, 1994), 107–42 and 143–202; all trans. in Sean Gilsdorf, *Queenship and Sanctity: The Lives of Mathilda and the Epitaph of Adelheid* (Washington: Catholic University of America Press, 2004). For a detailed history of Ottonian ruling women compared with ruling women in the eleventh and early twelfth centuries, see Penelope Nash, *Empress Adelheid and Countess Matilda: Medieval Female Rulership and the Foundations of European Society* (Basingstoke and New York: Palgrave Macmillan, 2017). See also Simon MacLean, *Ottonian Queenship* (Oxford: Oxford University Press, 2017); Paolo Golinelli, *Adelaide. Regina Santa d'Europa* (Milan: Jaca Book, 2001). For England in the eleventh century, see Pauline Stafford, *Queen Emma and Queen Edith: Queenship and Women's Power in Eleventh-Century England* (Oxford: Blackwell, 1997).

7 For powerful female rule in medieval Italy, see Patricia Skinner, *Women in Medieval Italian Society, 500–1200* (Harlow: Pearson Education, 2001); Amalie Fößel, "The Political Traditions of Female Rulership in Medieval Europe", in *The Oxford Handbook of Women and Gender in Medieval Europe*, ed. Judith M. Bennett and Ruth Mazo Karras (Oxford: Oxford University Press, 2013), 68–83; Amalie Fößel, "Adelheid", in *Die Kaiserinnen des Mittelalters*, ed. Amalie Fößel (Regensburg: Friedrich Pustet, 2011), 35–59; François Bougard, "Public Power and Authority", in *Italy in the Early Middle Ages: 476–1000*, ed. Cristina La Rocca (Oxford: Oxford University Press, 2002), 39–44.

8 Sean Gilsdorf, *The Favor of Friends: Intercession and Aristocratic Politics in Carolingian and Ottonian Europe* (Leiden: Brill, 2014), 173. The number of Adelheid's interventions in Otto I's diplomata cannot be precisely gauged because of interpretations in the meaning of the words of intercession in the diplomata and imprecision in the exact date of their wedding. Adelheid's proportion of interventions relative to Otto I's number of diplomata varies depending on her life circumstances. For example, the number of interventions is much fewer in the early child-bearing years and much greater in the later years. See Penelope Nash, "Empress Adelheid's Vulnerabilities as Mother and Ruler", in *Royal Mothers and Their Ruling Children: Wielding Political Authority from Antiquity to the Early*

Modern Era, ed. Elena Woodacre and Carey Fleiner (Basingstoke and New York: Palgrave Macmillan, 2015), 135–37.

9 Otto I, *Diplomata. Die Urkunden Konrad I., Heinrich I., und Otto I.*, ed. T. Sickel, *MGH, Diplomata regum et imperatorum Germaniae*, I (Hanover: Hahn, 1879–84, repr. Berlin, 1956), no. 257, S. Leo, 26 August 963; Johann Friedrich Böhmer, E. Ottenthal, and Hans K. Kaminsky, *Regesta Imperii II, 1 (Sächsisches Haus 919–1024): Die Regesten des Kaiserreiches unter Heinrich I. und Otto I. 919–973* (Hildesheim: Böhlau, 1967), no. 345, 163; Michael McCormick, "Where do Trading Towns Come From? Early Medieval Venice and the Northern *Emporia*", in *Post-Roman Towns, Trade and Settlement in Europe and Byzantium. Vol. 1: The Heirs of the Roman West*, ed. Joachim Henning (Berlin and New York: Walter de Gruyter, 2007), 47.

10 "... per Adeleidam dilectam coniugem nostrum ac per nuntios suos Iohannem Guntarinum et alium Iohannem diaconum", Otto I, *Diplomata*, no. 351, 2 December 967; Böhmer et al., *Regesta Imperii II, 1*, no. 460, 207; Amalie Fößel, *Die Königin im mittelalterlichen Reich. Herrschaftsausübung, Herrschaftsrechte, Handlungsspielräume*, Mittelalter-Forschungen 4 (Stuttgart: Jan Thorbecke, 2000), 282.

11 Otto I, *Diplomata*, no. 407, Ravenna, 8 January 972.

12 I have taken some time and effort to clarify the connections here because two closely connected women named Waldrada need to be disentangled and because information about female connections are not made as readily visible as are male connections.

13 Fößel, *Die Königin*, 283, n191.

14 Ibid., 156–57, 283.

15 Gilsdorf, *Favor*, 57. However, it was Pietro IV Candiano (doge 959–76), who married Adelheid's niece Waldrada, not Pietro I Orseolo (doge 976–78) as Gilsdorf states at note 45. The Petro about whom Althoff includes information from the Saxon chronologies is Pietro IV Candiano, not Pietro I Orseolo Vitale: Gerd Althoff, *Adels- und Königsfamilien im Spiegel ihrer Memorialüberlieferung. Studien zum Totengedenken der Billunger und Ottonen*, Münstersche Mittelalter-Schriften vol. 47 (1984), 165, 381. For more on the Orseolo and Candiano families, see Christopher Kleinhenz, ed., *Medieval Italy: An Encyclopedia*, 2 vols (New York: Routledge, 2004), 802, 1122.

16 Gilsdorf, *Favor*, 174.

17 Henry the Wrangler was nephew of Otto I through Otto's brother Duke Henry I of Bavaria. The brothers Lothair of West Francia and Charles of Lower Lotharingia were nephews of Otto I through Otto's sister, Gerberga. For the gradual shift from elective monarchy to hereditary monarchy during the tenth century in Germany, see Arnold, *Medieval Germany*, 174–75.

18 Gilsdorf, *Queenship*, 11. For studies in queenship in general, see Theresa Earenfight, *Queenship in Medieval Europe: Queenship and Power* (Basingstoke: Palgrave Macmillan, 2013). For studies of queenship in Merovingian and Carolingian times, see Janet Nelson, "Queens as Jezebels: The Careers of Brunhild and Balthild in Merovingian History", in *Debating the Middle Ages: Issues and Readings*, ed. Lester K. Little and Barbara H. Rosenwein (Malden: Blackwell, 1998), 219–53; Simon MacLean, "Queenship, Nunneries and Royal Widowhood in Carolingian Europe", *Past & Present* 178 (2003): 3–38.

19 Adelheid, Theophanu, and Abbess Mathilda are referred to as *dominae imperiales* in the *Annales Quedlinburgenses*, ed. Martina Giese, *MGH, Scriptores rerum Germanicarum in usum scholarum separatim editi* 72 (Hanover: Hahn, 2004), s.aa. 984, 985, pp. 473, 475. The *Annales Quedlinburgenses* records that the expression "*dominae imperiales*" was also applied to the two abbesses Sophia and Adelheid, daughters of Theophanu and grand-daughters of Adelheid, in AD 1000 and AD 1002 (pp. 511, 519).

20 "Illi tercius Otto, cum adhuc puer esset, in regnum substitutus annos XVIII forti et iusto exeptrum ornavit imperio": Adam of Bremen, *Gesta Hammaburgensis ecclesiae pontificum*, ed. Werner Trillmich and Rudolf Buchner, 2nd edn, *AQDG* 11: 137–499 (Darmstadt: Wissenschaftliche Buchgesellschaft, 1968), 2.24, 256, trans. Francis J. Tschan, *History of the Archbishops of Hamburg-Bremen* (New York: Columbia University Press, 1959), 69.

21 Josef Fleckenstein, *Early Medieval Germany*, trans. Bernard S. Smith (Amsterdam: North-Holland Publishing Company, 1978), 167–68; Reuter, "Ottonians and Carolingian Tradition", 279.
22 Fleckenstein, *Early Medieval Germany*, 167.
23 Johannes Fried, "Theophanu und die Slawen. Bermerkungen zur Ostpolitik der Kaiserin", in *Kaiserin Theophanu: Begegnung des Ostens und Westens um die Wende des ersten Jahrtausands*, eds Anton von Euw and Peter Schreiner (Cologne: Schnütgen-Museum, 1991), 370; Darius von Güttner-Sporzyński, *Poland, Holy War, and the Piast Monarchy, 1100–1230*, Europa Sacra (Turnhout: Brepols, 2014), 29–50; Przemyslaw Urbańczyk and Stanislaw Rosik, "Poland", in *Christianization and the Rise of Christian Monarchy: Scandinavia, Central Europe and Rus' c.900–1200*, ed. Nora Berend (Cambridge: Cambridge University Press, 2007), 263–66.
24 Otto III, *Diplomata. Die Urkunden Otto des III.*, ed. T. Sickel, *MGH, Diplomata regum et imperatorum Germaniae*, 2.2 (Hanover: Hahn, 1893, repr. Berlin, 1957), Theophanu, no. 1, Rome, 2 January 990; no. 2, Ravenna, 1 April 990. Theophanu's two extant charters, issued in her own name and not that of her son, are recorded in Otto III's printed charters.
25 Fleckenstein, *Early Medieval Germany*, 167.
26 After the initial disruption caused by Otto II's unexpected death, and order had been restored, Theophanu took the leading role as regent for her son, Otto III.
27 Otto III, *Diplomata*, no. 79, Pöhlde, 4 January 992; no. 130, Merseburg, 2 July 993.
28 Ibid., nos. 159 and 160, Erstein, 26 December 994.
29 Froumond, *Die Tegernseer Briefsammlung*, ed. Karl Strecker, *MGH, Epistolae selectae* 3:1–96 (Berlin: Weidmann, 1925, repr. 1964), no. 16, p. 16. For comments on the journey and its implications as well as arrangements for royal journeys in general, see Karl J. Leyser, "Ottonian Government", *English Historical Review* 96, 381 (1981): 747; John William Bernhardt, *Itinerant Kingship and Royal Monasteries in Early Medieval Germany, c.936–1075*, Cambridge Studies in Medieval Life and Thought, 4th series (Cambridge: Cambridge University Press, 1993), 59.
30 Johannes Laudage, "Das Problem der Vormundschaft über Otto III", in *Kaiserin Theophanu*, eds von Euw and Schreiner, 275.
31 Thietmar of Merseburg, *Chronicon*, ed. Werner Trillmich, 8th edn, *AQDG* (Darmstadt: Wissenschaftliche Buchgesellschaft, 2002), 4.19, 134, trans. David A. Warner, *Ottonian Germany: The Chronicon of Thietmar of Merseburg* (Manchester: Manchester University Press, 2001), 164–65; *Annales Quedlinburgenses*, s.a. 995, p. 486. For further information on the Abodrites and the Wiltzi (Liutzi), see the references in the *Quedlinburg Annals*, noted in Giese's edition. For the history of the Abodrites and the Wiltzi and their interaction with the Franks and the Saxons from the late eighth century, see also Ingrid Rembold, *Conquest and Christianization: Saxony and the Carolingian World, 772–888* (Cambridge: Cambridge University Press, 2017), 44–84.
32 For Otto III's activities in Italy between 996 and 999, see Penelope Nash, "Reality and Ritual in the Medieval King's Emotions of *Ira* and *Clementia*", in *Understanding Emotions in Early Europe*, eds Michael Champion and Andrew Lynch (Turnhout: Brepols, 2015), 251–53, 265–66.
33 Fried, "Theophanu und die Slawen", 370.
34 *Annales Quedlinburgenses*, s.a. 991, 478.
35 Thietmar of Merseburg, *Chronicon*, 4.20, 134–36, trans. Warner, *Ottonian Germany*, 165–66.
36 Karl J. Leyser, "Ritual, Ceremony and Gesture: Ottonian Germany", in *Communications and Power in Medieval Europe: The Carolingian and Ottonian Centuries*, ed. Timothy Reuter (London: Hambledon Press, 1994), 203; Thietmar of Merseburg, *Chronicon*, 5.3–5.4, 5.7, 196–98, 200, trans. Warner, *Ottonian Germany*, 207–08, 210.
37 For example, see Melissa R. Katz, "The Final Testament of Violante de Aragón (*c.*1236–1300/01): Agency and (Dis)empowerment of a Dowager Queen", in *Queenship in the Mediterranean: Negotiating the Role of the Queen in the Medieval and Early Modern Eras*, ed. Elena Woodacre (Basingstoke and New York: Palgrave Macmillan, 2013), 52, 56.

See also Mary Carpenter Erler and Maryanne Kowaleski, "Introduction: A New Economy of Power Relations – Female Agency in the Middle Ages", in *Gendering the Master Narrative: Women and Power in the Middle Ages*, eds Mary Carpenter Erler and Maryanne Kowaleski (Ithaca, NY: Cornell University Press, 2003), 1–2, 11–12, 16; Penelope Nash, "Women and Power: Thoughts Arising out of the Roundtable 'Debating Women and Power in the Middle Ages', International Medieval Congress, Leeds 2014", *Medieval Feminist Forum* 51, 2 (2015): ir.uiowa/edu/mff/vol51/iss2/6, accessed 7 May 2018.

38 Theresa Earenfight, "Medieval Queenship", *History Compass* 15, 3 (2017): 2–4, doi:10.1111/hic3.12372.

39 Bishop Thietmar's *Chronicon* was composed between 1013 and 1018. Henry II's coronation as emperor occurred in 1014: Warner, *Ottonian Germany*, 3; Herwig Wolfram, *Conrad II, 990–1039: Emperor of Three Kingdoms*, trans. Denise A. Kaiser (University Park: Pennsylvania State University Press, 2006), 152–53.

Bibliography

Primary sources

Adalbert of Magdeburg. *Continuatio Reginonis.* Edited by Albert Bauer and Reinhold Rau, *Ausgewählte Quellen zur deutschen Geschichte des Mittelalters* 8. Darmstadt: Wissenschaftliche Buchgesellschaft, 2002.

Adam of Bremen. *Gesta Hammaburgensis ecclesiae pontificum.* Edited by Werner Trillmich and Rudolf Buchner. 2nd edn, *Ausgewählte Quellen zur deutschen Geschichte des Mittelalters* 11: 137–499. Darmstadt: Wissenschaftliche Buchgesellschaft, 1968.

Annales Quedlinburgenses. Edited by Martina Giese, *Monumenta Germaniae Historica Scriptores rerum Germanicarum in usum scholarum separatim editi* 72. Hanover: Hahn, 2004.

Böhmer, Johann Friedrich, E. Ottenthal, and Hans K. Kaminsky. *Regesta Imperii II, 1: (Sächsisches Haus 919–1024): Die Regesten des Kaiserreiches unter Heinrich I. und Otto I. 919–973.* Hildesheim: Böhlau, 1967.

Froumond. *Die Tegernseer Briefsammlung.* Edited by Karl Strecker, *Monumenta Germaniae Historica Epistolae selectae* 3: 1–96. Berlin: Weidmann, 1925, repr. 1964.

Gilsdorf, Sean, trans. *Queenship and Sanctity: The Lives of Mathilda and the Epitaph of Adelheid.* Washington: Catholic University of America Press, 2004.

MacLean, Simon, trans. *History and Politics in Late Carolingian and Ottonian Europe: The Chronicle of Regino of Prüm and Adalbert of Magdeburg.* Manchester: Manchester University Press, 2009.

Odilo of Cluny. *Epitaphium domine Adalheide auguste or 'Das Epitaphium'.* Edited by Herbert Paulhart, *Die Lebensbeschreibung der Kaiserin Adelheid von Abt Odilo von Cluny*, 27–45. Graz and Cologne: Böhlau, 1962.

Otto I. *Diplomata. Die Urkunden Konrad I., Heinrich I., und Otto I.* Edited by T. Sickel, *Monumenta Germaniae Historica. Diplomata regum et imperatorum Germaniae.* I. Hanover: Hahn, 1879–1884, repr. Berlin 1956.

Otto III. *Diplomata. Die Urkunden Otto des III.* Edited by T. Sickel, *Monumenta Germaniae Historica. Diplomata regum et imperatorum Germaniae.* 2.2. Hanover: Hahn, 1893, repr. Berlin, 1957.

Thietmar of Merseburg. *Chronicon.* Edited by Werner Trillmich. 8th edn, *Ausgewählte Quellen zur deutschen Geschichte des Mittelalters.* Darmstadt: Wissenschaftliche Buchgesellschaft, 2002.

Tschan, Francis J., trans. *History of the Archbishops of Hamburg-Bremen.* New York: Columbia University Press, 1959.

Vita Mathildis reginae antiquior (Die Lebensbeschreibungen der Königin Mathilde). Edited by Bernd Schütte, *Monumenta Germaniae Historica Scriptores rerum Germanicarum in usum scholarum separatim editi* 66: 107–42. Hanover: Hahn, 1994.

Vita Mathildis reginae posterior (Die Lebensbeschreibungen der Königin Mathilde). Edited by Bernd Schütte, *Monumenta Germaniae Historica Scriptores rerum Germanicarum in usum scholarum separatim editi* 66: 143–202. Hanover: Hahn, 1994.

Warner, David A., trans. *Ottonian Germany: The Chronicon of Thietmar of Merseburg*. Manchester: Manchester University Press, 2001.

Secondary sources

Althoff, Gerd. *Adels- und Königsfamilien im Spiegel ihrer Memorialüberlieferung. Studien zum Totengedenken der Billunger und Ottonen*, Münstersche Mittelalter-Schriften Bd. 47, 1984.

Althoff, Gerd. *Otto III*. Translated by Phyllis G. Jestice. Pennsylvania: Pennsylvania State University Press, 2003.

Arnold, Benjamin. *Medieval Germany, 500–1300: A Political Interpretation*. Basingstoke: Macmillan, 1997.

Bachrach, David. "Exercise of Royal Power in Early Medieval Europe: The Case of Otto the Great 936–73". *Early Medieval Europe* 17, 4 (2009): 389–419.

Bernhardt, John W. "'On the Road Again': Kings, Roads, and Accommodation in High Medieval Germany". In *Every Inch a King: Comparative Studies on Kings and Kingship in the Ancient and Medieval Worlds*, edited by Lynette Mitchell and Charles Melville, 303–24. Boston: Brill, 2012.

Bernhardt, John William. *Itinerant Kingship and Royal Monasteries in Early Medieval Germany, c.936–1075*, Cambridge Studies in Medieval Life and Thought: 4th series. Cambridge: Cambridge University Press, 1993.

Bougard, François. "Public Power and Authority". In *Italy in the Early Middle Ages: 476–1000*, edited by Cristina La Rocca, 34–58. Oxford: Oxford University Press, 2002.

Earenfight, Theresa. *Queenship in Medieval Europe*, Queenship and Power. Basingstoke: Palgrave Macmillan, 2013.

Earenfight, Theresa. "Medieval Queenship". *History Compass* 15, no. 3 (2017). doi:10.1111/hic3.12372.

Erler, Mary Carpenter, and Maryanne Kowaleski. "Introduction: A New Economy of Power Relations – Female Agency in the Middle Ages". In *Gendering the Master Narrative: Women and Power in the Middle Ages*, edited by Mary Carpenter Erler and Maryanne Kowaleski, 1–16. Ithaca: Cornell University Press, 2003.

Fleckenstein, Josef. *Early Medieval Germany*. Translated by Bernard S. Smith. Amsterdam: North-Holland Publishing Company, 1978.

Fößel, Amalie. *Die Königin im mittelalterlichen Reich. Herrschaftsausübung, Herrschaftsrechte, Handlungsspielräume*, Mittelalter-Forschungen 4. Stuttgart: Jan Thorbecke, 2000.

Fößel, Amalie. "Adelheid". In *Die Kaiserinnen des Mittelalters*, edited by Amalie Fößel, 35–59. Regensburg: Friedrich Pustet, 2011.

Fößel, Amalie. "The Political Traditions of Female Rulership in Medieval Europe". In *The Oxford Handbook of Women and Gender in Medieval Europe*, edited by Judith M. Bennett and Ruth Mazo Karras, 68–83. Oxford: Oxford University Press, 2013.

Fried, Johannes. "Theophanu und die Slawen. Bermerkungen zur Ostpolitik der Kaiserin". In *Kaiserin Theophanu: Begegnung des Ostens und Westens um die Wende des ersten Jahrtausands*, edited by Anton von Euw and Peter Schreiner, Vol. II, 361–70. Cologne: Schnütgen-Museum, 1991.

between this support and publicly expressed desires, Philip IV felt it necessary to specifically exclude Juan José from the possibility of succession and regency in his will and testament, and "as a symbol of his exclusion, [he] did not permit him to be present at his death".[11] Silvia Mitchell speculates this was done in order to protect Mariana's authority; this surely must have fuelled tensions between Mariana and Juan José. Quintero explains that in the royal court the "roles for men and women are repeatedly renegotiated, and this negotiation frequently goes hand in hand with negotiations of political power".[12] This observation may be the most poignant and accurate statement to define the years following Philip IV's death. As Mariana's role became both officially and symbolically redefined, Don Juan José saw an opportunity to redefine his own role in the political sphere. These renegotiations, or attempted renegotiations, of political roles fuelled the tensions and negotiations of political power throughout the decade.

While Juan José sought to redefine his own role in courtly politics, women such as Mariana "were able to use their importance as the mothers or future mothers of heirs to the throne to influence the court",[13] and although Mariana's transition had happened smoothly and without grave issue or cause for concern, as Carlos' fourteenth birthday drew near unease brewed in the court. Concern grew for Carlos and the tight grasp Mariana had on him.[14] The young prince had a tendency to bend to her every whim, something that greatly concerned the Regency Council, among others. This is a problem that Carlos would struggle with throughout his entire reign; despite Carlos' reputation as physically and mentally impaired, Christopher Storrs posits that throughout Carlos' life, it was not that he did not make his own decisions or have his own will; rather, well into the 1690s he "failed to impose his will".[15] Either case would have made it easy for Mariana to impose her own will, and therefore, by the early spring of 1675, "efforts to monopolise the king's attention and direct it away from his mother and her supporters began immediately".[16] Less than two weeks from his fourteenth birthday Carlos himself reached out to his half-brother, Juan José, thirty-two years his senior and with a strong political and military reputation, and requested his presence at court. Carlos wrote that he was to assume his duties on his birthday, and in order to deal with matters of state, he stated: "I need your person at my side for this function and my *farewell* to the Queen, my Lady and my mother, therefore Wednesday at 10:45 you will report to my antechamber and I will entrust you with this secret."[17] Although Juan José did present himself at court, and it was noted that Carlos seemed happy to receive him, Mariana subsequently spent two hours with Carlos in private discussion, from which Carlos left apparently crying, and Don Juan José was ordered to leave the Palace.[18] Although the note to his half-brother shows Carlos' intent to establish independence from his mother at his coming of age, these subsequent events clearly demonstrate the tight grasp Mariana had on Carlos as well as the conflict Carlos faced in being stuck between two opposing political entities and their courtly interests.

In the final years of the 1670s, the political clash between Queen Mariana and Don Juan José would continue. Mariana asked for a two-year extension of her regency, claiming that Carlos was not ready to rule at the age of fourteen. While she was likely not wrong in her claim, this would have garnered her two more years as acting head of the monarchy. Carlos refused to sign the petition to extend her regency; rather, Mariana and Carlos came to a compromise that the Regency Council would remain intact for an additional two years, but his minority would not.[19] Finally, in 1677 Mariana was exiled to Toledo and Juan José was appointed Prime Minister with Carlos' kingly support. Dying only two years later, however, Don Juan José had little chance to implement significant changes,[20] and Mariana returned to oversee her son's court once more.[21]

It was those moments leading up to Carlos' fourteenth birthday in 1675 that shaped the political sphere in which *La estatua de Prometeo* was written and staged for the court. This context is as important as the work itself, and determined how it came to be staged.

The play and its scholarly reception

The primary figures of the Prometheus–Pandora story at the centre of *La estatua de Prometeo* were not new to the Habsburg Court, as Pandora's story even occupied the ceiling of the Hall of Mirrors in the Alcázar Palace in a five-scene fresco.[22] The fresco adhered to our common understanding of mythology in the depiction of Vulcan (Hephaestus) as Pandora's creator, Prometheus rejecting her advances, and Pandora marrying Epimetheus. However, the five scenes do not depict Prometheus' theft of fire for man, his punishment, or Pandora's opening of the urn. Pandora is presented with gifts from the gods, and rather than an urn, Jupiter gives her a golden vase.[23] Margaret Greer theorises:

> The fresco's depiction of a woman as a central figure in human civilization would certainly have pleased Mariana and may have been a factor in the selection of the Prometheus–Pandora story for the celebration of her birthday with one of the first court spectacles of the interregnum.[24]

However, as Elliott and Greer both remind us, there were strong ties between the courts in Vienna and Madrid,[25] and Greer hypothesises that court celebrations in Vienna may have sparked the extensive use of the Prometheus–Pandora story in this play.[26] This theory relies on the knowledge that an opera titled *Benche vinto, vince amore. ò il Prometeo* had been staged in Vienna at the end of 1669 in celebration of Mariana's birthday, and in February of the following year nine copies of the work were sent from Emperor Leopold I in Vienna to Ambassador von Pötting at the court in Madrid.[27] Leopold requested that Mariana be given four of those copies, which perhaps provoked her to ask Calderón to write his work, *La estatua de Prometeo*.[28] This patronage is testament to the fact that "'real queens,' whether contemporary or historic, had a profound influence on the production of the *comedia* in a variety of ways".[29] I support Greer's hypothesis that Mariana may have asked Calderón to write the play after the manuscripts from Vienna arrived, but, not surprisingly, Calderón does deviate from classic mythology. This is in fact one of the first observations scholars make, and Anne Pasero in her article "Male vs. Female: Binary Opposition and Structural Synthesis in Calderón's *Estatua de Prometeo*" explains that Calderón seems to rely on the previous works of Boccaccio and Pérez de Moya, but still deviates even from their works.[30]

In Calderón's play, Prometheus creates a statue in the image of Minerva for which he receives praise from the goddess herself, particularly on the reflection of Minerva's beauty in his work. This provokes jealousy in their twin counterparts, Epimetheus and Pallas. The characters Minerva and Pallas are twins, and are presented as two characters, despite more commonly held knowledge that Minerva and Pallas are two names for the same goddess. Calderón, however, does write Minerva and Pallas as counterparts in which knowledge and reason are represented by Minerva, while war is represented by Pallas. Prometheus' statue comes to life as Pandora using a ray of light Prometheus stole from Apollo, and a question of ethics comes into play at the end of the work as a debate surfaces in regard to Prometheus' potential punishment for stealing from the gods. One of the most important artistic choices Calderón makes in the creation of this play is his rewriting of Pandora as female, contrary to Boccaccio and Moya, who both wrote Pandora as male.[31] I link Pandora to the representation of Spain, and therefore Calderón's writing of Pandora as female links her to Spain through its physical land, or the grammatically feminine *tierra*.[32] It also returns to the more classical tradition of Pandora as female. Pasero suggests this may be one of the most notable changes.[33] However, it is not the most frequently analysed; rather it is usually the function of duality in this work.

Wasting no time, Calderón immediately presents the audience with a duality: twin counterparts for both the protagonists and antagonists. Within the first sixty lines, the audience learns that Prometheus has a twin brother, Epimetheus, and the audience will come to find out that, despite their apparent differences, power unites the brothers.[34] As the play unfolds, the spectator finds that most elements and characters in this play have a counterpart. Minerva and Pallas are also twins and the *gracioso*, or fool, Merlin has Libia, a villain. Minerva serves as inspiration for Prometheus' statue as well as his "compass" for knowledge and reason, while Pallas influences Epimetheus. These dualities have proved to be the fundamental question of this play for theatre historians of the last several decades. As Greer points out, academics tend to differ not on the presence of the duality, but on the identification of the central axis of tension.[35] The dualities that have dominated the studies of *La estatua de Prometeo* have included male and female binaries (Pasero), emotion versus intellect (Greer, W. G. Chapman), and the role of reason (Blue, O'Connor).

Greer subscribes to a mind–body principle that places emotion in opposition to intellect—mind is intellect and body is emotion. It is important to bear in mind that the material in these works does not present "'layers of meaning' arranged hierarchically from the superficial to the profound, but simultaneously present in an interrelationship of productive tension".[36] In his article "Desire and the Supplement in *La estatua de Prometeo*", William Blue agrees on this pluralistic approach, explaining: "We have in the men and gods in this play not good facing bad, not gods facing men, but rather a complication of all oppositions in one".[37] In contrast, Pasero focuses more on the stricter dualities, describing them as "pairs of categories" that "respond to a basic underlying polarization".[38] My approach favours this, but makes it a more political duality or polarisation: traditional rule versus progressive change, as well as acknowledging the multiple layers of meaning. All of these authors have had their sets of obstacles to overcome. Mine here is that in discussing the representation of political tensions at the time in which the play was written, it is imperative not to adhere solely to strict one-to-one character association with real-life figures of the court, but rather to explore them alongside the variety of ties that reveal themselves.

Considering the dualities of the characters does serve on a micro level to bring to light the tension, specifically between Mariana and Don Juan José. Here we can link Juan José to Prometheus, the progressive thinker who has produced his own creation, Pandora, or Spain as Don Juan José envisions his plans for it. This casts Mariana in the role of Epimetheus as he threatens to destroy Prometheus and Pandora, in an effort to restore the status quo. Mariana, on more than one occasion, had set out to eradicate Juan José and his progressive push for political change in an attempt to maintain a secure foothold in the political sphere. Although representative of the undoubted swirling tension between these two political figures, recalling warnings against strict one-to-one comparisons, this analysis falls short when Epimetheus covets Pandora. While Mariana certainly wanted to keep Spain in the hands of the pure and legitimate Habsburgs, the Spain Mariana longed for was a more traditional model of the Spanish monarchy. She did not covet the Spain Don Juan José imagined with new ideas such as a move toward a unified Spanish currency.[39]

Therefore it is possible to cast Don Juan José as both creator and coveter. As Prometheus creates Pandora and brings her to life, and Epimetheus covets the creation, Prometheus covets the higher perfection that is Minerva, as Juan José coveted a Spain that could and would never be entirely his.[40] Aligning Juan José with this duality also supports the mind–body axis of interpretation set forth by Greer in her reading of the practical text. Epimetheus and Prometheus serve as complements that represent an internal versus external struggle of man with and against himself; this is further apparent in the meaning of their names: forethought (Prometheus) and afterthought (Epimetheus). While Greer posits that it was most likely that seventeenth-century audiences would relate Juan José with Prometheus,[41] she also acknowledges that Don Juan José can be seen as "a compound of Prometeo and Epimeteo".[42] I agree with Greer in her second statement; this work was written for a courtly audience, an audience that would have known Don Juan José both as a man with a strong military background and as a thoughtful intellectual and political leader. Juan José embodied both the physicality represented by war and the cerebral nature of court politics. He was not just, as some still saw him, an illegitimate noble whose coup in Madrid in 1669 threatened civil war for Spain. He was a careful politician who most memorably managed to bring a twelve-year rebellion

It is perhaps this plot to steal the statue that prompts Blue to read this action as done out of love. Blue states: "So great is [Epimeteo's] love for the statue Prometeo sculpted, for instance, that he defies Pallas' direct order to destroy it".[57] My interpretation, however, is that Epimetheus does so out of jealousy of the praise Prometheus receives on the creation of his statue. O'Connor confirms that jealousy is fundamental in Calderón's work: "This mythological play underlines the role of hatred, jealousy and vengeance in the destruction of what harmony and peace we humans are capable of."[58] This is further proven by the fact that Epimetheus falls for Pandora—the physical manifestation of the statue created in Minerva's image; it is not simply love for the statue, and we have become further removed from a character coveting Minerva herself. Epimetheus' desire for the statue is not adoration, or simply love of its artistic nature. Rather, Epimetheus is jealous of the attention Prometheus receives and covets Pandora as Prometheus idolises Minerva.

Although Minerva and Pallas take opposing sides in this political model, Apollo has had no physical presence in the first two acts of this play. Minerva and Pallas are sisters of Apollo as much in this production as in mythology, and so, as such, nearing the end of this play Pallas seeks Apollo's support to punish Prometheus for the ray he has stolen. The two sisters each argue their case to Apollo, with Minerva acting in Prometheus' defence. Pallas' conservative wisdom argues that Prometheus has committed a moral error in stealing, while Minerva's progressive intelligence proposes that stealing for the good of the community is not a moral error, and posits the question: is a crime committed for the good of the community acceptable, and can the individual who does so still be considered just from a moral standpoint? Her argument can be viewed as an effort to protect herself, as it was Minerva who took Prometheus to the heavens for him to pick anything he liked as a thank-you gift for his statue. Minerva effectively usurps "Apolo's right to give fire to man"[59] as Mariana attempted to take over Carlos' right to rule when she sought an extension of her regency. Seeing both arguments as just, Apollo cannot decide between his two sisters, and demonstrates his indecisiveness when he states: "As I cannot intervene, continue your duel; as I am and am not, neither complicit nor in charge, I'll only say that they are and are not at a resolution".[60] He leaves them to resolve the issue themselves in the mortal world. He only returns later in the play to banish Discordia in order to express Jupiter's pardon of Prometheus. Apollo's actions reinforce the idea that both a ruler's concern for his populace (Minerva's argument) and a proper moral code (Pallas' argument) are admirable attributes, as he cannot decide between the two, and that Discordia will always threaten any political situation. In addition, while Apollo as the sun god evokes the imagery associated with Philip IV,[61] his indecisiveness is representative of Carlos II. Apollo's role in this play is arguably as small as Carlos II's role in the high-level political activity of the court at the time, and his indecisiveness reflects an inexperienced king not ready to rule, and heavily influenced by those around him. The myth of Apollo both affirms and rejects the kinship bond,[62] an experience witnessed in Carlos' struggle with his relationship with his mother. Just as Apollo "vacillates between the conflicting natures of Minerva and Pallas",[63] Carlos was pulled in two different directions, having to choose between his family members and unable to do so. Carlos both officially supports Don Juan José, and continues communications with his mother. Even during her period of exile in Toledo, Carlos gave written formal consent for Juan José to govern as Prime Minister while exchanging letters back and forth with Mariana, particularly concerning the issue of his marriage, an issue that I contend only Mariana could resolve tactfully.[64]

La estatua de Prometeo's open ending

Despite a seemingly tidy resolution to the play, *La estatua de Prometeo* ends on a note more akin to the notions of an ending *in medias res.*[65] The ending is not as neat or joyful as W. G. Chapman claims in his work "Las comedias mitológicas de Calderón", and O'Connor argues for a need to shift the scope of Chapman's summary of *La estatua* which posits that the play concludes with the restoration of order and reestablishment of harmony.[66] On the one hand, the happy ending is obvious and easy; it can be enticing to label it neatly as such. Merlin (the fool) and Libia (the villain) marry, as do Prometheus and Pandora, Apollo expresses Jupiter's pardon, and Epimetheus thanks Apollo for restoring peace. That is to say, it does check the stereotypical *comedia* resolution boxes: weddings, a godly—seemingly *deus ex machina*—imparting of peace, thanks, and the departure of the most toxic antagonists (Pallas and Discordia). Yet, there is still more work to be done: the supposedly "joyous" ending feels exceedingly artificial and leaves us questioning more than it actually resolves; for example, the imparting of peace and the purpose of marriage.[67] Greer doubts that the final resolution is truly representative of the a true *deus ex machina* ending due to the fact that when Apollo finally expresses authority, it is not his own but rather displays "his conception of an invisible supreme being"—the absent Jupiter.[68] Additionally, the audience is left feeling uneasy as the moments of resolution and happiness are tainted by the lingering threat of marital tension. Blue cites Merlin's proposal to Libia as an example of this tension. Merlin tells Libia he lives in the shadow of her loathing, and she returns the sentiment. They agree to marry due to this commonality of loathing, as opposed to love. Perhaps these lines are said in jest, but Blue notes that marriage, although capable of producing "conjugal happiness, [. . .] may also produce conjugal war".[69] This leaves the audience with a bitter feeling as it sours the traditional Baroque happy ending.

The problem we then face is: if this was an intentional political commentary on Calderón's part, we are not presented with a clear solution. We see Calderón questioning the ability of man to conduct himself without an overshadowing network of biases; the "reflection of the true rule of reason is significant for it reveals Calderón's pessimistic and realistic views concerning the ability we possess to conduct our affairs strictly according to reason's dictates".[70] That being said, while Calderón questions our abilities to conduct ourselves while adhering strictly to reason—a reference to courtly doubts of the capabilities of Carlos II and concern for the shadow his mother cast over him—that does not mean there cannot be peace in human relationships. O'Connor elucidates: "*La estatua de Prometeo* manifests reason's limits and acknowledges the need for some form of outside intervention in order to establish peace and harmony in human relationships."[71] Don Juan José certainly would be "outside intervention" as he was not a member of the inner circle of the royal family—in a literal sense, he introduces "new blood" from his non-royal mother—and therefore not a member of the court in Madrid, or its state of daily affairs in the early and mid-1670s. Or, is leaving Mariana in charge, in the hopes that Carlos himself will someday take his own power and not allow himself to be consumed by other courtly influences and biases the peace the court needed in the face of the threat of Don Juan and his prior coup? Carlos was after all the rightful heir to the Spanish Crown, although somewhat peripheral to the tensions between Juan José and Mariana. Calderón leaves us with the notion that he is nominally supporting Mariana, while simultaneously suggesting that something new is required: tradition must be supplanted by progressive intellect. This force will have to be Carlos II (Apollo) no matter how indecisive, and the ambiguity presented by Calderón functions so as not to risk his privileged position within the court. We know Calderón was rather politically conservative,[72] but obscuring his personal opinion one way or the other keeps this work from jeopardising his professional work and career, presents a play open to multiple readings, and reinforces the notion of duality.

La estatua de Prometeo was a play before its time. Pasero notes the play's tripartite structure of creation, destruction, and redemption,[73] which mirrors the status of Mariana and court politics from 1665–79. She would experience her elevation as Queen Regent in 1665. She then suffered two blows to her power; these were Don Juan José's seizures of power that would lead to her "destruction", as she was sent into exile from the court. Her redemption was her return to court in 1679. Regarding the action of the play, O'Connor comments: "Once jealousy ceases, so does the desire for vengeance: harmony is restored within man."[74] Although I would not stretch the comparison to say harmony was entirely restored once Don Juan José died, we can certainly see a reduction of the internal strife of the court. Mariana's greatest opposition had been eliminated through his death—the only way to restore harmony in this instance, as there was no hope of any sort of reconciliation between Juan José and Mariana as there is for Prometheus and Epimetheus. Perhaps, though, we can learn from the twin brothers' reconciliation. Harmony for Spain must come by striking a balance between passion and intellect or forethought and afterthought, as harmony for Pandora comes from the reconciliation of Prometheus and Epimetheus. This balance will have to be guided by royal authority however vague or indecisive, as Apollo roughly guides Minerva and Pallas. (Despite his indecisiveness, they both recognise the godly authority in Apollo as their brother, and he is the god that expresses Jupiter's pardon.) Although serious doubts about Carlos II lingered, these parallels then can be read as reinforcing royal legitimacy as Carlos II serves as the royal authority that must mitigate the tension between Don Juan José and Mariana of Austria.

Almost all of the scholars mentioned here highlight the fact that the characters in this play are more alike than they are different, particularly under the presentation of dualities. Although there are differences, and these are certainly representative of the divide between two political factions, we can also say that Don Juan José and Mariana are more alike than even they would have liked to admit. Don Juan José, although arguably more progressive, and who did have ideas for change, also adhered closely to Philip IV's memory at times,[75] and the tradition that surrounded his father's monarchy. Additionally, Mariana would not be completely averse to change. The 1680s saw gross tax reform—something that was badly needed—done under the supervision of Mariana.[76]

My analysis has shown that Calderón's work, although mythological in theme, as many of his other plays are, is also largely political. Through the careful tact of what Bances Candamo in the 1690s would name *el decir sin decir* ("to say without telling"),[77] Calderón weaves masterfully the concerns and tensions for the politics in Mariana's court into the strife and conflicts between his fictional creations. Calderón knew the court and its members well. He supported Mariana, Carlos, and the Crown officially, yet he provides us with the tools to analyse both sides of this political rivalry without overtly taking a side himself. Perhaps this was Calderón's most fundamentally important use of literary decorum: the characters that represent the real-life figures are not necessarily those we would most obviously and readily associate with those situations, and these correlations are not always so simple and clear. Designing his characters to divide between support of the traditional norms (hindsight) or that of progressive ideas (forethought), Calderón creates a timeless and universal work that posits two opposing political notions and leaves us to question their, and by consequence our, political future, making this work even more relevant than previously argued.

Questions about legitimacy would only grow as the Habsburg monarchy in Spain crawled toward its end, and court drama serves as a way in which we can continue to approach the political concerns of the era. Other Calderónian works of the 1670s, such as *Fieras afemina amor*, continued to highlight tensions between the regency court and Don Juan José. By the 1690s, despite efforts to father children with two separate wives, Carlos II did not produce the heir for which the court and royal family had hoped. As it had in the 1670s, politics and legitimacy would influence royal court productions, most notably in the works comprising the political trilogy of court dramaturge Francisco Bances Candamo: *La piedra filosofal*, *El esclavo en grillos de oro*, and *Cómo se curan los celos y Orlando Furioso*. While this chapter has been limited to the tensions within the court in Madrid in the early 1670s and Calderón's *La estatua de Prometeo*, it presents the beginning of an intensifying argument and concern for the future of the court in Madrid. In the final decade of the century the concern about the presence and status of figures like Don Juan José, and the legitimacy of the Regent, would evolve and expand into a European debate over the legitimate claim to the Spanish Crown itself.

Notes

1 Credit must be given at the start to Margaret Greer for her reading of the political text. Her work inspired my own reading of the text that supports the duality of traditional rule versus progressive change. Margaret Greer, "An Optimistic Answer: *La estatua de*

Lynch, John D. *Spain Under the Habsburgs: Vol. 2, Spain and America 1598–1700*. 2nd edn. New York and London: New York University Press, 1981.
McKendrick, Melveena. *Playing the King: Lope de Vega and the Limits of Conformity*. London: Tamesis Books, 2000.
Mitchell, Silvia Z. "Habsburg Motherhood: The Power of Mariana of Austria, Mother and Regent for Carlos II of Spain". In *Early Modern Habsburg Women: Transnational Contexts, Cultural Conflicts, Dynastic Continuities*, edited by Anne J. Cruz and Maria G. Stampino, 175–96. Burlington: Ashgate, 2013.
O'Connor, Thomas A. "Calderón and Reason's Impasse: The Case of *La estatua de Prometeo*". *La Chispa 81 Selected Proceedings* (1981): 229–37.
Pasero, Anne. "Male vs. Female: Binary Opposition and Structural Synthesis in Calderón's *Estatua de Prometeo*". *Bulletin of the Comediantes* 32, 2 (1980): 109–15.
Pfandl, Ludwig. *Carlos II*. Translated by Manuel F. Galiano. Madrid: Afrodisio Aguado, 1947.
Quintero, María Cristina. *Gendering the Crown in the Spanish Baroque Comedia*. London: Routledge, 2012.
Rabb, Theodore K. "Artists and Warfare: A Study of Changing Values in Seventeenth-Century Europe". *Transactions of the American Philosophical Society* 75, 6 (1985): 79–106.
Ruiz Rodríguez, Ignacio. *Juan José de Austria: Un bastardo regio en el gobierno de un imperio*. Madrid: Dykinson, 2005.
Shergold, N. D., and J. E. Varey. Introduction to *Representaciones Palaciegas: 1603–1699: Estudio y Documentos*, by N. D. Shergold and J. E. Varey, 13–39. London: Boydell & Brewer, 1982.
Slater, Philip E. *The Glory of Hera: Greek Mythology and the Greek Family*. Boston: Beacon Press, 1971.
Storrs, Christopher. *The Resilience of the Spanish Monarchy 1665–1700*. New York: Oxford: Oxford University Press, 2006.
Stradling, R. A. *Europe and the Decline of Spain: A Study of the Spanish System, 1580–1720*. London: George Allen and Unwin, 1981.
Stroud, Matthew D. "Pedro Calderón de la Barca". In *Spanish Dramatists of the Golden Age*, edited by Mary Parker, 39–50. Westport, Conn.: Greenwood Press, 1998.
Wilson, Edmund. "The Historical Interpretation of Literature". In *The Norton Anthology of Theory and Criticism*, edited by Vincent B. Leitch, 1127–40. New York: Norton, 2010.
Yun Casalilla, Bartolomé. "The Castillian Aristocracy in the Seventeenth Century: Crisis, Refeudalisation, or Political Offensive?" In *The Castilian Crisis of the Seventeenth Century: New Perspectives on the Economic and Social History of Seventeenth-Century Spain*, edited by I. A. A. Thompson and Bartolomé Yun Casallilla, 277–300. Cambridge: Cambridge University Press, 1994.
Yun Casalilla, Bartolomé. "Spain and the Seventeenth-Century Crisis in Europe: Some Final Considerations". In *The Castilian Crisis of the Seventeenth Century: New Perspectives on the Economic and Social History of Seventeenth Century Spain*, edited by I. A. A. Thompson and Bartolomé Yun Casallilla, 301–21. Cambridge: Cambridge University Press, 1994.

14

CATHERINE THE GREAT

How the question of legitimacy influenced her politics

Elena Teibenbacher

This chapter explores the importance of legitimacy in the life and politics of Empress Catherine II of Russia (1729–96). Born as Princess Sophia Augusta Fredericka of Anhalt-Zerbst, she married the future Tsar Peter III of Russia in 1745. Having overthrown her husband in 1762 without any dynastic claim to the throne herself, she needed to prove her legitimacy through other means. Catherine considered herself an enlightened monarch with the authority to exert absolute power for the benefit of the nation. Aware of her shaky claim in a country where rulers with much stronger ties to the throne had been deposed, she was careful not to lose necessary support from the most influential groups in her realm. Indeed, one major justification for her *coup d'état* had been to keep Russian traditions and culture alive. During the course of her reign she abandoned reforms under the pressure of domestic politics and under the influence of upheavals against authority in Russia and elsewhere. She governed in an autocratic manner, considering that her legitimacy was based on her ability, and hers alone, as the one most capable to rule.

Catherine II is one of the most controversial figures in political history, even within her lifetime. At the beginning of her reign, high hopes were invested in her by diplomats, statesmen, and philosophers all over Europe. Even the fact that she had usurped the throne from her husband Peter III seemed to be justified or at least tolerated. Catherine had gained the image of a charismatic and intellectual personality with great talent for diplomacy. However, historiography presents a very ambivalent picture that often oscillates between honest admiration and blistering criticism. Scholarly research has to span a bridge between the portrait of a clever actress who cared most about her public reputation and external political success, and the philosopher on the throne who clashed with political reality. According to her own testimony, Catherine had to abandon many of her enlightened ideas but always tried to implement as much reform as she could. Baljazin writes that since her arrival in Russia in 1744, Catherine had learned enough about the country, its history, and its people, that she was under no illusions about whom she was dealing with.[1] A more severe critic states that:

> Catherine sacrificed her first identity as a Protestant German princess to the role of the Russian empress, her morality as a wife to the complicity with her husband's murderers, [and] her enlightened intellect that had made her dream of great reforms at the beginning of her rule to the interests of the nobility [. . .] She was a perpetrator driven by ambition and a victim of the functionalities that constrained her and that she forced upon others.[2]

Yet in 1767, the same Catherine II issued a decree abolishing torture as a means of interrogation in all the courts of her realm, stating that a person in such physical pain was not master of himself and incapable of telling the truth.[3] A year later, the Empress and her son Paul were vaccinated against smallpox by the English physician Thomas Dimsdale (1712–1800), setting an example for medical reform. In doing so, Catherine defied the warnings of many, including Frederick II of Prussia.[4] Within ten years of the start of her reign, the number of pupils in Russian schools rose from 4,400 to 17,000.[5] She founded the first medical college in Russia and the first school of higher education for girls, the Smol'niy Institute.[6] These advances were made by Catherine alone, who justified her adherence to autocracy by stressing her own capability as a ruler. Her legitimacy was thus based on ability, not hereditary descent, which *is*, in its way, perfectly in line with the ideals of the Enlightenment. Yet, unlike Emperor Joseph II, Catherine did not abolish serfdom, though it would have been regarded by many as a great example of enlightened rule.

In Catherine's time, autocracy did not contradict a ruler's understanding of what we call today "Enlightened Absolutism". Frederick of Prussia, Maria Theresa, and Joseph II never considered abandoning their autocratic style of governance. This chapter will interpret some of Catherine's political decisions within this context, considering the Empress' political (self)conception as an enlightened monarch to support and defend the legitimacy of her rule. This chapter will equally argue that autocracy was at the same time a means to strengthen Catherine's position and to emphasise that her legitimacy was not to be questioned.

Creating legitimacy

In 1722, Peter I (r. 1682–1725) issued a law on imperial succession, permitting the ruling monarch to choose a worthy candidate who would not weaken what had been passed on, thus abandoning strict dynastic legitimacy as a precondition to inherit the throne. In so doing, Peter I strengthened the monarch's autocracy but also encouraged him (or her) to choose a successor for the benefit of the state rather than feeling bound by tradition. One could argue even further that Peter I had changed the image of the tsar by creating a new rule of legitimisation. The dynastic heir could be replaced by someone with greater ability to govern the state.[7] Peter had made his wife Catherine co-ruler in 1724 but did not formally name a successor before his death. He was survived by several Romanov family members, including descendants of his half-brother and co-tsar Ivan V (1666–96). The strongest claim was held by his infant grandson, the future Peter II (who would die childless in 1730, thus ending the direct male line of the Romanov dynasty). Catherine had strong supporters at court and promised to name Peter II her heir. Yet, this lowborn widow of Peter the Great proclaimed herself the first empress of Russia, her ascent facilitated by the new and unclear law of succession. Altogether, in one century, the female rule of four empresses, Catherine I (1725–27), Anna Ivanovna (1730–40), Elizabeth Petrovna (1741–62), and Catherine II, spanned more than sixty-seven years. None of them had an uncontested claim to the throne, nor had they been proclaimed as successors by their forerunners. Anna Ivanovna, daughter of Ivan V, had spent twenty years as regent to the duchy of Courland before ascending the throne in 1730. She named Ivan VI (1740–64), son of her niece Anna Leopoldovna (1718–46), as her successor. Anna Leopoldovna was the daughter of Duke Karl Leopold of Mecklenburg-Schwerin, and had married another German prince, Anthony Ulrich of Brunswick-Wolfenbüttel. But the reign of the infant Ivan was short, and the throne was taken in 1741 by his cousin, Elizabeth Petrovna. Elizabeth was a usurper, but as a daughter of Peter I and Catherine I she had her own claim to the throne.

Therefore, the case of Catherine II still constitutes a novelty. Unlike Anna or Elizabeth, she ascended the throne without any legitimate dynastic claim, having no Romanov blood and no direct kinship to any family member who had ever occupied the Russian throne. Her only connection in 1762 was being the estranged wife of Peter III. Therefore, it was paramount for Catherine II to prove that she herself had become a true Russian princess. Raised a Protestant but converted before her marriage, this display included a strong and public devotion to the Orthodox faith. Through her behaviour, Catherine emphasised that she was more Russian than Anna Ivanovna, Anna Leopoldovna, or even her own husband.

As son of Duke Charles Frederick of Schleswig-Holstein-Gottorp and Anna Petrovna (another daughter of Peter I), Peter III was half German. His aunt, Empress Elizabeth Petrovna, had no legitimate issue and named him her successor in 1742. At age fourteen, Peter was expected to fill big shoes. He was presented as heir to his grandfather's throne and as successor in his achievements. In fact, through his dynastic relations he also had a claim to the Swedish throne, and in her memoirs Catherine did not miss pointing out that, "The prince was educated for the throne of Sweden."[8] Furthermore, Peter III made no secret of his desire to reform Russia in the manner of his great idol Frederick II of Prussia. His desire to radically overturn old structures must have threatened the ruling classes, the military, and the influential Orthodox Church. Yet, it is still disputed whether he had really lost as much support as Catherine would later argue. Nolte, for example, accentuates the militarist attitude of Peter III as well as his preference for the Protestant religion and Holstein courtiers, but also admits that Peter's decisions in internal and foreign politics were well reflected and far reaching.[9] Peter's ideas to reform the Church and to abolish serfdom were quite in the spirit of Enlightened Absolutism, but Catherine proved to be more diplomatic in her endeavours. She promised reforms based on the teachings of the Enlightenment but also swore to uphold Russian culture and tradition as part of her efforts to legitimise her assumption of the throne. Moreover, Catherine II followed the tradition of previous usurpers, destroying the image of her overthrown predecessor, which has influenced the historiography of Peter III until today. Both Elizabeth Petrovna and Catherine II followed an inclination to adopt Western traditions and politics often generalised as "German", and to surround themselves with foreign favourites who supported their propaganda to legitimise their usurpations.

Legitimacy through ability and heritage

Reform policies historians label as "Enlightened Absolutism" were marked by a top-to-bottom approach. In a typical example, Emperor Joseph II is often quoted with his alleged motto, "everything for the people but nothing by the people". In Russia, Peter I had distanced himself from the Church but had not fully broken with the powerful and convenient tradition of a monarch "Dei gratia". In order to create the image of a secular and modernist reformer but at the same time enjoy the advantages of autocratic rule, he focused on the doctrine of divine duty rather than that of divine right.[10] However, the role of the Russian tsar was always of a strongly sacred nature, making it impossible to completely separate these two doctrines. If the rightful monarch distinguished himself through righteous rule, he would establish the most heaven-like realm possible on earth.[11] In the absence of a dynastic claim, Catherine II needed to create a different path of legitimacy and to defend her usurpation from a religious point of view as well. Her rule would be justified by her politics but also by her piousness, her benevolence, and her protection of the Orthodox flock. "When Catherine II [. . .] ascended the throne after a coup d'état, her claim to power was shaky and she worked to buttress it by projecting the image of a reforming tsar."[12] In the age of Enlightened Absolutism, she did so by emphasising her ability to rule for the benefit of the country. "One of the first tasks Catherine assigned to herself was to illuminate (*prosveshchat'*) the nation."[13]

In her memoirs, Catherine described herself as studious, intellectual, charming, and humble, always ready to please others and to learn from her betters. At the same time, she appears as an astute observer and severe critic of the society and circumstances around her. She conveys the image of an interested conversationalist, eagerly participating in the political and philosophical discussions of her time. She often compares her husband's character, disposition, and behaviour with her own, thus justifying her future actions against him. At several points, she mentions her desire to learn everything about the country, its people, and their culture.[14] Being Russian and proving it became one of the most important issues in Catherine's propaganda programme.

The introduction to Catherine's memoirs is decidedly revealing. It says that fortune is not as blind as one might think, that it depends largely on a person's qualities and behavioural traits, and that Catherine herself and Peter III were two remarkable examples of this idea.[15] Her husband is shown as an emotionally unstable and unpredictable personality, unfit to rule. Catherine described her conversations and meetings with Peter as insipid. "When he was gone, the most tiresome book appeared a delightful amusement."[16]

Frederick II had warned Peter not to feel too secure on the throne and had advised him to perform a public coronation that would strengthen his position by a spectacle of political and symbolical significance.[17] The Prussian king allegedly said later that "he [Peter III] let himself be overthrown like a child sent to bed".[18] Extraordinarily, the circumstances of Peter's removal from power and his subsequent death seem to have disappeared from public interest rather quickly.[19] Yet, the voices accusing Catherine of illegitimacy and of her husband's murder were never silenced for good, requiring the Empress to constantly employ propaganda. Catherine did not want to hold power by force alone but desired to establish herself as legitimate empress in her own right. Therefore, she needed everyone—her people and foreign observers alike—to understand why she had been the better choice. Pamphlets and manifestos were issued to justify her actions and to denigrate Peter III's image. In a manifesto from October 1762, Catherine expressed self-awareness and underlined her divine calling:

> We can say, without any praise of Ourself, in front of God and the entire world that We have received the Russian throne from the hands of God, not to our own pleasure but to enhance Russia's glory, to introduce order and to strengthen justice in our dear fatherland. [. . .] Everyday, We care about the common good and have just one thing in mind: the happiness, the content and the organized state of our subjects; to see the inner peace and welfare of the realm is Our recompense. Such, We aim to glorify God, such, We aspire to eternal merit.[20]

A pamphlet from 28 June 1762 stated that Peter III would have destroyed the Orthodox Church and that Catherine had protected Russia from a "foreign" religious system, a topic she deliberately exaggerated and exploited.[21] It argued that her husband would have endangered domestic order and thrown Russia into political and military turmoil through his foreign endeavours. He would have damaged the state's finances and threatened Russia's independence, strength, and glory. Catherine concluded by stating that she had taken the throne following the explicit wish of her faithful subjects who had already sworn allegiance to her.[22] The accusations against Peter III, true or not, together with the evidence of "sworn allegiance" provided Catherine the desired proof of her legitimacy. Johann Moritz Prasse, Saxon envoy to Russia, reported that the *coup d'état* was received in St Petersburg with great joy and that it did not surprise him given the dissatisfaction that had prevailed among all ranks. In his eyes, Catherine had acted heroically like a truly great spirit.[23]

Another manifesto, from 7 July 1762, underlined how ungrateful Peter III had been towards Empress Elizabeth Petrovna and how he had refused to pay his

themselves successors to the apostles they should be proud to be as poor as their predecessors had been.[51] The Empress continued in the style of Peter I by influencing the allocation of ecclesiastical positions and by consolidating the necessary steps of education for higher clerical ranks.[52] Catherine also supported the freedom of faith inside her realm, establishing religious communities for all major confessions, but she did not intend to turn Russia into a secular country. Unlike Emperor Joseph II, she was cautious about displeasing her citizens and was very sensitive regarding their devotion to the Church. She commented that in religious matters, her people's feelings were easily bruised, and she wanted to avoid anything that could offend this national idiosyncrasy that still dominated the masses.[53] Catherine also knew how to use the Church to her advantage. During the Pugachev Rebellion, she appealed to the archbishop of Kazan, urging him to make people understand that joining the rebellion would be a breach of their oath to their monarch and that the Church would condemn such criminals to eternal perdition.[54] As such, supporting Pugachev became a crime subject not only to worldly but to divine punishment.

Legitimacy justifies autocracy

"I might be good, usually soft, but by status I am obliged to want whatever I want terribly. [. . .] In for a penny, in for a pound."[55] These lines written by Catherine II to German philosopher Melchior Grimm (1723–1807) reveal a self-assured and decisive person who does not consider failure an option. Catherine lived according to the theory that a progressive ruler needed as much authority as possible to ensure that the good he or she intended was most effectively implemented. This did not comply with the principles of constitutionalism and limited monarchic power. "The idea of a 'suppression of absolute power' that Catherine had considered in her early years had eventually turned into the opposite."[56] Catherine was more inclined towards the idea that "it is better to be subject to the Laws under one Master, than to be subservient to many".[57] After all, Frederick II had said about France that it lacked systematic organisation; that every minister created his own system and that each of them overturned the setup of his predecessor.[58] At the same time, Catherine did not want to sacrifice her public image inside and outside Russia or threaten her legitimacy by pushing for reforms that would have provoked too much indignation, unsure of the desired outcome. The abolition of serfdom might have fallen into that category. Yet, it does not explain why Catherine left several projects unfinished or let them slide after an ambitious beginning. In a letter to Frederick II, she argued: "I beg that you remember that I have often accommodated myself to the present, without closing the path to a more favourable future."[59]

Shortly after her ascent to the throne, Catherine started to write a series of instructions that should become the foundation for a new universal set of laws. Her foreign minister, and tutor to Grand Duke Paul, Nikita Panin (1718–83), drafted a manifesto that envisioned the creation of an imperial council. He reminded Catherine "that she could not be an empress like any other; that she had to justify the choice of the Russian people by giving the nation more benefit than any other could have done".[60] Catherine did not establish such a council but she set up the Legislative Commission, although it was never turned into a permanent institution. A manifesto from December 1766 requested representatives of all classes and municipalities to elect deputies for a grand commission assigned to work out the details of a new universal code of law. A total of 564 members were appointed, with representatives of the bourgeoisie and free farmers being in the majority.[61] The introduction read that an empire of such vast dimensions needed an autocratic sovereign to act with sufficient vigour. Any other form of government than that of a monarch with absolute power would be the ruin of Russia;[62] efficiency in decision-making would have to make up for the loss of time caused by the vast geographic distances.[63] On the one hand, establishing the commission fit Catherine's portrayal as an enlightened monarch. On the other, the Empress illustrated her perception of absolute monarchic rule, one that did not entail the surrender of any significant political power, especially not to the different factions of nobility competing for influence.[64]

Sixteen expert committees met in session until the outbreak of the Russo-Turkish War of 1768–74.[65] The last session of the full assembly took place in January 1769, but certain subcommittees met until 1771.[66] Opinions differ on why Catherine lost her interest in the commission so quickly and why, in 1774, she began to work personally on a new set of civil laws. Some critics say that Catherine established the commission mainly to gain recognition and not to introduce legal reform. Once the first goal was achieved, Catherine had little need for the rest.[67] Some believe that Catherine lost interest in the work of the commission because the latter did not comply enough with her own instructions. Yet, she let many conclusions guide her during the work on her book of civil rights.[68] More optimistic voices may say that Catherine was disappointed in the slow process of the commission's work, considering it not the motor it should have been but rather a stumbling block to reform. She told Voltaire that it was easy to find common rules but difficult to agree on the details and that she felt as if she had to create, unite, and preserve an entire new world.[69] Denis Diderot (1713–84) visited Russia between October 1773 and March 1774 to advise the Empress on her reform policy.[70] He was generally opposed to the concept of autocratic rule even if the monarch possessed all necessary qualities of an enlightened sovereign.[71] He stated that Catherine had before her "a space free of all obstacles upon which to build according to her desires".[72] Like Panin, Diderot argued that the commission should be turned into a permanent institution, but his advice was equally overlooked. In his *Histoire des deux Indes*, the disappointed philosopher stated that Catherine was a "real autocrat" and "the Russians a nation that was rotten before it was ripe".[73] Catherine's decisions not to establish constitutional and controlling elements and to uphold serfdom made her legitimacy as enlightened monarch questioned in the eyes of some of her strongest supporters.

Nonetheless, the international feedback on the instructions was overwhelming. The text was translated into all major European languages and met with great success. Voltaire labelled it the "finest monument of the age" and mocked the French censors for banning the work, considering it a compliment that would guarantee its popularity. Frederick II of Prussia called it "a performance, worthy of a great man".[74]

For Catherine, legitimacy turned out to be a double-edged sword. On the one hand, she defended her legitimacy through capability, which included reforms according to enlightened thinking. On the other hand, the Empress did not want to weaken her authority by alienating influential groups and turning them into a threat. They should be satisfied without being actively involved in political decision-making. For example, she declared herself a "republican soul" who nevertheless transferred two million people into serfdom to please her courtiers. She "trumpeted her commitment to the liberal ideals of the Enlightenment while she reigned over the cruellest autocracy in history".[75] In her defence, Catherine stated once again how difficult it was to change a deeply rooted system. She argued eloquently that she did not even dare to introduce the Julian Calendar because people were whispering to each other that she was an atheist who questioned the infallibility of the Council of Nicaea.[76] The idea might have pleased Catherine to enter history as the monarch who abolished serfdom in Russia. According to her own testimony, she disliked it and considered it outdated.[77] At the same time, she understood that in Russia it was an established economic system, sustaining agriculture and industry alike. Abolishing serfdom meant not only overthrowing this structure but also making an enemy of the class that was still closest to Catherine in rank, power, and dignity. The debate about serfdom also involved the clash of two of the major ideologies of enlightened thinking: the right of individual liberty and the right to private property. If individual liberty was extended to the serfs, their owners' rights to private property would need to be restrained.[78]

> It was serfdom that troubled Catherine the most and that became the Achilles Heel of the Commission. As Voltaire's disciple, she despised it but as the sovereign of a country where it constituted the predominant kind of property, she acknowledged its expediency, the difficulty to reform it, and contented herself by putting her attention on the relationship between serfs and serf-owners hoping to humanise it.[79]

Catherine II did not abolish serfdom, but she tried at least to set examples. In 1767, the Empress wrote to her minister of justice: "If we do not consent to diminish cruelty and to moderate a situation which is intolerable to the human race, then sooner or later they will take this step themselves."[80] She abolished a law stating that children born out of wedlock, foundlings, and orphans would become serfs to those who "adopted" them. She allowed unfree people to study in public schools and, from 1787 onwards, also in universities. "The sciences are called free so that they can give everyone the freedom to study them but not to give this right to only those who are already free."[81] In 1768, Princess Dar'ya Saltykova was imprisoned for life for the murder of countless serfs.[82]

These actions show that, considering herself legitimised by her ability and her desire to reform, Catherine believed it her personal duty to improve the conditions of her more unfortunate subjects. She did not consider the Russian nobility educated enough to successfully modernise the state and therefore often circumvented her ministers and provincial governments.[83] Regardless of her personal opinions, Catherine might not have felt secure enough to challenge the nobility like Emperor Joseph II had done. Yet, their understanding of autocracy appears similar. The Prince de Ligne wrote about Joseph II that "He wanted the highest authority so that no one else had a right to do wrong".[84]

Threatened legitimacy

Many ideals were lost during Catherine's thirty-four years on the throne as her understanding of enlightened thinking clashed with her conviction that absolute rule was her legitimate right.

Like other sovereigns, Catherine was deeply concerned by the French Revolution and by the rebellions inside Russia, explicitly the Pugachev uprising. "I cannot believe in the superior talents of cobblers and shoemakers for government and legislation", the Empress wrote to Grimm.[85] In 1793, provincial governors were ordered to forbid the publication of books "which appeared doubtful, likely to corrupt morals, concerned with the government, and above all dealing with the French Revolution and the execution of the French king".[86] Having read Radishchev's *A Journey from Saint Petersburg to Moscow* in 1790, Catherine declared that "Its author infected and filled with the French madness is trying in every way to break down respect for authority and the authorities, to stir up in the people's indignation against their superiors and against the government."[87] Catherine might have reacted differently to the book had it been published earlier.

In 1796, all private printing presses were closed, having been allowed only thirteen years previously, and all books henceforth were to be submitted to a censorship office before publication.[88] Catherine was very sensitive about the criticism directed at herself. In such cases she had always censored rather quickly.[89] Yet, we can observe that her tone grew harsher towards the end of her reign.

The accusation that Catherine turned her back on domestic progress as soon as she got a chance to prove herself in foreign politics is probably too severe. Yet, she was not disinclined, at least temporarily, to abandon a critical or deadlocked matter for a more glorifying prospect. After all, Catherine seemed quite susceptible to praise and compliments. For that purpose, military conquest might have proven the safer bet and it could not be done without the support of the nobility.

Conclusion

In 1797, Catherine's son Paul I issued a new law of succession that codified primogeniture in the male line. Only after the extinction of the latter would the throne pass through a female line.[90] Paul's and Catherine's relationship had been strained,

31 Garstka, *Das Herrscherlob in Rußland*, 207: "I ot Petra moj stich tečet k Ekaterine"; "Pjotr' dal' nam bytie, Ekaterina dušu".
32 The State Russian Museum, St Petersburg [accessed June 2017]. http://en.rusmuseum.ru/collections/painting-of-xviii-first-half-xix-centuries/artworks/ekaterina-ii-zakonodatelnitsa-v-khrame-bogini-pravosudiya/?sphrase_id=73627.
33 Proskurina, *Creating the Empress*, 17.
34 Ibid., 37.
35 Christiane Hemer, *Herrschaft und Legitimation im Rußland des 17. Jahrhunderts. Staat und Kirche zur Zeit des Patriarchen Nikon* (Frankfurt/Main: Haag und Heerchen, 1979), 38.
36 Proskurina, *Creating the Empress*, 49ff. See also Klaus Maria Girardet, trans., *Konstantin. Rede an die Versammlung der Heiligen*, Fontes Christiani, vol. 55 (Freiburg: Herder, 2013), 201–07.
37 Garstka, *Das Herrscherlob in Rußland*, 207–08.
38 Simon Dixon, *Catherine the Great* (New York: Harper Collins, 2009), 17.
39 Proskurina, *Creating the Empress*, 181.
40 The British Museum, collection online, "An Imperial Stride!" [accessed June 2017]. www.britishmuseum.org/research/collection_online/collection_object_details.aspx?objectId=1462701&partId=1.
41 Jessen, *Katharina II. von Rußland*, 108.
42 Robert K. Massie, *Catherine the Great: Portrait of a Woman* (New York: Random House, 2011), 272.
43 Jessen, *Katharina II. von Rußland*, 109.
44 Proskurina, *Creating the Empress*, 25.
45 Garstka, *Das Herrscherlob in Rußland*, 204.
46 Erich Bryner, "'Respecter la religion, mais ne la faire entrer pour rien dans les affaires d'état'. Die orthodoxe Kirche als staatstragendes Element unter Katharina II", in *Russland zur Zeit Katharinas II.*, ed. Hübner, 154.
47 Bryner, "'Respecter la religion, mais ne la faire entrer pour rien dans les affaires d'état'", 151–52. See also Igor Smolitsch, *Geschichte der russischen Kirche 1700–1917, vol. 1*, Studien zur Geschichte Osteuropas, vol. 9, eds W. Philipp and P. Scheibert (Leiden: Brill, 1964), 251.
48 Ekkehard W. Bornträger, *Katharina II. Die Selbstherrscherin aller Reussen. Das Bild der Zarin und ihre Aussenpolitik in der westlichen Geschichtsschreibung*, Historische Schriften der Universität Freiburg Schweiz, vol. 13, ed. Urs Altermatt (Freiburg: Universitätsverlag, 1991), 63: "Elle n'a aucune religion, mais elle contrefait la devote."
49 Proskurina, *Creating the Empress*, 24.
50 Sellin, *Gewalt und Legitimität*, 99.
51 Cronin, *Katharina die Große*, 211.
52 Bryner, "'Respecter la religion, mais ne la faire entrer pour rien dans les affaires d'état'", 158.
53 Ibid., 152–53.
54 Ibid., 161.
55 Edmond Scherer, *Melchior Grimm, l'homme de lettres. Le Factotum–le Diplomate* (Paris: Calmann Lévy, 1887), 315–16.
56 Bornträger, *Katharina II. Die Selbstherrscherin aller Reussen*, 118.
57 Catherine II as quoted in John T. Alexander, *Catherine the Great: Life and Legend* (New York: Oxford University Press, 1989), 101.
58 Sellin, *Gewalt und Legitimität*, 155.
59 Massie, *Catherine the Great: Portrait of a Woman*, 351.
60 Georg Sacke, *Die Gesetzgebende Kommission Katharinas II. Ein Beitrag zu Geschichte des Absolutismus in Russland*, Jahrbücher für Geschichte Osteuropas, suppl. 2, ed. Hans Uebersberger (Breslau: Priebatsch, 1940), 45.
61 Günter Arnold, "Katharinas II. Große Kommission und Instruktion aus der Sicht Herders", in vol. 3 of *Europa in der Frühen Neuzeit*, ed. Erich Donnert (Weimar: Böhlau, 1997), 147.

62 Sacke, *Die Gesetzgebende Kommission Katharinas II*, 64; Catherine the Great, *The Grand Instructions to the Commissioners Appointed to Frame a New Code of Laws for the Russian Empire. Composed by her Imperial Majesty Catherine II Empress of all the Russias*, trans. Michael Tatischeff (London: T. Jefferys, 1768), 71.
63 Sellin, *Gewalt und Legitimität*, 152; *The Grand Instructions*, 71.
64 Georg Sacke, "Zur Charakteristik der gesetzgebenden Kommission Katharinas II. von Russland", *Archiv für Kulturgeschichte*, vol. 21, issue 2 (1931), 175–76.
65 Oleg A. Omel'čenko, "Die 'Kommission zur Verfertigung des Entwurfs zu einem neuen Gesetzbuch'. Einige neue Beobachtungen im Zusammenhang mit dem gesetzgeberischen Werk der Fachausschüsse", in *Russland zur Zeit Katharinas II.*, ed. Hübner, 171.
66 Massie, *Catherine the Great: Portrait of a Woman*, 361.
67 Arnold, "Katharinas II. Große Kommission und Instruktion aus der Sicht Herders", 151.
68 Omel'čenko, "Die "Kommission zur Verfertigung des Entwurfs zu einem neuen Gesetzbuch", 179.
69 Wunderlich, *Vernetzte Karrieren*, 184.
70 Sellin, *Gewalt und Legitimität*, 145.
71 Ibid., 145.
72 Ezequiel Adamovsky, *Euro-orientalism: Liberal Ideology and the Image of Russia in France (c. 1740–1880)*, French Studies of the Eighteenth and Nineteenth Centuries, vol. 19 (Bern: Peter Lang, 2006), 59.
73 Ibid., 61.
74 Alexander, *Catherine the Great: Life and Legend*, 101.
75 J. J. Mangan, *The King's Favour* (London: St Martin's Press, 1991), 221.
76 Cronin, *Katharina die Große*, 240.
77 Hélène Carrère d'Encausse, *Catherine II: un âge d'or pour la Russie* (Paris: Fayard, 2002), 107.
78 Robert E. Jones, "Catherine the Great and the Russian Nobility", in *Russland zur Zeit Katharinas II*, ed. Hübner, 111.
79 Carrère d'Encausse, *Catherine II: un âge d'or pour la Russie*, 107.
80 Catherine II, as quoted in Ian Grey, *Catherine the Great: Autocrat and Empress of All Russia* (London: Hodder and Stoughton, 1961), 164. See also Massie, *Catherine the Great: Portrait of a Woman*, 305.
81 Cronin, *Katharina die Große*, 221.
82 Ibid., 209.
83 Wunderlich, *Vernetzte Karrieren*, 176.
84 Hervé Hasquin, *Joseph II. Catholique anticlérical et réformateur impatient* (Brussels: Racine, 2007), 7.
85 Massie, *Catherine the Great: Portrait of a Woman*, 539
86 Catherine's order to the provincial governors, as quoted in Isabel de Madariaga, *Russia in the Age of Catherine the Great* (London: Weidenfeld and Nicolson, 1981), 546.
87 Massie, *Catherine the Great: Portrait of a Woman*, 552.
88 Ibid., 549.
89 Garstka, *Das Herrscherlob in Rußland*, 205.
90 *Polnoe Sobranie Zakonov Rossijskoj Imperii*, vol. XXIV (Saint Petersburg: 1830), 587, no 17: 910.
91 Massie, *Catherine the Great. Portrait of a Woman*, 340.

Bibliography

Adamovsky, Ezequiel. *Euro-orientalism: Liberal Ideology and the Image of Russia in France (c. 1740–1880)*. French Studies of the Eighteenth and Nineteenth Centuries, vol. 19. Bern: Peter Lang, 2006.

Alexander, John T. *Catherine the Great: Life and Legend*. New York: Oxford University Press, 1989.

Andree, Heike M. E. *Katharina II. im Spiegel der deutschen Zeitschriftenpublizistik des 18. Jahrhunderts.* Studien zur Geschichtsforschung der Neuzeit, vol. 35. Hamburg: Dr Kovač, 2003.

Anisimov, Evgenii V. *Five Empresses: Court Life in Eighteenth-Century Russia.* Westport and London: Praeger, 2004.

Aretin, Karl Otmar von. "Katharina die Große und das Phänomen des aufgeklärten Absolutismus". In *Russland zur Zeit Katharinas II. Absolutismis–Aufklärung–Pragmatismus.* Beiträge zur Geschichte Osteuropas, vol. 26, edited by Eckhard Hübner, 33–40. Cologne and Vienna: Böhlau, 1998.

Arnold, Günter. "Katharinas II. Große Kommission und Instruktion aus der Sicht Herders". In *Europa in der Frühen Neuzeit,* vol. 3, edited by Erich Donnert, 154–59. Weimar: Böhlau, 1997.

Baehr, Stephen Lessing. *The Paradise Myth in Eighteenth-Century Russia.* Stanford: Stanford University Press, 1991.

Baljazin, Vol'demar. *Ekaterina Velikaja i ejo cemejstvo.* Moscow: OLMA Media Grupp, 2007.

British Museum. Collection online. "An Imperial Stride!" [accessed June 2017]. www.britishmuseum.org/research/collection_online/collection_object_details.aspx?objectId=1462701&partId=1.

Bryner, Erich. "'Respecter la religion, mais ne la faire entrer pour rien dans les affaires d'état'. Die orthodoxe Kirche als staatstragendes Element unter Katharina II". In *Russland zur Zeit Katharinas II. Absolutismis–Aufklärung–Pragmatismus.* Beiträge zur Geschichte Osteuropas, vol. 26, edited by Eckhard Hübner, 151–69. Cologne and Vienna: Böhlau, 1998.

Bornträger, Ekkehard W. *Katharina II. Die Selbstherrscherin aller Reussen. Das Bild der Zarin und ihre Aussenpolitik in der westlichen Geschichtsschreibung,* Historische Schriften der Universität Freiburg Schweiz, vol. 13, edited by Urs Altermatt. Freiburg: Universitätsverlag, 1991.

Carrère d'Encausse, Hélène. *Catherine II: un âge d'or pour la Russie.* Paris: Fayard, 2002.

Catherine II, Empress of Russia. *The Grand Instructions to the Commissioners Appointed to Frame a New Code of Laws for the Russian Empire. Composed by her Imperial Majesty Catherine II Empress of all the Russias.* Translated by Michael Tatischeff. London: T. Jefferys, 1768.

Catherine II, Empress of Russia. *Memoirs of the Empress Catherine II. Written by Herself.* With a preface by A. Herzen. London: Trübner & Co, 1859.

Cronin, Vincent. *Katharina die Große.* Translated by Karl Berisch. Munich: Piper, 2012.

Dixon, Simon. *Catherine the Great.* New York: Harper Collins, 2009.

Dukes, Paul. *Catherine the Great and the Russian Nobility. A Study Based on the Material of the Legislative Commission of 1767.* Cambridge: Cambridge University Press, 1967.

Flocken, Jan von. *Katharina II: Zarin von Rußland.* Berlin: Verl. Neues Leben, 1991.

Garstka, Christoph. *Das Herrscherlob in Rußland. Katharina II., Lenin und Stalin im russischen Gedicht.* Heidelberg: Universitätsverlag Winter, 2005.

Girardet, Klaus Maria, trans. *Konstantin. Rede an die Versammlung der Heiligen,* Fontes Christiani, vol. 55. Freiburg: Herder, 2013.

Grey, Ian. *Catherine the Great: Autocrat and Empress of All Russia.* London: Hodder and Stoughton, 1961.

Hasquin, Hervé. *Joseph II. Catholique anticlérical et réformateur impatient.* Brussels: Racine, 2007.

Hemer, Christiane. *Herrschaft und Legitimation im Rußland des 17. Jahrhunderts. Staat und Kirche zur Zeit des Patriarchen Nikon.* Frankfurt am Main: Haag und Heerchen, 1979,

Hildermeier, Manfred. "Hoffnungsräger? Das Stadtbürgertum". In *Russland zur Zeit Katharinas II. Absolutismis–Aufklärung–Pragmatismus*. Beiträge zur Geschichte Osteuropas, vol. 26, edited by Eckhard Hübner, 137–51. Cologne and Vienna: Böhlau, 1998.

Jena, Detlef. *Die Zarinnen Russlands (1547–1918)*. Regensburg: Pustet, 1999.

Jessen, Hans. *Katharina II. von Rußland. Im Spiegel der Zeitgenossen*. Düsseldorf: Karl Rauch, 1970.

Jessen, Hans. *Katharina II. von Rußland in Augenzeugenberichten*. Munich: dtv Verlag, 1978.

Jones, Robert E. "Catherine the Great and the Russian Nobility". In *Russland zur Zeit Katharinas II. Absolutismis–Aufklärung–Pragmatismus*. Beiträge zur Geschichte Osteuropas, vol. 26, edited by Eckhard Hübner, 103–15. Cologne/Vienna: Böhlau, 1998.

Kopelew, Lew. "Lehrmeister und Rivalen, Kameraden und Fremdlinge". In *Deutsche und Deutschland aus russischer Sicht. 18. Jahrhundert: Aufklärung*. West-Östliche Spiegelungen. Russen und Rußland aus deutscher Sicht und Deutsche und Deutschland aus russischer Sicht von den Anfängen bis zum 20. Jahrhundert, Series B, vol. 2, edited by Dagmar Hermann, 11–53. Munich: Fink, 1992.

Madariaga, Isabel de. *Russia in the Age of Catherine the Great*. London: Weidenfeld and Nicolson, 1981.

Madariaga, Isabel de. *Katharina die Grosse: das Leben der russischen Kaiserin*. Wiesbaden: Matrix, 2004.

Mangan, J. J. *The King's Favour*. London: St Martin's Press, 1991.

Massie, Robert K. *Catherine the Great: Portrait of a Woman*. New York: Random House, 2011.

Montefiore, Simon Sebag. *Die Romanows: Glanz und Untergang der Zarendynastie 1613–1918*. Frankfurt am Main: S. Fischer, 2016.

Nolte, Hans-Heinrich. *Kleine Geschichte Russlands*. Stuttgart: Reclam, 1998.

Omel'čenko, Oleg A. "Die 'Kommission zur Verfertigung des Entwurfs zu einem neuen Gesetzbuch'. Einige neue Beobachtungen im Zusammenhang mit dem gesetzgeberischen Werk der Fachausschüsse". In *Russland zur Zeit Katharinas II. Absolutismis–Aufklärung–Pragmatismus*. Beiträge zur Geschichte Osteuropas, vol. 26, edited by Eckhard Hübner, 169–81. Cologne and Vienna: Böhlau, 1998.

Polnoe Sobranie Zakonov Rossijskoj Imperii. vol. XXIV. St Petersburg: 1830.

Proskurina, Vera. *Creating the Empress: Politics and Poetry in the Age of Catherine II*. Brighton, MA: Academic Studies Press, 2011.

Quellen zur Aufhebung der Folter. Rechtsgeschichte und Rechtsgeschehen–Kleine Schriften, vol. 25, edited by Jan Zopfs. Berlin and Münster: Lit. Verlag, 2010.

Sacke, Georg. "Zur Charakteristik der gesetzgebenden Kommission Katharinas II. von Russland", *Archiv für Kulturgeschichte*, vol. 21, issue 2 (1931), 166–91.

Sacke, Georg. *Die Gesetzgebende Kommission Katharinas II. Ein Beitrag zu Geschichte des Absolutismus in Russland*. Jahrbücher für Geschichte Osteuropas, suppl. 2, edited by Hans Uebersberger. Breslau: Priebatsch, 1940.

Scharf, Claus. "Tradition–Usurpation–Legitimation. Das herrscherliche Selbstverständnis Katharinas II". In *Russland zur Zeit Katharinas II. Absolutismis–Aufklärung–Pragmatismus*. Beiträge zur Geschichte Osteuropas, vol. 26, edited by Eckhard Hübner, 41–103. Cologne and Vienna: Böhlau, 1998.

Scherer, Edmond. *Melchior Grimm, l'homme de lettres. Le Factotum–le Diplomate*. Paris: Calmann Lévy, 1887.

Sellin, Volker. *Gewalt und Legitimität. Die europäische Monarchie im Zeitalter der Revolutionen*. Munich: Oldenbourg, 2011.

Smolitsch, Igor. *Geschichte der russischen Kirche 1700–1917, vol. 1*, Studien zur Geschichte Osteuropas, vol. 9, edited by W. Philipp and P. Scheibert. Leiden: Brill, 1964.

Voltaire (François-Marie Arouet). *Oeuvres complètes de Voltaire, avec des notes et une notice historique sur la vie de Voltaire. Tome Dixième. Correspondance avec le Roi de Prusse, l'Impératrice de Russie et d'Alembert.* Paris: Chez Furne, 1836.

Voltaire (François-Marie Arouet). *Voltaire Catherine II. Correspondance 1763–1778.* Edited by Alexandre Stroev. Paris: Non Lieu Editions, 2006.

Whittaker, Cynthia H. "The Reforming Tsar: The Redefinition of Autocratic Duty in Eighteenth-Century Russia". *Slavic Review* 51 (1992): 77–99.

Wunderlich, Dieter. *Vernetzte Karrieren.* Regensburg: Pustet, 2000.

INDEX

Page numbers in *italic* refer to tables.
Added to a page number, 'n' denotes a note.